**RENEWALS 458-4574**
**DATE DUE**

**WITHDRAWN**
**UTSA LIBRARIES**

# Communist Indochina

This book examines the history of communist Indochina from the foundation of the Indochinese Communist Party in 1929–30 to the end of the 1970s. It explores the impact of the Japanese invasion of Indochina in 1940, and the subsequent relationship between the Japanese occupiers and the Vichy French colonial regime. It considers why, following the Japanese surrender, the cause of Vietnamese independence was championed by the Communist-led Viet Minh movement headed by Ho Chi Minh, culminating in the August Revolution and the Viet Minh seizure of power and analyses the record of the Viet Minh Provisional Government of 1945–46. It goes on to consider key episodes of the Vietnam War which followed partition in 1954, including the Tet Offensive of 1967–68 – a crucial turning point in the course of the conflict – and the Cambodia Crisis of 1969–70. Throughout, it considers events within Indochina in the context of wider regional and international developments, focusing in particular on the role played by the Chinese, including their support to the Viet Minh in their struggle against the French from 1947, and the issue of Cambodia which eventually precipitated the Sino-Vietnamese War of 1979. The book also explores the main trends in social, economic and institutional development which characterised this period, including village and clan networks, economic and monetary developments, the contrasting systems of North and South after partition, and the consequences of choosing a Soviet economic alignment in preference to links with Japan and capitalist Asia. Written by the late Ralph Smith, a highly respected historian of Asia, this book is essential reading for anyone seeking to understand the history of Indochina.

**R.B. Smith** was Professor of the International History of South-East Asia at the School of Oriental and African Studies, University of London, where he taught from 1962–2000. His works include *Vietnam and the West* (1971); and the three-volume *An International History of the Vietnam War* (1983, 1985, 1990).

**Beryl Williams** is Emeritus Reader in History, University of Sussex, UK. She taught at Sussex from 1963–2003, and her publications include *The Russian Revolution 1917–1921* (1987) and *Lenin* (2000).

# Routledge studies in the modern history of Asia

1 The Police in Occupation Japan
Control, corruption and resistance to reform
Christopher Aldous

2 Chinese Workers
A new history
Jackie Sheehan

3 The Aftermath of Partition in South Asia
Tai Yong Tan and Gyanesh Kudaisya

4 The Australia–Japan Political Alignment 1952 to the present
Alan Rix

5 Japan and Singapore in the World Economy
Japan's economic advance into Singapore, 1870–1965
Shimizu Hiroshi and Hirakawa Hitoshi

6 The Triads as Business
Yiu Kong Chu

7 Contemporary Taiwanese Cultural Nationalism
A-chin Hsiau

8 Religion and Nationalism in India
The case of the Punjab
Harnik Deol

9 Japanese Industrialisation
Historical and cultural perspectives
Ian Inkster

10 War and Nationalism in China 1925–1945
Hans J. van de Ven

11 Hong Kong in Transition
One country, two systems
Edited by Robert Ash, Peter Ferdinand, Brian Hook and Robin Porter

12 Japan's Postwar Economic Recovery and Anglo–Japanese Relations, 1948–1962
Noriko Yokoi

13 Japanese Army Stragglers and Memories of the War in Japan, 1950–1975
Beatrice Trefalt

14 Ending the Vietnam War
The Vietnamese Communists' perspective
Ang Cheng Guan

15 The Development of the Japanese Nursing Profession
Adopting and adapting Western influences
Aya Takahashi

16 Women's Suffrage in Asia
Gender nationalism and democracy
Louise Edwards and Mina Roces

17 The Anglo–Japanese Alliance, 1902–1922
Phillips Payson O'Brien

18  **The United States and Cambodia, 1870–1969**
    From curiosity to confrontation
    *Kenton Clymer*

19  **Capitalist Restructuring and the Pacific Rim**
    *Ravi Arvind Palat*

20  **The United States and Cambodia, 1969–2000**
    A troubled relationship
    *Kenton Clymer*

21  **British Business in Post-Colonial Malaysia, 1957–1970**
    'Neo-colonialism' or 'Disengagement'?
    *Nicholas J. White*

22  **The Rise and Decline of Thai Absolutism**
    *Kullada Kesboonchoo Mead*

23  **Russian Views of Japan, 1792–1913**
    An anthology of travel writing
    *David N. Wells*

24  **The Internment of Western Civilians under the Japanese, 1941–1945**
    A patchwork of internment
    *Bernice Archer*

25  **The British Empire and Tibet 1900–1922**
    *Wendy Palace*

26  **Nationalism in Southeast Asia**
    If the people are with us
    *Nicholas Tarling*

27  **Women, Work and the Japanese Economic Miracle**
    The case of the cotton textile industry, 1945–1975
    *Helen Macnaughtan*

28  **A Colonial Economy in Crisis**
    Burma's rice cultivators and the world depression of the 1930s
    *Ian Brown*

29  **A Vietnamese Royal Exile in Japan**
    Prince Cuong De (1882–1951)
    *Tran My-Van*

30  **Corruption and Good Governance in Asia**
    *Nicholas Tarling*

31  **US–China Cold War Collaboration, 1971–1989**
    *S. Mahmud Ali*

32  **Rural Economic Development in Japan**
    From the nineteenth century to the Pacific War
    *Penelope Francks*

33  **Colonial Armies in Southeast Asia**
    *Edited by Karl Hack and Tobias Rettig*

34  **Intra Asian Trade and the World Market**
    *A.J.H. Latham and Heita Kawakatsu*

35  **Japanese–German Relations, 1895–1945**
    War, diplomacy and public opinion
    *Edited by Christian W. Spang and Rolf-Harald Wippich*

36  **Britain's Imperial Cornerstone in China**
    The Chinese maritime customs service, 1854–1949
    *Donna Brunero*

37  **Colonial Cambodia's 'Bad Frenchmen'**
    The rise of French rule and the life of Thomas Caraman, 1840–1887
    *Gregor Muller*

38  **Japanese–American Civilian Prisoner Exchanges and Detention Camps, 1941–1945**
    *Bruce Elleman*

39  **Regionalism in Southeast Asia**
    *Nicholas Tarling*

40 **Changing Visions of East Asia, 1943–1993**
Transformations and continuities
*R.B. Smith (edited by Chad J. Mitcham)*

41 **Christian Heretics in Late Imperial China**
Christian inculturation and state control, 1720–1850
*Lars P. Laamann*

42 **Beijing – A Concise History**
*Stephen G. Haw*

43 **The Impact of the Russo–Japanese War**
*Edited by Rotem Kowner*

44 **Business–Government Relations in Prewar Japan**
*Peter von Staden*

45 **India's Princely States**
People, princes and colonialism
*Edited by Waltraud Ernst and Biswamoy Pati*

46 **Rethinking Gandhi and Nonviolent Relationality**
Global perspectives
*Edited by Debjani Ganguly and John Docker*

47 **The Quest for Gentility in China**
Negotiations beyond gender and class
*Edited by Daria Berg and Chloë Starr*

48 **Forgotten Captives in Japanese Occupied Asia**
*Edited by Kevin Blackburn and Karl Hack*

49 **Japanese Diplomacy in the 1950s**
From isolation to integration
*Edited by Iokibe Makoto, Caroline Rose, Tomaru Junko and John Weste*

50 **The Limits of British Colonial Control in South Asia**
Spaces of disorder in the Indian ocean region
*Edited by Ashwini Tambe and Harald Fischer-Tiné*

51 **On The Borders of State Power**
Frontiers in the greater Mekong sub-region
*Edited by Martin Gainsborough*

52 **Pre-Communist Indochina**
*R.B. Smith (edited by Beryl Williams)*

53 **Communist Indochina**
*R.B. Smith (edited by Beryl Williams)*

# Communist Indochina

**R.B. Smith
Edited by Beryl Williams**

LONDON AND NEW YORK

First published 2009
by Routledge
2 Park Square, Milton Park, Abingdon, Oxon, OX14 4RN

Simultaneously published in the USA and Canada
by Routledge
270 Madison Avenue, New York, NY 10016

*Routledge is an imprint of the Taylor & Francis Group,
an informa business*

© 2009 individual chapters, R.B. Smith; editorial selection and matter,
Beryl Williams; introduction, A.J. Stockwell

Typeset in Times New Roman by Keyword Group Ltd
Printed and bound in Great Britain by TJ International Ltd,
Padstow, Cornwall

All rights reserved. No part of this book may be reprinted or reproduced or
utilised in any form or by any electronic, mechanical, or other means, now
known or hereafter invented, including photocopying and recording, or in
any information storage or retrieval system, without permission in writing
from the publishers.

*British Library Cataloguing in Publication Data*
A catalogue record for this book is available from the British Library

*Library of Congress Cataloging in Publication Data*

    p. cm. – (Routledge studies in the modern history of Asia ; 53)

The foundation of the Indochinese Communist Party, 1929-1930 –
The Japanese period in Indochina and the coup of 9 Mar. 1945 –
The Vietnamese revolution of Aug.-Sept. 1945 : a South-East Asian
perspective – The work of the provisional government of Vietnam,
Aug.-Dec., 1945 – China and Southeast Asia : the revolutionary
perspective, 1951 – The Tet crisis of 1967-68 in perspective – The
international setting of the Cambodia crisis, 1969-1970 – Cambodia in
the context of Sino-Vietnamese relations – Vietnam from the 1890s to
the 1990s : continuity and change in the longer perspective.

Includes bibliographical references and index.
ISBN 978-0-415-46804-6 (hardback : alk. paper)
1. Indochina–History–20th century. I. Williams, Beryl, 1940- II. Title.
DS549.S65 2008
959.704–dc22                                            2008026415

ISBN 13: 978-0-415-46804-6 (hbk)
ISBN 10: 0-415-46804-3 (hbk)

**Library
University of Texas
at San Antonio**

**In memory of Judy Stowe**

# Contents

| | | |
|---|---|---|
| *Preface* | | xi |
| *Acknowledgements* | | xii |
| | Introduction | 1 |
| 1 | The foundation of the Indochinese Communist Party, 1929–1930 | 5 |
| 2 | The Japanese period in Indochina and the coup of 9 March 1945 | 34 |
| 3 | The Vietnamese revolution of August–September 1945: a South-East Asian perspective | 70 |
| 4 | The work of the Provisional Government of Vietnam, August–December 1945 | 84 |
| 5 | China and Southeast Asia: the revolutionary perspective, 1951 | 115 |
| 6 | The TET crisis of 1967–1968 in perspective | 132 |
| 7 | The international setting of the Cambodia crisis, 1969–1970 | 149 |

8  Cambodia in the context of Sino-Vietnamese relations    178

9  Vietnam from the 1890s to the 1990s: continuity and change
   in the longer perspective    193

   *Index*    216

# Preface

Professor Ralph Smith died suddenly in London in December 2000, leaving a number of unfinished projects. The most important of these was later edited by one of his former research students and published by Routledge as: R. B. Smith, edited by Chad J. Mitcham, *Changing Visions of East Asia, 1943–93, Transformations and Continuities* (Routledge, 2007). Dr Mitcham also kindly agreed to compile the indexes for the two current volumes. An unfinished work on historiography has also led to the publishing of two articles in the journal *History of European Ideas* (no. 33, 2007 and forthcoming). The idea for a collected volume of Professor Smith's essays on Indochina, including a number of unpublished conference papers, was first put forward in 2003 by the late Judy Stowe. Assisted then by Professor Kevin Ruane of Canterbury Christchurch University, she selected items for a one volume collection, but problems with finding a publisher and her own declining health led to the project being put to one side. These two volumes are dedicated to her memory. I am most grateful to Peter Sowden of Routledge for enabling me to resurrect the project and for insisting that the material available justified two volumes rather than one. I am also grateful to Professor Anthony Stockwell for agreeing to write the introduction and to the various journals involved for permissions to reprint.

Beryl Williams<br>
University of Sussex

# Acknowledgements

The editor and publishers would like to thank the following for granting permission to reproduce material in this work:

Cambridge University Press for the reproduction of

'The Japanese period in Indochina and the coup of 9 March 1945', in *The Journal of Southeast Asian Studies* 9(2), 1978.
'China and Southeast Asia: the revolutionary perspective, 1951', in *The Journal of Southeast Asian Studies* 19(1), 1988.
'The foundation of the Indochinese Communist Party, 1929–30', in *Modern Asian Studies* 32, 1998.
'The Work of the Provisional Government of Vietnam August–December 1945', in *Modern Asian Studies* 12, 1978.

South East Asia Research for the reproduction of:

'Vietnam from the 1890s to the 1990s: continuity and change in the longer perspective', in *South East Asia Research* 4, 1996.

The International History Review for reproduction of:

'The international setting of the Cambodia crisis 1969–1970', in *The International History Review* 18, 1996.

Taylor & Francis for reproduction of:

'Cambodia in the context of Sino-Vietnamese relations', in *Journal of the Royal Asiatic Society for Asian Affairs* 72, 1985.

Every effort has been made to contact copyright holders for their permission to reprint material in this book. The publishers would be grateful to hear from any copyright holder who is not here acknowledged and will undertake to rectify any errors or omissions in future editions of this book.

# Introduction

Ralph Bernard Smith was born, an only child, in 1939 in the Yorkshire town of Bingley. He attended Burnley Grammar School and proceeded to the University of Leeds where he read History. Having graduated with first-class honours in 1959, he proceeded to research and completed his doctorate in 1963. The subject of his thesis was Yorkshire during the Henrician Reformation and it remained for years the single, authoritative work on the Pilgrimage of Grace. A subsequently revised version was published in 1970 as *Land and Politics in the England of Henry VIII: the West Riding of Yorkshire, 1530–46* (Oxford, Clarendon Press). By then, however, Ralph's career had taken an unexpected turn. In 1962, while a post-graduate student at London's Institute of Historical Research, he had successfully applied to the nearby School of Oriental and African Studies for a part-time job that held out the prospect of an established lectureship. He had two principal duties: to teach Early Modern European History to students majoring in non-European subjects, and to learn the history and language of a country on the South East Asian mainland.

Having selected Vietnam almost at random and in virtual ignorance, Ralph immersed himself in a new culture. He stayed with the Vietnamese community in Paris while working at the Bibliothèque Nationale. Then, in January 1966, he flew to Saigon with Beryl Williams (lecturer and later Reader in Modern Russian History at Sussex University) whom he had married in 1964. Bilingual in French, Ralph learned Vietnamese, and, notwithstanding the war, Beryl and he travelled extensively in Indo-China and elsewhere in the region (including Hong Kong and Malaya) although they were barred from North Vietnam. Smitten by the world east of Suez and with £5 between them, they returned to the United Kingdom in September. Ralph went to Vietnam at least one more time before 1975 but thereafter his exclusion from the country until the mid-1990s must have been a factor in the expansion of his interests from the national history of Vietnam to the international history of East Asia. He continued to visit other parts of Asia, and regularly presented papers at conferences there as well as in continental Europe and the United States.

A year after his field trip to Vietnam and now established at SOAS, Ralph published in the *Bulletin of the School of Oriental and African Studies* (30 (3), 1967) an introduction to Sino-Vietnamese sources for the Nguyen period.

2   *Communist Indochina*

Then *Vietnam and the West* (London, Heinemann, 1968) appeared. Full of insight and wisdom, this book had an immediate and enduring impact. After forty years it is still obligatory reading for undergraduates and a delight for all. The range of his interests is reflected in *Early South East Asia: Essays in Archaeology, History, and Historical Geography* (New York, OUP, 1979), a large volume of papers which he edited in collaboration with the scholar of ancient China, William Watson, and which had originally been presented to the colloquy on early South East Asia at SOAS in September 1973. His own research, however, came to focus on the rise of the Indo-Chinese Communist Party during the period of French colonial rule and on its struggle for supremacy after 1945.

It is as an historian of Vietnam and of the international dimension of the Vietnam War that Ralph Smith became best known. His purpose was to explain the origins and course of the conflict. His approach was to cut through the propaganda surrounding it – as a student his own political views had had an affinity with those of the Bow Group on the Conservative left. Using American and British archives as well as the media and monitored broadcasts from the Communist world, and demonstrating his mastery of great power strategy, he examined decision-making on both sides and situated the conflict in a wider context than either area-study or bipolar US–Vietnamese relations. The first volume of *An International History of the Vietnam War* (London, Macmillan) came out in 1983 and was followed in 1985 and 1990 by the second and third. Between them they covered the years 1955–66. Ralph had planned four volumes to take the story to its dénouement in 1976 and one may surmise why he did not reach the fall of Saigon in 1975 or even the Paris Peace Accords of 1973. Perhaps he felt that the release of Soviet archives in the 1990s had changed the methodological assumptions of his project but, in any case, his attention was moving to yet broader themes.

One was a grand survey of the changes in East Asia during the half-century between 1943 and 1993. This was an attempt to understand, as he himself put it, 'why the 1990s turned out to be so very, very different from both the world of the early 1940s and also from conflicting aspirations of those who "shaped destiny" in that far off age' and 'why even the aspirations of the early 1960s proved so wide of the mark, when measured against what actually came about by the 1980s and 1990s'. As a historian of the international relations of East Asia, Ralph regarded his subject as a region rather than as a collection of states, and he applied historical methods to its recent history which had so often been left to non-historians. This book would be the summation of his thinking over the previous thirty years and he provided a taste of what was to come in the Fourth Huang Hsing Foundation Distinguished Lecture in Asian Studies which he delivered at St Antony's College Oxford in November 1997. It was published the following year as 'Visions of the Future: East Asia in 1943 and 1993'. A second big theme which came to engross him was historiography but neither his writing on this nor his analysis of a half-century of change in East Asia had been completed before his untimely death on 20 December 2000.

When they examined Ralph's unfinished work, Beryl Williams (legal guardian of his papers) and the late Judith A. Stowe (former head of the Thai and Vietnamese sections of the BBC) were determined that it should be published. In addition to two articles on historiography and the book, *Changing Visions of East Asia, 1943–93* (edited by Chad J. Mitcham), a collection of essays on Indo-China was planned. Some of these had already appeared in diverse journals while others had remained unpublished. Such is their range and originality that the collection has grown to two volumes. The first starts with four essays on the pre-colonial period, including a pair which combines Ralph's interests in both Vietnam and England during the period 1300–1600. These are followed by five articles that discuss aspects of the Vietnamese response to French rule. Here local political developments are considered in relation to indigenous society and culture. The second volume focuses on the rise and victory of communism in Vietnam but also includes pieces on Cambodia and the impact of foreign intervention. The editors have adapted a discussion of the Tet Offensive, 'The Vietnam War from Both Sides: the Crisis of 1967–68', from a much longer paper which was delivered in Washington in March 1998. Meticulous respect for the evidence, fastidious care for chronology, together with bold handling of big themes are hallmarks of Ralph Smith's scholarship. So, too, is the clarity with which he interrogates the sources and develops his arguments.

As Lecturer, later Reader in the History of South East Asia and finally Professor of the International History of East Asia, Ralph Smith was an inspiring and caring teacher. For years his Special Subject on the Vietnam War, which he periodically revised in the light of new research, was one of the most popular in the undergraduate programme of the federal University of London. It was to his students that he dedicated his *International History*. Under his supervision graduate students from all over the world produced highly original doctoral dissertations, went on to distinguished careers and will for ever recall him with admiration and affection. Living within a few minutes' walk of the School of Oriental and African Studies, Ralph was unstinting with his hospitality and the time he bestowed on others. His high expectations and the warmth of his generosity were particularly in evidence at the research seminar on the Recent History of South East Asia which he convened during the 1980s and 1990s. This gathering was remarkable not only for the intellectual demands it made of its members but also for the sense of common endeavour and companionship that it fostered. In commemorating the life and work of Ralph Smith, this collection will ensure that his scholarship reaches a new audience, particularly among current students of Asia.

Anthony Stockwell<br>
(Emeritus Professor of Modern History,<br>
Royal Holloway, University of London)

# 1 The foundation of the Indochinese Communist Party, 1929–1930

Source: *Modern Asian Studies* 32(4) (1998): 769–805.

## I

For perhaps a quarter of a century, from the mid-1930s to the year 1960, the Indochinese Communist Party—later the Workers' Party of Vietnam and now the Vietnamese Communist Party—celebrated the anniversary of its foundation on 6 January each year.[1] The thirtieth anniversary (6 January 1960) was given special prominence in Hanoi and was marked by the publication of an official Party history in Vietnamese, French, English and other languages.[2] Then, quite abruptly in September of the same year, the Party's Third National Congress approved a resolution to the effect that in future the anniversary would be commemorated on 3 February, which thereafter was held to be the 'correct' date. The most authentic explanation for the change is probably that given by Hoang van Hoan, a member of the Party's Politburo from 1957 to 1976, in a memoir published following his flight to Beijing in 1979. He tells us that in 1960, 'records provided by the Soviet Union showed that the Communist Party of Vietnam was founded on February 3 instead of January 6'. The error had arisen because of the difference between the solar and lunar calendars: 'When President Ho said that the Party was founded on January 6, he didn't make it clear that it was the lunar calendar' and 'everyone present thought it to be the solar calendar.'[3] The anniversary continues to be celebrated in Hanoi on 3 February, although a further refinement had crept into official histories by the 1980s: the 'unified conference to found the Party' is now said to have taken place (in Hong Kong) between 3 and 7 February 1930.[4]

There is one genuinely contemporary record which seems to confirm that the reunification meeting did in fact occur in early February rather than early January 1930. Towards the end of that year the French Sûreté seized around forty Communist documents at a house in Hanoi, one of which was headed (in French translation) 'Compte Rendue Sommaire de l'Assemblée'. It relates to a meeting between two delegates of the 'Dong Duong' (Indochinese) Communist Party and two from the 'Annam' Communist Party, presided over by a 'delegate of the Communist International'. The purpose of the meeting was to unify the two groups to create a single Communist organization, on the basis of proposals put forward by the Comintern delegate. The place is not indicated, but the summary of the proceedings is clearly dated: '7.2.30'.[5] No names are given for either the Comintern representative or those of the rival Communist groups. But there is so far no reason to question the claim in later sources, including the account of 1938, that the meeting was presided over by Nguyen Ai Quoc.

What is much more problematic is the question why the date of the meeting was misremembered; and also, perhaps, the reason why the correction was not made until 1960. Decisions to change the historical record inevitably tease the historian's imagination—and in this case the official explanation seems a little suspect. Nguyen Ai Quoc was a Western-educated Marxist who had lived in France for at least seven years. A mistake of this kind on his part seems unlikely, and certainly no other example of confusion between calendars is known in the context of Vietnamese Communist history. But even if a genuine error occurred in 1930 itself—and went uncorrected during Nguyen Ai Quoc's absence between 1931 and 1938, first in a Hong Kong prison and then in Moscow—it seems surprising that it was allowed to persist throughout the years from 1945 to 1960, when he was undisputed chairman of the Party and president of the Democratic Republic of Vietnam. Doubts about the explanation are only reinforced by the discovery that in reality the sixth day of the first month of the lunar year of the Horse in 1930 coincided with the fourth, not the third of February.

While this puzzle may seem to be of relatively minor historical significance, it reflects our lack of precise knowledge regarding the circumstances in which the Party was founded; and it focuses attention on a number of larger questions regarding the status and context of the Hong Kong meeting. We need to ask not only why such a meeting was necessary, from the point of view of internal rivalries among the Vietnamese themselves, but also how it fits into the broader pattern of international Communist activity in East and Southeast Asia at this critical juncture. These questions require us to look not just at the historical record of the Indochinese Communist Party but also at its relations with the Comintern, the Profintern, the Chinese Communist Party, and the nascent Communist movement elsewhere in Southeast Asia.

The world revolution, as it affected East and Southeast Asia in the late 1920s, involved two different—albeit closely related—strategic perspectives. On one level the global nature of capitalism—in Leninist terms, imperialism—meant that bourgeois exploitation of labour was also worldwide. In that sense the working class in the colonial and semi-colonial countries stood in much the same relationship to capitalist enterprise as did the much larger proletariat of Europe and North America. Organizing strikes among workers on Asian plantations and in Asian factories and mines was an integral part of the international struggle against capitalism as a whole. But on another level it was possible to think of each Asian country in terms of a national struggle between classes, leading logically towards a national revolution under the leadership of its own Communist Party. In that context, it was the task of the Party to mobilize the peasantry, and possibly other classes, under the leadership of the proletariat—in order to defeat both feudalism and capitalism and to win national independence. The tension between the two perspectives was especially noticeable in Comintern thinking about China during the four years following the Shanghai Uprising (and the split between the Communists and the Guomindang) in the spring of 1927. It was also relevant to the creation of a Communist Party in Vietnam.

A general analysis of the revolutionary movement in the 'colonial and semi-colonial countries' was made in a series of 'Theses' drafted by Otto Kuusinen and formally adopted at the end of the Sixth World Congress of the Communist International (17 July–1 September 1928). They defined the ultimate objectives of the 'bourgeois democratic revolution' in those countries as:

> A shifting in the relationship of forces in favour of the proletariat, emancipation of the country from the yoke of imperialism and the establishment of national unity; . . . the overthrow of the power and the exploiting classes at whose back stands imperialism; the organisation of soviets of workers and peasants, and of a red army; the establishment of the dictatorship of the proletariat and peasantry; consolidation of the hegemony of the proletariat.

The relationship between the proletariat and the peasantry was crucial in areas of the world where conflict between the feudal elite and the rural masses still had to culminate in an agrarian revolution; that process must be encouraged and led by the Communist movement. But there was no doubt about the ultimate primacy of the proletarian workers as leaders of the eventual revolution. The national bourgeoisie, on the other hand, was no longer seen as a serious ally in the struggle, and grave reservations were expressed even about the role of the petty bourgeois intelligentsia.[6]

The importance of the proletariat was again emphasized in a section dealing specifically with Indonesia, where a planned uprising under Communist leadership had failed disastrously in 1926–27. The Indonesians were inclined to blame the Comintern for giving inadequate support at that time. The Comintern itself now advised the Indonesians to transfer the 'centre of gravity' of Party activity 'to the places where the town and village proletariat is aggregated— the factories and plantations'; and to concentrate on 'the restoration of the dissolved trade unions and the struggle for their legalization'.[7] Since the Indonesian Communist Party had grown out of the Dutch Communist Party as early as 1920, it was logical to expect the Dutch to continue to play a role.

The Theses of 1928 represent, in one respect, an important stage in the evolution of Comintern strategy in the direction of a long-term pursuit of 'national liberation' revolutions in the colonies, as against merely organizing labour unions and strikes as part of the global struggle against capitalism. In that context it was logical to think in terms of the establishment of Communist Parties in those countries of Southeast Asia which had not previously attempted to organize them: notably the Philippines, Malaya, Siam and Indochina. One contribution to the Sixth Congress debate was made by a Vietnamese delegate—referred to at the time as 'Comrade An' but now identified as Nguyen Van Tao—who was attending as a member of the French Communist Party delegation. He argued that 'Indochina had a strong and concentrated proletariat, and a revolutionary mass organisation would have to be created to take the lead; the Comintern must give its attention to founding a Communist Party and trade unions in Indochina, as well as peasant organisations'.[8]

Before turning in detail to consider Indochina, however, it is worth-while to notice briefly two cases where Marxist-led labour movements appear to have developed in advance of the creation of a Communist Party: those of the Philippines and of Malaya, both countries where Western capitalism could be directly damaged by strikes against enterprises such as plantations and mines. The international organization of labour was the responsibility of the Profintern; in Asia its work was assisted by the creation of the Pan-Pacific Trade Union Secretariat at a conference in Hankou (or Wuhan) in 1927, to which both the Philippine *Congresso Obrero* and the Nanyang General Labour Union (based in Singapore) became affiliated in the same year.[9] The Filipino labour leader Crisanto Evangelista attended the Fourth Congress of the Profintern, held in Moscow in March 1928, which sought to provide new impetus for proletarian mobilization in the colonies. On his return to Manila in June, he set to work to reinvigorate both the *Congresso Obrero* and its political arm, the *Partido Obrero*. An attempt by 'moderate' elements to seize control of the former, at its annual conference in May 1929, led to a split which left Evangelista and the Communist wing even stronger than before. A parallel effort to organize the peasantry was made by his colleague Jacinto Manahan, whose Philippine Confederation of Peasants was allowed to affiliate to the Krestintern early in 1929. But it was not until August 1930 that these developments led to the foundation of the Communist Party of the Philippine Islands. Its relationship to the United States Communist movement remained close.

Meanwhile the Philippine labour movement was prominently represented at the second conference of the PPTUS, which met in Vladivostok in August 1929, with a 'second section' being held concurrently in Shanghai for delegates unable to get to the main meeting. The organization's own propaganda organ noted, in advance of the conference, that the Philippine movement was due to send five delegates, compared with 12 for China, 10 for Japan, but only 3 for Indonesia and one for Indochina.[10] The meeting gave continued encouragement to the Filipino delegates. It would appear that the Shanghai section was also attended by four delegates from the Nanyang General Labour Union (or Federation of Labour) which had succeeded in organizing a strike in Singapore in March 1928 but had since been inactive owing to effective suppression by the British authorities. The PPTUS meeting of August 1929 seems to have attempted to give to that organization the same kind of reinvigoration as had been given to the *Congresso Obrero* in 1928. The possibility of securing support for the Nanyang labour movement from British Communists was mentioned. It was also being urged not to restrict its attention to Chinese workers but to organize Indian labourers on the Malayan rubber plantations. Again, as we shall see later, it was not until early 1930 that steps were taken towards the establishment of an effective Malayan Communist Party.[11]

In the case of China, it is not surprising that the 'Maoist' version of Party history in this period places most emphasis on the mobilization of peasant guerrilla forces, on the launching of armed insurrections, and on the establishment of soviet governments through an alliance of workers, peasants and soldiers. The key issues for Mao Zedong were already those of agrarian struggle against 'feudal' landlords and the building of a Red Army under firm political control.[12] The Comintern account of events in China during these years, on the other hand, stresses the need to mobilize the proletariat as well as the peasantry and to make greater efforts to counter Guomindang influence in the Chinese trade union movement; it also pays more attention to its own guiding role *vis-à-vis* the Chinese Communist Party. Both the 9th plenum of the Comintern Executive Committee (25 February 1928) and the Sixth Congress of the CCP (held in Moscow from 18 June to 11 July 1928) recognized the continuing importance of peasant recruitment, of local soviets, and of building up guerrilla forces in preparation for an eventual armed uprising. But they criticized the notion that success in the agrarian struggle alone meant that the Chinese revolution was already approaching the 'socialist' phase: an idea attributed explicitly at one point to Mao Zedong, already a significant figure in Hunan and Jiangxi, and probably also held by Li Lisan, who reported on peasant questions to the Sixth Congress. In reality, China was still at the stage of 'bourgeois-democratic' revolution: the eventual seizure of power from the Guomindang in China as a whole would depend on patient mobilization of the masses—and especially of the urban proletariat. That priority was reflected in the selection of Xiang Zhongfa, a man of genuinely proletarian origin, to be chairman of the CCP (a post which he held from mid-1928 to mid-1931). The same theme was also stressed in Comintern messages to the Chinese Central Committee in February and June 1929.[13]

In the wake of the Sixth CCP Congress the Comintern Executive Committee and its Eastern Department sought to extend their own activities in China. Until early 1929 the Far Eastern Bureau (or Dalburo) appears to have operated from Soviet territory, at Vladivostok or Khabarovsk. Those centres remained important links in the communications chain, but from April 1929 (according to an official Soviet account) the Bureau was based in China—probably in Shanghai.[14] The extent of the Comintern presence in China at that time, and of the operations of other Soviet Russian agencies, can be gauged from the regular reports sent to Paris by the French Sûreté in Shanghai. In April 1929, for example, they secured (from a contact with access to the Soviet telegraph system) a series of thirteen telegrams exchanged between Moscow, Vladivostok and Harbin during January and February that year. In the same report they noted that Rissine, a special representative of the Comintern's Eastern Secretariat, was about to leave Shanghai for Khabarovsk to report on the possibilities for organizing an armed uprising in the Chinese interior.[15]

The French had the impression, however, that direct Comintern influence within the Chinese Communist Party was exercised only at the level of the Central Committee, leaving lower level Party committees to be run entirely by Chinese cadres. They were able to gain an insight into provincial level organization in June 1929 when an incident in Zheli province (whose capital was Tianjin) led to a number of arrests and the seizure of documents by the Chinese police. There was no evidence of Russian involvement even in the provincial committee.[16] On the other hand, it is possible that the Comintern was beginning to exert influence at the provincial level in Shandong. Around 8–9 April 1929 the French noted an intensification of Communist effort in that province, including a transfer of funds (6,000 Mexican dollars) and the deployment of a number of Chinese and Korean agents of the Krestintern (Peasant International) who had been trained in the Soviet Union. Direction of the new campaign there, which was believed to have been authorized by Rissine, was to be in the hands of a triumvirate including two Chinese and one Russian.[17]

Taking all of this evidence together, it suggests that the year 1929 and the beginning of 1930 constitute a significant period in the growth of Asian Communism. On the one hand it was important for the Comintern's promotion of an active proletarian movement—and the first fully-fledged Communist Parties—in colonial Southeast Asia. On the other, it was also important for the expanding rural strength of the Chinese Communist Party and for its not always smooth relations with the Communist International. It is against this background that we must review what is known about the initial stages in the formation of an Indochinese Communist Party. Moreover, tension between the Comintern and the CCP did not prevent at least some Comintern officials from envisaging a Chinese role in guiding the Communist movement elsewhere in Asia. But there was also a (potentially contradictory) tendency for the Comintern to call on metropolitan Communist Parties to guide the labour movement in their own colonies.

## II

By comparison with China, Indonesia, and even the Philippines, French Indochina does not figure prominently in the published Comintern record of 1928 and 1929. Its one representative at the Sixth Comintern Congress was there only as a member of the French delegation, whereas Indonesia (which had its own Communist Party) had four delegates in its own right. Indochina also had only one delegate (whose identity is not known) at the Second PPTUS Conference in August 1929—compared with five Filipinos, three Indonesians, and four from the Nanyang. Moreover, until around October 1929 there seems to have been no question of recognizing the Vietnamese Revolutionary Youth Association, which Nguyen Ai Quoc had fostered in Guangzhou from 1925 to 1927, as an official Comintern organization.

Moscow appears to have begun to take serious notice of Indochina only in February 1930, initially as a result of the Yen Bay Insurrection of 9–10 February—which was the work of the non-Communist Viet-Nam Quoc Dan Dang (VNQDD). Two weeks later, on 26 February, articles on Indochina appeared in two Soviet newspapers: *Izvestiya* and *Biednota*. The latter proclaimed that 'a new fire of revolutionary struggle has been lit in the oppressed East: Indochina . . . has entered the ranks of colonial and semi-colonial countries which are starting to act against world imperialism'. The author went on to note the possible influence in Tonkin of recent Chinese Communist successes in neighbouring Guangxi province. Neither article made any mention of the 'reunification' of the Indochinese Communist Party earlier the same month, but conceivably an awareness of that move may have contributed to Moscow's new optimism about the struggle there. The *Izvestiya* article, however, recognized that a revival of the revolutionary movement in Indochina had been going on during the preceding 18 months and noted that an 'illegal Communist Party' had been established there 'at the end of 1928'.[18]

If we wish to understand the sequence of events which culminated in the relaunching of the Indochinese Communist Party as a unified organization in early 1930, we must examine in as much detail as possible this preceding period of 18 months. A useful point of departure might be to analyse the somewhat fragmented pattern of Vietnamese Marxist activity around the time of the Sixth Comintern Congress (July–August 1928), starting in Moscow itself. At the time when Nguyen Van Tao attended that meeting there were probably at least a dozen Vietnamese students in the Soviet capital enrolled at the 'University of the Toilers of the East' or receiving political training at other institutions.[19] They included two protégés of Nguyen Ai Quoc who later held the position of secretary-general of the ICP: Le Hong Phong, who had gone to Moscow in 1926 and had been trained as an aviator before starting his political studies; and Tran Phu, who had arrived a year later and stayed until early 1930.[20]

These Moscow trainees had reached the Soviet Union by way of either Paris or Guangzhou, which were the two main centres of Vietnamese political activity outside Vietnam. Those coming via Paris were sponsored by the French Communist Party, but in 1928 the latter was by no means convinced of the value of creating a separate Vietnamese Communist organization, even as a section within its own ranks. According to one source, Nguyen Van Tao and others held talks on the subject with the French Communist, Henri Lozeray, in April 1928, but no decisions emerged.[21] The principal left-wing political organization of the Vietnamese in France at that time was the Dang Viet-Nam Doc-Lap ('Annamite Independence Party') which had been founded in June 1927 and flourished until it was dissolved by the authorities in March 1929. It received a measure of encouragement from the French Communists, but several of its leading members—notably Ta Thu Thau—were already beginning in 1928–29 to express support for Trotsky rather than Stalin.[22] Other Vietnamese students in France at this time, who became prominent later, included the Trotskyist Ho Huu Tuong (at Aix-en-Provence) and the Stalinist Duong Bach Mai (in Paris until he left for Moscow in mid-1929).[23] However, while Paris was certainly an important link in the transmission to Vietnam of Marxist ideas and Communist revolutionary techniques, it was unlikely to play a role at this point in the actual creation of an independent Indochinese Communist Party.

In that respect, Southern China was a more important centre for the Vietnamese Communists. A French Sûreté analysis of the situation in Guangzhou in June 1928 recognized two main revolutionary groups there. One was described as 'le parti de la "vieille révolution"' because it consisted mainly of former supporters of the veteran leader Phan Boi Chau (arrested by the French in 1925 and still detained in Hue). The current leader of that group was Nguyen Hai Than (also called Vu Hai Thu), who had been in southern China since 1905. The other group was the Viet Nam Thanh Nien Cach Menh Dong Chi Hoi ('Vietnamese Revolutionary Youth Association', often known simply as the 'Thanh Nien') which had been built up by Nguyen Ai Quoc during his stay in Guangzhou from early 1925 till April 1927. At this time (mid-1928) it was led by Ho Tung Mau and also included Le Quang Dat, Truong Van Lenh and Lam Duc Thu. Another prominent member, Le Van Phan (more usually known as Hong Son), had been imprisoned by the Guangdong authorities since spring 1927; yet another, Le Hong Phong, was by this time studying in Moscow as we have seen. The Thanh Nien group was believed by the French to receive a subsidy from the Comintern, and also to draw income from property in Guangzhou owned by Lam Due Thu. With those resources it was able to maintain around 100 young Vietnamese cadets in the military schools of Whampoa and Nanjing, who appear to have remained there despite the break between the Chinese Communists and the Guomindang in 1927.[24]

The combined influence of these left-wing exiles in France and southern China inevitably shaped, but also complicated, the early stages of Communist activity inside Vietnam. The influence of Paris and Aix-en-Provence was felt most strongly in Saigon. Phan Van Truong, for example, a former associate of Nguyen Ai Quoc in Paris, had returned to Saigon in 1926 and had published a Marxist newspaper, *L'Annam*, between then and January 1928. Arrested in mid-1927 he had originally survived a trial on charges of incitement to revolt; but the authorities had appealed, and in March 1928 he was sentenced to two years in prison.[25] Another Paris-educated intellectual, the celebrated Nguyen An Ninh, was active in mid-1928 as the organizer of a radical secret society, the Cao-Vong Thanh-Nien Dang ('Hope of Youth Party'), which was especially strong among peasants and artisans in the Hoc-Mon area. But it did not last long: following his arrest in Saigon at the end of September that year, over a hundred of his followers were also detained (and put on trial with him in April–May 1929).[26] As things turned out, the activities of these elite intellectual radicals were to be of much less consequence in the events of 1929–30 than the conversion to Marxism of a growing number of young people whose education had been confined to French-run schools in various parts of Vietnam, or who had been expelled from school altogether for joining in anti-French strikes around 1926–27. They too, however, were sometimes inclined to look for inspiration to the French Communist Party as much as to the exiles in China.

Another important element in Vietnam itself—especially in Central Vietnam—was the revolutionary movement which had originally supported Phan Boi Chau in the first two decades of the century and which had already experienced its own revival in the years since 1925. The Viet-Nam Cach-Menh Dang ('Vietnamese Revolutionary Party') was originally strongest in Nghe-An province but had subsequently gained a following in Thua-Thien and Quang-Nam. At a congress held in Hue in mid-July 1928 it was reorganized as the Tan-Viet Cach-Menh Dang ('New Vietnam Revolutionary Party') with Dao Duy Anh as secretary.[27] Since Nguyen Ai Quoc's group in Guangzhou had also grown up among former supporters of Phan Boi Chau, it was logical for the Thanh-Nien Association to cultivate links with the Cach-Menh Party—and to seek to win over its followers both to Marxism and to membership of their own more disciplined organization. Some individuals were recruited, but the year 1928 was characterized by continuing tension between the (non-Communist) Cach-Menh leadership inside Vietnam and the Thanh-Nien bureau—essentially Ho Tung Mau—in Guangzhou. It was not until late 1929, after its own activity had been largely disrupted by arrests and detentions, that the rump of the Tan-Viet decided to become Communist; by then, the Thanh Nien were the more powerful group in Nghe An and Ha Tinh. The Cach Menh/Tan Viet also had a branch in Saigon, two of whose leaders—Tran Ngoc Danh and Ha Huy Tap—were later trained in Moscow and became active in the ICP.

In the meantime the Thanh-Nien had made other converts both in Tonkin and in Cochinchina. In the North, where by 1928 it was probably strongest in the port of Haiphong, the leading figures included Ngo Gia Tu, Nguyen Duc Canh and Do Ngoc Du (also known as Phiem Chu). They appear to have paid more attention at this stage to mobilizing urban workers than peasants in rural areas, and were already beginning to organize strikes in capitalist enterprises: for example, one by four hundred labourers of the French-owned oil company at Haiphong on 13 March 1928. Something of the flavour of the movement in Haiphong is given in a memoir by Hoang Quoc Viet (alias Ha Ba Cang), who was employed as a turner in the Caron Works there and was inducted into the Thanh-Nien Association by Nguyen Duc Canh in early 1928. He remained active in Haiphong until the second half of 1929, when he went south to Saigon.[28] A parallel memoir by Nguyen Luong Bang—who worked in Saigon for much of 1928 but returned to Haiphong before the end of that year—tells us that early in 1929 the North Vietnamese regional bureau of the Thanh-Nien Association 'directed all its members to proletarianise themselves'.[29] He himself was unable to get a job at the Caron Works and instead became a rickshaw driver, as did several other comrades. Bang's statement establishes a context for Hoang Quoc Viet's claim that in the early months of 1929 the movement was able to establish 'primary' level organizations in most capitalist enterprises in the port city; and also for the split within the Thanh-Nien leadership which was to come into the open a few months later. What is not at all clear is how and why the 'proletarianisation' decision was taken: whether, perhaps, it was based on some kind of contact with the Comintern or the Profintern even at that stage. Certainly the decision was in line with those of the Sixth Comintern Congress, and with what was happening in the Philippines and Malaya at this time.

Meanwhile, in the South the Thanh Nien had both a Saigon organization and a Regional Committee for Cochinchina by mid-1928. There, too, the issue of 'proletarianisation' was probably making itself felt towards the end of that year. The Saigon Committee was beginning to organize strikes in such enterprises at the Larruc ice-plant (19 February), a Cholon rice-mill (23 February), and a Saigon printshop (14 May 1928).[30] Among the leading labour organizers was Ton Duc Thang, a veteran of the Toulon Arsenal to which he was sent during the First World War (but not, as he later claimed, a participant in the Black Sea mutiny of the French fleet). Another Thanh-Nien activist in Saigon from late 1927 was Nguyen Luong Bang, who had previously worked as a seaman on a vessel plying regularly between Haiphong, Guangzhou and Hong Kong. Both were later prominent in the Democratic Republic of Vietnam; but at the time they were probably less senior in the labour movement than Ngo Thiem, a native of Nghe An with whom they both worked in Saigon.[31]

Outside Saigon, the Thanh Nien was also active among the peasants in certain provinces of Cochinchina. Three areas were particularly important at this stage. One was the Hoc Mon area of Cholon province, where Nguyen An Ninh had had a strong following. Another was the district of Cao Lanh in Sa Dec province, where Nguyen Ai Quoc's father (Nguyen Sinh Sac) had settled after leaving Central Vietnam: he died there in October 1929. The third was Ben-Tre, the native province of Le Van Phat, who had been trained (then imprisoned) in Guangzhou and returned to become the chairman of the Thanh-Nien regional committee for Cochinchina in mid-1928. All three of these areas would later figure prominently in the Communist-led rural unrest that occurred—starting in Nghe-Tinh but soon spreading to the South—in 1930–31.[32]

The complexity of political and personal relations within the Thanh-Nien movement in Cochinchina eventually became apparent to the French Sûreté as the result of an incident that occurred in Saigon towards the end of 1928, and which is usually known as the 'Rue Barbier Affair'. It arose out of a decision by the members of the Saigon 'provincial committee' (*tinh bo*), who seem to have forced the hand of members of the 'regional committee' (*ky bo*), to order the 'execution' of the chairman of the latter body, Le Van Phat. He was accused of having forced a young female recruit to become his mistress, but it is possible that the incident also reflected political tensions within the southern leadership. A Sûreté enquiry began when Phat's (initially unidentifiable) body was found at a house in the Rue Barbier on 9 December 1928.[33] The case was immediately complicated by the discovery, in the next street, of a clandestine printing operation run by the Tan Viet group—at that stage unrelated to the Thanh Nien—and the consequent arrest of two members of that organization. One of them was Nguyen Duy Trinh (who later became planning minister and then foreign minister in Hanoi in the 1960s and 1970s). Two other Tan Viet members, Ha Huy Tap and Tran Ngoc Danh, immediately escaped to Guangzhou and from there to Moscow. But it was not until mid-July 1929 that the police eventually succeeded in solving the original murder mystery. At that point (starting on 23 July) they proceeded rapidly to a series of arrests which took in not only members of the Thanh Nien but also some more adherents of the Tan Viet, and a number of members of the southern branch of the Viet Nam Quoc Dan Dang ('Vietnamese Nationalist Party').[34]

In the meantime, immediately following the 'execution' of Le Van Phat, another key member of the Thanh Nien regional committee (Ngo Thiem) appears to have left Saigon for Guangzhou to make a report to the central committee. The latter concluded that although Phat had erred, the death sentence had been too harsh; it therefore ordered both the regional and the (Saigon) provincial committees to be dissolved. An enquiry into the affair was undertaken by Pham Van Dong (the future prime minister of the Democratic Republic of Vietnam, who had been trained by Nguyen Ai Quoc in Guangzhou in 1926 or 1927). At that point—early in

1929—it would seem that the labour leader Ton Duc Thang—on being expelled from the Thanh Nien—decided to found a new organization: the Nam Ky Cong Hoi ('Southern Labour Association') which presumably remained active from then until his arrest on 23 July 1929.[35] Ngo Thiem, Thang's earlier mentor, did not return immediately to Saigon; he was still at Vinh when he was arrested in late June. During the first half of 1929, therefore, the affairs of the Thanh Nien in Cochinchina were dominated by Pham Van Dong, until he too was arrested in late July. But it was probably Ton Duc Thang's new group that was responsible for much of the labour activity in Saigon in that interval. His group, moreover, was more closely in line with the 'proletarianisation' of the Communist movement then taking place in Tonkin.

One further element which must be included in this survey of Vietnamese Marxist activities during 1928 and early 1929 was the mobilization of support amongst the Vietnamese community in Siam. There too it was possible to build on a rudimentary organization previously created by Phan Boi Chau, which still had close ties with his own native province of Nghe-An. The likelihood that the Thanh-Nien leadership was paying new attention to Siam by mid-1928 is suggested by the memoir of Hoang Van Hoan, who had been trained in Guangzhou in 1926–27 and had then returned to work in Nghe-An. In May 1928 he was instructed to travel across the mountains to North-East Siam, where he worked in Udorn from then till 1933.[36] A few months later (August 1928) Nguyen Ai Quoc himself arrived in the same area and appears to have remained there for at least the next twelve months.

It is not easy to say why Nguyen Ai Quoc was assigned to such an apparently unimportant area for so long, after playing a seemingly far more prominent role under Borodin in Guangzhou between 1925 and 1927. Conceivably he was 'put out to grass' for a while, having been too closely associated with a 'united front' line which the Comintern was about to abandon. That impression is confirmed by new evidence of Quoc's correspondence with the Krestintern in Moscow between December 1927 and April 1928.[37] It shows him living in Berlin during that period and experiencing some difficulty in securing the Comintern's permission to return to Asia. Possibly a decision was taken in mid-1928 to send him to Bangkok, with the task of establishing liaison between the Comintern and the whole South-East Asian region, rather than confining his attention to Indochina alone.[38] He was certainly not providing direct guidance to the Thanh Nien Association and its various branches during the critical first half of 1929.

## III

The split which occurred within the Thanh Nien Association at its 'First Congress', held in HongKong from 1 to 9 May 1929, has long been a recognized landmark in the history of Vietnamese Communism.[39] At the time of the meeting it would appear that the organization had around 1,000 members and active supporters in the different regions of Vietnam, including perhaps 200 who had received training in Guangzhou and had then returned home. There was a regional committee for each of the three *ky* (Tonkin, Annam, Cochinchina) as well as urban committees in Haiphong, Hanoi and Saigon; and a number of provincial committees, notably in Nam Dinh, Bac Ninh and Thai Binh (in Tonkin) and in all the provinces of northern Annam. In Cochinchina, inter-provincial committees existed at Saigon, My Tho and Can Tho. The social composition of the movement differed from region to region: in the North it included mainly workers and had few peasant supporters; whereas peasants were more important in the Centre and South, along with low-level school teachers and other 'petit bourgeois' elements, in addition to workers' organizations at Vinh and in the Saigon-Cholon area.[40]

The congress of May 1929 was presided over by Le Hong Son, who was now out of prison. (Ho Tung Mau and Le Quang Dat, however, had themselves been arrested the previous December and were in prison in Guangzhou until August 1929.) The other delegates representing the Central Committee included Lam Duc Thu and Le Duy Diem (sometimes referred to as Le Huy Diem, and also known as Le Loi). From inside the country there were at least three delegates from Tonkin, three or four from Annam, and two or three from Cochinchina; as well as two participants from Siam. The names of the three dissidents are well known: Ngo Gia Tu (alias Ngo Si Quyet) and Nguyen Tuan (alias Kim Ton) from Tonkin; and Tran Van Cung (alias Quoc Oanh) from Vinh. It was they who proposed the immediate formation of a Communist Party, to be based inside Vietnam, and who left the meeting when their proposal was rejected. It is noticeable that there were no dissidents among the delegates from Cochinchina—perhaps because Ton Duc Thang and the other 'proletarian' labour leaders in Saigon had by then been expelled from the Thanh Nien organization altogether.

Ho Tung Mau (despite his absence from the meeting) and Le Hong Son both had important positions in the new central committee; but the Sûreté noted the remarkable absence of the name of Nguyen Ai Quoc, both from the Congress and from the new central committee. Among the other participants who stayed on at the Congress, and who constituted the majority, mention should be made of Pham Van Dong, coming from Saigon; Nguyen Nghia, one of the delegates from Annam; and Duong Hac Dinh, a delegate from Haiphong. All three were named to the new central committee of the association, with Dong and Dinh having responsibility for coordinating activity in their respective regions.[41] There was perhaps a hope that in Cochinchina Pham Van Dong would be able to repair the damage that had arisen from the Rue Barbier affair; instead, as we have seen, he was arrested following his return to Saigon and spent the years 1929–36 in prison. At that point, around August, it would seem that Nguyen Nghia was sent to Saigon—perhaps to take over Dong's role.[42]

Duong Hac Dinh was subsequently identified by the French as the cadre who, soon after the Hong Kong meeting, gave orders for the execution of two female members of the movement in Haiphong at the end of May 1929: an incident known as the 'crime de la ruelle de Metz'. Later in the year he was recalled to Hong Kong to work closely with Ho Tung Mau and Le Hong Son. He seems to have taken over some of the responsibilities assigned in May to Le Duy Diem, who was said by the Sûreté report to have been criticized for his conduct towards the wife of a comrade and to have been sent 'in disgrace' to Siam. Following the released of Ho Tung Mau from prison and his expulsion from Guangzhou, on 19 August 1929, he and Duong Hac Dinh withdrew to Macao—which became their headquarters until early 1930—leaving Hong Son in charge in Guangzhou.[43]

Immediately following the Hong Kong Congress the dissident minority returned to Haiphong and set up, on 17 June, the first organization to call itself the Dong-Duong Cong-San Dang ('Indochinese Communist Party', or ICP).[44] It proceeded to step up its own trade union activities: at Hanoi, Haiphong, Nam Dinh, in the Hon-Gay coal-mines, and also at Vinh and Danang. Between mid-May and late July 1929 eight strikes were recorded in those places—one or two involving several hundred workers—compared with only one in Saigon in that period.[45] The ICP leaders also proceeded to try to win over the existing membership of the Thanh Nien in Northern Annam and Cochinchina. To that end, Ngo Gia Tu himself went to Saigon in July; followed by Hoang Quoc Viet and probably Le Van Luong (another Haiphong activist) in the autumn.[46] They found a Saigon organization badly hit by French moves to suppress pro-Communist activity of all kinds.

In July 1929 the government-général ordered a crackdown which, as we have seen, started with the series of arrests arising from the Rue Barbier Affair and related activities; to be followed by a large number of arrests in other regions between then and October. One tally put the totals at 27 in Tonkin, 48 in Cochinchina, and as many as 265 in Annam. This last figure included a group of 45 people who were put on trial at Vinh and sentenced (on 11 October 1929) either to death or to long terms of imprisonment: among them one of the leading Hong Kong dissidents, Tran Van Cung (alias Quoc Oanh), whose death sentence was commuted to life imprisonment on appeal. On the same occasion, four others were sentenced to death *in absentia*: Ho Tung Mau, Le Duy Diem, Tran Phu, and Nguyen Ai Quoc himself.[47] Meanwhile the Rue Barbier interrogations continued in Saigon, including those of Ngo Thiem (transferred from Vinh), Ton Duc Thang and Pham Van Dong; but their trial was delayed I until July 1930. Likewise the case was prepared against members of the Tan Viet and of the southern branch of the VNQDD. The one Communist group inside the country which seems to have remained unaffected by the crackdown at this stage was the 'Dong Duong', or ICP, group.

The differences between the 'mainstream' of the Thanh Nien and the 'dissidents' at the Hong Kong meeting may be attributable to some extent to tensions that were bound to arise between activists working within Indochina and a central bureau permanently situated abroad. But they seem also to have involved genuine disagreements about strategy, and possibly also different assessments of the current stage of social contradictions in Indochina. It is clear that by the time of the May Congress both 'factions' in the leadership were fully committed to Marxism–Leninism. They disagreed mainly about the steps that were deemed necessary before a true Communist Party could be established. The resolution actually approved in Hong Kong on 9 May 1929 analysed the development of capitalism in Indochina and recognized that eventually the emergence of sharper class conflicts would make the establishment of a Communist Party necessary; but it argued that the proletariat in Indochina was still too weak for that step to be taken, and that the immediate need was to reorganize the existing association. Another resolution, however, required the new central committee to send a representative to Moscow with a letter seeking formal relations with the Comintern.[48] Very probably the dissidents also intended to seek such recognition, but we have no record of their own communications—if any—directly with the Comintern.

## IV

The French Sûreté probably began to gain some understanding of this internal conflict around mid-October 1929, when they arrested another of the dissidents—Nguyen Tuan, alias Kim Ton—in the vicinity of Nam Dinh. Unlike other detainees he was not put on trial: instead he was released in late January 1930, after the French had confirmed the truth of his 'revelations'.[49] An even fuller picture began to emerge by the latter date, following the Sûreté's chance interception of a secret document dated 13 January 1930 in which the leaders of the ICP in Tonkin were apparently intending to communicate detailed information to their comrades in the South, Concealed in the form of a school exercise-book, in which a long message was written in invisible ink, it included: first, a series of letters exchanged between the ICP leaders in Tonkin and the Than Nien bureau (in Hong Kong or Guangzhou) between late July and mid-November 1929; second, a record of decisions taken by the ICP central committee on 5 December 1929 and 7 January 1930; and third, a covering letter which included the warning that Kim Ton (that is, Nguyen Tuan) had betrayed many of their secrets to the French.[50]

The first two letters in the sequence, dated 25 and 28 July 1929, were addressed by the Thanh Nien bureau to the 'comrades of Tonkin' in one case and to 'comrades of the three ky' in the other—the signatories being identified by the Sûreté as Le Hong Son and Le Duy Diem. The third letter, dated 21 August, was signed by Ho Tung Mau and Le Quang Dat (again using pseudonyms), and announced their release from detention in Guangzhou. The two former communications criticized the Tonkin group for splitting the movement and so weakening it, then went on to justify the central leadership's own position at the Hong Kong congress. They offered an alternative procedure for building a Communist Party, starting in secret at the lowest level and gradually working towards the holding of a national congress which would definitively launch the new Party sometime during the following year. The Thanh Nien leaders also criticized the ICP for being too heterogeneous in its composition, insisting that its membership should be purged and that greater discipline be observed in future.

Letters written by the Tonkin leaders in the opposite direction are less well represented in the early part of the sequence—although it is clear that they had already written to the Guangzhou group before the end of July. The first of their letters to be included is one dated 1 September, and its signatories are identified as Nguyen Duc Canh, Trinh Dinh Cuu and Phiem Chu: all three of them members of the original ICP preparatory committee formed in early 1929. They eventually set forth their own version of the Hong Kong split in a letter of 4 October, which placed emphasis on the rapid evolution of a proletariat in Indochina and asserted that the Thanh Nien organization was no longer adequate to provide effective class leadership. This suggests that an underlying issue between the two groups may have been, from the outset, the question of 'proletarianisation'. Another Sûreté report (later the same year) suggested that one of the problems faced by the Thanh Nien, when it sought 'recognition' from the Comintern, or from the Chinese Communist Party, was that too few of its adherents were willing to meet the criterion that all full members of a Communist Party should have had the experience of working in a factory.[51] As we have seen, that was one of the strengths of the Tonkin membership as early as 1928.

By the time of this 4 October letter the situation had clearly entered a new phase—probably starting in September, when the Comintern appears to have made its first indirect response to the Thanh Nien's appeal for recognition. The Sûreté learned that Hong Son had at that point received a letter from Le Hong Phong (still in Moscow) informing him that the International would not even consider recognizing the Thanh Nien as a Communist organization until after an 'inspection' of its activities.[52] That information may have spurred the leadership in Southern China to press ahead with the idea of creating its own lower-level Communist network. In a further letter to the Tonkin group, dated 29 September, Ho Tung Mau informed them not only that 'the Vietnamese Communists in China have formed themselves into a Communist cell' but also that they had entered into contact with the Chinese Communist Party in order to work together. 'The Chinese,' he added, 'have promised to do their best to help us to found a Communist Party.' He was also able to report that 'the Communist International has sent its delegates to us and will proceed to an enquiry into our case'. The same letter indicated that low-level cells had been organized (presumably amongst loyal Thanh Nien members) in Cochinchina, in Annam, and in Siam. In emphasizing that these were only lower-level cells, Ho Tung Mau went on to warn against the danger of the definitive creation of two complete Communist Parties in Indochina—perhaps one in the North, the other in the South—which would then become impossible to unify. In order to avoid such an impasse, he urged the Tonkin group to send a delegation to southern China to bring about unification—through talks which should also involve the Chinese and the Comintern.[53]

The letter of 4 October, which was addressed by the 'Central Committee of the Indochinese Communist Party' to the 'Members of the "Annamite" Communist Party in China', may have been a reply to the above communication. In addition to giving the ICP's version of the Hong Kong split, it also set forth their views on relations with other parties. As far as the Thanh Nien itself was concerned—and likewise the Tan Viet—it was necessary to divide the existing membership into three categories. Those individuals who were genuine Communists would be accepted immediately into the ICP; those who were not yet ready for such acceptance but belonged to an appropriate class should be sent to work within their own class, and should be organized into 'red cells' which might in due course be admitted to the ICP as full participants; lastly, people who did not possess the qualities required for Party membership should be organized into 'support cells' or 'defence cells' and asked to provide financial or technical support. The ICP would welcome as 'true Bolsheviks' those who chose to abandon the 'Annamite' CP immediately; but it did not recognize the latter as a 'true Communist Party'. In the same spirit the letter added that if 'comrade Vuong' (that is, Nguyen Ai Quoc) returned, he would be treated in the same way as other members of the Thanh Nien—without specifying whether he would be recognised immediately as a 'genuine Bolshevik'.[54]

The precise moment at which the Thanh Nien leaders decided to establish their own Communist Party cannot be determined, but the above evidence shows that it was certainly in existence by October 1929. Nguyen Luong Bang describes how in that same month, after working for a time as liaison between Hong Kong and Guangzhou, he was admitted to the 'Annam' Communist Party. He was then sent to Shanghai, where he lived in the French concession and worked in collaboration with Chinese comrades to conduct propaganda amongst Vietnamese soldiers and sailors in French service.[55] Another memoir however—that of Nguyen Nghia— tells us that the Thanh Nien leaders authorized the creation in Cochinchina of an 'Annam Cong San' group (not yet a Party) as early as August 1929.[56] He himself was a leading member of that group, and some time afterwards was summoned to Hong Kong by Ho Tung Mau in order to meet a representative of the ICP from Tongking. He calls this the 'first'—but abortive—unification meeting and says that his interlocutor was Phiem Chu (Do Ngoc Du). No date is given, but evidence from Ho Tung Mau's letter of 14 November 1929 implies that Phiem Chu was indeed in Hong Kong towards the end of October; the meeting may have occurred then, and its failure may have spurred on the effort to build up an 'Annam' Communist Party.

By the end of October the guiding role of both the Comintern and the CCP was assuming fundamental importance in the developing effort to establish an effective Communist Party in Indochina. On 27 October 1929 the Comintern addressed a letter to the various Communist organizations in Indochina, deploring the 'divisions and controversy' that had arisen among them and insisting that 'the key problem ... which brooks no delay, is to establish a revolutionary proletarian party, a massive Communist Party a single Communist organisation for the whole of Indochina'. The directive went on to recommend the immediate formation, 'under the leadership of a representative from the Executive Committee of the Communist International', of an 'intergroup committee composed of representatives from all organisations recognising the principles, regulations and resolutions of the Comintern and working actively among the workers and people.'[57]

It is not known precisely how this message was transmitted from the Comintern nor when it was received by either the Thanh Nien or the Tonkin groups. Nor, indeed, do we know whether it was sent directly from the ECI in Moscow or—perhaps more likely—was a communication from the Far Eastern Bureau (by this time operating in Shanghai). We do, however, have evidence to indicate that it was only one strand in a wider pattern of Comintern thinking, embracing the whole of colonial South-East Asia. Another letter from Ho Tung Mau to the ICP leaders in Tonkin, dated 14 November 1929, reported to them details of a meeting he had had (on 2 November) with an unnamed delegate from the Eastern Bureau of the Comintern, coming down from Shanghai. The delegate had informed him of a recent decision by the Eastern Bureau to organize a new 'Secrétariat de la Fédération Communiste des Peuples Faibles d'Extrême-Orient', whose role would be to give direct leadership in the early creation of Communist Parties in Malaya, Java, Burma, Siam and Annam. (Interestingly the list did not include the Philippines.) The individual parties, when they were eventually formed, would become independent of the umbrella organization. But the first step would be to summon delegates from these various countries to attend a meeting in two months' time (mid-January?) to launch the new organization. In the meantime, Ho Tung Mau suggested that it would be advisable for the Vietnamese themselves to achieve a reunification of their own organization before sending delegates to the larger meeting. Mid-January was thus emerging as a likely deadline by which that process must be completed. The letter went on to ask the comrades in Tonkin to send their proposals for unification (presumably to Ho Tung Mau) well before the meeting of the new secretariat.[58]

The same letter indicates that Ho Tung Mau, in addition to his contacts with the CCP, was making an effort to keep in touch with the French Communist Party. He says that he has sent to France some photographs of comrades Quoc Anh (Tran Van Cung) and Tong Oanh (Vuong Thuc Oanh, son-in-law of Phan Boi Chau), who had been sentenced to death by the tribunal at Vinh the previous month. The gesture was not in vain: on 11 December the photographs appeared, alongside an article denouncing the sentence, in the French Communist newspaper *L'Humanité*.[59] For their part, the leaders of the ICP seem also to have been anxious to put their case to their French comrades. Hoang Quoc Viet tells us that in November 1929, while still in Saigon, he was appointed to go to Paris to make contact with the FCP. Accompanied by a close colleague, Luu Ba Ky, he got a job on board the *Chantilly* and travelled to Marseilles; but circumstances prevented him from going to Paris himself, and it was Ky who established the direct contact. They did not get back to Saigon till early February 1930.[60] The French response was sympathetic, but it should be noted that their own Party organization was passing through a difficult time during the second half of 1929. Plans for massive demonstrations in France on 1 August 1929—to mark the 'Red International Day against War'—had been disrupted by mass arrests in July, including that of Party leader Maurice Thorez. By the end of the year the Party was still in a weakened state, from which it recovered only gradually during 1930. It was unlikely to find the energy for a major effort on the colonial front.[61]

In any case, it was the Chinese Communist Party which began to loom larger in the Comintern's Asian plans during the last two months of 1929. This became evident at a further meeting between Ho Tung Mau (accompanied by Duong Hac Dinh) and a 'Comintern delegate charged with the inspection of all groups in the Far East', which the French believed took place in Hong Kong on 16 December 1929. The 'delegate'—again unnamed—appears to have given some very firm instructions to the Vietnamese Communists. First, it had been decided that the Thanh Nien Association could not yet claim to call itself

Communist. Nor, secondly, could the Comintern recognize as affiliates any of the groups inside Indochina: only Vietnamese affiliated, as individuals, to either the Chinese or the French Communist Party would be recognized. Finally, direction of the affairs of the Thanh Nien was to be entrusted to the Central Committee of the CCP—to whom it must turn for both directives and subsidies, at least for the time being.[62]

In the meantime the ICP leadership in Haiphong had been taking stock of its own organization, still stronger in Tonkin than elsewhere, and seeking to define more clearly its criticisms of the rival organization in Cochinchina. A meeting of the leaders in Tonkin on 23 November recognized that they had so far had more success in Haiphong than in Hanoi and that more effort was needed in the latter city. The situation was 'stationary' in Nam Dinh, and even 'regressing' in Bac Ninh; but progress was now being made in Thai Binh and Hung Yen. In Vinh Yen and Phuc Yen it was reported that new cells had been established, made up of former members of the VNQDD.[63] On 5 December, by which time they had presumably received Ho Tung Mau's letter of 14 November, they held another meeting before sending yet another letter to the comrades in southern China. The ICP side were now inclined to argue against any proposal for immediate unification of the two groups. Instead there should be a further (fixed) period of competition between them, at the end of which—if both groups had proved themselves—unification could take place. Their main concern regarding an early merger of the organizations was that in Cochinchina the membership (presumably of the 'Annam' CP) had been recruited too rapidly and was too heterogeneous; it would take time to decide who were the genuine Communists among them.[64] On 13 December, Ho Tung Mau replied directly to the letter of 5 December, to the effect that he would transmit these criticisms to the comrades in Cochinchina and ask their opinion. At the same time, he observed that if the ICP wanted to send a delegation of its own to the forthcoming meeting organized by the Comintern's Eastern Bureau, he would ask the Chinese Communists to introduce them. But they would need to pay their own expenses and should expect their delegate to be away for one month. Another remark in the same letter suggests that Ho Tung Mau was expecting further news regarding the decisions of the Comintern delegates: possibly an allusion to the meeting with them which—as we have seen—probably took place three days later, on 16 December.[65]

After receiving this last letter—but not necessarily any news yet of the 16 December meeting—the ICP leadership took some further decisions on 20 December. They continued to insist that the leaders of the 'Annam' CP 'are not Communists' and will never have 'the Bolshevik spirit'. It was therefore necessary for the ICP to press ahead with its own plans to establish new cells amongst the members of the 'Annam' party: initially, from January, by creating cells of 'stagiaires'; and then, starting in April (1930), by admitting some of them to full membership of the ICP as 'titulaires'. (A worker might progress from 'stagiaire' to 'titulaire' in three months, but a peasant would need six; and an intellectual a whole year.) This process would allow the holding of a nation-wide general assembly at the end of June 1930.[66]

By the latter part of December 1929, therefore, two rival Communist Parties were operating inside Vietnam. The 'Indochinese' Communist Party, formally established in June 1929, was by far the stronger of the two in Tonkin—and had some support in Cochinchina. Its leading figures were Nguyen Duc Canh, Trinh Dinh Cuu and Do Ngoc Du (Phiem Chu) in Haiphong and Hanoi; and Ngo Gia Tu (Ngo Si Quyet) in Saigon. The 'Annam' Communist Party, closely identified with the older Thanh Nien Association, had its principal following in Cochinchina; but its leadership organization (*tong-bo*) was based outside the country, in the region of Guangzhou, Hong Kong and Macau. Its organization in Saigon had suffered a serious setback during the year, following the Rue Barbier affair and the resulting spate of arrests. So, too, had the Tan Viet party—both in Saigon and in Annam. Sometime towards the end of 1929, the rump of this latter group appears also to have decided to become Communist and to have changed the name of the organization to the 'Indochinese Communist Federation'. But it remained weak and its alignment in relation to the other two groups is unclear.

Of the old Thanh Nien leaders, Ho Tung Mau and Duong Hac Dinh appear to have still been based at Macau, and Le Hong Son in Guangzhou (apart from a visit to Hainan around the end of the year). Another key figure, Le Quang Dat, had by this time moved to Nanning (Guangxi) where he hoped to set up a staging-post for overland liaison with Tonkin. That operation may have found new encouragement around 11 December, when a CCP group led by Deng Xioping and Zhang Yunyi led an uprising at Bose in Guangxi.[67] In addition there was some kind of Thanh Nien liaison group in Shanghai, working closely with the Chinese Communists. They also had a cell in Nanjing, where they could rely on support from Ho Hoc Lam—a Vietnamese staff officer in the Guomindang army, not himself a Communist but the uncle of Ho Tung Mau. For a time there had been a small group of Vietnamese cadets training at the Guomindang military school there, including Truong Van Lenh, a founder member of the Thanh Nien; but they had recently left Nanjing.[68]

Finally, the Thanh Nien group in Siam had remained loyal to the leadership in southern China and appears to have had no contact with the ICP leadership. Its organizers included Hoang Van Hoan, who has left us some account of its activities in the North-Eastern provinces at this time. Nguyen Ai Quoc, however, appears to have left Siam in September 1929 and did not return until the following March.[69] These external bases and connections in China and in Thailand would later play an important role in the survival of the Vietnamese Communist movement during difficult periods in the 1930s and 1940s.

## V

It is clear from the tone of the secret correspondence between the ICP in Tonkin and the 'Annam' CP (former Thanh Nien) leaderships in southern China that neither of the two rival organizations was willing to accept absorption by the other. There are signs that as late as 13 January 1930 the ICP leaders still believed their own efforts at reorganization would gain recognition, once they had an opportunity to explain their position directly to the Comintern delegates rather than having to communicate with them through Ho Tung Mau and Le Hong Son. An ICP meeting on 7 January appears to have decided on a thorough reorganization of 'the Party', and to have called for the complete overthrow of the Thanh Nien *tong-bo*. By 13 January their secret letter to Bach (now identifiable as Ngo Gia Tu) in Saigon indicates that the Comintern had at last instructed them to send representatives to a direct meeting, and two ICP delegates were due to leave Haiphong for that purpose on 17 or 18 January.[70]

There seems no reason to doubt that a 'unification' meeting did indeed take place in Hong Kong in the first week of February 1930; and subsequent Vietnamese memoirs state unequivocally that it was convened by Nguyen Ai Quoc (using the name Vuong) in his capacity as a delegate of the Comintern. Vietnamese sources of the early 1960s also tell us the names of the four delegates from Vietnam who attended the conference.[71] The ICP was represented by two of its founding members, Trinh Dinh Cuu (alias Chi) and Nguyen Duc Canh (alias Trong). These were presumably the delegates mentioned as planning to leave Haiphong around 17–18 January. The representatives of the 'Annam' CP, coming from Saigon, were Chau Van Liem (alias Viet) and Nguyen Thieu (alias Nghia): probably men of lesser standing than some of those—for example Pham Van Dong—who had been arrested in July 1929. Nghia's memoir says that they arrived in Hong Kong at Tet, the start of the lunar new year (30 January 1930), and that the ICP delegates were already there. The 1960s sources confirm the main outlines of the conference, as they were recorded in the document seized by the Sûreté in December 1930.[72] The two sides accepted the Comintern's criticism of their previous errors and agreed to cooperate in the establishment of a unified organization, to be called the 'Viet Nam Cong San Dang' (Vietnamese Communist Party). Practical steps towards unification were also worked out, as we shall see.

There is rather less certainty regarding the immediate consequences of the Hong Kong meeting. Before we try to assess its true significance we need to re-examine the wider context. In particular, we must explore the external relations of the new organization, not only with the Comintern—which continued to withhold formal recognition until April 1931—but also with the Chinese Communists and with other emerging Communist Parties in colonial South-East Asia. Secondly, we must look more closely at what actually happened inside Vietnam during the two or three months following the 'unification' conference.

The presiding role of Nguyen Ai Quoc might easily lead to an assumption that the formation of a single, unified Party represented a victory for the old Thanh Nien group (which he had himself originally founded) and a defeat for the ICP group (which had in a sense 'rebelled' in mid-1929). However, we have only very limited knowledge about Nguyen Ai Quoc's own status and movements during the interval between his departure from Siam in autumn 1929 and his return there the following March. The terms in which he was mentioned in the ICP letter of 4 October 1929 suggest that he was not at that stage accorded any very high status by the Tonkin leaders. The only other firm reference we have to him in this interval is a remark by Nguyen Luong Bang that, during the time when the latter was working in Shanghai between October or November 1929 and late 1930, he met 'comrade Vuong' four times—the first occasion probably being fairly early in that period.[73] Since Vuong was presumably still working under the auspices of the Comintern's Far Eastern Bureau, his presence in Shanghai from time to time is not surprising. Nevertheless it seems rather unlikely that, being himself Vietnamese, he would have been appointed to 'inspect' the affairs of rival Vietnamese groups; or that he was the 'delegate of the Comintern' who met with Ho Tung Mau either on 2 November or on 16 December 1929. His intervention in the affairs of the divided Communist movement of his own country may have begun only in early January 1930; and although it must have had Comintern authorization in some form, it may have been undertaken partly on his own initiative.[74]

Nor can it be assumed that the Hong Kong meeting in itself settled the future relations of the unified Vietnamese Communist Party with either the Chinese Communist Party or the new Comintern 'Secretariat of the Federation of Weak Peoples of the Far East', whose planned inauguration had been communicated to Ho Tung Mau in early November. A Chinese role in the promotion of Communist Parties in South-East Asia was logical, in that the CCP had probably already established its own branches among the various Chinese communities of the region—including that of Indochina. Such branches would be in a good position to maintain liaison between the different colonial countries, as well as with Guangzhou or Shanghai, and there were growing signs of such coordination by December 1929. In relation to the second anniversary of the Canton Uprising of 7 December 1927, for example, the French authorities in Cholon came across leaflets (in Chinese characters) issued by the 'Executive Committee of the League of Oppressed Peoples of "Insulinde" and Indochina'. They also acquired a letter, dated 6 November 1929, which had been addressed by the 'Provisional Committee of Chinese Communist Youth in Annam' to the 'Provisional Committee of the Chinese Communist Party of Singapore'.[75] According to Ho Tung Mau, the new Secretariat about to be formed in Shanghai was to have at least provisional responsibility for the new Parties which would soon be established in Siam, Malaya and Java, as well as for that of Indochina. In mid-December he was also informed that, for the time being, his own group must accept direct guidance—as well as financial support—from the Chinese Communist Party. But the precise relationship between the Secretariat and the CCP remained unclear.

The possibility that the CCP was in effect taking on leadership of the whole Asian Communist movement finds some confirmation in French Sûreté reports from Shanghai itself at this period. On the night of 6–7 February 1930 leaflets distributed in that city called for commemoration of the 'February 7 massacre', which had occurred when the warlord Wu Peifu crushed a strike on the Beijing–Hankou railway in 1923. Some of them were signed by the 'Preparatory Committee for the Anti-Imperialist Federation of the Oppressed Oriental Peoples', which the French report said had recently been created in Shanghai to coordinate 'the revolutionary movement of the Hindus and the Koreans'.[76] The following month information came into their possession which allowed them to construct a chart of the various sections of the CCP Central Committee, together with the Committees for Shanghai and for Jiangsu Province. An important new component of the Central Committee, alongside its Secretariat, Organization Department and Propaganda Department, was a 'Committee of Races' which had responsibility for the 'Anti-Imperialist Association of Oppressed Oriental Peoples' and also for the 'Korean Independence League'. The former of these two organizations had, in turn, four subdivisions: looking after the Koreans, the Formosans, the Indians, and the 'Annamites' (who apparently numbered only about a dozen members so far).[77]

As far as Vietnamese representation in the new Secretariat was concerned, the Sûreté believed that the departure of Duong Hac Dinh from Hong Kong on 20 January 1930 might mean that he was being sent as the delegate of the Thanh Nien to attend its opening meeting in Shanghai. They also had information that he would afterwards go on to Vladivostok, where he would continue to plead the case of the Thanh Nien for direct recognition by the Comintern.[78] It is possible that such a plan was overtaken by the Hong Kong meeting in early February. But we do not know how the latter affected the unified Party's representation in the new regional organization; nor do we have any information about its formal relationship to the CCP. The Vietnamese Communist Party's historical publications are, perhaps not surprisingly, silent on both matters.

Nguyen Ai Quoc's own responsibilities do not appear to have included the task of detailed guidance of the newly unified Vietnamese Communist Party. He apparently issued an 'appeal' on its behalf on 18 February 1930, which is usually included in selections of his writings.[79] But by late March he had returned to Siam; after again visiting the Northeast, he was once more in Bangkok on 20 April. There, 'in his capacity as representative of the Communist International', he 'convened a meeting at which the founding of the Siamese Communist Party was announced'.[80] This would fit in with the belief of British officials in Malaya that his next move was to travel to Singapore. On 30 April 1930 he is said to have again represented the Comintern at a meeting there, which dissolved the (wholly Chinese) Nanyang Communist Party and founded a Malayan Communist Party in its place.[81] By then, too, it is possible that he had succeeded in bringing about a situation where all three of these Parties, in Vietnam, Siam and Malaya, were linked directly to the Comintern—perhaps through the new Shanghai secretariat—rather than being placed entirely under the supervision of the Chinese Central Committee. But that remains a matter for speculation.

Returning to the question of how the decisions of the Hong Kong unification meeting were implemented inside Vietnam, we can again draw on the Hanoi accounts of the early 1960s. One of these tells us that—as an interim measure before the establishment of a single central committee for the whole Party—the delegates in Hong Kong agreed to the formation of two provisional executive committees: one for the North and one for the South. The former included the two delegates from Haiphong (Nguyen Duc Canh and Trinh Dinh Cuu), together with Tran Van Lan (alias Giap) whose previous affiliation is unclear. They took charge of the organization in Haiphong and Hanoi until the return to Vietnam of Tran Phu, one of the more senior Moscow-trained figures, in April 1930.[82]

However, the provisional committee in the South did not include either Nguyen Thieu (Nghia) or Chau Van Liem (Viet), who were sent to reorganize provincial echelons of the Party in Cholon and My Tho. The new committee in Saigon was headed by Ngo Gia Tu (Bach), whom we have met as the senior ICP figure there during the period from July 1929 to January 1930. He was assisted by Pham Huu Lau, Nguyen Van Loi and Ung Van Khiem (who subsequently became a minister in the Hanoi government after 1954); and also by a representative of the Chinese community in Cholon, known simply as A Lau.[83] Thus the impression given by the 1962 account is that—at least in the immediate aftermath of the Hong Kong conference—leadership of the Party organization in both the northern and southern areas of Vietnam itself was in the hands of former 'Indochinese' Communist Party activists, rather than members of the former 'Annam' (or Thanh Nien) group. That need not be cause for great surprise when we recall that throughout 1929 the political line of the ICP—with its strong emphasis on proletarian activity and leadership—had been much closer to the line of the Sixth Comintern Congress than that of its rivals.

The Sûreté does not appear to have kept immediately abreast of these developments in the Indochinese Communist movement. Not until around 20 April did it become aware of what, at first sight, appeared to be the 'fusion of all secret anti-French associations in Indochina'. Two days later, it observed the distribution of leaflets in various parts of Tonkin signed by the 'Dang Cong San Viet Nam'.[84] Probably around the same time it also acquired a document, believed to emanate from the Cochinchina committee of the new Party, which implied that a member of the old Thanh Nien association, Truong Van Lcnh, had visited Cochinchina earlier in the year, but had been obliged to flee again to Siam. On doing so, he had entrusted responsibility for his own comrades to representatives of the ICP. It was therefore six members of the latter group, led by Trinh Dinh Cuu, who—around the middle of March—attended a meeting with another (unnamed) Thanh Nien delegate from Canton and a representative of the Chinese Communist Party, in order to 'realise the unification of the "Indochinese" and "Annamite" Communist Parties under the tutelage of the Chinese Communist Party'.[85] The precise significance of that arrangement still cannot be assessed. One other thing, however, seems fairly certain: the new situation involved at least a temporary loss of influence for Ho Tung Mau, if not for Le Hong Son. The same Sûreté report tells us that Mau, together with his wife (Ly Phuong Tuan) and Le Quang Dat, left Macau secretly for Hong Kong on 22 March 1930. From there they were to be accompanied by a Chinese Communist to Vladivostok, where for six months they would 'perfect their education as Communist militants'.[86]

Such evidence as we have, therefore, suggests that the 'unification' of the Vietnamese Communist Party, although it was brought about by the intervention of Nguyen Ai Quoc, did not in fact amount to a victory for his own immediate protégés. While he himself was occupied elsewhere, in an essentially regional role, the people who mattered inside Vietnam were those who had founded the Indochinese Communist Party in June 1929. It is likely, too, that when Tran Phu arrived directly from Moscow in April 1930, he would have confirmed a 'proletarian' line that was more in keeping with Stalin's current policies than the line with which Nguyen Ai Quoc had previously been identified. In April 1930 the party seemed poised for a new 'high tide' of proletarian struggle. Unfortunately for the new leadership, however, the proletarian element in the Party was the most vulnerable to both surveillance and eventual suppression by the French. Their carefully made plans for a coordinated strike movement against French capitalist enterprises, to begin on 1 May 1930, was nipped in the bud. Hoang Quoc Viet, having returned to Haiphong in time to meet Tran Phu himself, was arrested before the end of April. He tells us how he was joined by numerous other comrades in early May, and that the cells in Haiphong were soon 'crammed with prisoners'.[87]

As the summer wore on, the aspect of the struggle which eventually developed more fully was the peasant movement in the country-side: anti-tax revolts in numerous provinces from Thai-Binh in the North to Ben-Tre and Long-Xuyen in the South, which eventually culminated in a peasant rebellion, now remembered as the Nghe-Tinh Soviet movement—from the name of the province where it became most intense. How far that struggle was deliberately promoted by those elements in the Vietnamese Communist Party which had survived the repression of May 1930—and how far it was influenced by the Chinese Communist thinking of Mao Zedong and Li Lisan—are questions which deserve more thorough study. What has been demonstrated in this paper is that the early history of the Indochinese Communist Party is both internally more complex than many secondary writings suggest and also more interesting, when seen in the wider context of a changing Comintern strategy that sought to take account of all the countries of Asia and was concerned with anti-imperialism as a global phenomenon—rather than with purely national revolutionary aims.

## Notes

1 The earliest reference I have found to the commemoration on this date is an article published for the eighth anniversary, in *Le Peuple* (Saigon), 8 January 1938; it was reprinted one year later in the Hanoi socialist weekly *Notre Voix*, 8 and 15 January 1939.
2 *Thirty Years of Struggle of the Party* (Hanoi: Foreign Languages Publishing House, 1960); for the account of the foundation meeting on 6 January 1930, see p. 24.
3 *A Drop in the Ocean: Hoang Van Hoan's Revolutionary Reminiscences* (Beijing: Foreign Languages Press, 1988; preface dated February 1986), pp. 52–3. Hoan was in Northeast Thailand in 1930 and learned of the unification meeting from Nguyen Ai Quoc himself towards the end of March that year. The explanation based on a confusion of calendars is also mentioned in Huynh Kim Khanh, *Vietnamese Communism 1925–1945* (Ithaca: Cornell University Press, 1982), p. 125, n. 66.
4 See *Lich-su Dang Cong San Vietnam* (Hanoi, 1989), vol. ii, p. 48; also *Tap Chi Cong San*, no. 2, Feb. 1982: article by Nguyen Van Phong, translated in *Vietnam Report* (Washington D.C.), no. 2363, 3 May 1982, p. 23.
5 Centre des Archives d'Outre-Mer (CAOM), Aix-en-Provence: SLOTFOM Series III, dossier no. 6, item 40. The translated documents were sent to Paris on 9 April 1931, the originals having been seized at the residence of a Party member, Nguyen Vu, on 6 December 1930.

6 See the formal record reprinted in Jane Degras (ed.), *The Communist International 1919–1943: Documents*, Vol. ii, 1923–28 (London: Royal Institute of International Affairs, 1960), pp. 530–48.
7 For a discussion of the Sixth Congress debate on Indonesia, and its advice for the future, see Charles B. McLane, *Soviet Strategies in Southeast Asia: an Exploration of Eastern Policy under Lenin and Stalin* (Princeton, 1966), pp. 98–102.
8 Degras, *op. cit.*, p. 527. See also I. A. Ognetov, 'The Comintern and the Revolutionary Movement in Vietnam', in R. A. Ulyanovsky (ed.), *The Comintern and the East* (Moscow, 1979), pp. 472–3.
9 The somewhat limited activities of these unions, in relation to the meetings of the PPTUS, are discussed in McLane, *op. cit.*, pp. 113–36. The general secretary of the PPTUS from 1927 to 1929 was the American Communist Earl Browder: *ibid.*, p. 71.
10 *Pan Pacific Monthly*, April 1929; cited in McLane, *op. cit.*, p. 122, n. 114.
11 'Malayan Labour steps out onto the World Stage', *Pan Pacific Monthly*, December 1929–January 1930; cited by McLane, *op. cit.*, p. 133, and by Gene Z. Hanrahan, *The Communist Struggle in Malaya* (New York, 1954; 2nd edn, Kuala Lumpur, 1979), pp. 36–7. A South Seas (Nanyang) Communist Party of some kind was established in 1926–27, but was not very successful. Its status remains problematic; possibly it was little more than a Singapore branch of the Chinese CP. See sources cited in note 81 below.
12 The secondary literature on this subject is too extensive and well known to, require specific reference. For a brief outline of the official record of Party activity in these years—which makes no reference at all to the role of the Comintern—see *History of the Chinese Communist Party—A Chronology of Events (1919–1990)* (Beijing: Party History Research Centre, 1991).
13 See A. M. Grigoriev, 'The Comintern and the Revolutionary Movement in China under the Slogan of the Soviets (1927–31)' in R. A. Ulyanovsky (ed.), *The Comintern and the East* (Moscow: Progress Publishers, 1979), pp. 345–88.
14 *Ibid.*, p. 361. Development of a secret financial base for the activities of the Comintern's OMS (Otdel Mezhdunarodnoi Svyazi, or 'International Liaison Department') had taken place during 1928—involving, among others, the Comintern agent usually known as Hilaire Noulens or Paul Ruegg: see Frederick S. Litten, 'The Noulens Affair', *China Quarterly*, no. 138 (June 1994), pp. 499ff.
15 'Renseignements sur l'Action Bolchevique et Etrangère en Chine', Shanghai, 15 April 1929: in archives of Ministère des Affaires Etrangères (Quai d'Orsay), Asie 1918–29, Chine, Vol. 209. Four volumes in that series (208 to 211) cover the year 1929; for the early part of 1930, see Asie-Oceanie 1930–40, Chine, Vol. 592.
16 Report from the French Consul in Tianjin, 30 June 1929: Asie 1918–29: Chine, vol. 210.
17 Renseignements, etc. . . . 15 April 1929'; as cited in note 9, above.
18 The articles were spotted by the French embassy in Moscow which sent translations to Paris: Ministère des Affaires Etrangères: Asie 1930–40, Indochine, Volume 28, pp. 51–4.
19 A French Sûreté report of 22 March 1933 notes that seventeen Vietnamese had been admitted to the University of Toilers of the East during the years 1925–28, but some of them arrived late in the latter year; another nine arrived in 1929, and eight more during 1930–31: CAOM, Aix-en-Provence: SLOTFOM III/Carton 131.
20 See their biographies in Tran Van Giap *et al.*, *Luoc Truyen Cac Tac Gia Viet Nam*, vol. ii (Hanoi, 1972), pp. 162–3, 190–1. Tran Phu (1904–31) was secretary-general from mid-1930 to spring 1931; Le Hong Phong (1900–42) held that position from 1935 to 1939.
21 Hue-Tam Ho Tai, *Radicalism and the Origins of the Vietnamese Revolution* (Cambridge: Harvard University Press, 1992), p. 237; she cites the subsequent confession to the

30  *Communist Indochina*

police by Nguyen The Vinh, another Vietnamese Communist, who claimed to have attended the meeting but had left the movement by 1931.
22 Tai, *op. cit.*, pp. 233–8. Trotsky had been expelled from the Soviet Communist Party in 1927; he spent 1928 in exile in Alma Ata before being expelled from the USSR altogether in early 1929.
23 See Daniel Hemery, *Révolutionnaires vietnamiens et pouvoir colonial en Indochine: Communistes, Trotskyistes, Nationalistes à Saigon de 1932 à 1937* (Paris, 1975), pp. 443ff.
24 'Note sur la Situation des Révolutionnaires annamites de Canton, 6 June 1928', CAOM, Aix-en-Provence: Sûreté file 7F.2 (GGI, 65,434). See also: Gouvernement-Général de l'Indochine: Direction des Affaires Politiques et de la Sûreté-Générale, *Contribution à l'histoire des mouvements politiques de l'Indochine française: Documents*, Vol. iv (Hanoi, 1933), pp. 14ff (the latter source will be cited hereafter as *Contribution*).
25 *Tribune Indochinoise*, 25 July, 28 October 1927; 12 and 28 March 1928. Cf. also Hemery, *op. cit.*, p. 64.
26 Tai, *op. cit.*, pp. 191ff.
27 A detailed account of the history of this group was given by the Sûreté, in *Contribution*, vol. i (Hanoi, 1933), on the basis of information from one of its founding members, Hoang Duc Thi.
28 See his memoir in *A Heroic People: Memoirs from the Revolution* (2nd edn: Hanoi, 1965) pp. 151ff.
29 *Ibid.*, pp. 22–3.
30 For these and other strikes during 1928, mentioned below, see *Contribution*, vol. iv, p. 122.
31 See Nguyen Luong Bang's memoir in *A Heroic People*, esp. pp. 19–22. On Ton Duc Thang, see discussion of the Rue Barbier Affair, below.
32 On Nguyen Sinh Sac, see report of the erection of a memorial to him in 1977, at Hoa An village, Cao Lanh: BBC, *Summary of World Broadcasts, Far East*, 5441/B/6. The geography of unrest in Cochinchina in 1930–31 is discussed in R. B. Smith, 'The Development of opposition to French rule in Southern Vietnam, 1880–1940', *Past and Present*, no. 54, February 1972. (For Le Van Phat, again see discussion of Rue Barbier Affair, below.)
33 The affair is covered in considerable detail by a series of files in the French archives: CAOM, Aix-en-Provence: Gouvernement-Général Sûreté Files, 7F.55. See especially the section headed 'Affaire No. 200'. The incident eventually led to a trial, covered by the Saigon newspapers (*La Tribune Indochinoise, La Dépêche d'Indochine*, etc.) in mid-July 1930; and was reported in *Indochine*, 5 October 1930. A short account of the case is given by Tai (*op. cit.*, pp. 215–17) who accepts the interpretation that it was a case of personal jealousy intruding into politics. (I am grateful to Ms Nho Young Soon, who is working on a more detailed analysis, for assistance in unravelling the political dimensions of the incident.)
34 This latter group included Tran Huy Lieu, who became firmly committed to the Communist Party by the time of his release from the island prison of Con Son in 1934.
35 See the information obtained from his interrogation: CAOM, Aix-en-Provence: Gouvernement-Général Sûreté Files, 7F.55: 'Affaire No. 200', pp. 28–9; several others among those arrested appear to have joined it.
36 *A Drop in the Ocean* (see note 3, above), pp 30–1 and 34ff.
37 Sophie Quinn-Judge, 'Ho Chi Minh: New Perspectives from the Comintern Files', *Vietnam Forum*, no. 14, 1994, p. 66; citing documents from the Krestintern files in Moscow (Fond 535/opis 1/delo 42) and also *Ho Chi Minh Bien Nien Tieu Su* (Hanoi, 1992), vol. i.
38 One Soviet work says explicitly that 'from 1928 to 1931' he worked in Siam 'as the Comintern's representative in Southeast Asia': USSR Institute of Oriental Studies,

*Indochinese Communist Party 1929–1930* 31

*Lenin and National Liberation in the East* (Moscow: Progress Publishers, 1978), p. 259. Interestingly this account mentions the reunification conference in Hong Kong, on 3 February 1930, *without* indicating that Nguyen Ai Quoc presided over it.

39  For the standard account, followed by most secondary sources, see the Sûreté publication, *Contribution* etc. (note 24, above), vol. iv (Hanoi, 1933), pp. 20ff; and documentary annexes, *ibid.*, pp. 52ff. As will become clear, the actual Sûreté files now available in the archives at Aix-en-Provence give a more complete picture and raise additional questions.

40  *Contribution*, vol. iv, pp. 19–20.

41  For these and other details, see the Sûreté report, undated but probably of late 1929, 'Les Associations anti-françaises en Indochine et la Propagande communiste: Historique': CAOM, Aix-en-Provence, SLOTFOM III, Carton 48, no. 1 ; esp. pp, 37–41 (also found in Sûreté files, 7F.2: GGI, no. 65,434). That report was followed by a series of monthly (or six-weekly) reports under the same title, referred to hereafter as 'Les Associations anti-françaises . . .' with date and location.

42  Nguyen Nghia (alias Nguyen Thieu) subsequently wrote a series of memoir articles in the Hanoi periodical *Nghien Cuu Lich Su*, nos 59, 62 and 67 (Feb., May, Oct., 1964). We shall meet him again as one of the delegates at the Hong Kong 'unification' meeting of February 1930. See below, section V.

43  *Ibid.*, pp. 44–5 (for the 'ruelle de Metz' incident); and 'Note complémentaire . . . 19 novembre 1929': CAOM, Aix-en-Provence, SLOTFOM III, Carton 48, no. 2 (also in GGI no. 65,434).

44  This date is given in *Lich Su Dang Cong San Viet Nam* (Hanoi, 1989), vol. i, p. 47. The Sûreté later acquired a copy of a manifesto calling for that move, dated 1 June 1929: translated in *Contribution*, vol. iv, pp. 70–2. Another report indicates that copies of that or some similar manifesto were distributed at Vinh on the night of 17 June 1929; followed by the distribution of leaflets announcing the formation of the party on the night of 31 July–1 August 1929: 'Rapport sur la Situation politique de la Province de Nghe An, 2eme et 3eme trimestres 1929', CAOM, Aix-en-Provence, Sûreté files 7F.30 (6).

45  *Contribution*, vol. iv, pp. 122–3. Of the four strikes listed in September and October 1929, all occurred at enterprises in Tonkin.

46  Hoang Quoc Viet, in *A Heroic People*, pp. 154–5; and *Contribution*, vol. iv, p. 23.

47  'Associations . . . Historique' (see note 41 above): SLOTFOM III, Carton 48, no. 1, pp. 67–8; also in GGI 65,434.

48  The texts of these resolutions, and of the letter sent to Moscow, will be found in Sûreté file 7F.2, no. 1: now GGI No. 65,434, no. 1 (CAOM, Aix-en-Provence).

49  See note 50, below. His arrest was initially mentioned in 'Note complémentaire . . . 19 novembre 1929': SLOTFOM III, Carton 48, no. 2. It was one of a number of arrests made in the vicinity of Nam Dinh at that time, and documents seized then indicated that that town was to be a special target of Communist activity on the 7 November anniversary.

50  A translation of the whole document, together with explanatory footnotes, was forwarded by the Government-General from Paris to Hanoi (in Report no. 895 SG, with Annexes) on 12 February, 1930: hereafter as Report no. 895 SG. The collection of letters is noticed in Huynh Kim Khanh, *Vietnamese Communism 1925–1945*, p. 182, n. 93; but he gives few details and appears not to have fully appreciated their significance.

51  'Associations . . . décembre 1929': SLOTFOM III, Carton 48, no. 3.

52  'Note complémentaire . . . 19 novembre 1929': SLOTFOM III, Carton 48, no. 2.

53  Report No. 895 SG (see note 50: Annexe I, Letter 7).

54  *Ibid.*, Letter no. 13.

55  *A Heroic People*, pp. 25–30. He had remained in Haiphong until mid-May 1929 and had met Ngo Gia Tu on the latter's return from Hong Kong; but shortly afterwards was himself sent to work in Hong Kong.

## 32  Communist Indochina

56 Nguyen Nghia, 'Additional Documentation: The Unification of the First Communist Organisations in Vietnam and the Role of Comrade Nguyen Ai Quoc' (in Vietnamese), *Nghien Cuu Lich Su*, no. 59, February 1964, pp. 3–8. For his attendance at the May 1929 meeting in Hong Kong, see above.

57 Quoted (from an official Vietnamese history of 1961) in *Lenin and the National Liberation in the East* (see note 38, above), p. 260; the directive was published in full in *Nhan Dan* (Hanoi), 6 January 1970, and is partly translated (from that source) in R. F. Turner, *Vietnamese Communism: Its Origin and Development* (Stanford: Hoover Institution Press, 1975), p. 16.

58 Report no. 895 SG (see note 50): Annexe I, Letter no. 10.

59 'Associations . . . janvier 1930': SLOTFOM III, Carton 48, no. 4. That report notes other articles in *L'Humanité* (7, 12 December 1929) suggesting that the French were keeping in touch with both of the Vietnamese Communist groups, without choosing between them.

60 *A Heroic People*, pp. 156–7.

61 See Gerard Walter, *Histoire du Parti Communiste Français* (Paris, 1948), pp. 206ff.

62 'Associations . . . janvier 1930': SLOTFOM III, Carton 48, no. 4, pp. 5–6.

63 'Associations . . . décembre 1929': SLOTFOM III, Carton 48, no. 3, pp. 11–12.

64 Report no. 895 SG (see note 50): Annexe, Letter no. 14, dated 5 December 1929; at another point in the same sequence of documents (seized on 13 January and forwarded on 12 February 1930), we find a record of the decisions of the meetings of 5 and 20 December, and that of 7 January 1930.

65 *Ibid.*, letter no. 12, dated 13 December 1929.

66 As note 58, above; but in this case we have no evidence of the decisions being communicated to Ho Tung Mau.

67 For Le Quang Dat, see 'Associations . . . décembre 1929': SLOTFOM III, Carton 48, no. 3, p. 6. On the Bose rising, and further CCP successes in the area, between then and February 1930, see *History of the Chinese Communist Party, Chronology* (note 12, above), p. 65.

68 'Associations . . . décembre 1929': SLOTFOM III, Carton 48, no. 3. See also Hoang Van Hoan, *A Drop in the Ocean* (Beijing, 1988), pp. 75–6, 88–90.

69 Hoang Van Hoan, *ibid.*, pp. 51–2. See also *Contribution*, vol. iv, p. 24.

70 Report no. 895 SG (see note 50): Annexe no. 1 (separate dossier); neither the identity nor the destination of the two delegates was known to the Sûreté.

71 See in particular two articles published in *Nghien Cuu Lich Su*: that by Nguyen Nghia (cited in note 56, above) in no. 59, February 1964; and one by T.C. (not otherwise identified), 'The Secret Leadership Structure of the Indochinese Communist Party, 1930–1935' (in Vietnamese), in no. 37, February 1962.

72 See above, note 5. It should be noted that in that document, the ICP ('Dong Duong') appears *before* the 'Annam' CP at each stage of the record.

73 *A Heroic People*, pp. 28–31.

74 Ms Quinn Judge found a letter in the Comintern records in Moscow (Fonds 495/opis 154/delo 462), from a Vietnamese party official writing from Saigon on 17 April 1931, which criticized Nguyen Ai Quoc explicitly for having convened the unification conference before the formal Comintern directive had been received: see *Vietnam Forum*, no. 14, pp. 70–1.

75 'Associations . . . décembre 1929': SLOTFOM III, Carton 48, no. 3, pp. 13–14.

76 'Renseignements sur l'Action Bolchevique . . . 15 février 1930' (see note 9 above): AMAE (Quai d'Orsay), Asie 1930–40, Chine: vol. 592, pp. 178–9.

77 *Ibid.*, pp. 245–6 and 258–60. The chart was forwarded by the French consul in Shanghai to the Ambassador in Beijing on 21 March 1930. A copy later found its way to the Governor-General of Indochina, who forwarded it to the Minister of Colonies on 13 April: SLOTFOM III, Carton 129.

78 'Associations 1 février et mars (1ère quinzaine) 1930': SLOTFOM III, Carton 48, no. 5, pp. 12–13; also 'Associations . . . mars et avril 1930', *ibid.*, no. 6, p. 2.
79 See for example: Ho Chi Minh, *Selected Works*, volume II (Hanoi, 1962). However, the version included in Robert F. Turner, *Vietnamese Communism* (Stanford, 1975), Appendix B, is slightly different—being based on a revised version published in *Hoc Tap*, no. 5, 1971, with the note that previous versions contained inaccuracies. The main difference is that the 1971 version includes an explicit reference to Nguyen Ai Quoc's having 'fulfilled my task', after 'receiving the Communist International's instructions to solve the revolutionary problem in our country'.
80 Hoang Van Hoan, *A Drop in the Ocean*, pp. 52–5.
81 This meeting is referred to in an official party history of 1942: *Nan Dao Zhi Chun*, translated in Cheah Boon Kheng, *From PKI to the Comintern: the Apprenticeship of the Malayan Communist Party: Selected Documents and Discussion* (Ithaca: Cornell University Press, 1992), p. 103; and also in 'Communism in Malaya up to 1933', in *Malayan Command Intelligence Notes*, No. 75 (15 Jan. 1933) in file FO 371/17147: F1191/1191/61 (Public Record Office, Kew). (The date 30 April also appears to come from British special branch sources.) See also C. F. Yong, 'Origins and Development of the Malayan Communist Movement, 1919–1930', *Modern Asian Studies* (Cambridge), vol. 25, no. 4 (1991).
82 *Nghien Cuu Lich Su*, no. 37 (Feb. 1962): article by T.C. cited in note 71, above, p. 21, Tran Phu subsequently became secretary-general of the Party in mid–1930.
83 *Ibid.*, pp. 21–2. A Lau was also a member of the Party's central committee in October 1930; it is noted at one point that he did not know Vietnamese and needed an interpreter.
84 'Associations . . . mars et avril 1930', SLOTFOM III, Carton 48, no. 6, p. 3. This report, finalized on 16 May 1930, highlighted the 'unification des sociétés secrètes anti-françaises à forme communiste et leur reconnaissance par la IIIe Internationale'; at least some of the Sûreté's information seems to have come from Chinese sources.
85 *Ibid.*, p. 9. The Sûreté thought the meeting took place somewhere in southern Annam.
86 'Associations . . . mars et avril 1930': SLOTFOM III, Carton 48, no. 6, p. 18.
87 *A Heroic People*, pp. 158–9. He shared a cell with Le Thanh Nghi, another leading figure in Hanoi after 1954, who had been active in the mining area north of Haiphong.

# 2 The Japanese period in Indochina and the coup of 9 March 1945

Source: *Journal of Southeast Asian Studies* 9(2) (1978): 268–301.

## I

For the greater part of the period from 1940 to 1945, French Indochina occupied a peculiar place in the Co-Prosperity Sphere of Great East Asia. Following the capitulation of France before the German army in June 1940, the northern part of Indochina became the first area in Southeast Asia to admit Japanese troops — at that stage, as an extension of the Japanese campaign in southern China. In July 1941 the Japanese advance into southern Indochina marked the first step towards a full-scale attack on European and American possessions in the whole region, which materialized in December 1941. But this military advance into Indochina, precisely because it took place before the general assault on Southeast Asia and the Pacific, had to be achieved by means of agreements and treaties with an established government. These were possible only because the French in Indochina decided to recognize the pro-German government at Vichy, so that the Japanese were able to apply diplomatic pressure both in France and at Hanoi. Once the agreements had been made, the Japanese saw no need to change the basis of their occupation of Indochina even after December 1941; they were by then preoccupied with establishing their presence in other areas. Consequently they continued to recognize the French administration in Indochina and to maintain diplomatic relations with it, so long as diplomatic pressure was sufficient to ensure that Japanese military needs were fully met. This situation lasted until early 1945. Relations between Tokyo and Hanoi (or, when the Governor-General was in the South, Saigon) were governed throughout the years 1942–44 by two agreements: the Kato-Darlan protocol signed at Vichy on 29 July 1941, and the military agreement on the defence of Indochina, which Admiral Decoux was obliged to accept on 9 December 1941.[1] The latter made a broad distinction between northern and southern Indochina, laying down that the defence of the north was primarily the responsibility of French forces, whilst responsibility for the south lay with the Japanese. By that time the headquarters of the whole Southern Region Armies, commanded by General Terauchi Hisaichi, was in Saigon. On the economic side, agreements on trade and navigation and on the position of Japanese business in Indochina were signed at Tokyo on 6 May 1941, and were supplemented by several later agreements on trade in specific commodities from year to year.[2] On the financing of trade between the two countries, the Laval-Mitani agreement of 30 December 1942 established a system of payments in "special yen" based on the transfer of gold reserves merely to the account of the Bank of Indochina in Tokyo.[3] In effect, the Japanese were able to treat French Indochina as a separate country, without actually removing the French administration.

One consequence of this was that Indochina, like Thailand, remained the concern of the Foreign Ministry (and later the Great East Asia Ministry) in Tokyo; it was not placed under military administration, even though it had a Japanese garrison army in addition to Terauchi's headquarters. The military dealt with the civilian population through the French, and the French army was allowed to remain under arms until March 1945. This status was reflected in the presence in Indochina of a Japanese diplomatic mission, headed by an ambassador-extraordinary who from September 1941 to December 1944 was Yoshizawa Kenkichi. He had previously been ambassador in France in 1930 and had more recently led the Japanese mission to Batavia which had failed to negotiate a satisfactory economic agreement with the Netherlands East Indies. He was succeeded in 1944 by Matsumoto Shunichi, who was then Deputy Foreign Minister in Tokyo and who returned to that post in May 1945.[4] Another consequence of the continuing relations with the Japanese Foreign Ministry is that there has survived an important sequence of archival material in Tokyo relating to the years 1940–41, 1943, and 1944–45.[5] It ends with the *coup d'etat* of 9 March 1945, but it provides valuable insight into the background to that coup and the development of Japanese thinking about Indochina up to that point. Foreign ministry archives are not available for countries in Southeast Asia that were placed under military rule after the Europeans had been driven out; nor for Indochina after the French were overthrown.

The continuing presence of a French administration in Indochina did not however mean that there was continuity in all respects with the period before 1940. Economically Indochina was cut off from France after the end of 1941 and was obliged to participate in the Japanese economic sphere. Whilst Decoux did his best to prevent complete economic annexation to Japan, and was criticized by the Japanese in 1943 for raising discriminatory barriers to Japanese business in Indochina, he was able to do so only by a series of policies which virtually gave Indochina a centralized controlled economy, with marketing monopolies in rubber and cereals and a state-sponsored importers' federation. On the other hand, the difficulty in transporting goods at all between Japan and Indochina meant that in certain fields production within the country declined (for example, in the coalfields of Tongking), whilst there was a scarcity of imported manufactured products. This led Decoux to sponsor types of industrial production (notably in the pharmaceutical, chemical, and metal-plating fields) of a kind which had been steadfastly resisted under the protectionist principles that had prevailed before 1940.[6]

In the political and administrative spheres, Decoux was also free from detailed direction from France and was able to make a series of reforms which streamlined and to some extent modernized the government of Indochina. During 1942–43 he admitted Vietnamese to higher levels of administrative responsibility than had been permitted before, and he modernized the old mandarinate at Hue. He also embarked upon, but never completed, a grandiose plan to make Dalat the administrative capital of the Indochinese Federation.[7] Politically, he adopted a number of measures which demonstrated his loyalty to Vichy and his approval of the new style of right-wing mobilization that was taking place in France itself. An Indochinese branch of the "Légion Francaise des Combattants" was established during 1941, and other political organizations were abolished. Press censorship was imposed, and Decoux took steps to root out dissidents amongst the French community, justifying his policy by the publication in February 1943 of a book entitled *Les Responsables*.[8] During the year 1942 he encouraged a naval officer called Ducoroy to develop a Movement for Sport and Youth, and to create sports associations and facilities for young people. Participation was open to middle- and upper-class Vietnamese as well as to French.[9]

But what of the Vietnamese? They were not seriously affected by the specifically pro-Vichy policies that imposed censorship and rooted out dissidents, since they themselves had had few rights even before 1940. The short period of relative liberalization following upon the Popular Front Government of 1936 had been rapidly ended with the outbreak of war in Europe in 1939. Elsewhere in Southeast Asia, during 1943 the Japanese encouraged the development of "nationalism" by granting nominal independence to Burma and the Philippines and by convening the Great East Asia Congress held in Tokyo in November of that year.[10] Indochina was largely ignored in this regard; it remained French. The only significant formal change was the reconstitution on 31 May 1943 of the Federal Council, orginally created in 1941, which was now to have thirty "native" members as against twenty-three Frenchmen. Since they were all to be nominated, through consultation with the professional organizations that Decoux had created, and since the Council itself was given no executive or legislative powers, the change did not signify a great deal. It was probably no more than a means of rewarding those Vietnamese who had contributed to the advancement of Decoux's policies, especially in the economic field.[11]

There are nevertheless signs that at least one school of thought amongst the Japanese would have had it otherwise: that some were eager to give the Vietnamese a greater role in their own affairs, if not to overthrow the French altogether. Decoux records the embarrassment he suffered in July 1943 when General Matsui Iwane (well known as an "idealist" for Great East Asia) made a so-called private visit to Saigon during which he went out of his way to make a strongly anti-French speech to an audience of Vietnamese journalists. At about the same time, Decoux noted, there were a number of clashes in Saigon between the police (sometimes French, sometimes Vietnamese) and Vietnamese members of the teams of auxiliaries who by this time were employed directly by the Japanese. He says that he even heard of plans for demonstrations, under *Kempeitai* protection, to demand independence for Annam; but these did not materialize.[12]

Philippe Devillers, who was also in Saigon at this period, remarks that during 1943 the Japanese increased their encouragement of nationalist groups in Cochinchina, despite the disapproval of the French. They persuaded the pro-Japanese Caodaist leader Tran Quang Vinh to form a new committee for that sect, and to declare his support for the southern branch of the *Viet-Nam Phuc-Quoc* movement which had been formed (also under Japanese auspices) the previous year by Tran Van An.[13] There was talk in May 1943 of these two groups holding a joint congress the following September, but it did not take place. These few clues suggest that in the summer of 1943 the Japanese were already debating the question whether to overthrow the French and set up a Vietnamese state, to be run by nationalist leaders who were willing to collaborate with Japan. If so, they must have decided against such a step. It is possible that it was for this reason, as well as because of French moves to suppress nationalist groups, that in October and November 1943 the Japanese rescued several pro-Japanese figures from arrest by the French, and spirited them away to Singapore and other places. Devillers mentions in this category Tran Van An, Tran Trong Kim, and Nguyen Van Sam.[14]

It is not easy, unfortunately, to go beyond the published French material to reconstruct a detailed picture of the various unofficial relations which undoubtedly existed between Japanese agencies and Vietnamese nationalists during the years 1940–44. With one important exception, the Japanese have provided hardly any information on this subject, whilst the French archives are not yet open beyond the year 1940. We must rely on the few indications contained in Vietnamese sources (mostly published memoirs), which are far from adequate even if they are wholly reliable so far as they go.

Probably the best known, but not necessarily the most important, Vietnamese nationalist figure to collaborate with the Japanese in this period was Prince Cuong-De, a member of the Nguyen imperial family who had escaped from Hue with the help of the nationalist Phan Boi Chau in 1905 and had lived in exile for most of the time since then. By the late 1930s he was once more in Tokyo, but in March 1939 he made a brief trip to Shanghai to meet some of his former supporters, and together they set up the *Viet-Nam Phuc-Quoc Dong-Minh Hoi* (Vietnamese League for Restoration of the Nation).[15] Some of its members then went to Kwangtung to gather new members for the organization, and by the autumn of 1940 had raised a military unit. It was this group which played a small part in the Lang-Son incident of 22–26 September 1940, when the Japanese army sought to put pressure on the French by invading Indochina and attacking Lang-Son. The officers responsible for this attack were reprimanded by the Japanese command, since they went into action after the French had already signed an agreement; their force quickly withdrew. But not before part of the *Phuc-Quoc* force of Vietnamese had made its own miscalculation and tried to start a revolt against the French in the border area. After suffering serious casualties they were obliged to withdraw to Kwangsi, where they subsequently became detached from allegiance to the Japanese and went to work with the Kuomintang General Chang Fa-kuei.[16] But if the French had been less cooperative, and if the Japanese invasion had developed into a major military operation to seize Tongking by force, it is possible that the Vietnamese unit could have played a role comparable to that of Aung San and his "thirty heroes", recruited in Burma by Colonel Suzuki Keiji at precisely this period (summer 1940) in order to accompany the eventual Japanese invasion of Burma.[17] Since the French continued to cooperate, there was no need for such a Vietnamese group even in 1941–42.

Cuong-De himself returned to Tokyo after the Shanghai meeting, but in September 1939 he was asked to go to Taipei to help the Japanese set up a Vietnamese-language radio programme in Taiwan — for example, by recruiting suitable personnel. He remained there until May 1941, then once again returned to Japan.[18] For the remainder of the period down to March 1945 he seems to have stayed there, acting as a symbolic focal point for Vietnamese loyalty and from time to time receiving visitors (or recruits) from Indochina. One of these was Vu Dinh Dy, a native of Tongking, who in 1936 had organized a group called "Eastern Independence Party", perhaps already with Japanese assistance. In 1941, he became associated with the *Ai Quoc Doan* (Patriots Group), which Devillers mentions as one of the pro-Japanese groups in Hanoi, and which the Viet-Minh Provisional Government was later to proscribe by a decree of 12 September 1945.[19] At some point he was taken from Indochina to Hainan Island and given military training, before being sent back to Saigon to assist the Japanese army. He went to Japan to meet Cuong-De, perhaps in 1941, and appears to have been again in Tokyo in 1944. In July of that year he was again sent to Saigon, this time at the suggestion of General Matsui's *Kisaragi Kai*, a private association which had submitted to the Japanese Imperial Headquarters a proposal for the recruitment of a group of twenty to thirty Vietnamese nationalists, who would be brought to Japan for training. Vu Dinh Dy was supposed to arrange this in Saigon, but was prevented from doing so by the commander of the Garrison Army, General Machijiri, who was advised that such a blatant move would merely arouse French suspicions and achieve nothing.[20] It is not clear whether Dy played any further part in Japanese planning, but he is not heard of in Vietnamese sources relating to the period after 9 March 1945.

Cuong-De had relationships with other Vietnamese in Indochina itself during these years. We have seen that in 1942–43 there was a southern branch of the *Phuc-Quoc* in Cochinchina, headed by Tran Van An. The latter, born in Long-Xuyen province in 1903, had studied for a time in France in the 1920s and had been associated for a while with the Constitutionalist group of Bui Quang Chieu. He had been detained by the French in 1940–41, and was recruited by the Japanese following his release. Although he was obliged to leave Vietnam in October 1943, he was later to return and to play a part in the final days of Japanese rule in Saigon.[21] Another pro-Japanese leader said to have been in touch with Cuong-De was the Caodaist Tran Quang Vinh. The Tay-Ninh sect of the Caodaists, headed by Pham Cong Tac, is reputed to have had dealings with the Japanese before 1940; and for that reason the French took measures against it as early as the spring of 1941. The "holy see" at Tay-Ninh was occupied by French troops, and Pham Cong Tac himself was exiled to the Comoro Islands in the Indian Ocean. Tran Quang Vinh emerged in February 1943 when the Japanese encouraged him to form a new Caodaist Committee, and, as we have seen, later in the year he was in touch with Tran Van An.[22] In July 1944 Decoux asked General Machijiri to arrest Vinh and hand him over to the French authorities, but the Japanese refused. By the end of 1944, according to a French source, the Japanese were organizing Caodaist supporters to work in small shipyards in Saigon, to build wooden boats that might be used if the Japanese had to fight a war against the Allies within Indochina itself. They were also giving Caodaists training in martial and guerrilla warfare.[23]

By 1944, the Caodaists were probably collaborating much more closely with the Japanese than was the other important religious sect of Cochinchina, the *Hoa-Hao* (also known as the *Dao-Xen*). Although formally "founded" in 1939 by Huynh Phu So, the sect could trace its origins back to the *Buu-Son Ky-Huong* movement of the years 1911–16, and beyond that to the teachings of a master who had lived in the area as long ago as the 1840s. In May 1941, when Pham Cong Tac was being exiled, the French transferred Huynh Phu So from semi-detention near Saigon to house-arrest in Bac-Lieu. In October 1942 he was to have been moved still further away, to Laos, but was kidnapped by the *Kempeitai* and installed in a house in Saigon under their protection.[24] By 1944, however, he does not appear to have figured very seriously in their plans although he was used for propaganda purposes amongst his own following.

In Tongking, and possibly also Annam, the best-known pro-Japanese movement is that generally known as the *Dai-Viet*, so called after the name by which Vietnam was known in the fourteenth and fifteenth centuries. There were in fact several parties of this name, some of which seem to have been established by former supporters of the Chinese Kuomintang who now rallied to the Japanese. The *Dai-Viet Quoc-Xa Dang* (Dai-Viet National Socialist Party) is said to have been founded as early as 1936 by Nguyen Xuan Tieu. The *Dai-Viet Quoc-Dan Dang* was founded in 1940 by a group of former members of the *Viet-Nam Quoc Dan Dang* (that is, the Vietnamese K.M.T.); whilst another such group led by Nguyen Tuong Tam created the *Dai-Viet Dan-Chinh Dang* at about the same time. In 1944 these three groups joined together to form the *Dai-Viet Quoc-Gia Lien-Minh* (Dai-Viet National Alliance), probably as a result of Japanese efforts to merge them into a single movement.[25] But very little is known of their membership or internal structure. What is remarkable is that none of the personalities mentioned in connection with them seems to have played any part in the creation of a Vietnamese government after 9 March 1945.

Finally mention must be made of Ngo Dinh Diem, the former Minister of Interior under Bao-Dai in 1933, who had also emerged by 1944 as a Japanese collaborator and as a supporter of the claims of Cuong-De to the throne at Hue. In July 1944, whilst living at Hue, he received advance warning of French plans to arrest him and so sought the protection of the Japanese. He too was taken to Saigon by the *Kempeitai* and given their protection, living in a hospital until March 1945.[26] He is mentioned by Cuong-De as having sent an envoy to Tokyo in 1943, but we do not know what his formal position was in relation to other Cuong-De supporters. About the end of July 1944, a *Kempeitai* officer arranged a meeting between him and Vu Dinh Dy, which was apparently their first contact with one another. The two men quarrelled and perhaps both lost ground with the Japanese as a result.

The impression that emerges from all these fragments of information is that by the end of 1944 there was quite a number of Vietnamese nationalist groups which had contact with the Japanese and which were ready to collaborate with them if called upon to do so, but who were not necessarily in harmony (or even in contact) with one another. It is possible, indeed, that they were in touch with different and even rival groups or agencies within the Japanese command structure itself; such a situation is certainly known to have arisen in Java during 1942–43, where different Indonesian religious and nationalist groups had quite different Japanese sponsors.[27] Unfortunately we know very little about the Japanese side of this relationship in the case of Vietnam.

The available sources suggest that there were at least three Japanese organizations in Indochina during the years 1941–44 which had unofficial (and political, or semi-political) contact with Vietnamese groups. The first was the *Kempeitai* or "Military Police" within the Imperial Army, which is mentioned several times by Devillers. But he indicates no names, and in Japanese published material only one name is mentioned: a "Mr. H", who helped Ngo Dinh Diem in 1944. This was Colonel Hayashi Hidezumi; but since he did not go to Vietnam until early in 1944, he cannot have been involved in events before that date.[28] In general the *Kempeitai* seems to have had contacts with the Caodaists and with Tran Van An, but the full extent of its relationships cannot at present be defined.

Secondly, on the civilian side there was a commercial enterprise known as the Dainan Koosi (or, in Vietnamese, *Dai-Nam Cong-ty*) which operated in Saigon and perhaps other places from 1941. A press report from Saigon on 9 November 1945 says that the firm was "believed to be behind the Japanese Secret Service" in Indochina. The British had arrested the manager of its Phnom Penh office, but the Saigon manager (named here as Sumita Nichu) "who was believed to head all Japanese intelligence in Indochina", had escaped to Taiwan before the British arrived.[29] This function of the Dainan Koosi is also noted by Devillers, who names its head as Matsushita, and says that he was in Saigon in the 1930s and again from 1941.[30] He too had contact with the Caodaists, and possibly other groups. According to Colonel Hayashi, he was born about 1892 in the Amakusa area of Western Kyushu and went to Indochina as early as 1909 to work for the Japanese enterprise Mitsui Busan. He knew the country and the Vietnamese language very well by the 1940s; but there is no means of knowing the extent of his authority within the Japanese decision-making structure.

Thirdly, also on the civilian side, there existed a Japanese Cultural Institute in Saigon which may also have played a part in maintaining unofficial contacts with Vietnamese. Its head during 1944–45 was Yokoyama Masayuki, a man of considerable experience and probably a more important figure than this post might suggest; he subsequently became the principal Japanese adviser to Bao-Dai after 9 March 1945. Born in 1892, he had held diplomatic posts in France in the early 1920s, and was Japanese minister in Egypt in 1936. His first known connection with Indochina was his appointment in 1941 to supervise the Japanese inter-ministerial survey of the colony's natural resources. Unfortunately nothing is known of his activity in Indochina between then and 1945, except for references to his attending ceremonial occasions.[31] Another man who was connected with the Cultural Institute, probably as its Director at one time, is referred to in a Vietnamese source as "Komashu" and appears to have been Komatsu Kiyoshi. He too had been in France in the early 1920s, and is said to have met the young Nguyen Ai Quoc in Paris in 1919; but he became a writer rather than a diplomat, and is noted for his translations of French authors (including André Malraux) in the late 1940s and 1950s, as well as for a book on Vietnam published in Tokyo in 1955. But there is not a great deal of information about his work in Vietnam in the early 1940s, beyond the fact that he was a friend of Pham Ngoc Thach, the Saigon doctor who in 1945 was to become both leader of the Japanese-sponsored youth movement and a secret member of the Indochinese Communist Party.[32]

To sum up, during the period down to the end of 1944 Japanese policy in Indochina had two aspects. On the one hand the Foreign Ministry and the Army recognized the French position there and were content to leave the civil administration to Governor-General Decoux, so long as he cooperated in meeting the essential requirements of the Japanese army. On the other hand a number of Japanese organizations had unofficial relationships with Vietnamese nationalists, which could be brought into play if it were ever thought necessary to overthrow the French administrators and establish either direct Japanese control or an "independent" Vietnamese regime. By the beginning of 1945 the need for this was recognized by almost all Japanese involved in Indochina policy, but there was still room for much disagreement over precisely how it should be done.

## II

The initial Japanese penetration of Indochina had begun immediately after the defeat of France by Germany, and had been based on negotiations with the Vichy regime. When France was liberated by the Allies and a new provisional government was formed by De Gaulle, in August/September 1944, it was unlikely that the colony would remain completely unaffected for very long, and the Japanese attitude was liable to change. Decoux had earlier taken precautions against a situation of this kind. In February 1943 he had secured from Vichy a decree authorizing him to take over independent responsibility for Indochina in the event of his being cut off from metropolitan France. The Japanese followed the German example of pretending that the Vichy regime still existed despite the liberation, and on 20 August 1944 (the day after the Allies reached Paris), Decoux invoked the decree and assumed full authority.[33] For the time being the Japanese accepted this arrangement and were willing to carry on as before. But as the autumn went on it would seem that they began to face up to the probability that in due course they would need to seize direct control of Indochina.

One development which obliged them to think in those terms was the creation of a Resistance movement amongst the more adventurous elements within the French community, and especially within the French army in Indochina. In July 1944 a French officer working with the British Force 136 in India (in effect, and Asian arm of S.O.E.) was parachuted into Tongking and made contact with the commander of French forces in Indochina, General Mordant.[34] As a result, Mordant agreed to take steps towards organizing a resistance movement; and to that end, without informing Decoux of the real reason, he obtained permission to retire from his command on grounds of age. On 10 September 1944 Mordant was formally appointed by De Gaulle to head the Resistance within Indochina, directly under General Blaizot who was the senior French commander for the Far East and head of the French military mission attached to South East Asia Command.[35] There was in fact some confusion on the Allied side, since the Americans were unwilling to recognize Blaizot's status, or even to accept that French Indochina was within the geographical limits of South East Asia Command. Whilst it was agreed that in certain cases Force 136 might operate within Indochina, the Americans were still insisting in January and February 1945 that the country was formally within the China Theatre and that its eventual liberation was primarily the responsibility of Wedemeyer and the Chinese troops under Chiang Kai-shek.[36] Mordant however maintained his links with Ceylon and India, and in November he received a further visit from the same officer, Major de Langlade. By this time Decoux had been informed of the existence of Mordant's organization, and of his authority under De Gaulle. On 19 November 1944 Decoux received Langlade at the Governor-General's palace in Hanoi.[37] The Admiral resented a situation in which Mordant had authority in the eyes of Paris, but where he himself was obliged to continue formally as Governor. But there was still some hope of deceiving the Japanese, if Decoux carried on ostensibly as usual; and in fact the Japanese did not decide to act until the following January, even though they were probably aware of some kind of secret activity amongst the French long before then.

More important in Japanese calculations, however, were general strategic considerations in a war which was beginning to go badly for them. During 1944 the Japanese had made their last two significant offensives of the war. In March they had begun an offensive towards the Burma-Assam border, with an advance towards Kohima and Imphal.[38] The battle which thus began lasted until late in the year, but already by July it was clear that the Japanese could not force their way through and would ultimately be obliged to withdraw. In April 1944 came the Ichi-go operation in China, directed against the airfields from which the Fourteenth U.S. Army Air Force had been bombing Japanese supply lines with devastating effect.[39] That offensive was more successful, and by June the Japanese had captured Changsha. In October and November 1944, they captured the Kwangsi bases of Kweilin and Liuchow, but then appear to have decided against making any major offensive against Kunming where General Chennault had his headquarters. But if they were still capable of offensives in China and Burma, the Japanese were on the defensive in the Western Pacific. At the Second Quebec Conference in mid-September 1944, the Allied leaders approved an American proposal to land on the Philippine island of Leyte in October, an operation which had previously been envisaged for late December.[40] About the same time, the new Japanese prime minister, Koiso Kuniaki, compared the forthcoming battle on Leyte with the battle of Tennozan in 1582, which had marked the decisive emergence of Hideyoshi as the most powerful lord in Japan.[41] But if Leyte was decisive, it was to be in the opposite sense of that intended by Koiso. The Japanese lost the naval battle of Leyte Gulf on 24–26 October 1944, and by 10 November General Yamashita was advising General Terauchi (in vain) that Leyte was going to be lost.⁴² More Japanese reinforcements were sent, but the Americans gained final control of the island on 26 December 1944.

It was against this background that the Japanese had to decide what to do about Indochina. They did not have much knowledge of Allied planning, and were therefore not in a position to know that there was in fact no immediate threat to the area. It is very likely that the Chinese, with American support, had been planning an advance into Tongking from Kwangsi before the fall of Liuchow and Kweilin; but that was no longer a practical possibility for the time being. From the West, there was also the beginning of a threat from South East Asia Command, and we now know from the British archives that there were serious hopes for a French-led uprising in Indochina in the Spring of 1945, if only the Americans would agree to it.⁴³ But for the Japanese, the main threat seemed to come from the Americans. In a conversation between Yoshizawa and the Frenchman Boisanger, in November 1944, the Japanese ambassador is reported as saying that if Manila were to fall to the Americans, policy towards Indochina might have to be revised.⁴⁴ The Allies in fact had no plan to make Indochina a part of the South Western Pacific Theatre: they had already decided to advance northwards from Luzon after Manila had been taken. But in their ignorance the Japanese feared American landings, and saw the French Resistance as part of a plan to support that move when the time came. It was for that reason that they took very seriously the American air raids on Indochina on 12 January 1945. Already since 1943 the northern area of Indochina, as far south as Vinh, had been bombed by planes coming from Chennault's airfields to the North. But this was the first time that Indochina had been attacked by planes based on carriers in the Pacific, and they saw it as the first step towards an eventual American invasion.⁴⁵

Already by November 1944 a Japanese officer on the staff of the garrison army (known as *Shin* headquarters), which was distinct from the Southern Army headquarters of Terauchi, although both were in Saigon, had been instructed to prepare a plan for a Japanese take-over in Indochina. He had the plan ready by the end of the year, although it was subsequently revised.⁴⁶ Also towards the end of the year, two military moves were made which indicated the new importance the Japanese were giving to the defence of Indochina. In December 1944 General Machijiri, who had commanded the garrison army (the Thirty-eighth Army) since 1942 or earlier, was replaced by General Tsuchihashi.⁴⁷ At about the same time, part of the forces which had been successful in Kwangsi in October and November began to move into Tongking. By 20 January 1945, further units were crossing into Indochina, namely, the Hikari Corps led by General Nagano, who established his headquarters to the west of Hanoi. Soon afterwards the Ambassador Matsumoto (himself a new appointee in December 1944) complained to Tokyo of the rough behaviour of the new arrivals, implying that the forces which had occupied Indochina thus far were of a more gentle disposition.⁴⁸ The importance of Tongking in the new situation becomes clear when it is recalled that under the joint defence agreement of December 1941, the French had been made responsible for the security of northern Indochina. It was there that General Sabattier (under Mordant) was responsible for organizing the Resistance and for a plan which would have used French troops to defend the Lang-Son border area against any Japanese move to disarm them.[49] If the Japanese were to implement any plan for direct control over Tongking, they needed the reinforcements.

By the end of January, therefore, the question of Indochina had assumed some urgency in Japanese eyes. On 1 February 1945, the Supreme War Leaders' Conference in Tokyo decided in principle that action must be taken to establish direct Japanese control of the country at some date which was still to be decided.[50] Throughout February the Japanese debated among themselves the detailed plan for the take-over: the terms of the ultimatum to Decoux; plans for the two contingencies of his accepting or rejecting the ultimatum; the question of future administration in Indochina and the relationship between the military and the diplomatic staff; and the issue of independence for Annam, Cambodia, and Laos.[51] In the meantime, Matsumoto was instructed to open discussions on the question of greater French financial support for the Japanese army in Indochina, as a first step towards putting new pressure on Decoux.[52] On their side, the French were also aware of the need for greater urgency, but they were still woefully unprepared. As early as July 1944, it would appear that Mordant had told Langlade that any effective action against the Japanese by a French Resistance force would depend on the arrival of well-trained reinforcements. By February there was a force of six hundred French officers, all familiar with Indochina, ready to be shipped from North Africa to India and eventually to Southeast Asia. It was intended at one point to move them to India on 15 February 1945. But whereas the British within South East Asia Command were willing, the Combined Chiefs of Staff in Washington — that is, in effect, the Americans — vetoed the proposal.[53] The force was therefore still in North Africa when the Japanese coup occurred. In its absence, Mordant and his colleagues had to devise plans for resistance without them, and it was evident that their options were very limited.

In the communique in which the Japanese later justified their action of 9 March 1945, they drew attention to a meeting of French leaders which had taken place on 20 February at Hanoi, of which they seem to have had some inside knowledge. They asserted that many of the Frenchmen present had advocated an immediate armed attack on Japanese positions, and also that French forces had received supplies dropped by air on 20–22 February 1945.[54] The French documentation, available from subsequent memoirs, shows in fact that on 19 February Decoux prepared a set of instructions to the civilian administration in the event of military action against Japan.[55] But he added the observation that he did not consider the danger imminent, which suggests that he had very little inkling of actual Japanese planning. On the same day (19 February 1945), the most determined of the generals, Sabattier, wrote to Mordant of the need for greater preparedness, but even he did not envisage short-term readiness before 15 March.[56] He himself took the precaution of creating a secret command post at Phu-Doan (between Viet-Tri and Tuyen-Quang), and it was no accident that Sabattier was the one senior general to escape the Japanese net.

The Japanese in fact resolved most of their problems of detail about Indochina by the end of February. As late as 26 February, Matsumoto — unhappy at the way the disagreements between the army and the diplomats were being settled — argued for postponement of the action until after 25 April 1945, the date when Russian intentions regarding the Soviet-Japanese Non-Aggression Pact would become clear.[57] But on the very same day it would seem that the Supreme War Leaders' Conference decided on action in the near future; the precise date was probably left to be decided by the local military commanders. All the final details were completed by 3 March 1945, which suggests that initially that was the date set for the coup. Indeed, it would appear that American intelligence sources had reason to believe it would occur then, for on 3 March we find Shigemitsu writing to Matsumoto to report a monitored radio broadcast out of San Francisco—a report that on 3 March, at 11.00 a.m. Japanese troops had disarmed the French forces in Indochina without any resistance by the Governor-General![58] If the plan was postponed, it was probably because on that day Decoux was in Dalat, whereas the plan required his presence in Saigon. Conditions were not finally right until 9 March.

The events of the coup itself and its immediate aftermath have long been known from the French point of view, notably through the memoirs of Decoux and Sabattier. There is also by now a small amount of material published in Japanese: in particular, a section of a volume in the series produced by the War History Office of the Self Defence Agency; and a chapter by Tominaga Toyofumi, a journalist who witnessed the coup in Hue.[59] As one would expect from what has been said so far, the coup went very smoothly for the Japanese in the South, but was slightly less easy to accomplish in Tongking.

On the evening of 9 March 1945, Matsumoto called on Decoux at his palace in Saigon, ostensibly to finalize the financial negotiations which had been going on for the past month or more. At 7:00 p.m. he presented the Frenchman with an ultimatum demanding that all French forces be placed immediately under Japanese command, together with control of all transport systems and all war materials in Indochina.[60] Two hours later, when the ultimatum expired, Decoux gave a reply which the Japanese interpreted as rejection of their conditions, and they gave the order to attack. In the South there was virtually no fighting at all, and Decoux himself and his senior officials submitted to arrest and internment. At Hue, the situation was more complicated because of French superiority of numbers and because it was essential for the Japanese plan to establish swift control over the palace and the physical presence of the emperor.[61] By a stratagem, they gained entry into the main fortified position within the old citadel, and were lucky enough to kill the most senior French officer at an early stage in the fighting. They had reduced most points of any military importance in the city by the afternoon of 10 March, and on the same day Bao-Dai received a Japanese delegation led by Yokoyama Masayuki, which virtually took the place of the French Resident and his staff.

At Hanoi there was also a certain amount of fighting, but the Japanese were quickly masters of the situation and were able to arrest Mordant and most of the other senior French officers. Sabattier, who had given more credence than the others to an informant's report of Japanese plans for imminent action, escaped from Hanoi with a small number of French troops. Also alerted was the French base at Tong, under the command of General Alessandri. And there were attempts at resistance at various places along the northern Tongking border from Cao-Bang to Mon-Cay. Once again, further details are now available from the British archives, which make it clear that the various pockets of resistence in Tongking and in northern Laos were in radio contact with Force 136 and its French counterpart and that some attempt was made by the British to drop supplies and arms.[62] As has always been suspected, it was the Americans who refused to give any significant support, on orders from Washington, despite their continuing claim that Indochina belonged to the China Theatre and that Wedemeyer was the responsible Allied commander.[63] Without American support, the resistance at Mon-Cay could not last long, and by 19 March the Japanese had forced the French to withdraw across the Chinese border. At Lang-Son the fighting lasted only a short time, and the Japanese had Cao-Bang by about the 22nd. Further South, Alessandri escaped from Tong with over a thousand men and made his way to Son-La, where the Resistance still held an airfield and which became their temporary stronghold. But that too was taken by the Japanese about 26 March, and Alessandri and Sabattier had to make their way to Dien-Bien-Phu. In the end, again lacking American assistance, they were obliged to flee with the remnants of their force into Kwangsi.

Thus by 12 March 1945 the Japanese had established effective control of all the main lowland centres in Indochina, and by the beginning of April they faced very little resistance even in border areas. Their planning had paid off. In a Japanese news agency broadcast of 13 March 1945, they claimed to have taken 8,500 prisoners, to have killed 1,000 Frenchmen and French colonial troops, and to have captured 54 aircraft, 274 motor trucks, and substantial quantities of arms and ammunition.[64]

## III

The situation which actually emerged in Vietnam following the coup of 9 March 1945 was the result of several compromises. In the broadest sense, it was a compromise between military necessity, which required as little interference with smooth administration and as great a measure of direct military control as possible, and political idealism which favoured the creation of an independent Vietnam under Japanese tutelage that could take its place among the other nations of Great East Asia. But also it was the product of compromises in detail between the various groups involved in Japanese policy-making, both in Saigon and Hanoi and in Tokyo. Fortunately the debate which went on within Japanese circles between mid-January and the beginning of March 1945 can be followed in some detail from the archives of the Japanese Foreign Ministry, of which the relevant portions were seized by the Americans after the surrender but were later returned to Japan. Underlying the debate were two conflicts, one of principle and the other between institutions. The conflict of principle was between two points of view which had been interacting ever since 1942: between advocates of independence within Great East Asia and advocates of military or colonial rule such as existed in Korea and Taiwan. The conflict between institutions was between the military and the diplomatic services, and it was there that the most difficult compromises of detail had to be worked out. On the whole, the military seem to have had the upper hand in the final arrangements; but it should be noted that all our records are from the diplomatic side, since day-to-day communications within the military between Tokyo and Indochina have not survived.

We have seen that a member of the staff of General Machijiri, commander of the garrison army in Saigon, was asked to prepare a plan for handling the Indochina question at the end of October 1944; the officer in question appears to have been Colonel Hayashi Hidezumi.[65] His plan was ready by the end of December, and was forwarded to the new commander, General Tsuchihashi. The plan included proposals for granting some form of independence to the Vietnamese, but we do not know precisely what was intended at that stage. What seems clear is that by the second half of January, following the air raids of 12 January 1945, an influential section of the military (including perhaps also members of the staff of General Terauchi, located in Saigon but in command of all Southern Region Armies) was opposed to the idea of independence and wanted something more like the direct military rule which still prevailed in Malaya and the former Dutch East Indies. It seems that at some point in January, Tsuchihashi overruled the original plan and substituted a draft of his own which was in due course forwarded to Tokyo and became the basis of the decision of the Supreme War Leaders Conference on 1 February 1945.[66] Meanwhile the diplomats were also formulating their opinion on the future of Indochina, which was outlined in a telegram from Tsukamoto (Matsumoto's deputy) to Shigemitsu, who was then Minister of both Foreign Affairs and Great East Asia, on 16 January 1945.[67] Tsukamoto accepted as a matter of necessity that something like the existing administrative machinery would have to function in the first instance, and also that in all circumstances the requirements of the war effort must be paramount. But he challenged the military insistence on direct control of the administration and instead put forward a blueprint for the eventual creation of an independent Indochinese Federation. The first step would be for the kings of Annam, Cambodia, and Laos to declare their independence of France, and in due course the regions of Tongking and Cochinchina would be incorporated into the kingdom of Annam. The long-term goal would be a Federation uniting all three countries, which would be bound to Japan by a Treaty of Alliance comparable to those already signed with Thailand, Burma, and the Philippines. The Ambassador to Annam, assisted by a staff of Japanese advisers, would guide the new state but Japanese would not be appointed to formal positions within the state. The capital would be Saigon, where the main embassy would be situated, with branch offices in Hanoi, Hue, Haiphong, Phnom Penh, and either Vientiane or Luang Prabang.

As time went on it became clear that the military leaders were set upon delaying or abandoning altogether the more ambitious features of the diplomats' plan. About 10 or 11 February 1945, at a meeting with Tsukamoto in Saigon, General Tsuchihashi argued that it was quite unnecessary to appoint an ambassador after the coup had been accomplished. The military commander himself would take the place of Decoux as Governor-General, and military officers would be appointed as "mayors" of the chief towns; the ambassador and the other diplomats could then be appointed to be advisers to the Governor-General (which meant, in effect, making them subordinate to the military).[68] For the next two weeks, Ambassador Matsumoto fought a rearguard action to prevent the implementation of Tsuchihashi's proposals, and to preserve the independent existence of a diplomatic mission directly responsible to the Foreign Ministry in Tokyo; this issue became linked to the diplomats' insistence on granting some form of immediate independence to Annam. A chief of bureau from the Ministry in Tokyo, Ishizawa, was sent to report on the situation later that month. His reports of 22–23 February indicated that by now the military were opposed to any measure of independence at all, and he feared that unless some separate diplomatic mission was allowed to survive, the question of independence would be permanently shelved.[69] There would appear to have been a parallel debate going on at the same time between the Foreign Ministry and the Army in Tokyo. A further stage of the compromise was reached by 24 February, when Shigemitsu reported to Matsumoto that it was now agreed to place under military administration the areas presently ruled directly by the French, but to allow a token declaration of independence by the emperor of Annam.[70] He had also by this time conceded the point that the main responsibility for "guidance" of the new administration would lie with a military man rather than with an ambassador responsible to the Foreign Ministry. On 26 February, Matsumoto tried to argue in favour of postponement of the whole operation, on the grounds that there was now no longer a serious threat of American landings; he hoped that this would allow time for a more gradual transition to independence.[71] But that same day (26 February) the Supreme War Leaders' Conference decided to go ahead with the coup, on the basis of the compromise plan which had by now emerged.[72] The only major issue left was that of the status of the embassy staff after the coup, and a further telegram from Matsumoto to Shigemitsu (28 February) indicates that the conflict was serious enough to require a special visit to Indochina by Vice-Minister Takeuchi.[73] The final compromise which emerged gave the position of Governor-General to Tsuchihashi, and placed the diplomats under his authority, but it allowed for most of the top positions formerly held by Frenchmen to go to civilian officials rather than to military officers. Some diplomats at this point sought permission to resign and return to the French, but in the end, with some changes of detailed assignments, it was the plan of 28 February that was put into effect.

Throughout the sequence of telegrams back and forth between Tokyo and Indochina during January and February, the diplomats were shaping their recommendations not merely in terms of Indochina itself nor even of military needs in Southeast Asia. They were concerned also with the world situation and with possible external reactions to Japanese policy in Indochina. They had based their relationship with Decoux on formal treaties with France, and on the principle of French independence. They were aware that any move to disarm the French in Indochina was a reversal of that position and required some kind of justification. In particular, they were concerned about the possible reactions of the Soviet Union.

The secret decision of the Russians at Yalta to enter the war against Japan at the appropriate time was presumably not yet known to the Japanese and they still hoped that the Russians would agree to continue the Non-Aggression Pact between the two countries when it came up for renewal in April 1945. They did not wish to take any action in Indochina which might offend the Russians, who were now (following the overthrow of the Vichy regime) allies of France.[74] Whilst the Foreign Ministry was unable to get its way on many of the issues of substance between it and the Army commands in Indochina, their argument about international recognition does appear to have carried some weight. Conceivably it was the principal reason why the military were finally willing to accept at least a token declaration of independence.

The result of all these compromises was that the situation after the coup of 9 March 1945 was both complicated and ambiguous. But there was no doubt in any one's mind that the Japanese held the real power and that the Vietnamese were not in any effective sense independent. Soon after the coup, a number of appointments were announced. Tsuchihashi became Governor-General, with Matsumoto as his supreme adviser; however, Matsumoto withdrew to Tokyo in May, and the work of general adviser was actually in the hands of his deputy Tsukamoto. The other key appointments were:

| | |
|---|---|
| Supreme Adviser to Annam: | Yokoyama Masayuki |
| Supreme Adviser to Cambodia: | Kubota (a former diplomat) |
| Adviser to the Imperial Delegate of Tongking: | Nishimura Kumao |
| Governor of Cochinchina: | Minoda Fujio |
| Mayor of Saigon: | Kawano Tatsuichi |
| Mayor of Hanoi: | Kobase Hirosui |
| Inspector of Police: | Kasuga (of *Kempeitai*).[75] |

A number of other senior positions were held by Japanese, but it was obvious that there were not enough Japanese civilians (or even available officers) to take over all the positions previously occupied by Frenchmen in the administration. Many of these positions were now taken over by Vietnamese, including high-level judicial positions and that of province-chief in each of the provinces of Cochinchina.

The coup was followed by proclamations of independence by the Kings of Annam, Cambodia, and Laos. In Laos it had been decided to take direct control of Vientiane but to allow the northern areas to be governed from Luang Prabang. It was not until 5 April 1945 that a Japanese column finally reached the royal Lao capital, after a sixteenth-day march from Vinh (Nghe-An) and a certain amount of fighting against French resistance groups. But by 8 April they were in firm control of Luang Prabang and on that day King Sisavang Vong made a proclamation renouncing the French protectorate. Later in the month he sent his heir-apparent (Savang Vathana) to Saigon, ostensibly to provide liaison between his government and the Japanese, but perhaps in reality to become a hostage for his good behaviour towards Japan.[76] In Cambodia, there was no need to delay so long. King Norodom Sihanouk proclaimed his independence of France on 13 March 1945, and a week later appointed a new government whose ministers would function with Japanese advice.[77]

It was at Hue that the Japanese faced their most difficult problems. We have seen that they had given sanctuary and assistance for many years to Prince Cuong-De, who since 1905 had been pretender to the throne of Annam. It would have been logical if the Japanese had now deposed Bao-Dai, who had been emperor since 1925 and was thoroughly French in his education and apparent loyalties, and put Cuong-De on the throne in his place. When Yokoyama came to the imperial palace to visit him on the evening of 10 March, it seems that Bao-Dai was expecting to be obliged to abdicate. Instead, the following day he was instructed by the Japanese to issue a proclamation abrogating the protection treaty of 1884 and proclaiming the independence of his kingdom.[78] On 12 March this was followed by a formal ceremony in the throne-room and popular demonstrations in the city outside. A week later (17 March 1945), Bao-Dai issued his first decree under the reign-name *(hieu)* of Dan-Vi-Quy, which he had chosen to replace that of Bao-Dai.[79] By then it was evident that for the time being he was to remain on the throne, and Cuong-De was to stay in Japan. Once again the Japanese need for stability and continuity, which had been given so much emphasis by the army, prevailed over the more idealistic notions of those who wanted to encourage Vietnamese nationalism. In any case, these proclamations by Bao-Dai did not affect the treaties of 1862 and 1874, by which the then "six provinces" of Cochinchina had been ceded outright to France as a colony. Nor did they change the status of the cities of Hanoi, Haiphong, and Danang (Tourane), which had also been treated as French territory on the basis of the trading concessions granted by the 1874 treaty; these places were given Japanese mayors who took over the powers previously held by the French. (The municipal councils had been abolished in 1941.) The status of Tongking was more ambiguous, in that since 1900 it had been virtually detached from Annam and ruled separately under a French Resident. At first the Japanese may have intended to keep it under the their direct control, but towards the end of April they allowed Bao-Dai to appoint an Imperial Delegate (Phan Ke Toai), who was to be advised by a Japanese Resident. The area to be directly controlled by the newly "independent" regime at Hue was therefore no larger than Annam (that is, Central Vietnam).

## IV

The period between 9 March and 19 August 1945 has been dealt with only very superficially by most writers on Vietnamese history. It was in fact a period of the greatest importance for the subsequent development of the situation in Vietnam. To begin with, it saw the sudden and complete collapse of French prestige. Throughout the lifetime of all but the very oldest inhabitants of Indochina the French had been able to command obedience and outward respect from everyone: even the French-educated "native" did not enjoy real equality with the colon, except in certain legal respects if he were also a French citizen. Now the Frenchmen were quite suddenly reduced to impotence, as their highest officials were taken away to prison and the large majority of the 40,000 or so Europeans in the country were concentrated into restricted areas. In Saigon, where their numbers were greatest, they were obliged to live within a clearly defined locality and were forbidden to congregate in numbers of more than three or to move around after dark.[80] Their prestige was taken over by the Japanese.

Paul Mus, who by early 1945 was responsible for liaison between the French Resistance group and the Vietnamese, remarked upon this in the course of the lectures he gave a year or two later.[81] In February, as he was making a clandestine journey from Saigon to Hanoi, an incident at a ferry convinced him that even at that stage the Vietnamese still had respect for French strength. But when they were so quickly removed less than a month later, it was clear to the Vietnamese that they had lost the Mandate of Heaven and could now be treated with contempt. Long-term French residents found the change impossible to understand and would afterwards speak bitterly of "ingratitude", and when Sainteny visited Paris (from his post in Kunming) the following August he had great difficulty in convincing those responsible for Indochina policy there that the Vietnamese were not simply waiting to welcome back their former colonial rulers.[82] This transformation of attitude was probably an essential preliminary to the revolution which was to follow. Not merely were the French removed from positions in which they had the initiative against any opposition movement; they also lost their power over the minds of ordinary Vietnamese and this made possible the growth of a new spirit in the country at large. Vietnam may not have gained real independence in the fullest sense, but for the first time genuine independence became a real possibility.

In the first instance, the political aspirations of the Vietnamese willing to co-operate with the Japanese were centred upon the imperial capital. It soon became clear that at Hue the Japanese could not ensure (perhaps did not want) complete political continuity despite their decision to keep Bao-Dai on the throne for the time being. The government of Annam was vested in a "Secret Council" *(Co-Mat Vien)* whose origins went back to 1834, but which under the French had operated in the presence of Frenchmen as advisers to the various ministries, who manipulated its decisions. The membership of this council had been reshuffled by Decoux in May 1942, when Pham Quynh (a solidly pro-French figure who had been minister of education since 1933) was made minister of the interior and virtually head of the government. He had proved his ability to move with the times, about one month before, by giving a public lecture on the relationship between the thinking of Confucius and the ideas of Charles Maurras![83] But he was not at all acceptable to the pro-Japanese Vietnamese nationalists, nor to the intellectuals who were hoping that Vietnamese culture might at least abandon its colonial colouring under a new regime. On 19 March 1945 Pham Quynh and the other ministers in the council were obliged to resign in order to allow the emperor (and his Japanese advisers) to choose a new government.

Bao-Dai (it is more convenient to continue using his old title) summoned a number of Vietnamese personalities to Hue to advise him on what to do next. According to Hoang Xuan Han, who was later to become minister of education in the new government and was one of those consulted, they unanimously advised him to invite Ngo Dinh Diem to serve as prime minister. Since July 1944, Diem had been under *Kempeitai* protection in Saigon and it was therefore necessary to communicate with him through the Japanese. Dr. Han, who was then in Hue, says that Bao-Dai made two efforts to invite Diem to come but that he did not reply.[84] Colonel Hayashi, on the other hand, who was looking after Diem in Saigon apart from a short visit to Hanoi at the time of the coup itself, insists that Diem did receive the invitation and that he sent a reply declining the office on grounds of ill health. Whatever the truth of this matter, it is clear that Diem was not in a position to accept. He had quarrelled with Bao-Dai in 1933, when he resigned as minister of the interior, and was well known as a supporter of Cuong-De. Since the Japanese had decided against the return of Cuong-De from Japan, one must conclude that they had also decided against promoting Diem to office at this time. What seems most likely is that the Vietnamese close to Bao-Dai knew this, but also had to demonstrate the fact clearly by sending their invitation, before they were in a position to form a government without him.

It is somewhat remarkable that the Japanese did not at this point advise Bao-Dai to select a prime minister from among the Dai-Viet groups in Tongking; perhaps they too could not be relied on to work with Bao-Dai, or perhaps there was no personality within their ranks who could command wide enough support. The Japanese eventually chose a relatively obscure figure whose career had been not unlike that of Pham Quynh, in that he had devoted most of his life to culture and education. This was Tran Trong Kim (1882–1951), a native of Ha-Tinh province who had been educated in Chinese as well as French and had entered the education service on his return from studies in France in 1911.[85] He held a series of teaching posts, then became inspector of elementary schools, and from 1933 till his retirement in 1943 he served as director of boys' schools in Hanoi. He had long been interested in the development of new teaching materials in the Romanized form of Vietnamese (known as *quoc-ngu*) and had himself written a number of books. The most famous of them were an outline of Vietnamese history (1925) and a study of Confucianism in three volumes which had appeared between 1930 and 1933. Thus where Pham Quynh promoted the study of French philosophy during this period, Tran Trong Kim sought to instil greater understanding of traditional values and of Vietnamese national history. We know nothing of his actual contacts with the Japanese before 1943, but it is easy to see the connection between his values and theirs. For some reason in the autumn of 1943 he felt threatened by the French and sought asylum with the Japanese army, who flew him first to Singapore and then to Bangkok. Now, in April 1945, he was flown back to Saigon. On being told at the airport by Kawamura (Chief of Staff under Tsuchihashi) that he was being invited to serve as chief minister under Bao-Dai, he at first refused. Eventually he agreed and on 17 April it was announced that he had formed a government at Hue.[86]

The Tran Trong Kim Cabinet has been much criticized by historians, and its achievements were certainly limited. But its full history has never been adequately explored and it probably deserves at least more careful attention than it has previously received. Its membership was diverse, but not wholly without talent: its lack of achievement should perhaps be put down to lack of experience and limited opportunities, rather than to personal failings on the part of individuals. Three of the ministers, at least, belonged to an intellectual group which had grown up at Hanoi since about 1940 and was closely associated with the journal *Thanh-Nghi*, founded in 1941. Some members of that group were too left-wing to contemplate association with Bao-Dai or the Japanese, and were later prominent amongst either the Viet-Minh and its supporting organizations, or within the parties supporting the Chinese nationalists. The three who joined the Tran Trong Kim Cabinet were Vu Van Hien (Minister of Finance), who had written about taxation; Hoang Xuan Han (Minister of Education), a graduate of the Ecole Polytechnique and also a specialist in Vietnamese history; and Phan Anh (Minister of Youth). Two of these, Phan Anh and Hoang Xuan Han, were natives of the same province as Tran Trong Kim, Ha-Tinh. At least two of the other ministers were lawyers: Tran Van Chuong, previously nominated to head the judiciary in Tongking but now made Foreign Minister (he was later well known as Ngo Dinh Diem's ambassador to Washington and father of Madame Ngo Dinh Nhu); and Trinh Dinh Thao, originally a native of Tongking who had moved to Saigon, who became Minister of Justice in 1945, but was subsequently more famous as an opponent of Ngo Dinh Diem and leader of the "third force" in South Vietnam from 1968 to 1975.[87] At least one minister was a businessman: Nguyen Huu Thi (Minister of Supplies), a native of Danang who trained as a medical assistant but later became a merchant exporting goods to France, and for a time was also proprietor of a rice-mill at Cholon. Vu Ngoc Anh (Minister of Welfare), who was to die in an air-raid in Tongking in July, was a Paris-trained doctor and a former member of the Grand Conseil and then of Decoux's Conseil Federal.[88] The biographical data available about the various ministers indicate that they were mostly members of the elite which had grown up in the 1920s and 1930s, and could be classified as "bourgeois" nationalists. But in other circumstances they might well have given a better account of themselves.

The new council of ministers met for the first time at the premier's official residence in Hue on 4 May 1945.[89] Its initial concerns were the constitutional question and matters of protocol such as the flag and national anthem. The latter seem to have involved a certain measure of controversy, and a commission was set up to settle the issues which arose — for example, whether the country should have a plain yellow flag or one of red and yellow bands. Decisions were not finally announced until the end of June, when it was also announced that the name of the country would be Viet-Nam. The creation of a constitution raised even more complicated issues, and on 8 May the emperor established a committee of fifteen people (under the chairmanship of Phan Anh) to work towards preparing a constitution. Since those appointed were living in several different places, it was up to Phan Anh to correspond with them and to centralize their advice in a report to be submitted eventually to a plenary meeting. It was likely to take considerable time, and it is hardly surprising that no report was produced before Bao-Dai's abdication in August.[90]

However, it should not be supposed that the Hue Government did nothing more than talk about generalities and issues of protocol. The record of its decisions, represented by a series of Domei announcements published in the Saigon newssheet *Opinion-Impartial* (the only French one to survive in Saigon), shows that the ministers were also concerned with practical matters. They had problems of effective control over all areas of the country, owing to the destruction of many railway bridges and difficulties of transport. But one should not imagine that Vietnam in this period was in a state of total chaos: despite the difficulties, organized life continued and could therefore be changed by administrative decrees. The record indicates four areas in which the Government tried to make some impact during the months of May and June: the food problem, the problem of corruption, reform of taxation, and the mobilization of youth. Of these the first was by far the most urgent, especially in the northern half of Annam (and also, as we shall see, in Tongking). The harvest of late 1944 had been inadequate, and the problem of transport made it difficult to move rice as fast as usual from south to north. Moreover, the Japanese were anxious to commandeer as much as possible of available supplies for military use, including the use of rice-fuel in place of petrol for vehicles. During 1943–44, the French had been obliged to introduce a system of government purchase of rice, which was extremely unpopular. On 13 May 1945 an imperial decree abolished the system of government purchase throughout Annam, and replaced it by new methods of controlling the rice market, which permitted relative freedom of sale and purchase (but not of storage) within four economic zones. It also set up for each province a committee to advise on problems of transportation and pricing, and an agricultural union which was permitted to buy and stock surplus rice for later sale when the market required it.[91] We have no means of knowing how far the new measures were implemented, but they represented a new approach to a serious problem. There was certainly an effort to bring more rice into the region of Annam, and by July this was bearing fruit; but it may have been as much the work of the Japanese in Cochinchina as of the Minister of Supply at Hue. Between 30 June and 7 August there is record of the arrival at the ports of northern Annam (from Danang to Quang-Khe) of fifty-four junk-loads of rice from the south; another fourteen junk-loads went to Nam Dinh between the end of June and the middle of July.[92] They were not enough to prevent serious famine, however, especially in Thanh-Hoa and Nghe-An. The situation was one which was beyond the capacity of a new government to solve by the means at its disposal, unless the Japanese had decided to abandon their military requirements altogether.

In terms of the actual workings of the economy of Annam, one cannot ignore the fact that decrees and decisions in Hue were always subject to the grassroots characteristics of the society, and above all the almost natural tendency towards official and private corruption and extortion at all levels. The kind of social inequalities and extortion which could exist in a Vietnamese village at this period have been well illustrated in the selection of literary extracts published by Ngo Vinh Long.[93] It was appropriate that a government claiming to be leading Vietnam towards a new age of independence and progress, albeit one based on traditional virtues rather than principles of social revolution, should at least make some attempt to reform abuses of this kind. On 30 May an imperial order abolished the practice which allowed people condemned to punishment to "purchase" the penalty with money, and at the same time increased the penalties against extortion. A further order, on 6 June 1945, provided for the dismissal of officials found to be dishonest, disloyal, or incapable of performing their duties.[94] Later in the month the Hanoi newspaper *Ngay-Nay*, in an article assessing (in highly critical tones) the limited achievements of the Hue government, noted that five province chiefs in Annam (as well as six in Tongking) had been removed from office by the Minister of the Interior.[95] It was in a similar spirit that the government promulgated a fiscal reform on 23 May 1945, by which those who had no property at all (a very large number of the poor of Annam) were to be exempt from the "impot personnel", together with all employees with wages of less than 1,200 piastres a year.[96] But this too was an area in which the government was not in office for long enough to make any serious impact. It was generally agreed amongst critics of the old taxation system, among whom Vu Van Hien himself was one, that a thorough overhaul of the system was required. But that too could only be effective if official and local corruption could be eliminated, and in a situation of dislocation and famine that was hardly possible at a stroke of the imperial pen in Hue.

The Government at Hue was slower than the authorities in the other two regions to implement any efforts towards political mobilization, of young people. Nevertheless, on 16 June it was reported that Phan Anh (the Minister for Youth) was to institute an *"ecole de jeunesse"* in each province which give one-month courses to people aged between eighteen and twenty-five.[97] The emphasis was on a combination of physical and moral education, and the inspiration may have come as much from the earlier work of Ducoroy as from the Japanese. But the morality involved was now very definitely that of Confucius rather than of Charles Maurras.

In some respects developments in Tongking during May and June paralleled those in Annam, except that there the mandarins were still responsible to a *Kham-Sai* (Imperial Delegate) advised by a Japanese official, rather than to a council of ministers. The food question was especially acute in Tongking, where typhoons on the coast had severely reduced the crop gathered in the fifth month of 1944, so that in some areas starvation was already setting in as early as October of that year. By the time of the coup in March 1945 the famine had killed vast numbers of people; the lowest estimate given is usually 500,000, and there is some reason to accept a figure much nearer the two million deaths which appears in communist accounts of the period, for the whole of Tongking and northern Annam.[98] The question of how the fifth month harvest of 1945 should be handled was therefore of the greatest importance. On 7 June 1945 the *Kham-Sai* (in effect the Japanese adviser) issued a decree abolishing government collection of paddy throughout Tongking, and replacing it with a system of marketing through the agricultural bank of each province. Merchants were not allowed to purchase directly from farmers or landlords, and private houses were permitted to store only two months' supply, but transport of up to fifty kilos of rice was allowed. There was also an official price-scale, but the attempt to regulate prices was almost futile in a situation of gathering inflation.[99] As in Annam, it was much easier to change the regulations than to reform morals and ensure fairness of conduct between different classes within society.

Compared to Annam, there was greater emphasis in Tongking on the creation of a new elite through education and mobilization of youth. The model for this elite was no longer the French professional trained in the Grandes Ecoles, but the Japanese military man devoted to the ideals of the emperor, or the scholar-official steeped in Confucian forms of loyalty. On 12 May 1945 *Thanh-Nghi* carried an announcement that on the 15th a youth-camp would open in Son-Tay province, of two months' duration, which would (it was hoped) be attended by young men willing to take up a life of hardship and self-sacrifice.[100] On a different level, plans were made to create a new school for government officials, which opened at Hanoi on 1 June 1945.[101] The problem of Japanese cultural influence however was still one of language. It would seem that very few Japanese — prominent among them being Matsushita — had any knowledge of Vietnamese. Also, the French had not encouraged the development of Japanese language teaching for Vietnamese; although cultural institutes existed in Hanoi and Saigon at which lessons could be had, until March 1945 there was no attempt to spread Japanese teaching to all schools, such as occurred in Indonesia at an early stage of Japanese rule. A first step towards remedying this was the opening of a special Japanese language school at Dalat on 1 June, which had places for 200 pupils.[102] As in other spheres, the first steps were taken but the war ended before they could produce any significant results.

Unlike Annam, Tongking had in Hanoi an important urban middle class which had to be appealed to and mobilized if the new arrangements were to be effective from the Japanese point of view. But that same class also found a kind of political awakening of its own as a result of the disappearance of French control and the possibility of evolution towards independence. Whereas Hue had its court and bureaucratic politics, Hanoi developed a plethora of political parties and the beginnings of political debate. On 5 May 1945 the two leading journals of Hanoi were allowed to reappear: *Thanh-Nghi*, edited by Vu Dinh Hoe, whose frequent contributors included not only a group represented in the government (Hoang Xuan Han, Phan Anh, Vu Van Hien), but also a number of people later prominent within the Viet-Minh regime; and *Ngay-Nay*, edited by Nguyen Tuong Bach, with frequent contributions from Khai-Hung and Hoang-Dao, who together with Hoang Dao's brother (Nhat Linh, alias Nguyen Tuong Tam) had formed the *Tu-Luc Van Doan* literary school in the 1930s and were now associated with the Vietnamese *Quoc Dan Dang*.[103] From the pages of these journals one learns that during April and May political groups had been growing like a bamboo in spring rain. Some were pro-Japanese, others were thinly disguised revivals of pro-Chinese (Kuomintang) groups. The most significant of the new parties or associations seems to have been the *Tan Viet-Nam Hoi*, launched on 5 May 1945, whose leaders included members of both the principal journalistic groups.[104] Its programme consisted of working towards independence and national unity within Great East Asia, and developing "national construction". Judging by some of the articles in the two main journals, its members were highly critical of the efforts being made towards those ends by Tran Trong Kim and his ministers in Hue.

It was, nevertheless, the latter who had Japanese backing for the time being. Towards the end of June 1945 there are signs that the Japanese were beginning to change their attitude towards the Annam government, to allow it to embrace a wider range of functions and to absorb the government of Tongking (but not yet Cochinchina). On 20 June 1945 there was an elaborate ceremony in Hue to commemorate Unification Day, which was the day on which Gia-Long unified the present territory of Vietnam for the first time in 1802. The proclamation made by Bao-Dai on that occasion foreshadowed the eventual administrative reorganization of the territories beyond Annam, and made the inevitable expressions of gratitude to the Japanese.[105] By the end of the month decrees had been issued by the Governor-General (still Tsuchihashi) transferring to "local" governments and their budgets (that is, to Annam, Tongking, Cochinchina, Cambodia, and Laos) certain government responsibilities previously regarded as "general". The changes were announced on 12 July.[106] The following day Tran Trong Kim and four other ministers arrived in Hanoi to negotiate the transfer of most of the remaining general services to his government, which was completed by 1 August 1945 and was due to take effect on the 15th. Whilst in Hanoi, the premier also negotiated the transfer to Vietnamese mayors of the cities of Hanoi, Haiphong, and Danang.[107] But it was one thing to sign papers creating a more unified system, quite another to hold it together as an effective unit. The acute problems of transportation were worse than ever by now, and it was announced on 26 July that a system of cycle couriers, organized by members of the Tongking youth movement, had begun to operate between Hanoi, Hue, and Saigon.[108]

Cochinchina, which had been ceded to France by the treaties of 1862 and 1874 and had since been a colony as opposed to a protectorate, was not affected by the changes made in Annam and Tongking. Until August it continued to be administered by a Japanese governor, Minoda Fujio, with a small staff of his fellow-countrymen and a body of Vietnamese officials. At the beginning of April he appointed Vietnamese province chiefs for each province — a move which merely gave Cochinchina the kind of mandarinate which Annam and Tongking had kept throughout the French period; but the change was striking because previously these positions had been filled by Frenchmen.[109] On 9–10 April 1945, Minoda held a conference of the new province chiefs and briefed them on Japanese needs and the policy to be followed in the immediate future. At about the same time, Vietnamese were appointed to fill the highest legal positions in the colony.[110] There was no question of constitutional changes or reforms in taxation, and Cochinchina was not suffering the extremes of economic hardship which affected the Centre and North. The main development in that area was the creation of a Committee of Mutual Aid, to assist the poor of northern Indochina by collecting money to buy rice to send there. There is no indication that the Japanese themselves were willing to organize major relief operations to help the North.[111]

This does not mean however that there were no political developments in the South. The nationalists who had been willing to collaborate with the Japanese whilst the French were still in power now had hopes of playing a more prominent part in political life, if not actually achieving independence. Less than ten days after the coup, on 18 March 1945, a large but orderly demonstration was held in Saigon by a number of pro-Japanese groups. It was addressed by the Caodaist leader Tran Quang Vinh, and by Ho Van Nga as leader of the newly formed *Viet-Nam Quoc-Gia Doc-Lap Dang* (Vietnam National Independence Party). Also on the rostrum was Nguyen Vinh Thanh, who made a speech thanking the Japanese for returning to Saigon the remains of the patriot Duong Ba Trac who had once been exiled to Poulo Condore for his anti-French activities and who had died in Singapore at the end of 1944 after being helped to escape from the French authorities at about the same time as Tran Van An and Tran Trong Kim.[112] Meanwhile Tran Van An was still in Singapore, from where according to Devillers he made a broadcast welcoming the overthrow of the French (21 March 1945) in the name of the *Phuc-Quoc Dong-Minh-Hoi*.[113] For the time being, none of these figures was given any role in the actual administration of Cochinchina.

A somewhat different group of people began to acquire prominence towards the end of May, when the Japanese appear to have decided to develop a youth movement not unlike the one we have already noticed in Tongking. On 22 May 1945 there was established a Committee on Physical Education, Sports and Youth, whose president was an engineer called Kha Van Can and secretary-general Dr. Pham Ngoc Thach (a secret communist who was able to turn this position to good effect during the August Revolution).[114] This was in effect the origin of the *Thanh-Nien Tien-Phong*, known in French sources as "Jeuness d'Avant-Garde". An English observer in the following October saw a conflict for leadership within the group between Dr. Thach and Kha Van Can, and identified the latter as a member of the "Caodaist Annamite Independence Party".[115] In any event, it was probably strongly influenced at the top by Iida, who is mentioned as the Japanese successor to Ducoroy as Director-General of Youth and Sports for the whole of Indochina.[116] The fact that a Japanese sponsored organization could be so thoroughly penetrated by the Communists is symptomatic of the problem of control which they experienced after the 9 March coup. The youth movement became increasingly prominent, and on 1 July 1945 a grand oath-taking ceremony was held in Saigon in the presence of Minoda Fujio and other Japanese officials, at which about 4,000 young people were on parade. Iida made the principal speech, attacking the individualism and egotism of those Vietnamese who had been too much influenced by France, and predicting that Vietnam was about to return to the greatness it had enjoyed under Minh-Mang. Each of the participants then took an oath to serve the fatherland.[117]

Also in early July, Minoda announced the formation of a Council of Cochinchina whose ten members included Tran Van An, Kha Van Can, and Ho Van Nga. It held its inaugural session on 21 July 1945, in the chamber of the old Colonial Council, and listened to a speech by Minoda instead of to one by a French governor. A reply on behalf of the Council was made by its senior member (and former

Constitutionalist) Luu Van Lang. They then proceeded to elect Tran Van An to be president of the standing bureau, Kha Van Can as vice-president, and Ho Van Nga as one of the two secretaries.[118] Once again Tran Van An was prominent when a new newspaper was founded on 2 August 1945, the *Hung-Viet*.[119] These moves were probably an indication that by July the Japanese were almost ready to begin the process of integrating Cochinchina into the new state of Vietnam. In fact, they decided to speed up the process as events began to move rapidly during August, and on 14 August 1945 Bao-Dai was allowed to proclaim the abrogation of the treaties of 1862 and 1874, thus declaring Cochinchina part of independent Vietnam.[120] The same day a decree appointed Nguyen Van Sam, another of the exiles of 1943, to be *Kham-Sai* in the South. Ho Van Nga was made acting delegate until Sam arrived in Saigon.[121] But by then the war, and the Japanese period, was over.

## V

One further element in the situation after the 9 March 1945 remains to be considered, perhaps the most important of all: that is, the growth in the power of the Viet-Minh. It had been founded in May 1941, following the eighth plenary session of the Central Committee of the Indochinese Communist Party, and since 1943 had made increasingly effective efforts to attract non-communists into its ranks, at least in Tongking. Contrary to the belief of some Western commentators that its leadership operated only in Kwangsi during the years 1941–45, the Indochinese Communist Party was in fact run by a Standing Bureau of its Central Committee whose members were living in the area to the North of Hanoi; the most important of them being the Secretary-General, Truong Chinh, who went to the Chinese border area only once, to attend the eighth plenum itself.[122] By March 1945, the Viet-Minh had two base areas, which had both been subject at different times to clearing operations by French forces but which had survived and remained active after the French had left. One was the Cao-Bac-Lang base area, centred on Cao-Bang province, where the leading figures were Vo Nguyen Giap, Pham Van Dong, and Ho Chi Minh himself.[123] The other was an area of Thai-Nguyen and Lang-Son provinces which had begun to develop after the Bac-Son insurrection of 1940 under the leadership of Chu Van Tan and Hoang Van Thu.[124] However the communists were chastened by the failure of their revolt in the South, the Nam-Bo Uprising of November/December 1940, and throughout the Japanese period they had been very cautious about risking their strength in another open confrontation with the colonial power.

In March 1945, they were ready to carry their activities one stage further towards a full-scale rising. The decision to prepare for such a rising was taken at the meeting of the Standing Bureau of 9–12 March, held at two successive village hide-outs in the province of Bac-Ninh.[125] The leaders of the Party Central Committee, including at this time Truong Chinh, and Nguyen Luong Bang, adopted an "Instruction" to the effect that the Japanese were now the number one enemy, and even envisaging the possibility of alliance with the French Resistance against the Japanese. They also decided to prepare for insurrection by using more aggressive forms of propaganda and struggle, and by mobilizing people to demonstrate against the Japanese and to storm the supply-depots where rice collected for the Japanese forces was being stored. In areas where guerrillas were already active, People's Committees should be set up; in other areas, liberation committees should be formed in villages, factories, offices, etc.; and the guerrilla base areas should be expanded. The communists also resolved to support the expected Allied landings or invasion, and to welcome the Allies when they arrived.[126]

The events of the next few days in a number of different places suggest that the communist leaders had in fact anticipated a Japanese coup some time earlier, and that they had already discussed what to do. In certain places, they went into action very rapidly. In western Bac-Giang province, which was the centre of activity of the Central Committee at this time, the first village liberation committee was formed on 13 or 14 March 1945 and was quickly followed by a number of others. In nearby Bac-Ninh province, similar committees were formed from 10 March onwards, and the local Party committees began to organize attacks on paddy stores. The latter policy very soon spread to Hung-Yen and Ninh-Binh provinces. In the principal guerrilla base area at this time, which stretched from southern Tuyen-Quang province across Thai-Nguyen province to southern Lang-Son, action was taken by the Viet-Minh which resulted in their controlling at least five district towns of the remoter areas by the beginning of April.[127] But activity was not confined to this area. In the Cao-Bac-Lang base area the Interprovincial Party Committee met on 10 March 1945 and adopted a policy similar to that of the Central Committee. Following this the Propaganda Brigade created by Ho Chi Minh and Vo Nguyen Giap in December 1944 divided into sections; one of these moved into Lang-Son province and eventually linked up with the central base area forces (the National Salvation forces) there; the main one marched south under Vo Nguyen Giap, and reached northern Tuyen-Quang province perhaps by early April.[128] In one other area of Vietnam action was taken with equal speed after the Japanese coup; at the Ba-To prison camp (Quang-Ngai province), a communist-led group seized control on the night of 11 March and three days later created the famous Ba-To guerrilla detachment. It moved off into the hills pursued by the Japanese.[129]

It is evident from the pattern of events immediately following the coup that the Viet-Minh were strongest in the above areas, and had still to organize effectively in other places (including the Nam-Bo). It is not surprising therefore that preparations for the coming insurrection were concentrated on the North. Following the link-up of military leaders from the two base areas, a Military Revolutionary Conference was held in Hiep-Hoa district (western Bac-Giang), from 15 to 20 April 1945. It created a unified Liberation Army, formally established a month later, under the leadership of Vo Nguyen Giap, Chu Van Tan, and Tran Dang Ninh.[130] Meanwhile in Bac-Giang, Thai-Nguyen and Lang-Son the Viet-Minh took over another seven district towns by the middle of May, whilst the forces coming south from Cao-Dang continued to advance. It was at this point, probably during the latter part of May, that Ho Chi Minh reappeared on the scene and established a new headquarters at Tan-Trao (Tuyen-Quang province). It appears to have been thanks to his efforts that on 4 June 1945 the Viet-Minh held a conference of cadres at which a Free Zone was formally established, embracing a large part of the provinces of Cao-Bang, Bac-Kan, Lang-Son, Ha-Giang, Tuyen-Quang, and Thai-Nguyen; the two base areas were not in effect amalgamated into one.[131] The area of operations outside this Free Zone was also expanding, with liberation committees and growing support in the provinces of Bac-Giang, Bac-Ninh, Hai-Duong, Vinh-Yen, etc. From about 8 June, moves were made to create a "fourth maquis" zone in the provinces of Hai-Duong and Quang-Yen.[132]

Thus by the end of June the Viet-Minh movement was growing from strength to strength in the North, and had a foothold in Quang-Ngai province. It also, as we have seen, had infiltrated the new youth movement in the South. A major question which has still to receive a proper answer from historians is the extent to which the Viet-Minh received support from the Allies, with whom it was so anxious to cooperate. American archives which may provide a full answer are not yet open, but two recent American works written by people who have had at least some access to the secret record suggest that from May 1945 the Viet-Minh and the Americans were in close contact and collaboration. At the time of the coup of 9 March, Ho Chi Minh was in Yunnan, where he had gone towards the end of 1944 in the hope of making contact with the American OSS mission and other organizations.[133] He appears to have made little progress at first. It was the coup itself which changed things, because it destroyed overnight the intelligence network amongst French resistance officers and civilians, which since at least 1943 had been supplying information to the American Fourteenth Air Force and perhaps to other Allied agencies in southern China. The Americans needed intelligence. Ho Chi Minh, through the networks created within the country by Vo Nguyen Giap and Pham Van Dong, and by Truong Chinh, Chu Van Tan, and Tran Dang Ninh, was in a position to offer help which at last the Americans were willing to accept. In the first instance, his contacts were with the Air-Ground Aid Section of the U.S. Fourteenth Army Air Force; by May they had sent in a team of wireless operators and other equipment. Ho himself was back in Cao-Bang province by that time, and together they advanced southwards to Tan-Trao.[134] By the middle of July, however, the Viet-Minh had made contact with OSS itself and the latter had agreed to help. At that point, an OSS team was sent in to Tan-Trao, headed by Major Allison Thomas; and two weeks later it is said that an OSS medical officer saved the life of Ho Chi Minh when he became gravely ill with a combination of fevers that might easily have killed him. This mission proceeded to train some of the Liberation Army troops, and supplied a battery of weapons flown in from Kunming.[135] One should not overestimate the significance of this aid, but it probably helped the Viet-Minh to act with greater speed and effectiveness at the time of the Japanese surrender in mid-August. Also the fact that this aid had been negotiated by Ho Chi Minh probably gave his faction (notably Vo Nguyen Giap and Pham Van Dong) greater influence than they would otherwise have enjoyed within the Viet-Minh itself, previously dominated by comrades close to the secretary-general of the Indochinese Communist Party, Truong Chinh.

A much more difficult question still is that of the relationship between the Viet-Minh and the Japanese. Until the end of the Second World War, the two were implacably opposed to one another, in line with communist policy; and this opposition was reinforced by the Soviet declaration of war on Japan on 8 August 1945. It is very likely that the Japanese sought to defeat the Viet-Minh preparations for an uprising during the months of direct Japanese rule. This is indicated briefly by the Vietnamese communist source materials. Unfortunately on the Japanese side no archival or memo material has become available to scholars on this subject, and none of the publications of the period makes any reference to anti-Viet-Minh security operations. Presumably the Japanese took over the French Sûreté and other records in Hanoi, but we have no information about Japanese security organization during the period.

After the Japanese surrender, the situation was quite different. Japanese troops were in the country, and from 14 August onwards they were simply waiting for Chinese and British forces to arrive to receive their formal surrender. The French remained interned or disarmed — there was no question of restoring them to their former position, in either half of Indochina. But what of Japanese–Vietnamese relations at this time? In Hue, Tran Trong Kim's government sought to continue but in fact lost control of the situation very rapidly; its position was undermined completely when Bao-Dai abdicated on 25 August 1945.[136] In Hanoi, a meeting of officals originally intended to back Tran Trong Kim's government, held on 17 August, was virtually taken over by the Viet-Minh; and two days later the Viet-Minh took over the whole city and occupied government buildings. Phan Ke Toai, the imperial *Kham-sai* since late April, went over to the Viet-Minh and subsequently (from 1947) served as their Minister of Interior; so too did a number of former supporters of Tran Trong Kim's government, including Phan Anh, the Minister for Youth. There is no evidence to suggest that the Japanese in Tongking made any effort to hand over control of the government to any of the pro-Japanese groups, in the Dai-Viet union. It would seem rather that they were content to allow the Viet-Minh a free hand, and not to interfere. The one building which they appear to have effectively guarded in Hanoi was the Bank of Indochina, which the Viet-Minh did not take over; and the fact that they did not suggests that Japanese connivance was a necessary element in their rapid takeover of the administrative services at Hanoi.[137]

In the South, on the other hand, the closing days of the War saw the Japanese taking steps to create a new authority which was Vietnamese but not associated with the Viet-Minh. The communists had used the period since March 1945 to reactivate their organizations in the Nam-Bo, moribund since 1940, and by the second half of August they were ready to act. But whereas Hanoi was in their hands by 19 August, it was not until 25 August 1945 that they were able to set up a Provisional Executive Committee, which virtually superseded the Executive created by the Japanese ten days earlier.[138] In the next few days, they established revolutionary committees in most of the southern provinces. Thus even here the structure created by the Japanese collapsed very quickly. But the Viet-Minh were not the only organized body with support in the countryside of the Nam-Bo. The Cao-Dai and Hoa-Hao sects were probably more effectively organized at this stage, and they supported the Viet-Minh out of patriotism rather than political convictions. They had their own links to the Japanese, and they may have hoped that eventually the independence movements in Saigon would come under their own leadership. After the arrival of the British and the return to power of the French in Saigon on 23 September 1945, the alliance between the communists and the sects seems to have begun to break down.[139] Neither the Japanese nor the Viet-Minh had succeeded in creating a Vietnamese political entity capable of resisting the combination of British and French forces.

What of the suggestion that, apart from acquiescence in the Viet-Minh seizure of power, the Japanese also actively assisted the Viet-Minh — or indeed other nationalist groups — in their attempts to resist the return of the French? News reports of September and October 1945 certainly suggested that was the case, and there are other indications which lead one to take the idea seriously even though there is very little hard evidence. Some of the reports were based on allegations by French officials. A Reuter report from Kandy (Ceylon, or Sri Lanka) on 13 September 1945 alleged that 10,000 or more Japanese had abandoned their uniforms and joined the ranks of Vietnamese "rebels" instead of surrendering to the Chinese.[140] This must refer to Tongking, since it is the Chinese who are mentioned. Other reports concerned Cochinchina (Nam-Bo). On 7 October 1945 Reuter reported that General Terauchi had just been placed under house arrest by the British, "following proof of Japanese participation in Annamite uprisings".[141]

A week later more specific assertions were made about the Japanese "secret service" sponsoring the "Annamite Army" in the South, but it was admitted that there could in the nature of things be no proof of their involvement. The French, on the other hand, claimed that two Japanese officers were captured and shot (but not in uniform) in a battle within Saigon on 12 October 1945.[142] On the 15th, General Terauchi admitted that some deserters may be helping the nationalists, but that this did not reflect the true Japanese attitude; he called on his officers to obey the Allied command. For their part the British denied as "baseless" reports that a secret Japanese headquarters directing the nationalists had recently been discovered in Saigon.[143] By the end of October, Japanese troops in uniform were collaborating with the British in the fighting to recover control of Saigon, Bien-Hoa and other centres.

Two more concrete pieces of evidence were offered by Paul Mus in his lectures of 1947, although they were never referred to by him in subsequent publications.[144] They suggest a more complex situation than that indicated by the press reports. At a Vietnamese post taken by French troops on 12 October 1945, a copy of a tract written by a Japanese was found. It was addressed (in French?) to the peoples of Great East Asia and called on them to "grit their teeth" and harass the Europeans, promising that one day the Japanese would return to Indochina to chase out all the Europeans. The other document, also captured by the French, was a circular from the general staff of the Viet-Minh at Bien-Hoa to all unit commanders, dated 24 September 1945. It called for an attack on Saigon, now that the efforts of the executive committee to install itself in

Saigon had been defeated. But it also included an analysis of the likely attitudes of the Japanese to the new situation, distinguishing between three groups. One group of Japanese was primarily concerned with loyalty to the Emperor and would obey the Allies; its only concern was to save their ruler from further humiliation. Another group had thoughts only for their eventual return to Japan, and would sell arms for money to anyone who could buy them; the Viet-Minh should seek to make contact with them solely for that reason. The third group were those of the "Black Dragon" party, determined upon resistance against the Allies, and willing to give active assistance to the Viet-Minh; it was already providing arms and incorporating Japanese officers into the Viet-Minh forces as instructors. This document suggests a high degree of sophistication on the part of the Vietnamese leaders. There is no reason to regard it as not genuine, even though it may have been used by the French to prove points of their own against the Viet-Minh.

Once again, the evidence is meagre but it all points in the same direction. Some Japanese did help the Viet-Minh, and some almost certainly gave arms to the Caodaists and to the Hoa Hao sect leaders. But there is no means of quantifying the degree of assistance, or for that matter the degree of dependence of the various groups on the help they received from that Japanese. It would certainly be a travesty of the evidence to suggest that without Japanese help in August and September 1945 there would have been no revolution against the French. The principal contribution of the Japanese to the Vietnamese Revolution was not at that stage, but earlier on: their overthrow of the French army and administration in March 1945 was the key to the whole situation which developed after their own defeat later that year. One might almost write the history of the Vietnamese revolution in terms of two stages: a "bourgeois" stage, which effectively began with the coup of 9 March 1945 and was dominated throughout by the presence of the Japanese; and a "communist" stage which began with the Viet-Minh Congress of 16–17 August 1945. They would correspond to the February and October Revolutions in Russia in 1917.

## Notes

In writing this article, I am greatly indebted to Mr. M. Shiraishi and to Mrs. M. Nakahara for their assistance during a visit to Tokyo in November/December 1975; and to Mr. M. Shiraishi and to Miss M. Takemoto, for translation and interpretation of Japanese source materials.

1 F.C. Jones, *Japan's New Order in East Asia* (London, 1954), pp. 225ff. For the text of the agreement of Dec. 1941, see Japanese Foreign Ministry Archives, A.7.0.0.9–2–3 (=*Checklist* S.I.7.0.0.–17/2–5); See n. 5 below.
2 A. Decoux, *A la Barre de l'Indochine, 1940–1945* (Paris, 1949), pp. 427–48, 435, 438–39.
3 Ibid., pp. 443–44.
4 *Opinion-Impartial* (Saigon), 25 Nov. 1944, 14 May 1945; for biographical details, see *Japan Biographical Encyclopedia* (Tokyo, 1958).
5 For a list of this material, which was taken to Washington in 1945 and later microfilmed by the Library of Congress, but which has now been partly restored to the Japanese Foreign Ministry, see Library of Congress, *Checklist of Archives in the Japanese Ministry of*

*Foreign Affairs* (Washington, 1954). There is some confusion regarding the numbers in this list and those used at the Foreign Ministry Archives; where documents have been consulted in Tokyo, in what follows, the numbers given are those used in Tokyo.

6  For these aspects of Decoux's policy, see Decoux, op. cit., pp. 431ff.
7  Ibid., pp. 401ff, etc.
8  On these aspects of Decoux's policy, one must consult his critics; e.g. J. Pedrazzini, *La France en Indochine* (Paris, 1972), pp. 111 ff.
9  M. Ducoroy, *Ma Traison en Indochine* (Paris, 1949).
10  Jones, op. cit., pp. 368, 470–71.
11  Decoux, op. cit., p. 393.
12  Ibid., pp. 236–40.
13  Ph. Devillers, *Histoire du Viet-Nam de 1940 à 1952* (Paris, 1952), p. 92.
14  Ibid., p. 93.
15  Cuong-De, *Cuoc Doi Cach Mang* (Saigon, 1957), pp. 129–31. This volume of his memoirs is said to have been written for the Prince whilst he was in Japan in 1943; it gives very little information after 1941. For the earlier career of Cuong–De, see D.G. Marr, *Vietnamese Anti-Colonialism, 1885–1925* (Berkeley, 1971).
16  Cuong-De, op. cit., pp. 134–35; Devillers, op. cit., p. 78.
17  F.N. Trager (ed.), *Burma: Japanese Military Administration, Selected Documents, 1941–45* (Philadelphia, 1971).
18  Cuong-De, op. cit., pp. 133–34.
19  Ibid., pp. 137–38; Devillers, op. cit., p. 93.
20  Information from Col. Hayashi Hidezumi, Dec. 1975. See n. 28 below.
21  He was still alive in Saigon in the 1960s and his biography appears in *Who's Who in Vietnam, 1967* (Saigon, 1967).
22  Devillers, op. cit., pp. 89, 92. For the background to the Caodaists in the 1930s, see R.B. Smith, "An Introduction to Caodaism", *Bulletin of School of Oriental and African Studies* (London), XXXIII (1970).
23  P. Mus, *Problèmes de l'Indochine Contemporaine: la Formation des Parties Annamites* (Paris, n.d., mimeo), Lecon ii, pp. 4–5. This was originally a series of lectures given at the College Libre des Sciences Sociales et Economiques in Paris, probably after Mus's return to France in 1947. Consulted at the Bibliotheque d'Afrique et Outre-Mer, Paris.
24  Devillers, op. cit., pp. 89–91.
25  Hoang Van Dao, *Viet-Nam Quoc-Dan Dang: Lich-su dau-tranh can-dai* (Saigon, 1965), pp. 189–90. Two of these parties were proscribed by the Viet-Minh Provisional Government in early September 1945; *Viet-Nam Dan-Quoc Cong-Bao* (Hanoi), 29 Sept. 1945, p. 6.
26  Tominaga Toyofumi, in Ikeda Yu (ed.), *Daitoa Senshi* [History of the Great East Asia War], vol. II (Tokyo, 1968). He refers to Col. Hayashi Hidezumi, who was responsible for looking after Diem in Saigon and who would appear to be the original source of the information. See n. 28 below.
27  This is apparent from the information given in H.J. Benda, *The Crescent and the Rising Sun* (The Hague, 1958).
28  Col. Hayashi kindly permitted an interview with the author in Dec. 1975; I am greatly indebted to him both for specific factual information and for the insight he gave into the situation in Saigon during 1944–45.
29  *South China Morning Post*, 10 Nov. 1945.
30  Devillers, op. cit., pp. 89–91.
31  *Who's Who in Japan, 1937* gives details of his diplomatic career to that date; see also Japanese Foreign Ministry Archives, E.4.0.0.–13 (=S.5..4.0.0.2), for his role in charge of the Enquiry into Natural Resources, Sept. 1941; *Opinion-Impartial*, 21 Oct. 1944, for his position at the Japanese Cultural Institute; and *Opinion-Impartial*, 22 May 1945 for his role after 9 Mar. 1945.

32 Phuong Lan, *Nha Cach-Mang Ta Thu Thau, 1906–1945* (Saigon, 1974), p. 272. For his meeting with Ho Chi Minn (Nguyen Ai Quoc), see I. Lacouture, *Ho Chi Minh* (Paris, 1967), p. 19. Until his death, Komatsu was Professor of French at Tokyo University.
33 Decoux, op. cit., pp. 300–301. Text also in J. Legrand, *L'Indochine a l'Heure Japonaise.* (Cannes, 1963), pp. 224–25.
34 Devillers, op. cit., p. 118.
35 G. Sabattier, *Le Destin de l'Indochine: Souvenirs et Documents, 1941–1951* (Paris, 1952), pp. 387–90. Sabattier was placed in charge of the Resistance troops in northern Indochina. On Blaizot's position, see n. 36 below.
36 The dispute on this issue, and the question of Blaizot's position, is covered in some detail in the British archives, although the full story of relations with the U.S. at this point has yet to be revealed. See FO 371/46304, P.R.O., London.
37 Decoux, op. cit., pp. 319–20; Legrand, op. cit., p. 233. Langlade transmitted to Decoux the instructions of the new Minister of Colonies in Paris, for which see Sabattier, op. cit., pp. 99–100.
38 S.W. Kirby et al., *The War against Japan*, vol. III (London, 1961).
39 C.F. Romanus and R. Sunderland, *Stillwell's Command Problems* ("U.S. Army in World War II" Series, Washington, 1956), pp 316 ff. On the bombing of Indochina before Jan. 1945, see C. Chennault, *The Way of a Fighter* (New York, 1949), pp. 248–50, etc.
40 J.P.W. Ehrman, *Grand Strategy, August 1943–September 1944* ("History of the Second World War" Series, London, 1956).
41 R.J.C. Butow, *Japan's Decision to Surrender* (Stanford, 1954), pp. 42–43.
42 Kirby, op. cit., (London 1965), IV, 85–86.
43 W.O. 203/5608, P.R.O., London.
44 Legrand, op. cit., pp. 229–33; Boisanger's note on the conversation is dated 20 Nov. 1944. Boisanger was in charge of diplomatic affairs under Decoux.
45 U.S. Strategic Bombing Survey: *Fifth Air Force, in the War against Japan* (Washington, 1947), p. 21. For Japanese reaction, see the various telegrams between Indochina and Tokyo cited below.
46 The making of the plan is reported in a telegram from Matsumoto to Shigemitsu, 25 Feb. 1945, following an investigation of the situation in Indochina by a Foreign Ministry official named Ishizawa. A. 7.0.0.9-54 (=S.0.0.54), pp. 191–93, Japanese Foreign Ministry Archives, Tokyo. The identity of the officer is not given, but it appears to have been Col. Hayashi Hidezumi; see n. 65 below.
47 He had previously been in Timor. He took over command in Indochina on 14 Dec. 1944. *Sittan Meigo Sakusen* [The Sittang and Mei-go Operations], (Tokyo, 1969), pp. 594–95.
48 Matsumoto to Shigemitsu, 25 Jan. 1945. A.7.0.0.9-54, pp. 26–27, in Japanese Foreign Ministry Archives, Tokyo.
49 Sabattier, op. cit., ch. 5–6.
50 IMT Document no. 501 (=IPS no. 2664), from the Japanese Foreign Ministry Archives.
51 See below for more details of this debate, and references.
52 Japanese Foreign Ministry Archives, A.7.0.0.9–54, pp. 50ff.
53 British archives, FO 371/46305/F1563, P.R.O., London: secret correspondence between the French and British governments on 12 Mar. 1945.
54 Domei broadcast, in English for Europe, 10 Mar. 1945, as monitored by the B.B.C.; copies of monitored reports are to be found in the P.R.O. files: FO 371/46305/F1569.
55 Sabattier, op. cit., pp. 118–23.
56 Ibid., pp. 115–18.
57 Japanese Foreign Ministry Archives, A. 7.0.0.9.–54, pp. 194–96.
58 Ibid., p. 280.
59 Defence Agency, Office of War History: *Sittan Mei-go Sakusen* and Tominaga Toyofumi, "The Coup d'Etat in Hue" in Ikeda Yu (ed.), *Daitoa Senshi*, vol. II. I am grateful to Miss Takemoto for a translation of the latter.
60 For text, see Decoux, op. cit., 330.

*Japanese in Indochina and the coup of 9 March 1945*  67

61  Tominaga, as above, gives a fairly detailed account of this from the Japanese side.
62  See the Situation Reports of 10–29 Mar. 1945, forwarded to the Foreign Office by the War Office, in FO 371/46305/F1642 etc., P.R.O. London.
63  Note the telegram from Churchill to Roosevelt, 17 Mar. 1945, on this question: FO 371/46305/F1714, P.R.O., London.
64  Domei in English, 13 Mar. 1945, as monitored by the B.B.C.; copy in FO 371/46305/F1569, P.R.O., London.
65  See n. 46 above.
66  Matsumoto to Shigemitsu, 25 Feb. 45, Japanese Foreign Ministry Archives, A.7.0.0.9. 54, pp. 191–93.
67  Tsukamoto to Shigemitsu, 16 Jan. 1945, ibid., pp. 9–14.
68  Tsukamoto to Shigemitsu, 11 Feb. 1945, ibid., pp. 102–3.
69  The reports are contained in telegrams from Matsumoto to Shigemitsu, 22–23 Feb. 1945, ibid., pp. 168–71, 173–75.
70  Shigemitsu to Matsumoto, 24 Feb. 1945, ibid., pp. 181–85. For a discussion of the Japanese conception of "independence within the New Order of East Asia", as opposed to "independence based on the idea of liberalism and self-determination", see W.H. Elsbree, *Japan's Role in Southeast Asian Nationalist Movements, 1940–1945* (Harvard, 1953), pp. 25ff. The phrases quoted are from Exhibit 1336 of the International Military Tribunal of the Far East, i.e., the Total War Research Institute's "Draft basic plan for the establishment of the Great East Asia Co-prosperity Sphere", 27 Jan. 1942.
71  Matsumoto to Shigemitsu, 26 Feb. 1945, ibid., pp. 194–96.
72  Shigemitsu to Matsumoto, 26 Feb. 1945, ibid., pp. 197–98.
73  Matsumoto to Shigemitsu, 28 Feb. 1945, ibid., pp. 220.
74  This point is referred to in a memorandum by Ogijima, chief of the second political section of the Foreign Ministry, 30 Jan. 1945 (ibid., pp. 44–49); and in several telegrams, e.g., Shigemitsu to Matsumoto, 7 Feb. 1945 (ibid., pp. 70–80); Matsumoto to Shigemitsu, 26 Feb. 1945 (ibid, pp. 194–96).
75  *Domei* news agency reports, 14 Mar. 1945, based on proclamation of Tsuchihashi in Saigon the previous day, as monitored by the B.B.C. Copy in British archives, FO 371/46305/F.1569. Nishimura is not mentioned there, but see also *Opinion-Impartial* (Saigon), 23 Mar. 1945.
76  *Opinion-Impartial*, 10, 11, 30 Apr. 1945.
77  *Opinion-Impartial*, 21, 22 Mar. 1945.
78  Devillers, op. cit., p. 125, reproduces the French version of the text. See also *Ngay Nay* (Hanoi), 5 May 1945; and the account by Tominaga.
79  *Ngay Nay*, 5 May 1945.
80  Proclamation of Japanese authorities, 15 Mar. 1945, as reported by Domei news agency; see FO 371/46305/F1569, and also *Opinion-Impartial*, 19 Mar. 1945.
81  Mus (1947?), Lecon 3, pp.2–3.
82  J. Saintany, *Histoire d'une Paix Manquee, Indochine, 1945–1947* (Paris, 1967), p. 54.
83  *La Tribune Indochinoise* (Saigon), 15 Apr. 1942, 20 May 1942.
84  Cited in Huynh Kim Khanh, "The Vietnamese August Revolution Reinterpreted", *Journal of Asian Studies*, XXX, no. 4 (1971), 766.
85  Pham Van Dieu, *Viet-Nam Van-hoc Giang-binh* (Saigon, 1961), pp. 477–80.
86  *Opinion-Impartial*, 20 Apr. 1945, based on Domei report of previous day. A full list of ministers is given. See Devillers, op. cit., p. 127.
87  See *Who's Who in the Republic of South Vietnam* (Giai-Phong Editions, South Vietnam, 1969), p. 42.
88  Biographies of the following ministers will be found in *Souverains et Nota bilites de l'Indochine* (Hanoi, 1943): Hoang Xuan han, Nguyen Huu Thi, Tran Van Chuong, Vu Ngoc Anh. For the death of Vu Ngoc Anh on 23 July 1945, see *Opinion-Impartial*, 26 July 1945.

89 *Opinion-Impartial*, 9 May 1945.
90 Ibid., 16 July 1945; See Devillers, op. cit., 127.
91 *Opinion-Impartial*, 25 May 1945.
92 Ibid., various issues during July/August; figures based on numbers given at different dates during period.
93 Ngo Vinh Long, *Before the Revolution: The Vietnamese Peasants under the French* (Cambridge, Mass., 1973).
94 *Opinion-Impartial*, 12 June 1945.
95 *Ngay-Nay*, 23 June 1945.
96 Devillers, op. cit., p. 127.
97 *Opinion-Impartial*, 28 June 1945.
98 Ngo Vinh Long, pp. 122ff; he translates sections of an eyewitness account of the famine by Tran Van Mai, pp. 221ff.
99 *Opinion-Impartial*, 12 June 1945; *Ngay-Nay*, 23 June 1945.
100 *Thanh-Nghi*, 12 May 1945.
101 *Opinion-Impartial*, 23 May 1945.
102 Ibid., 8 June 1945.
103 Series of *Thanh-Nghi* and *Ngay-Nay* for 1945 were consulted by the author at the then "National Library" in Saigon, 1972.
104 *Thanh-Nghi*, 5 May 1945.
105 *Ngay-Nay*, 23 June 1945.
106 Communique of 12 July, reporting decrees dated 29 June 1945; *Opinion-Impartial*, 16 July 1945.
107 *Opinion-Impartial*, 18 July, 1 Aug. 1945.
108 Ibid., 26 July 1945.
109 *Opinion-Impartial*, 4 Apr. 1945.
110 Ibid., 10,12 Apr. 1945.
111 Ibid., 15 Apr. 1945.
112 Nguyen Ky Nam, *Hoi-Ky 1925–1964: II, 1945–54* (Saigon, 1964), pp. 151–63. Devillers merely says that permission for such a demonstration on the 16th was refused by the Japanese (p. 125); but it is clear that it did take place on the 18th. For Duong Ba Trac, see Tran Van Giap, *Luoc-Truyen cac Tac-Gia Viet-Nam* (Hanoi, 1972), II, 112–13.
113 Devillers, op. cit., p. 125–26.
114 *Opinion-Impartial*, 25, 27 May 1945.
115 Probably written by a British political officer named Meiklereid who arrived in Saigon about that time: FO 371/46309/F9525, P.R.O., London.
116 *Opinion-Impartial*, 2 July 1945.
117 Ibid., same issue.
118 Ibid., 9, 23 July 1945.
119 Ibid., 2 Aug. 1945.
120 Ibid., 18 Aug. 1945.
121 Ibid., 20 Aug. 1945.
122 Although there is no formal account of his movements during these years, it is evident from the published Vietnamese accounts by such people as Nguyen Luong Bang and Hoang Quoc Viet. For his journey to Kwangsi *and back* in 1941, see the account in Hoang Quoc Viet, *A Heroic People* (Hanoi, 1965), pp. 195–213.
123 For a relatively detailed account of this base area, see Vo Nguyen Giap's contributions to *A Heroic People* (Hanoi 1965), pp. 91–149; and to *Days with Ho Chi Minh* (Hanoi). See also K.C. Chen, *Vietnam and China, 1938–1954* (Princeton, 1969), ch. for the movements of Ho Chi Minh throughout this period.
124 Some information about the development of this base area can be gleaned from the essay by Hoang Quoc Viet in *A Heroic People*, cited in n. 123, and also from *Thirty Years of Struggle of the Party* (Hanoi, 1960), IX, 72ff.

125 *Thirty Years of Struggle of the Party*, pp. 84–86. See also the essay by Nguyen Luong Bang in *Heroic People*, p. 62.
126 For an English translation of the text, see *Breaking Our Chains: Documents on the Vietnamese Revolution of August 1945* (Hanoi, 1960), pp. 7–17.
127 *Histoire de la Revolution d'Aout* (Hanoi, 1972), pp. 85ff.
128 Ibid., 83–84.
129 Ibid., 88–89.
130 *Breaking Our Chains*, pp. 22–42; *Histoire de la Revolution d'Aout*, pp. 99–100.
131 *Breaking Our Chains*, pp. 52–57.
132 *Histoire de la Revolution d'Aout*, pp. 104–5; *Thirty Years of Struggle of the Party*, p. 88.
133 C. Fenn, *Ho Chi Minh* (London, 1973), pp. 75–82. Fenn was working for OSS and AGAS in Kunming in the first half of 1945, and was responsible for Ho's success in securing cooperation with AGAS; they first met, in Kunming, on 17 Mar. 1945.
134 The date of Ho's move to Tan-Trao is not firmly established, but this appears the most likely date; see Vo Nguyen Giap's contribution to *Days with Ho Chi Minh*.
135 The only information concerning this mission so far published is in R. Harris Smith, *OSS: The Secret History of America's First Central Intelligence Agency* (Berkeley, 1972), pp. 331–34.
136 For more detail on this period, see Devillers, op. cit., pp. 136ff and *Histoire de la Revolution d'Aout*, pp. 127ff.
137 Ibid., pp. 138–39. The failure to seize the bank was remarked upon critically by Truong Chinh in his assessment of the August Revolution, written in Sept. 1946; see Truong Chinh, *Primer for Revolt* (New York, 1963), p. 42.
138 Devillers, op. cit., pp. 140–42.
139 Even as early as 4 Sept. 1945, Tran Van Giau, the communist leader in Saigon, was having great difficulty in securing a policy of conciliation towards the British forces, in view of the more belligerent attitude of the non-communist groups. Devillers, op. cit., 155–56.
140 Included in Report to Foreign Office, P.R.O., London, FO 371/46308/F7054.
141 *South China Morning Post* (Hong Kong), 8 Oct. 1945; See also report of 28 Sept. 1945. A week later, Terauchi is quoted as admitting that some deserters were helping the "nationalists", but this "did not reflect the true Japanese attitude"; he claimed that senior officers were all cooperative with the British, but he had had to reprove some junior officers. Ibid. 17 Oct. 1945.
142 Ibid., 16 Oct. 1945.
143 Ibid., 17 Oct. 1945.
144 Mus, op. cit., pp. 9–11.

# 3 The Vietnamese revolution of August–September 1945
## A South-East Asian perspective

Source: Paper for Workshop on Comparative Perspectives on Revolutions and Nationalism in Indonesia and Vietnam, Nordic Institute of Asian Studies, Copenhagen, 26–27 April 1996.

## I

The central question to be addressed in this paper is why, following the Japanese surrender in 1945, the independence of Indonesia was proclaimed (on 17 August) by an essentially non-Communist national movement, led initially by the pro-Japanese Sukarno; while that of Vietnam (proclaimed on 2 September) was undertaken by the strongly anti-Japanese, Communist-led Viet Minh movement headed by Ho Chi Minh. It is important to distinguish this relatively narrow contrast from a much broader question which can also be asked: why did Indonesia later become, by the 1950s, an essentially non-Communist country, while the Vietnamese revolution continued to be led by the Indochinese Communist Party (and its successor the Vietnamese Workers' Party) until 'final victory' in 1975?

The two levels of discourse are not unrelated. The answer to the narrower question will always constitute one element in the efforts of historians to get to grips with the larger one. On the other hand, we should not take the events of the period 1946–50 too much for granted. In the case of Indonesia we must not forget that the eventual success of Sukarno, Hatta, Sjahrir and the other nationalists of 1945 depended on their ability to defeat, first the opposition of Tan Malaka's group in 1946, and then the Communist-led uprising, which began at Madiun in September 1948. The outcome of events also owed much to the fact that during the Dutch 'police actions' of 1947–49 the Indonesian National Army had to deal only with the forces of the former colonial power, while the British and the Americans were pressing for a negotiated solution. The problem of Indonesian independence was resolved by the end of 1949, before the 'Cold War' internationalisation of conflicts elsewhere in the region during the first half of 1950. Equally, in Vietnam, it must be recognised that in itself the August Revolution of 1945 by no means guaranteed an eventual Communist triumph. The initial revolution virtually collapsed by the end of 1947, leaving the subsequent ability of the Viet Minh to oppose the French increasingly dependent after 1949 on assistance from the Chinese People's Liberation Army.

Nevertheless, the more specific question relating to the events of August and September 1945 in the two countries has importance in its own right and deserves closer attention than it has usually received. Approaching that question in its own terms, without necessarily concerning ourselves with what came later, we need to take account of at least three different contexts: that of longer-term political and cultural differences between Indonesia and Vietnam; that of the differing histories of their anti-colonial movements down to 1941; and that of international as well as national developments during the 'Japanese period' from 1941 to 1945. I shall suggest that of these three contexts it is probably the third which matters most for an understanding of the actual course of events in 1945.

The longer-term historical and cultural context is frequently invoked to explain differences between Vietnam and other countries in South-East Asia. 'Chinese Confucian influence' over many centuries is seen as having shaped Vietnamese culture and politics at every stage of its history, making it appropriate – for some purposes at least – to treat Vietnam as belonging, like Korea and Japan, to the 'Confucian world' of East Asia. Indonesia, on the other hand, was for centuries one of those 'Indianised' parts of the region which eventually became converted to Islam. Among Western political scientists in the mid-20th century, it seemed logical to invoke the Confucian background as an explanation for the rise of Communism in China, Vietnam and the northern half of Korea; and to regard Islam as the main buttress against the success of Communism in countries like Indonesia. *Quod erat demonstrandum*, perhaps? No more need be said, according to that reasoning, with regard to the unavoidable misfortune of any Indonesian who happened to be impressed by Marxism; or of any Vietnamese who might wish to see that country develop along non-Communist lines.

It has become a *cliche* for scholars writing about Vietnam to emphasise both its long-standing connections with China and the distinctiveness of its own national identity. The legacy of several centuries of Chinese rule, from the Han to the Tang, was that as late as the 19th century Vietnam's scholarly elite studied the Confucian classics and passed formal examinations in order to qualify for status in the bureaucratic hierarchy. Consequently anyone wishing to study Vietnamese history before the French conquest must depend for much of the time on sources written in classical Chinese characters; and even when it came to be written in *quoc-ngu*, in the 20th century, the Vietnamese language itself owed much of its political and religious vocabulary to Chinese influence. It was natural for Vietnamese nationalists in the 20th century to respond to French domination by looking to China for revolutionary models; and beyond that to Japan, whose successful 'modernisation' had begun to attract China's own political intellectuals by 1900. In due course that led some Vietnamese towards an interest in Chinese Communism and its Soviet source.

Yet it is also true that Vietnamese history, from the 11th to the end of the 18th century, was marked by a series of wars against Chinese invaders; and that Vietnamese poets, at least from the time of the *Binh Ngo* Proclamation of 1428, prided themselves on the fact that 'the mountains and rivers of the South (Vietnam) are distinct from those of the North (China)'.[1] Where the classical Chinese histories look back to the Shang and Zhou dynasties, the Vietnamese *Dai-Viet Su-Ky* takes as its starting-point the ancient Hung Vuong dynasty which flourished, if only in mythology, long before the Han conquest. Past conflicts with China, moreover, were given special emphasis among Vietnamese nationalist writers of the 1940s as one means of identifying a nationalist patriotic tradition without running foul of French colonial censorship. But that also reinforced the tendency to define Vietnamese independence as independence from China.

Vietnam appears in a quite different perspective, however, if we compare it with other countries in South-East Asia rather than with the vast Chinese empire under the Ming and Qing. The apparent 'uniqueness' of its traditional relationship with China seems less important when we appreciate that every country of the region is unique in some way: the Philippines because it was conquered early on by Spain and became a predominantly Christian country; Thailand because it alone escaped Western colonial rule in the 19th century; Cambodia because its territory was truncated by Thai and Vietnamese expansion and then fought over by rival armies; Malaysia because it owed its eventual unity to constitutional processes of the period 1946–65; Indonesia because it is so much larger and more ethnically diverse than its neighbours. Vietnam was 'Sinicised' in much the same sense as the Philippines were 'Hispanised', or the Malayo-Javanese world was 'Indianised', and later 'Islamised'. The external influence on Vietnam's culture cannot be denied; but the Vietnamese are no more Chinese as a result than the Filipinos became Spaniards or the Indonesians became Indian Muslims.

In scale, certainly, Vietnam has more in common with its South-East Asian neighbours than with the 'Chinese model'. The geographical extent of Vietnam, even after the unification of its territories for the first time in 1802, remained no greater than that of many Chinese provinces. Its traditional administrative structure was far less complex than that of China; while the Vietnamese *xa* (or *lang*), with its council of elders and its communal lands, had more in common with the villages of Java and Bali than with those of southern China. This difference of scale also finds reflection in pre-colonial architecture. Visitors to the 19th century *dainoi* at Hue who have also seen the 'forbidden city' of Beijing are likely to be struck by the lower profile and more human dimensions of the Nguyen capital. So much so that it seems not entirely unreasonable to compare Hue with the Javanese *kratons* of Surakarta and Yogyakarta. The latter contrast is certainly no greater than that between Hue and Beijing.

Thus even before the colonial period – when it was completely detached from its 'Chinese' past by the imposition of French colonial rule – Vietnam had certain features which make it logical to consider it as part of South-East Asia rather than of an exclusively Confucian world. The similarities with Java are particularly interesting. Once the possibility of this comparison is acknowledged, however, it becomes necessary to find other explanations than 'traditional characteristics' for the different course taken by political events in Vietnam and Indonesia in 1945. The contrast between Confucian and Islamic traditions is not enough to justify an explanation solely in terms of cultural determinism. We cannot, of course, disregard on this basis the geo-political significance of Vietnam's greater proximity to China: as we shall see, that was an important consideration during the period after mid-1940 – when both Vietnam and Indonesia were cut off from many of their previous colonial links by events in Europe. But that must be counted as an aspect of the geography of international relations rather than a consequence of different cultural traditions.

A comparison between European colonial rule in French Indochina and in the Netherlands East Indies reveals both differences and similarities. Vietnam remained free of European domination until the mid-19th century, by which time its 'traditional' rulers had expanded into former Cham and Cambodian territory and had achieved the 'unification' which gave the country its modern shape. (An attempt by Manila to establish a Spanish protectorate over lower Cambodia in the 1590s had proved very short-lived.) By the time the French began their conquest around 1860, the cultural unity of Cambodia was already well defined – despite threats to its political independence coming from both Hue and Bangkok; most of Laos also had closer ties to Bangkok than to Hue. Although it was possible for the French to invoke traditional Vietnamese claims to suzerainty over those two countries, and to deploy military power to eliminate Thai claims, it was too late to bring about a cultural fusion of either Cambodia or Laos with Vietnam except by promoting actual Vietnamese colonisation of their territory. It was also too late for a single 'Indochinese' nationalism to develop – as opposed to an anti-colonial movement, which owed its coherence largely to the presence of the French themselves. Despite the claims of the Indochinese Communist Party to embrace the whole of French Indochina, it was the independence of Vietnam alone that was proclaimed in 1945: first by the emperor Bao-Dai on 11 March, then by Ho Chi Minh on 2 September.

In the case of Indonesia, however, the presence of the Dutch at Batavia after 1619 – and especially following their defeat of Sultan Agung's siege in 1628–9 – prevented the unification of Java under a single Javanese ruler. It also prevented any Malay (or Javanese) state from gaining control of the spice trade and other commercial activities in the archipelago, which might have provided the basis for the establishment of Malay domination over an area wider than Java. The Dutch themselves gradually came to control the Muslim ports of northern Java and to assert their own hegemony over southern Sumatra, southern Sulawesi and southern Kalimantan – long before they finally imposed unity on Java in the early 19th century. Already before 1850, therefore, they had created the geo-political framework within which Indonesia eventually acquired its own national unity. By the 1920s and 1930s, Jakarta had become a capital of 'the Indies', rather than of Java alone: a meeting place for the emergence of a genuinely Indonesian national elite. (Bandung shared that position, in the educational sphere.) This historical evolution helps to explain why it was a 'Republik Indonesia' that was proclaimed on 17 August 1945, and why its subsequent national unity has proved more viable than Western sceptics were willing to allow.

By the 1930s there were nevertheless certain similarities between French and Dutch colonial rule in South-East Asia, which are evident from comparisons with that of the British in India and Burma or that of the Americans in the Philippines.

Both France and the Netherlands imposed on their Asian colonies a far more systematic regime of institutional discipline and economic exploitation than the 'Anglo-Saxons' found necessary. They were also far more reluctant to respond to Asian demands for constitutional advance towards self-government. The result was that, whereas the Philippines, India and even Burma had by 1940 been allowed a measure of administrative autonomy based on elective assemblies, neither French Indochina nor the Dutch East Indies had been permitted to progress in that direction. (Ironically, when the British were preparing a new stage of constitutional devolution for Burma in 1936–7, the French Popular Front government was at that time releasing large numbers of Vietnamese political prisoners – and allowing them greater freedom of political expression – while doing nothing to promote a significant role in government even for the French-educated elite.) Neither French nor Dutch policy gave any encouragement to 'moderate' opposition leaders who might have collaborated in constitutional change; instead they strengthened the national appeal of more radical movements. That may count as one reason why Vietnam and Indonesia were the two countries in South-East Asia where a genuine 'revolution' was proclaimed in 1945.

However, while these longer-term historical considerations may help us to gain greater insight into events in both Vietnam and Indonesia in that year, they do not go far towards answering our central question: why was the independence 'revolution' led by a Communist movement in one case and by non-Communist nationalists in the other? The quest for general 'causes' of specific events and contrasts may lead to fascinating and endless academic debates. But no adequate explanation of what happened in 1945 will emerge without a close analysis of the actual course of events in the preceding decade.

## II

The question why the Communist movement was relatively strong in Vietnam by 1945, but very weak in Indonesia, has tended to be answered partly in terms of the cultural contrasts already noted, and partly by looking at political events in the two countries during the late 1920s and 1930s. The Indonesian Communist Party, although it was founded as early as 1920, had suffered a major setback following its abortive uprising of 1926–27. It had probably become further isolated from the nationalist mainstream by the proletarian 'class line' imposed at the Sixth Congress of the Communist International in 1928.[2] It was therefore unable to participate in the 'high tide' of Communist evolutionary activity which swept across Asia in the late 1920s. Instead it was leaders like Sukarno and Hatta who expressed the aspirations of Indonesian nationalism most effectively at that time. The Indochinese Communist Party on the other hand, growing out of Nguyen Ai Quoc's Revolutionary Youth Movement of 1925–27 in Guangzhou, was able to benefit from the failure of the nationalist-led Yen Bay uprising of February 1930 and to play a leading role in the 'Nghe-Tinh Soviet' movement of 1930–31. Nevertheless, the ruthless French suppression of that revolt left the Party almost as weak as its Indonesian counterpart. Moreover, the ICP may itself have suffered some degree of isolation through its application of the proletarian class line during the 1930s, and its consequent alienation of the Vietnamese 'bourgeoisie'.[3]

The years 1936–39 are generally regarded as especially important for the Indochinese Communist Party, which benefitted from the decision of the Popular Front Government in Paris to release substantial numbers of political prisoners from Con-Son island and other prisons and to allow them to take part in legal activities. That period saw the emergence of Truong Chinh, Vo Nguyen Giap, Pham Van Dong and Tran Huy Lieu as leading figures in Hanoi, all of whom were to play a prominent role in 1945. At the time, however, it would appear that the Party was in fact much stronger in the South; and its Central Committee usually met in the Saigon area during those years, when such figures as Le Hong Phong, Nguyen Thi Minh Khai and Ha Huy Tap (all of them trained in Moscow) were active in its 'illegal' work. It was in Cochinchina that the Party sought to develop a mass peasant and worker base for the 'Indochinese Congress' of 1936–7; there, too, that Nguyen Van Tao and Duong Bach Mai (also Moscow-trained) took part in legal activities in Saigon, including participation in the *La Lutte* group (till mid-1937) and running for election to the Municipal Council.

The period of southern ascendancy lasted at least until the French crackdown on Communist activities and the arrest of numerous key figures in 1939–40. It was terminated completely after the ill-fated Nam-Ky Uprising of November 1940, which was suppressed even more thoroughly than the revolts of 1930–31, leaving the Party in the South virtually without leadership for several years. Its former following at the grassroots seems to have drifted towards other movements, notably the various branches of the Cao Dai religion, and the Hoa Hao sect, which had been founded by Huynh Phu So in 1939. By the time of the famous '8th plenum' of the ICP Central Committee in May 1941, when Nguyen Ai Quoc again made contact with the Party, its leadership inside Vietnam had passed to a northern group associated with the new secretary-general Truong Chinh whose base was in the countryside north of Hanoi.

Despite the setback of 1940, however, the memories of its activity in the late 1930s probably gave the ICP – even in 1945 – a stature which could not be claimed by the Indonesian Communists. The history of the PKI during the later 1930s remains extremely obscure, despite the efforts of Musso to revive its fortunes during the year or so (1935–36) which he spent in and around Surabaya – before returning once again to Moscow.[4] In the absence of any leftward swing in Holland comparable with the rise of the French Popular Front, the 'illegal PKI' had to keep its tracks carefully covered. It may nevertheless have attempted to pursue the same essential line as the ICP – that of forming a united anti-fascist front with other classes – following the Comintern's Seventh Congress of 1935. For example Amir Sjariffuddin, who later claimed to have been already a secret member of the PKI at this period, was a leading figure in the *Gerakan Rakyat Indonesia* of 1937–39: a movement which had much in common with the abortive 'Indochinese Congress' in Saigon. But it is clear that the PKI was unable to survive as a mass movement in any significant form, and after 1940 its role was more marginal than ever.

Returning briefly to the theme of longer-term cultural factors, what has been said so far is not incompatible with the suggestion that the widespread importance of Islam in the archipelago made it difficult if not impossible for the Communists ever to become the *principal* voice of Indonesian nationalism. But that argument does not, in itself, demonstrate the converse: that there was some kind of cultural continuity between Confucianism and Communism in Vietnam. Perhaps the most important question to be asked about Vietnam in 1945 is not why the Viet Minh was so strong, but why non-Communist nationalism was so weak. Again the tendency of many writers has been to focus on the years around 1930, and in particular to observe the catastrophic consequences of the Yen Bay revolt and its suppression for Nguyen Thai Hoc's nationalist movement. The *Viet Nam Quoc Dan Dang* did not re-emerge as a serious revolutionary group until 1945, and even then still depended to a considerable extent on protection from the Chinese Nationalist forces, which occupied northern Indochina from mid-September. Another 'factor' in the weakness of non-Communist movements was the inability of the Constitutionalists to secure any real concessions from the French, which left them increasingly powerless after 1930: an elite of would-be 'collaborators' whose concern for their own welfare gave their cause little appeal to a wider following or to a younger generation.

In the Vietnamese case, however, the events of the 1930s can be counted as only partly explaining the situation that existed by 1945. At the beginning of 1941, following the collapse of the Nam-Ky rising, the recovery of the Communists was by no means assured. The emergence of a non-Communist mass movement in Vietnam, oriented towards Japan rather than towards either Paris or Moscow, was still a possibility during the Japanese occupation, which was about to begin.

## III

A fundamental contrast between Vietnamese and Indonesian political experience during the years 1941–45 arose from the nature of the Japanese occupation itself, which had very different consequences for the two countries. The Japanese military advance into French Indochina, which was completed in July and August 1941, took place as a result of diplomatic negotiations between Tokyo, Vichy and Hanoi; it did not involve the overthrow of the colonial regime. It is true that already in 1940 there were Japanese idealists who would have liked to sponsor a Vietnamese nationalist revolt against the French, but they were overruled by higher authority. Once the French had agreed to provide military facilities to Japan in September 1940, a group of Vietnamese supporters of Cuong De who tried to start an uprising around Lang-Son were left to their fate by the Japanese command. Even after the start of the Pacific War in December 1941, the Japanese decided to leave the French in administrative control of Indochina rather than to establish their own military regime.[5] In Indonesia, precisely the opposite happened. In accordance with plans drawn up in November 1941, when Dutch forces were overwhelmed the following March the East Indies were placed under Japanese military or naval administration and most Dutch officials and other residents were interned.

The consequence of this sudden change in Indonesia was that the Japanese immediately established direct relations with the mass of the population and looked for intermediaries to mobilise Indonesian support for their own war effort. They brought Sukarno and Hatta back to Jakarta from internal exile, and promoted the formation of a number of new mass organisations.[6] Although Tokyo refused to countenance any moves towards even nominal independence, when Burma and the Philippines were granted that status in 1943, the effect of Japanese policy was to produce a growing consciousness of national identity and of the possibility of cultural and social change without any European presence. The establishment of the *Pembala Tanah Air* (PETA) in October 1943 gave a taste of ideological discipline and limited military training to a significant number of young Indonesians, who were able to play their part in the creation of a genuine national army two years later. (The PETA was formally dissolved and disarmed by the Japanese between 18 and 25 August 1945; but the youths who had gained experience through it were in a position to form spontaneous groups, and to use any weapons they could acquire, in late August and September that year.) The Consultative Council of Indonesian Muslims (*Masjumi*), also formed in October 1943, played an important role in harnessing religion to the war effort. Since the PKI was in no position to gain influence over these Japanese-sponsored organisations, their nationalism was inevitably non-Communist in character even when a growing number of Indonesians became disillusioned with the Japanese during 1944–45.

In Vietnam, the survival of the French administration – including the Sûreté-Générale and its offshoots – rendered impossible such direct contact between the Japanese military and the indigenous population. Insofar as there was an attempt at mass mobilisation, it was organised by the French themselves along lines inspired by Petain's leadership of Vichy France. More Vietnamese were given education than before 1940, and some were allowed a measure of administrative responsibility. But there was no encouragement of Vietnamese nationalism; and Japanese attempts to promote such awareness in the summer of 1943 led to a crackdown the following October which forced a number of pro-Japanese figures to leave the country or to seek virtual sanctuary with the Japanese military. Prince Cuong De, who had lived in Japan for much of the time since 1905, was not allowed to return home to play a role that might in other circumstances have become comparable with that of Sukarno or Hatta.[7]

That situation continued until the coup of 9 March 1945, following which the French military were finally disarmed and interned, along with a large number of French civilians. At Japanese behest the treaty of 1884, which had established the French protectorate over Annam and Tonkin, was abrogated by Bao Dai. But despite his previous identification with the French, he was allowed to remain on the throne and to appoint the Confucian educationist Tran Trong Kim as prime minister of a new cabinet. There was still no move to bring back Cuong De, who remained in Tokyo till the end of the war; nor to give any role to Ngo Dinh Diem, his staunchest supporter in mandarin circles. The treaties of 1862 and 1874 which had ceded the 'six provinces' of Cochinchina to French colonial rule were left in place until 14 August 1945, which meant that Tran Trong

Kim's writ did not run there. In the meantime Governor Minoda gave greater administrative responsibilities to Vietnamese officials in Cochinchina, encouraged the formation of a 'Vanguard Youth' movement, and probably authorised a measure of paramilitary training for members of the pro-Japanese Cao Dai and Hoa Hao sects. But these moves, coming three years later than the Japanese takeover in Indonesia, were too late to allow a comparable mobilisation of Vietnamese nationalism oriented principally towards Japan. It was not merely that the Japanese were by now visibly losing the war, nor that (as things turned out) only another five months were left before Japan's surrender. (The swiftness of the final outcome could certainly not have been predicted at that stage.) What probably mattered most was that by March 1945 the Viet Minh had already become a formidable political movement. Its exclusion from such a significant role might have been possible had pro-Japanese mobilisation begun as early as 1942; by now, in that respect also, it was too late.

Opposition to Japanese military rule in Indonesia was never very strong, the only significant anti-Japanese plot being uncovered and rendered harmless in January 1943. One of its leaders was, it is true, the (probably) Communist figure Amir Sjariffudin; but even if we accept that he was already a PKI member in the late 1930s, and was thus acting according to a 'correct' international line, there was no possibility that the PKI could form the nucleus of an eventual liberation movement capable of serious collaboration with the Allies. In that respect Indonesia differed not only from Vietnam but from most other parts of South-East Asia. Left-wing anti-Japanese movements developed from about 1942 in the very different countries of Malaya and the Philippines, and later also in Burma, as well as in Vietnam.

In Malaya and the Philippines the Communist Party followed a line of opposing the Japanese, mobilising and training a peasant guerrilla force, and preparing to assist advancing British and Americans if the need should arise. Thus the Malayan Communist Party, even before the end of 1941, took the lead in creating a Malayan People's Anti-Japanese Army, which cooperated with the British 'Force 136' from 1943 till the end of the war. (By 1945 the MPAJA may well have had a greater level of preparedness for guerrilla warfare than the much more recently established Vietnamese Liberation Army.) In the Philippines, too, the Communists took the initiative to establish the *Hukbalahap* Anti-Japanese Army in 1942; but the Americans were less eager to cooperate with them than was the case with the British and the MPAJA. The situation in Burma was more complicated, since some Communists there cooperated with the Japanese at least until August 1944; but thereafter, it too can be added to the list. By late March 1945, as British forces advanced down the Irrawaddy towards Rangoon, the Anti-Fascist League of Aung San (and the Communist Party leader Than Tun) declared its opposition to the Japanese army and began a guerrilla uprising.

The situation of the Indochinese Communist Party was more complicated, at least in the earlier stages of the war, in that the French colonial administration not only remained in power but was actively collaborating with the Japanese. In forming the Viet Minh front in 1941, therefore, the ICP was in effect opening a new phase of the anti-colonial struggle rather than declaring itself ready to cooperate with a former colonial regime against the Japanese. The parallel with other areas became more obvious with the Japanese coup of 9 March 1945, which made it possible for the ICP to declare Japan its principal enemy. At that point it also became possible for the Viet Minh to offer assistance to the American OSS, based in Kunming. The relationship which developed between Ho Chi Minh and Archimedes L. Patti, from April to September that year, is well known; as is the arrival of the Deer Mission at the Viet Minh base in northern Tonkin in mid-July 1945. I am inclined to agree with Stein Tonnesson's view that, as late as the beginning of August when it was still impossible to predict an imminent Japanese surrender, Ho Chi Minh's real purpose in calling for the 'liberation' of Indochina was a guerrilla campaign in support of the Allies rather than an immediate seizure of power in the cities and a Viet Minh declaration of independence.[8]

Whether one accepts that interpretation or not, there can be little doubt that by March 1945 the Viet Minh front – and behind it the Indochinese Communist Party – had a much more extensive network throughout the country than had been the case in early 1941 or throughout 1942; while the constraints placed on pro-Japanese nationalist activity by the continuing French presence had hindered the growth of rival organisations. Moreover, in addition to the Viet Minh movement, it now appears that a separate Communist network was functioning in the Saigon area under the leadership of Tran Van Giau.[9] Although the latter did not accept the authority and line favoured by Truong Chinh in the North, its ability to infiltrate Japanese sponsored organisations (after 9 March) would play a significant role in undermining any attempt by such groups to oppose the eventual Viet Minh seizure of power. In particular leadership of the 'Vanguard Youth' movement, created by the Japanese in Saigon after 9 March, was in the hands of the secretly recruited Communist Dr Pham Ngoc Thach. The period from March to August 1945 was thus one of acute competition between political movements, in which the Communists had the edge. Only the Hoa Hao and the Cao Dai religious movements, active mainly in the southern provices, could be relied on to play an anti-Communist role at grass-roots level; and possibly even some branches of the Cao Dai were open to Viet Minh infiltration. The *Dai-Viet* and *Phuc-Quoc* also made some progress during these months, but they were essentially intellectual movements without any significant mass following.

One further aspect of the comparison between Indonesia and Vietnam in August 1945 remains to be considered: that of the role of the Japanese themselves. Their encouragement of Sukarno and Hatta to take action in Jakarta is well known. In early August the two leaders were summoned to meet Marshal Terauchi in Saigon. They returned home on 14 August ready to proclaim national independence – with Japanese approval – on the 24th; and they received further encouragement from Admiral Maeda, the liaison officer of the Navy in Jakarta. Even when Sukarno acted outside the originally approved scenario by declaring independence on 17 August, the Japanese army did not oppose the move; it even gave limited assistance to some of the youth groups which acted spontaneously in the chaotic situation that ensued. But what of the Japanese role in Indochina, and what of their attitude to the Communist-led Viet Minh which had previously been vigorously anti-Japanese?

Since Vietnam's 'independence' had already been proclaimed on 11 March 1945, the Japanese presumably saw no need for any new declaration in mid-August. But in whom should that independence be vested, if its Japanese sponsors were no longer in a position to protect it? At this point we need to take account of the geographical complexity of the two revolutions. To the extent that the Netherlands East Indies had a single political centre, with authority to dominate the whole archipelago, there was never any doubt that such power lay in Jakarta. Other centres mattered only for their own immediate areas; even Yogyakarta dominated only the central part of Java. The declaration of independence, once uttered by Sukarno in the capital, had immediate significance for the nation as a whole – whose unity was greatly enhanced by the role of Radio Republik Indonesia. In Vietnam, however, political and financial power was dispersed among three different centres. The most ancient political centre, embodying Vietnam's historical traditions, was Hanoi: the former Thang-Long. But although it had been made the official seat of the Indochinese Union, Hanoi was still a relatively small city by Asian standards, dependent on Haiphong as its port. The imperial capital of the current dynasty – the place where Bao-Dai had proclaimed independence in March and where the government of Tran Trong Kim was installed – was Hue. Thirdly, however, the largest Vietnamese city (and the most important in economic terms) was Saigon, whose excellent location and communications had made it the logical place for the Japanese to establish their military headquarters for the whole southern region. Which of these three centres could be made the most effective seat of an independent government, with or without Japanese encouragement?

The logic of political continuity might suggest that Hue would retain that status. But as soon as the Japanese surrender became known, Bao Dai and Tran Trong Kim were too deeply aware of their own weakness – *vis-à-vis* both the Allies and the Viet-Minh – to seize the kind of initiative that was open to a Sukarno or a Hatta. On the same day that Indonesian independence was proclaimed, Bao Dai was holding what would be virtually the last meeting of the Tran Trong Kim Cabinet; while Kim himself was already drafting a statement of resignation. By 20 August the emperor was aware that a new government would be needed and that his Court was no longer in a position to take the lead in the country as a whole. The Viet Minh leaders in Hue were in fact already getting ready to seize power, and it would not be long before the fate of Louis XVI at the hands of the French Revolution of 1789 began to seem more than a little relevant.[10] In these circumstances it was unlikely that the Vietnamese figures appointed to act as imperial delegates (*kham-sai*) in Hanoi and Saigon would be able to derive much authority from the throne.

The Vietnamese city that was most comparable with Jakarta was Saigon, where the Japanese sponsored the creation of a United National Front on 14 August. It embraced several pro-Japanese organisations, including the *Phuc-Quoc* (led by Tran Van An), the Vanguard Youth (of Pham Ngoc Thach) and the Hoa-Hao and Cao-Dai religious sects; the Trotskyists of the former *La Lutte* group also joined.

The Japanese appear to have envisaged that it would be led by the newly appointed *kham-sai*, Nguyen Van Sam, after his arrival in the city on 19 August. The highpoint of its success was a rally of 100,000 people in Saigon on 21 August. But at that point the Communists, no doubt encouraged by news of the Viet Minh seizure of power in Hanoi on 19 August, intervened to assert their own revolutionary ambitions. Having hesitated during a series of secret meetings of an Uprising Committee (formed by Tran Van Giau as early as the 16th), the Communist leadership decided on 21 August to seize power first in the provincial town of Tan An the following day. When that proved successful, eliciting no opposition from the Japanese, they decided to go ahead with the seizure of power in Saigon itself on 25 August. Meanwhile on the 24th, according to Giau's own account, he and Pham Ngoc Thach met Marshal Terauchi himself on the 24th and secured his tacit approval; also on that day the United National Front agreed to lend its support to the Viet Minh. The result was at least a measure of unity – all too fragile, as it would turn out – behind Tran Van Giau's announcement at a rally in Saigon (on 25 August) of the creation of a Provisional Administrative Committee for the South.

That was also the day on which Ho Chi Minh and Vo Nguyen Giap arrived in Hanoi, having journeyed for a week through the flooded lowlands of Tonkin, from the town of Tan Trao where Ho had presided over the Liberation Congress of 15–16 August. On the way, Giap's forces (accompanied by OSS officers) had become involved in clashes with the Japanese at Thai-Nguyen; the resulting stand-off there was not finally ended until the 26th. Thus the seizure of power in Hanoi, which had been planned on 16–17 August and was accomplished on the 19th, was not led in person by Ho Chi Minh or any of the other top leaders of the Viet Minh. Nor do they appear to have had any hand in the 'Assembly of Intellectuals and Students' which met at the Cite Universitaire of Hanoi on 21 August and which issued a declaration calling for the abdication of Bao Dai and the formation of a republican government by the Viet Minh in consultation with other parties. It was immediately telegraphed to Hue and probably determined Bao Dai's decision to abdicate. The four signatories were: Nguyen Xien, who emerged shortly afterwards as titular chairman of the Bac-Ky Administrative Committee and was later leader of the pro-Viet Minh Socialist Party founded in 1946; Nguyen Van Huyen, a Frenchtrained professor of history who in 1946 became titular Minister of Education and still held that post in Hanoi in the 1960s; Ho Huu Tuong, a Trotskyist of the 'October' group; and Nguy Nhu Kontum.[11] Behind the scenes, the most important ICP figures in Hanoi at this time seem to have been Nguyen Khang and Tran Tu Binh (both of whom may have had ties to the Chinese Communist movement, since they both later served as ambassadors to Beijing). But it is by no means certain that even they were in control of everything that happened.

The picture which seems to be emerging from recent research on the August Revolution in Hanoi is thus one of considerable ferment during the ten days following news of the Japanese surrender; but one in which Ho Chi Minh and Truong Chinh (and the leaders closest to them) were neither present on the scene nor directing the key decisions day by day. The attitude of the Japanese commander

Tsuchihashi is by no means clear. There was no direct contact between him and Ho Chi Minh or Vo Nguyen Giap at this stage, comparable with Terauchi's meeting with Giau and Thach in Saigon. (Nor did Tsuchihashi meet any OSS representative until the arrival of Patti in Hanoi, by plane from Kunming, on 22 August.) But there can be no doubt that Japanese troops did little to prevent the Viet Minh seizure of power beyond ensuring that they kept clear of the Bank of Indochina and a few other key buildings. In acquiescing to the takeover, however, the Japanese in Hanoi may not have been aware of the Viet Minh's Communist connections.

If we consider the situation of 25 August from the point of view of events in the three main centres of power in Vietnam, it was already clear that neither Hue nor the emperor would play a leading role in the revolution that was by then under way. But it was by no means yet certain that, in the long run, Hanoi would matter more than Saigon. That eventual outcome may not become evident until after the arrival of British forces, and their decision on 20 September to work with the French community to establish a measure of order in Saigon. More significantly, it may not have been until after 25 August that Ho Chi Minh himself began to assert firm control over the situation across the country as a whole. His declaration of independence on 2 September, undertaken partly as a means of impressing the Americans in the hope of winning their endorsement, may also have been a necessary step in the consolidation of his own leadership of the revolution.

## Notes

1 See translation and discussion in Stephen O'Harrow, 'Nguyen Trai's *Binh Ngo Dai Cao* of 1428: the development of a Vietnamese National Identity', in *Journal of Southeast Asian Studies* vol. x, no. 1 (March 1970).
2 For the role of the PKI at the Sixth Congress, and other details of its activities in the following decade, see C.B. McLane, *Soviet Strategies in Southeast Asia: an Exploration of Eastern Policy under Lenin and Stalin* (Princeton, 1966), pp. 188ff and 231ff.
3 The disadvantages of 'internationalism' are emphasised especially by Huynh Kim Khanh in *Vietnamese Communism 1925–1945* (Cornell, 1982).
4 Mentioned in G. McT Kahin, *Nationalism and Revolution in Indonesia* (Cornell 1952), pp. 86–7.
5 The Japanese decision to negotiate with the French rather than to 'expel' them from Indochina in 1940, and their policy of retaining French administrative control even in 1941–2, are discussed by Minami Yoshizawa, 'The Nishihara Mission in Hanoi, July 1940' (1984), and Masaya Shiraishi and Motoo Furuta, 'Two features of Japan's Indochina Policy during the Pacific War' (1975); both translated in T. Shiraishi and M. Furuta (eds), *Translation of Contemporary Japanese Scholarship on Southeast Asia: Indochina in the 1940s and 1950s* (Cornell, Southeast Asia Program, 1992).
6 The importance of this policy was recognised by historians as long ago as Harry J. Benda, *The Crescent and the Rising Sun: Indonesian Islam under the Japanese Occupation 1942–1945* (The Hague, 1958).
7 See, among other writings on this period: R.B.Smith, 'The Japanese Period in Indochina and the Coup of 9 March 1945', *Journal of Southeast Asian Studies* vol. ix, no 2 (September 1978).
8 Stein Tonnesson, *The Vietnamese Revolution of 1945: Roosevelt, Ho Chi Minh and de Gaulle in a World at War* (Oslo: PRIO, 1991), chapter 10.

9 The separateness of this group was first noted by Tonnesson in his work of 1991 (see note 8) and is now confirmed by David Marr's *Vietnam 1945: the Quest for Power* (Berkeley 1995), pp. 217ff and 453ff. Both authors based their interpretation partly on interviews with Giau himself.
10 This parallel is noted by Marr, *op. cit.*, pp. 443ff. I have relied for many details of events in August 1945 on Marr's account and on that of Tonnesson, *op. cit.*
11 This document, which is not mentioned in any subsequent Party versions of the events of 1945, was printed in the Hanoi newspaper *Le Peuple* in a special 'first anniversary' edition published on 19 August 1946. It is also reproduced in Philippe Devillers, *Histoire du Viet-Nam de 1940 a 1952* (Paris 1952), p. 137.

# 4 The work of the Provisional Government of Vietnam, August–December 1945

Source: *Modern Asian Studies* 12(4) (1978): 571–609.

## I

THE main outlines of the Vietnamese Revolution of 1945–46 are by now well enough known to Western scholars, through the writings of Philippe Devillers, B. B. Fall, K. C. Chen and J. T. McAlister.[1] But the detailed history of Vietnam during that period remains to be written; in particular only very scant treatment has so far been accorded to the actual political record of the Viet-Minh Provisional Government, which was established in Hanoi by Ho Chi Minh on 28 August 1945 and which lasted until the formation of the Coalition Government (or Government of Union and Resistance) in February 1946.

The omission is the more remarkable for the fact that there exists a printed record of its work, in the form of a decree book or official gazette. The *Viet-Nam Dan-Quoc Cong-Bao*, of which the first volume consists of weekly parts from 29 September to 29 December 1945 (but covering the period beginning 1 September 1945), was published officially (in Vietnamese) by the Provisional Government itself.[2] It takes up as close as we can get to contemporary 'internal' documentation of the government's activities. Other contemporary documents published in Hanoi have also survived from this period. One of these contains the original Vietnamese texts of speeches made by various Provisional Government leaders on 2 September 1945 on the occasion of the celebration of Independence Day in Hanoi, as well as the proclamation of independence itself.[3] There are also a number of Hanoi-printed newspapers, of which two may be specially mentioned: the French-language *La République*, organ of the 'Association Culturelle pour le Salut du Viet-Nam', which appeared weekly or slightly more often from 18 October to at least 25 November 1945;[4] and the opposition newspaper *Viet-Nam*, published by the Viet-Nam Quoc-Dan Dang ('Vietnamese Nationalist Party') from 15 November 1945.[5] Unfortunately, foreign news reporting from Hanoi during the early period of the Provisional Government was very limited. No Western journalist at all was present before mid-October, it would seem; but the reports filed by Palmer Hoyt, Jr. for United Press towards the end of November 1945 provide some interesting insights on the situation at that stage.[6] The purpose of the present article is to examine this and other material, and in particular the *Cong-Bao*, in order to define more clearly the character of the revolution which the Provisional Government was trying to implement during the second half of 1945.

By way of introduction, however, it is necessary to make three general points about the situation that existed in Vietnam by September 1945. In the first place, it needs to be understood that continuity with the French colonial period had been broken by the Japanese *coup d'état* of 9 March 1945.[7] The French, who had been masters of Indochina since the late nineteenth century, and who had still enjoyed the power of life and death over the Vietnamese population during the Japanese occupation after 1941, were swept aside in a mere couple of days. Their armies were defeated, their generals and top officials were interned, and in their place the Japanese held the whip hand. Although a formal declaration of independence was made by Bao-Dai on 11 March 1945 and a new Vietnamese era was proclaimed a week later, it was not until June and July that the Japanese began to allow any significant measure of authority to pass to the government of Tran Trong Kim; and not until 14 August 1945 that Bao Dai was permitted to abrogate the treaties which had ceded Cochinchina to the French in 1862 and 1874. Nevertheless, the effect of Japanese action was to bring to an end French rule, and to create a situation in which the future of the country was an open question. It was therefore not possible for the Viet-Minh, when they took control in Hanoi on 19 August 1945 (and throughout the country between then and the end of the month) simply to take over the French administration intact and to run the country along the same lines until they had time to make gradual reforms. In all revolutions, one of the essential features is that the *ancien régime* has already begun to crumble when the revolutionary régime arrives: in that respect, the situation of Vietnam by August 1945 was genuinely revolutionary.

Secondly, however, it must be said that Vietnam was not hermetically sealed from the outside world. The Japanese were not defeated by anything that happened in Vietnam; indeed, compared with other parts of South East Asia such as the Philippines or Burma, Indochina had seen relatively little ground fighting throughout the whole course of the war (although there were campaigns against the Viet-Minh in northern Tongking in 1943–44). The Vietnamese knew well enough that Japan had been defeated by the United States, and that the Americans were now the greatest power in the area. They knew, too, that the United States regarded Indochina as an extension of the China Theatre of the war against Japan, and that Chinese armies were due to enter the country in order to receive the Japanese surrender.[8] A long-standing conflict with the British (and French) on this question was settled at Potsdam in July 1945, by a compromise which made Indochina south of the 16th parallel part of the South East Asia Theatre, and so conferred on Mountbatten the responsibility for receiving the Japanese surrender there. A permanent partition was neither envisaged nor inevitable at this time. But the Viet-Minh knew that the arrival of Chinese and British troops would seriously complicate matters, and that they must race against time if they were to lay the foundations of an effective régime—and a revolutionary one, at that — before the arrival of the Allied armies. In the case of the Chinese, Ho Chi Minh had already foreseen this contingency and had made what preparations he could during his two periods in China during 1942–44 and 1944–45.[9] But the threat of a British presence in the South was less easy to deal with, and beyond it lay the strong possibility that the British would help the French to return. In the South, indeed, the French were able to restore their own power in Saigon by a *coup d'état* on 23 September 1945.[10] The revolution there was consequently very short-lived, and most of our attention will be concentrated on events north of the 16th parallel. Never at any time, however, did the Viet-Minh accept the possibility that Vietnam could be permanently partitioned into two separate polities.

Thirdly, it must be understood that the internal situation of Vietnam in August 1945 was seriously disorganized and presented grave problems for any government in Hanoi. Although it had escaped ground fighting, and had not actually been invaded by Allied forces before the end of the war, it had not escaped the effects of what was happening elsewhere in the region. Its economy had been dislocated, first by being cut off from France since late 1941, and then by the growing pressures suffered by the Japanese-oriented economy of Great East Asia into which it had been absorbed. Japan's war needs, combined with her inability to control the sea routes between Indochina and Japan, resulted in great scarcities in Vietnam which were only to a limited degree compensated by Admiral Decoux's policy of encouraging new industries and seeking to control internal markets.[11] There were also problems of currency, and after the coup of 9 March 1945 these got completely out of hand. The money supply increased dramatically and there was severe inflation. Disruption was made worse by Allied bombing raids, which had knocked out most of the transport system by 1945: they came first from Chennault's bases in southern China (from 1943) and then, across the whole country, from planes based on US carriers beginning in January 1945. The general effect of all these developments was that during the first half of 1945 Vietnam suffered a major economic disaster. The central and northern provinces were unable to produce enough rice both to feed themselves and to meet Franco-Japanese military needs. The bad harvests of 1944 led to serious food shortages from October of that year, and to a major famine during the early months of 1945. The death toll was put at two million by some observers, and cannot have been less than 500,000 on any estimation.[12] Worse still, the dykes had been broken during the rainy season of 1945 and the floods meant that an even worse famine was in prospect for the winter of 1945–46. The country which the Provisional Government began to administer in September 1945 therefore was in desperate straits.

The analysis which follows will attempt to relate the various aspects of the Provisional Government's work to one another, and to decide how far it is reasonable to speak of the events of 1945 as a 'Revolution' at all. It will look first at constitutional and administrative changes, and then at the politics of the Revolution. It will then proceed to examine the changes which were made, and the problems faced, in the fields of education and culture, propaganda, finance, industry and agriculture. A full account of the period would require also a study of the work of the Coalition Government of 1946, but that lies beyond the scope of the present article.

## II

The first and most fundamental task of a revolutionary party is to establish its power throughout the country, and then to establish machinery which will ensure that its power continues and is accepted by the population as a whole. In the second place it must also establish its own law, and this often includes the writing of a constitution and the holding of elections. All these things were important for the Viet-Minh in 1945, and the *Cong-Bao* indicates some of the administrative and constitutional steps which they took.

As early as 8 September 1945 a Decree laid down that an election for a National Assembly should be held within two months (which would have meant before 8 November).[13] All Vietnamese over the age of eighteen would be entitled to vote, with the exception of people who had been deprived of their civil rights and those deemed to be of unsound mind. The Assembly, to consist of 300 representatives in a single chamber, would have authority to decide upon the constitution of the Democratic Republic of Vietnam; in the meantime, committees were to be set up to draft a constitution, and also to devise regulations for the election. The constitutional committee was created by a Decree of 20 September 1945, and was composed of seven people, including Ho Chi Minh himself and the ex-emperor Bao-Dai (who now used the name Nguyen Vinh Thuy). Of the other five, three were members of the Indochinese Communist Party: its Secretary-General, Dang Xuan Khu (better known as Truong Chinh); the Secretary-General of the Viet-Minh, Nguyen Luong Bang; and the Minister of Labour, Le Van Hien. The others were Dang Thai Mai, a Socialist who was close to Vo Nguyen Giap and a leading figure in the field of education; and Vu Trong Khanh, who had been named by Tran Trong Kim to be Mayor of Haiphong on 16 July 1945 and who was presumably 'non-party'.[14] They set to work to prepare a Constitution, and it was eventually approved by the National Assembly during the course of 1946. The committee to draw up regulations for the election was set up by a further Decree on 26 September.[15] Interestingly, there was no overlap between its membership and that of the constitutional committee. It had nine members, including the Minister of Propaganda (Tran Huy Lieu), the Minister of Justice (Vu Dinh Hoe), the Minister of National Economy (Nguyen Manh Ha) and a Minister without Portfolio (Cu Huy Can). The other five members represented the various National Salvation mass organizations: culture, youth, women, workers, and peasants. It is worth noticing that even at this early stage there was a clear idea in the minds of the leaders that the election of a National Assembly was closely associated with the work of mass organizations and with propaganda. Tran Huy Lieu, one of the hardline Marxists in the Party, played a prominent role during these early days but drops from view after about December 1945. He later became head of the Historical Institute in the 1950s and 1960s, suggesting a permanent decline in his political influence; but in 1945 he was important enough to be ranked second after Ho Chi Minh in the list of ministers.

The actual regulations for the election were embodied in a decree dated 17 October 1945, by which time it had been decided that election day would be 23 December 1945; shortly before the latter date it was again postponed and was finally held on 6 January 1946, the sixteenth anniversary of the (by then dissolved) Indochinese Communist Party.[16] The election has been a subject of some controversy on the part of Western writers about Vietnamese affairs, who have often tended to regard it as completely 'bogus'. In practice, it is very likely that in certain parts of the southern zone of Vietnam (south of the sixteenth parallel) it could not be held at all; and in other areas it may have been held without the full rigours of the Election Decree being applied. But in the northern half of the country there is no reason to believe that in the majority of districts it was not held in accordance with the formal regulations. The seventy seats later allocated to the VNQDD and Dong-Minh-Hoi political groups by agreement between their leaders and those of the Viet-Minh would seem to have been simply added to the total and nominated by those two parties.[17] The Election Decree laid out a table of seventy-one provincial and municipal constituencies, for which there were to be 329 representatives (including thirty for ethnic minorities). Detailed regulations were to govern the nomination of candidates and the establishment of polling lists. Whereas the nominations would be the responsibility of provincial committees (since the provinces were the constituencies except for six municipalities), the drawing up of voting lists and the actual conduct of the ballot was the responsibility of village committees. It seems very probable that the conduct of the election was itself a part of the process by which the local administrative structure was mobilized by the revolution.

In considering the results of the election, which undoubtedly were overwhelmingly in favour of the Viet-Minh, it should be remembered that this was the first occasion on which an election of this magnitude had been held in Vietnam. During the French period, it is true, the Colonial Council of Cochinchina was directly elected from 1922 onwards, and by the 1930s there was also an elective element in the representative assemblies of Annam and Tongking, as well as in the municipal councils of Hanoi, Haiphong and Saigon. But these elections were based on very small electorates, since the franchise was strictly limited to a tiny élite. The election of 6 January 1946 was the first time that ordinary people had voted. That being so, the Viet-Minh success can probably be attributed to two simple aspects of the regulations. First, the fact that candidates had to present themselves at the level of a large constituency: this allowed the lists of candidates to be influenced by the provincial administrative committees (which were those set up by the Viet-Minh). Secondly, the fact that the voting was at village or basic level and that the vast majority of the population were illiterate meant that in effect the village administrative committee could influence the way people voted despite the secrecy of the ballot. The decree laid down precise procedures to be adopted where voters were illiterate, and no doubt the vast majority of peasants sought advice before telling their literate neighbours how they wished to vote. Indeed, the general election should be seen as an elaborate ritual by which the population was called upon to endorse the revolutionary government and its activities, rather than a means for popular choice of a government. What really mattered for the ordinary people were the elections for village and higher level administrative committees.

The origins of these grass-roots committees must be sought at an earlier stage. For although their formal creation was the subject of a decree in November 1945, they began to emerge at the very beginning of the revolution, even before the Viet-Minh reached Hanoi. The initial Viet-Minh decision to prepare to seize power in 1945 was taken at an enlarged meeting of the Standing Bureau of the Central Committee of the Indochinese Communist Party, presided over by the Secretary-General Truong-Chinh, which took place immediately after the Japanese *coup d'état* of 9 March 1945 and which approved the 'Instructions' of 12 March.[18] In the areas where guerrillas were already active, it was agreed to set up 'People's Revolutionary Committees' straight away. In other areas, the appropriate organization at grassroots level was to be the Liberation Committee, which would be set up wherever possible in villages, streets, factories, mines, public offices, etc. The Instructions also envisaged the eventual emergence of a National Liberation Committee, which would take on the form of a Provisional Revolutionary Government for the whole country. The pattern of committees which was sketched out on this occasion gradually took clearer shape, and was translated into reality, between then and the famous Tan-Trao Conference of 16 August 1945 which actually established the National Liberation Committee. The role and composition of the grassroots Liberation Committees was defined in a document of the Viet-Minh General Committee dated 16 April 1945.[19] By June the guerrilla areas had grown into the Free Zone (comprising large parts of the provinces which later became the 'Viet-Bac') and it was decided that it should be run by a Provisional Committee with various departments to deal with political and military affairs, and with economic, cultural and social (welfare) matters. At the same time there was to be a three-month programme, within the Free Zone, for the creation of elected People's Committees at the levels of the village, the district, and finally the province.[20]

The sudden ending of the war in mid-August forced the Viet-Minh leaders to speed up their programme, and it is likely that at that stage the creation of committees proceeded from the top down. But already by then grass-roots committees had been created at least in some provinces: either as people's committees in the fullest sense, or as liberation committees. The first village Liberation Committees are reported to have been established at the villages of Xuan-Bieu and Trung-Dinh, in western Bac-Giang province, which appears to have been the main centre of clandestine operations of the Party's Standing Bureau and Central Committee.[21] The process began as early as 13 or 14 March 1945, and involved the holding of a mass meeting in the village, at which the former notables were obliged to hand over their seals of office and village archives to representatives of the new committee. Immediately afterwards, in many cases, the peasants raided the local depot or store in which the village had kept rice due to be collected by government officials for the supply of the French and Japanese armies. This forced collection of rice was one of the greatest grievances in northern Tongking at a time when many families were starving in the serious famine. During March and April the creation of village Liberation Committees spread to other provinces of the North—certainly to Bac-Ninh and Vinh-Yen and probably further afield. In June a large area of Hai-Duong and Quang-Yen provinces was added. These were all provinces outside the Free Zone itself, where presumably the creation of local committees went ahead even more rapidly. Unfortunately, however, the limited information available does not permit us to measure with great precision the territorial extent of Liberation Committees by mid-August.

When the decision for an immediate insurrection was taken, on 13 August 1945, it became important to set up provincial revolutionary or liberation committees in as many provinces as possible. Between the decision to act and the actual seizure of Hanoi (i.e. 14–19 August 1945), village and district committees were established in 18 provinces of Tongking (Bac-Bo), in five provinces of Annam (Trung-Bo), and in two provinces of Cochinchina (Nam-Bo). On 18 August, provincial power was seized in Bac-Giang, Hai-Duong, Ha-Tinh and Quang-Nam; the next day the Viet-Minh moved into the provincial headquarters of Yen-Bay, Thai-Binh, Phuc-Yen, Thanh-Hoa and Khanh-Hoa; and on the 20th it was the turn of Bac-Ninh, Thai-Nguyen and Ninh-Binh. During the next week the movement spread rapidly to other provinces, reaching the South (Nam-Bo) by 23 August when provincial committees were established in Tan-An and Bac-Lieu, followed by My-Tho and Go-Cong on the 24th and Can-Tho on the 26th.[22] By the beginning of September the Viet-Minh had established its presence in the vast majority of province centres throughout Viet-Nam. There were a few exceptions, notably (in Tongking) Vinh-Yen, Mon-Cay, Ha-Giang and Lao-Kay, and for a while Phuc-Yen, where they were prevented from taking any action by the forces of their rivals, the Viet-Nam Quoc-Dan Dang or the Dong-Minh-Hoi.[23] It is likely, too, that in many southern provinces their success depended on their alliance with other groups, notably the religious sects of Hoa-Hao and Cao-Dai, who were the effective leaders at grass-roots level in certain areas. That alliance began to crumble as the French succeeded in restoring their power in the provinces of Cochinchina.

The formalization of this movement to create popular revolutionary committees at all levels did not come until 22 November 1945, when Decree no. 63 established administrative committees and also popular assemblies at all levels from the *xa* (village or 'commune') to the *ky* (the three divisions known to the French as Tonkin, Annam and Cochinchina).[24] By this time it was possible to lay down detailed rules about the composition of the committees and the election of the assemblies, and the implementation of the system in as many areas as possible was probably seen as a necessary preliminary to the holding of elections in December. But it is evident from other sources that the committees were already operating in many places, and that an important part in the government of the country was being played by the Administrative Committee of Bac-Ky (or Bac-Bo), whose chairman was the socialist leader, Nguyen Xien.[25] Later on, when the Viet-Minh had to fight the French for control of the country, these various committees evolved into the Resistance and Administrative Committees of the war period.

Whilst the hierarchy of committees operated as a structure for making and implementing many decisions, they did not in themselves constitute a government.

At the centre it was necessary to establish or reconstitute administrative machinery capable of holding the country together and carrying out the overall policies of the Viet-Minh. Several decrees recorded in the *Cong-Bao* relate to the administrative structure of the central government. On 13 September a Decree abolished the whole cadres of administrative and judicial officials which had operated under the French, and clearly some officials saw their careers brought to an abrupt end.[26] But not all, for the decree allowed for those officials who were acceptable to carry on under the new order, perhaps in new posts. The same was true for the cadre of education officials, dealt with separately (but similarly) in a Decree of 8 September 1945.[27] In a few cases we know that named individuals carried on in their existing posts. A notable example was Trinh Van Binh, previously director of customs for Tongking, who became Director-General of the Office of Customs and Indirect Taxes.[28] His subsequent career suggests that he was regarded as a reliable supporter of the Viet-Minh, and one account says that Ho Chi Minh stayed secretly at his house in Hanoi for a time in August 1945.[29] Probably there were others like him who continued to work for the new régime. By December, the government was concerned less with weeding out unacceptable officials than with ensuring that those holding office stayed at their posts. The reason was probably financial, as we shall see. On 17 December 1945 Decree no. 75 ordered that until further notice all officials on active duty in all parts of Vietnam should behave as if their services had been requisitioned by the state, unless expressly granted permission to resign.[30]

In the administration of justice, too, there was probably a considerable measure of continuity. A Decree of 10 October 1945 ruled that the existing law codes should remain in force for the time being, with a certain number of exceptions which the Decree itself specified. Another provisionally maintained the existing legal profession, to carry on the work of the courts.[31] There were, however, important changes in the style of government control over the administration and its officials, and in the maintenance of security; and in this connection an additional set of courts or tribunals was set up. This was accomplished by a series of Decrees dated 13 September 1945, which was the first series to be signed by the President himself, Ho Chi Minh.[32] One of them created nine military tribunals: at Hanoi, Haiphong, Thai-Nguyen, Ninh-Binh, Vinh, Hue, Quang-Ngai, Saigon and My-Tho; a tenth at Nha-Trang was added by a further Decree of 29 September. Their jurisdiction was to cover any action 'against the independence of Vietnam', and the range of sentences they could impose included the death penalty, with only very limited possibilities of appeal.[33]

Two other Decrees of 13 September indicate that powers of arrest in such cases lay with either the regular police (*so Canh-Sat*) or with the security agency (*ty Liem-Phong*). The latter body is not very fully documented but its existence is first attested by these Decrees, and it had the greatest importance for the power of the new government. It is evident from opposition newspaper articles of Spring 1946 that an important reason why the Coalition Government (created in March of that year) was still effectively a Viet-Minh government was that the *ty Liem-Phong* remained under their control despite the appointment of a 'non-Party' personality as Minister of the Interior.[34] Its powers were nevertheless defined to some extent, and it was obliged to report on anyone arrested so that a decision could be taken by the local People's Committee; or else it must hand over the arrested person to a military tribunal within twenty-four hours. Since we have no detailed information about how these institutions actually operated under the September Decrees, it is impossible to know whether they were as sinister as they sound. But in a revolutionary situation where the government was still insecure, some arrangements of this kind were inevitable.

A further measure was introduced on 23 November 1945 which implied a desire on the part of government leaders to gain more effective control over the bureaucracy. Decree no. 64 of that date, following hard upon the Decree which formalized the structure of administrative committees, established a Special Tribunal comprising the President, the Minister of Interior and the Minister of Justice (i.e. Ho Chi Minh himself, Vo Nguyen Giap and Vu Trong Khanh).[35] This body would pass judgement on anyone brought before it by a Special Inspection Committee (set up by the same Decree) whose function was to review the work and personnel of all government departments and administrative committees; it had full powers to inspect government papers and to investigate complaints brought to it by ordinary people. The potential implications of this measure were very great indeed, but once again we have no information about how the arrangements operated in practice. What seems clear is that all these decrees on security and control constitute a significant part of the explanation why the Viet-Minh leaders were able to keep control of the government machinery despite the great complexity of the political situation which developed after the middle of September 1945.

## III

An area of policy which was relatively uncontroversial in the first instance, and where the Provisional Government was able to demonstrate its energy without arousing political debate, was that of educational development. Universal education had been one of the points of the programme put forward by the Communists at the time of the unification meeting organized by Ho Chi Minh (then Nguyen Ai Quoc) in February 1930, and it also figured in the ten-point Viet-Minh policy approved at the Tan-Trao Party Congress in August 1945.[36]

Vu Dinh Hoe, who was Minister of Education in the Provisional Government, could be relied upon to carry out such a policy with vigour, and with the full support of many of the intellectuals in Hanoi whom the Viet-Minh was anxious to win over to its cause. Hoe himself had been editor of the journal *Thanh-Nghi*, founded in 1941, which had been one of the main focal points of intellectual life in Hanoi during the Japanese occupation. Some of its contributors had joined Tran Trong Kim's government in Hue in April 1945, but they were by no means committed to Japanese fascism. Others, like Hoe, joined the new government in August 1945 and became members of either the Democratic Party (founded in 1944) or the Socialist Party (founded in 1946), which supported the Viet-Minh without being Communist.[37] Another figure prominent in the educational field at this time was Dang Thai Mai, formerly a teacher at the Thang-Long private school, where Vo Nguyen Giap had also been a teacher and Hoang Minh Giam director, in the period 1936–39.[38] He now became inspector of middle schools under the Minister; he also had the distinction of being the only person to be invited to serve on both the constitutional committee set up by Bao-Dai on 8 May 1945 and that established by the Viet-Minh on 20 September.[39] The Director of Administration in the Ministry was Do Duc Duc, also a contributor to *Thanh-Nghi* and a leading figure in the Democratic Party.[40] Mention should perhaps also be made here of Nguyen Van To, who was Minister of Welfare in the Provisional Government but who in the 1930s and early 1940s had been president of the Association for the Spread of *Quoc-Ngu* and had worked hard for the movement against illiteracy. He was a contributor to the 'moderate' intellectual journal *Tri-Tan* and a member of the Ecole Française d'Extrême-Orient. His support was therefore even more valuable to the Viet-Minh in their attempt to appeal to uncommitted intellectuals.[41]

With men of this calibre working on educational policy, it is not surprising that one of the first series of decrees to be signed by Vo Nguyen Giap on behalf of the new government related to education and the literacy drive. In his policy speech of 2 September 1945, on Independence Day, Giap had talked of the need to lay the foundations for a new education, with compulsory elementary schooling and the provision of scholarships to enable poor pupils to go on to middle school. He envisaged, too, a campaign of adult education to eliminate illiteracy. At the same time his emphasis was on practical education, rather than on culture for its own sake, or for that matter the spread of ideology.[42] Changes in the pattern of schooling, and decisions about specific institutions, were no doubt taken at a lower level than that of the Presidential Decree. For example, a ministerial decision of 13 September 1945 set up a committee to reorganize the School of Industry at Hanoi, and another on the following day abolished fees for education and examination at all levels.[43] A ministerial decision of 17 September created scholarships for study at middle schools. But a Decree of 8 September 1945 established a whole new area of educational endeavour, by laying down that within one year from that date every Vietnamese over the age of eight years should learn to read and write; any adult unable to read *quoc-ngu* after that date would be fined. The details were to be worked out by the ministry, and the cost was to be divided equally between village and provincial level funds. The same day, Nguyen Cong My was appointed to become Director of Mass Education, and a further Decree created a new type of 'People's evening classroom' which should be formed in every town and village within six months.[44] As is so often the case, we do not have any official reports or detailed information about the extent to which these laws were put into effect. It seems highly improbable that, even in the areas firmly under Viet-Minh control, every single adult was able to read by September 1946. But we do know from press reports of 1946 that serious efforts were being made to spread literacy amongst ordinary people. On 20 May 1946, for example, the Mass Education Service organized at Nam-Dinh a day for checking illiteracy, supported by the town's youth groups: twenty check-points were set up at various places and everyone passing was invited to read a few sentences; those who failed were invited to attend an open-air course in reading, conducted by microphone.[45] Such news items may have had a propaganda purpose, but they reflect determination to carry through the policy.

Education was one thing. Cultural policy, however, also included the more complex question of state direction of cultural activities and censorship of publications and teaching material, which by 1945 was an established part of Soviet policy and which was likely to be imitated in Vietnam. In the speech of 2 September already cited, Vo Nguyen Giap insisted upon the need to eliminate corrupt habits which work against progress, and to outlaw all literature which tended to confuse and to poison the minds of the masses. On the other hand, he promised that the press censorship currently in force was merely a temporary measure occasioned by the political situation, and that eventually the government would ensure complete freedom of speech.

The record of the *Cong-Bao* enables us to go a little beyond these generalizations to see what was actually done. These matters were not in any way the responsibility of the Minister of Education or his staff, who were concerned with people's ability to read, not what they should be encouraged or permitted to read. The executive responsibility for censorship lay with Vo Nguyen Giap himself, as Minister of the Interior, with his chief administrator Hoang Minh Giam, and with a (possibly interministerial) Committee on News, Propaganda and Newspapers. This is clear from a series of decisions of the Minister of the Interior (in fact signed by Giam), beginning on 8 October 1945 and continuing to about the middle of November.[46] These were the formal registrations (and authorizations to publish) individual newspapers and periodicals. The titles authorized, and the personalities named, show that they were by no means all Communist newspapers, although they included the well-known *Cuu-Quoc* ('National Salvation') and *Quan Giai-Phong* ('Liberation Army'). Altogether twenty-six titles were approved on 8 October and another thirty or so during succeeding weeks, most but by no means all being published in Hanoi. By mid-November, however, the system of registration and authorization appears to have broken down. The VNQDD newspaper *Viet-Nam*, which first appeared on 15 November 1945, was not registered in this way. Perhaps the change reflects the growing political difficulties of the Provisional Government by that time, resulting from Chinese support for the VNQDD and the Dong-Minh-Hoi: difficulties which had to be resolved before the government could confidently impose the stamp of a single political movement on the country's press and culture.

Another organization concerned with cultural matters was the Ministry of Propaganda, headed by Tran Huy Lieu.[47] A native of Nam-Dinh (Tongking), born in 1900, he had been politically active in Saigon in the 1920s and had been imprisoned by the French on Poulo Condore from 1929 to 1934 following the incident known as the Rue Barbier Affair. After completing a sentence of five years, during which time he became a Communist, he returned to Hanoi and was active in journalism and politics from 1935 to 1939; he appears to have become a hard-line Marxist, and possibly an associate (though not a close comrade) of Dang Xuan Khu. He was again in prison from September 1939 until his escape in

March 1945, and after that he was once again active in the North. His first public action during the course of the August Revolution was to represent the Party at Hue (together with Nguyen Luong Bang and Cu Huy Can) on the occasion when Bao-Dai abdicated; and a few days later he was named as Minister of Propaganda.[48] Yet we do not know enough detail about his activities or affiliations to explain why he should figure so prominently in the list of ministers. Still less do we know why he was pushed out of the limelight in late 1945 or early 1946. In the Coalition Government of 1946, and in the Viet-Minh government of November 1946, not only does his name not appear but his ministry was also abolished. It is possible that he was an 'extremist' who could be sacrificed to the objections of non-Communists at this time. Moreover, the evidence of the *Cong-Bao* suggests that even at the beginning he was not given very important executive powers. The only notable recorded decision of his ministry was one of 2 October 1945 which repealed a French decree that had banned certain left-wing books (including some of his own).[49] He played a part in drafting the Election Decree, and it is possible that his main role was in relation to the National Assembly and the mass organizations.

One of the latter was very much concerned with culture: the National Salvation Cultural Association. It published *La République* from 18 October 1945, and also from November a Vietnamese journal *Tien-Phong* in which a number of leading intellectuals, not all of them Communist, served as members of the editorial board.[50] Its first president was Tran Huy Lieu himself, but it is noticeable that at the second annual meeting on 11–13 October 1946 he was replaced in that capacity by Dang Thai Mai.[51] The Association had its own representative on the electoral committee, Nguyen Huu Dang, but he, too, drops from view in 1946. The Cultural Association does not appear to have had any executive responsibilities; its function was to mobilize intellectuals in support of the revolution.

## IV

One of the most important subjects to appear in the *Cong-Bao* is that of finance. It is also one of the most difficult to deal with, partly because of the limitations of the source material and partly because of the sheer complexity of the situation which arose in Hanoi during this period. The verdict of historians that finance was one of the weak spots of the Provisional Government is probably a fair one; but it is not at all easy to reconstruct what went wrong.

In his 2 September speech, in effect a general policy statement by the chief administrator of the new government, Vo Nguyen Giap was frank about the great difficulties which faced the revolution in the financial sphere, but insisted that the government would find ways of overcoming them. In particular, an army was necessary and it would require a lot of money; the government would depend a great deal on the patriotism of the people. At the same time, he spoke of the desirability of reforming the taxation system and promised the abolition of the hated poll-tax and market-tax.[52] This promise led to a Decree of 7 September 1945 which ordered the immediate abolition of the poll-tax, whilst pointing out that other aspects of the taxation system must be changed gradually.[53] However, there is at least one small piece of evidence to suggest that the decree was not actually implemented: a British report of 16 October 1945, based on information recently obtained in Hanoi, said that the government there had been obliged to reinstate the poll-tax in order to meet government expenditure.[54] There can be no doubt that already by that stage the government was critically short of money, and from the financial point of view it was far from the best time to fulfil revolutionary aspirations to reduce or abolish the tax burden. According to one report, when the Viet-Minh arrived in Hanoi they found only 1,230,720 piastres in the state treasury; a figure which should be compared with the Indochinese budget (expenditure side) of 267.3 million piastres in 1944, and 299.7 million piastres estimated for 1945.[55]

The first substantive financial measure of the new government was a Decree of 4 September 1945 establishing, at the Centre and in each province, an Independence Fund which would receive donations (money and goods) from the population.[56] The Central Fund was to be managed by a director (Do Dinh Thien) and the province funds by the People's Committee at that level; but the directors were permitted only to receive and deposit money and valuables, whilst withdrawal from the fund was to be undertaken only by the Minister of Finance (Pham Van Dong). It was presumably within the framework established by this decree that Ho Chi Minh, on 17 September 1945, inaugurated the famous 'Gold Week' during which people were invited to contribute gold to the government in order to help solve the problem of national defence. According to Fall, commenting on the President's appeal, the gold was needed (and used) to purchase from the Chinese Nationalist forces now entering Tongking, weapons which they were perfectly willing to sell; this included the weapons which the Chinese were responsible for after the surrender and disarming of the Japanese Army.[57] Presumably, therefore, the gold was spent on armaments, and the other financial problems of the government remained to be solved by other means.

The central issue was, in fact, the question of control of the Bank of Indochina. The ten-point Viet-Minh programme adopted at Tan-Trao in August 1945 included the objective of founding a National Bank.[58] Seizure of the state and private banks had been one of the first principles of the Russian Revolution in 1917, after Lenin's own criticism that failure to seize the banks in Paris was the reason for the downfall of the Commune of 1871. But in practice it proved impossible for the Viet-Minh to seize the Bank of Indochina building in Hanoi. The reason given by the Vietnamese historians themselves, that it was surrounded by Japanese troops and therefore was not entered, seems to be the whole explanation.[59] Despite Truong Chinh's criticism of this failure in his later analysis of the August Revolution, it seems clear that the Viet-Minh take-over of Hanoi was predicated entirely on Japanese acquiescence: if the Japanese had chosen to oppose the forces coming down from Thai-Nguyen, the Viet-Minh would have had to fight a major battle before reaching Hanoi and would have lost time even if they had won the battle. Moreover, we now know that Ho Chi Minh had direct American support at this time. The Japanese probably understood well enough that the Americans would disapprove if they handed over the Bank, and so they kept it under guard.[60] Truong Chinh himself noted that the failure to seize it was due in part to the fact that it was 'a financial institution acting not only on behalf of the French and the Japanese but also of other countries.'[61] However, the Bank of Indochina did not close. It appears to have continued to do business, not only with Frenchmen and with the Chinese forces who arrived in the second half of September but even with the Provisional Government itself. The Treasury was empty, but the Government-General had kept an account with the Bank which the Vietnamese seem to have been able to use. The American journalist who wrote a series of reports from Hanoi for United Press in late November 1945 was quick to point out that the new government was 'still by its own admission under the control of the French through the Bank of Indochina.'[62] By then, indeed, the financial crisis had come to a head.

The monetary situation in northern Vietnam during the autumn of 1945 was extremely complicated. The Indochinese piastre, which had been the currency throughout most of the French period and which by 1940 was linked to international currencies through the French franc at the rate of 1:10, was issued by the Bank of Indochina. The latter was both the 'central bank' of the colony and a major investor in its principal economic enterprises. It had continued to maintain this function during the Japanese period, but had been obliged to hold reserves in special *yen* in Tokyo (through the Yokohama Specie Bank) and had had to issue additional currency to meet the requirements of the Japanese army. The quantity of money in circulation rose from 280 million piastres at the end of 1940 to over 1,300 million piastres by the end of 1944. During 1944 alone, the Bank of Indochina made available 360 million piastres to the Japanese forces; altogether, from mid-1940 to March 1945 the total of such allocations came to over 723 million piastres. During the period of direct Japanese control between March and August 1945, an additional sum of 720 million piastres was made available by the Bank.[63] In particular the Bank of Indochina was obliged to issue large numbers of notes of the denomination of 500 piastres, whose only backing consisted of special *yen* reserves in Tokyo. Inevitably this expansion of the money supply was accompanied by serious inflation, which continued during the second half of 1945. For Hanoi the information available about price changes is very limited, but a calculation (made after the French had returned to Hanoi) for the cost of living of Europeans in the city, showed that on an index starting at 100 in 1939 the figure of 2,130 was reached by December 1945. In Saigon, where the inflation was less severe, the comparable figures were 100 for 1939 and 1,026 for April 1946.[64] That a large part of this increase came during the year 1945 itself is suggested by the figures later published for wholesale prices at Saigon: an index starting at 100 in early 1939 stood at 296 by December 1944, but rose to 812 by December 1946.[65]

In August 1945, the Japanese ceased to be in a position to dictate policy to the Bank of Indochina. But as far as Hanoi was concerned (and the whole of northern Indochina) their place as the army of occupation was quickly taken by the Chinese forces from Yunnan which arrived during the second half of September. They, too, had to finance their activity in Indochina, but it would appear that they refrained from taking over the Bank of Indochina—presumably for the same reason as the Viet-Minh: such a move was precluded by the presence of the Americans and by the international situation. They did, however, make demands on the Bank, which the French management were not in a position entirely to ignore. At first, according to a later Vietnamese account, the Chinese army demanded that the Bank make available (over a period) the sum of 4,500 million piastres in exchange for 3,000 million *quan-kim* ('gold units', the most recently introduced Chinese currency).[66] This same writer says that, since there were at the time only 2,172 million piastres in circulation throughout the whole of Indochina, this was impossible. The Bank and the Viet-Minh were therefore obliged to agree to the supplementary Chinese demand, that the *quan-kim* itself should be accepted in northern Indochina as a medium of exchange, making it possible for the Chinese army to meet its needs by using its own currency for purchase of supplies. They were also able to oblige the authorities in Indochina to accept a rate of exchange of 1 *quan-kim* for 1.50 piastres.[67]

It was this latter decision that opened the way to speculation on the part of the Chinese army, aided and abetted by the Chinese residents of Tongking who were the one group to welcome the occupation with any degree of sincerity. The *quan-kim*, or 'gold unit', had its own exchange rate with the US dollar in China (and presumably also at Hong Kong): it was reported by Hoyt that in Kunming the rate was 50 *quan-kim* to one US dollar.[68] However, the international rate of exchange for piastres was 20 piastres to one US dollar. This meant that it was possible to use one dollar's worth of *quan-kim* to purchase 75 piastres in Indochina, then to take the 75 piastres back to China and sell them for 3.25 US dollars, thus more than trebling the initial value of the *quan-kim*. It is hardly surprising that the period from September 1945 to June 1946, which was the length of the Chinese occupation, saw the transfer to southern China (or Hong Kong) of large quantities of Indochinese piastres. As late as March 1947 the Hong Kong *Far Eastern Economic Review* noted that there were still a lot of Indochinese piastres in the colony (perhaps as much as 80–90 million piastres) which had been exported from Indochina by the Chinese troops during the occupation, and whose holders were now waiting for a recovery of Indochina's economy and trade in order to be able to use them.[69]

The Chinese also speculated in gold bullion, which they bought in Indochina more cheaply than they could sell it elsewhere. Hoyt says that the price of gold at Hanoi was fixed at 1 tael for 1,200 piastres on 1 October 1945, but that the unofficial price had risen to 2,500 piastres two weeks later.[70] We have already seen that the Chinese were willing to sell arms to the Viet-Minh for gold; now we can see the wider economic context of Ho Chi Minh's 'gold week'. Presumably one result was that large quantities of gold also left Indochina during the months that ensued. On the other hand Chinese who were resident in Indochina were anxious to buy property in this favourable situation, and Sainteny had difficulty dissuading Frenchmen from selling their urban land at the inflated prices.[71]

It was not merely the Viet-Minh Provisional Government who were alarmed by these monetary developments. The French, who had every intention of restoring at least their economic presence in Indochina, were anxious to maintain the value of the piastre on which the strength of the Bank of Indochina depended. They were unable to prevent the Chinese from doing whatever they wanted in Tongking, pending an agreement between the French and Chinese governments (which was not negotiated until February 1946); but they did control the policy of the Bank. On 17 November 1945 the French High Commissioner in Saigon, Admiral d'Argenlieu, supported a decision by the Bank to eliminate the 500 piastre notes issued during the Japanese period.[72] Those issued before 9 March 1945 could, within a definite period, be exchanged for Bank deposits at 70 per cent of face value, with the deposits remaining blocked for the time being. Those issued between 9 March and 23 September 1945 simply lost their value immediately. Both types of note therefore ceased to be legal tender. Unfortunately they made up a large part of the savings of the better-off Vietnamese, and of the Provisional Government's currency holdings, as well as of the stores of piastres bought up by the Chinese. Moreover, it was explicitly stated that the decision applied north as well as south of the sixteenth parallel, which divided the two zones of occupation.

In the meantime, Sainteny had been negotiating with the Chinese army command, following their presentation of new demands to be met by the Bank of Indochina. On 14 November 1945 he was obliged to agree to a monthly advance of 40 million piastres by the Bank to the army, and a daily exchange of piastres for *quan-kim* (at the official rate), to be limited to 50 *quan-kim* (i.e. 75 piastres) per person and to a daily total of 600,000 piastres.[73] The reason for this was probably that without such an opportunity for *quan-kim* to be exchanged at the official rate by Hanoi traders, it was becoming impossible for the latter to accept *quan-kim* in payment for goods; for anyone except the Chinese army, the *quan-kim* was worth less than half the official 1.50 piastres.

Both problems came to a head together on 20 November, the day when the exchange arrangements should have come into force. It was on that day that Sainteny announced the decision regarding the 500 piastre notes, and the Bank refused to operate the exchange arrangements until the situation became clearer. The Chinese protested, and Sainteny went to Saigon for discussions. He returned on 26 November, accompanied by several financial experts, and was greeted by a Vietnamese demonstration outside the Bank of Indochina's premises. Precisely what happened on that afternoon is still uncertain. The Vietnamese insist that the French opened fire from the Bank; a French source, written by someone present in Hanoi at the time but not actually on the scene, says that trouble began when Chinese troops opened fire and threw grenades, following one 'mysterious' shot.[74] The Viet-Minh were certainly responsible for the demonstration, and for strikes in opposition to the Bank's policy, and it is clear that their interests in the matter coincided with those of the Chinese: they wished to see a revision of the decision on the 500 piastre notes. On 29 November they began an anti-French boycott in Tongking which lasted into December.[75] It was not until 4 December 1945 that the Chinese and the French, following mediation of the dispute by the American mission in Hanoi, reached agreement. The exchange facilities demanded by the Chinese were not granted, but an additional monthly 15 million piastres was made available to the Chinese army by way of loan; and the 500 piastre notes would remain in circulation north of the 16th parallel, with special procedures laid down for changing them.[76]

The impotence of the Provisional Government during this crisis period was very marked. Moreover the outcome may have served to resolve temporarily the problems of both the Bank and the Chinese army, but it did nothing to help the Vietnamese. They were as dependent as ever on the Bank's facilities to carry on the finances of government, and it is noticeable that the Chinese command did not make any demands on the French to make more money available to the Viet-Minh. By this time, indeed, the Chinese were putting pressure on Ho Chi Minh to negotiate with the other nationalist parties whose leaders were closer to the Kuomintang. On 30 November 1945, in the middle of the crisis, we find the President signing a decree (no. 68) on the regulations for requisitioning private property for government use.[77] Then on 17 December, even after the Bank crisis was resolved by the French and Chinese, came the decree already referred to which 'requisitioned' all government officials and obliged them to remain in service.[78] It seems highly probable that the main reason why the Viet-Minh were obliged to reach agreement with the VNQDD and the Dong-Minh-Hoi on 23 December 1945 was that they were under such severe financial strain.

There is at least one small indication that the Viet-Minh leaders took immediate action, so far as they could, to reverse their dependence on the Bank, as a direct result of this crisis. On 1 December 1945 it was decided to send the Minister of Labour, Le Van Hien (subsequently appointed the Viet-Minh finance minister), to the southern zone in order to provide liaison with the Administrative Committees there and to reorganize and unify the administration.[79] No mention is made of financial matters in the decree appointing him to this task. But it is noticeable that on 31 January 1946 the Provisional Government issued its own currency for the first time. Ironically, this was one field in which its powers were greater in the South than in the North, and it was not until August 1946, following the departure of the Chinese, that the coalition government in Hanoi was able to authorize the circulation of the new currency in the northern zone.[80] But even then, it did not have the reserves of the Bank of Indochina to back its own currency, and it seems likely that in Hanoi itself and many other areas the old piastre was still the principal medium of exchange.

## V

The question of control of the Bank of Indochina was a crucial one for the August Revolution, not merely for its financial consequences but also in relation to the whole character of the revolution in its historical perspective. How far can one say that the August Revolution was 'Communist'? There need be no doubt that its leadership was in the hands of Communists, for the Viet-Minh was from its inception a Communist-organized front with a programme which was anti-fascist and anti-imperialist, along the lines indicated by the Comintern resolutions of 1935 and subsequent Communist thinking about the world situation. It had, indeed, some features in common with the type of front organizations that emerged in the Soviet-liberated countries of Europe in 1944–45, except that it achieved power without the presence of a Soviet Army. Its leading figures, notably Vo Nguyen Giap, Pham Van Dong, Truong Chinh and Nguyen Luong Bang (not to mention Ho Chi Minh) were all members of the Indochinese Communist Party in the 1930s. But how far was the content of the revolution, judged by its actual political measures, truly Communist in character?

In order to answer this question we must look eventually at the evidence relating to the economic measures of the Provisional Government, and to its policies regarding property. But first it is necessary to consider carefully the theoretical background, for by this time there had emerged a number of specific ideas within the Communist movement about how a revolution in this situation should develop. In his essay of 1946 on the August Revolution, Truong Chinh observed that it was first and foremost a 'revolution for national liberation'; at the same time it was also a 'democratic revolution'.[81] He made a distinction between two aspects of revolution in a colonial country, saying that it must be both anti-imperialist and also an agrarian revolution. In this he was following the line of reasoning developed by Mao Tse-tung in his essays of 1939–40, which were in turn a reinterpretation of the theses on colonial and semi-colonial countries formulated at the Sixth Comintern Congress in Moscow in 1928. Mao emphasized that there must be a close relationship between the anti-imperialist (or 'national') and the anti-feudal (or 'democratic') revolutions in China. He saw the domination of the landlord class in Chinese society as something which depended on imperialism, so that to end it would require the defeat of the imperialists. But at the same time, 'the feudal landlord class is the main social basis of imperialist rule', and consequently 'unless help is given to the peasants in their struggle to overthrow the feudal landlord class, it will be impossible to build powerful revolutionary contingents to overthrow imperialist rule'.[82] In Vietnam, as in China, the power of the Europeans had come to depend very much on the support of the 'feudal' elements amongst the Vietnamese population, who were either mandarins in the bureaucracy or landlords in the countryside, or both. The implication of Mao's line, which Truong Chinh eventually came to support wholeheartedly, was that in order to defeat the French once and for all it was necessary also to destroy the economic base of the 'feudal' élite and of the 'comprador' bourgeoisie. This meant the application of a policy of land reform, which in turn raised serious issues about how severe it should be: whose land should be confiscated, and how it should be redistributed. In view of the great local influence exercised at village level by the rich peasants (both as producers and as money-lenders) this meant a debate about the position of that class in relation to both revolutionary attitudes and economic exploitation. These issues had already begun to affect the thinking of Vietnamese Communists at the time of the celebrated Nghe-An Soviets of 1930–31.[83] They were even more important in China, where large areas were conducting land reform in the early 1930s and again by 1945.

However, the question of land reform and the 'anti-feudal' revolution could not be resolved without reference to that of patriotism and the 'anti-imperial' revolution, or 'national liberation'. In 1935 the Comintern had developed a new concept, that of a united front against fascism; and during the early 1940s this was extended to include the policy of creating a united front against imperialism, in countries such as China and Vietnam where there was foreign occupation of part or all the territory. The complexities of the Chinese National United Front policy which was developed from 1937 onwards cannot concern us here.[84] In Vietnam, a comparable policy was being developed by Ho Chi Minh when he organized the foundation of the Viet-Minh in 1941. The implications of this policy were that, under Communist (that is, proletarian) leadership, all classes except the worst kind of collaborator should be drawn into the anti-imperialist front in order to make it as strong as possible. That included the rich peasants, the patriotic landlords, and the 'national bourgeoisie' (as opposed to the 'compradors' whose business interests derived from imperialism itself). But if they were to be drawn into a front organization, it was necessary to abandon for the time being the policy of seizing their lands and destroying their economic base in the countryside. Consequently the anti-imperialist and anti-feudal tasks had to be separated. Inevitably there was controversy within Communist circles as to how far the separation should go. Truong Chinh, like Mao himself, would appear to have favoured relating them as fully as possible. Ho Chi Minh, along with his closest followers led by Pham Van Dong and Vo Nguyen Giap, preferred to emphasize unity and to avoid issues that might tend to break up the coalition of the classes they were trying to draw into the revolution. The tension between these two points of view was, indeed, to be one of the central themes of Vietnamese Communist development from 1945 until the 1960s; it has its parallel in the different approaches of Mao Tse-tung and Chou En-lai to many issues during the same period in China.

Such evidence as we have suggests that in Vietnam in 1945 it was the view of Ho Chi Minh and his group which prevailed. It does not enable us to reconstruct in detail the debates which must have been going on within the Party and Government, but it does record a number of decisions which indicate the results of the debate. One important policy question was that of foreign property, other than that belonging to the French. It would appear that the Viet-Minh had no choice but to follow the Soviet line, which seems to have been to recognize the rights of the British and Americans, who had been their allies since 1941. In his speech of 2 September 1945, Vo Nguyen Giap assured everyone that the new government would respect fully the property and livelihood of both Vietnamese and foreigners. He noted that 'some people' believed the government ought immediately to nationalize all business activity, but he disagreed: that would not be done. Priority must be given to developing the economy in a way that would allow everyone to carry on business freely.[85] On 10 September 1945 a decree was signed which revoked the two decisions of Decoux in December 1941 compelling British, Dutch and American enterprises and individuals to declare their property to the authorities as a preliminary to confiscation, including also the Franco-Asiatic Oil Company. The same decree ordered that the administrative confiscation of such property should no longer continue.[86] Presumably, during the course of the autumn, control was re-established by representatives of the various companies involved. One of them, it may be noted, was Socony, the American oil corporation, whose installations at Haiphong had been managed by a man who from 1941 to 1945 ran a private intelligence organization (with OSS connections) in Kwangsi and Kwangtung.[87] A month later another decree, dated 9 October 1945, granted full permission to foreign companies to continue their business operations in Indochina.[88] There were, however, a few specific exceptions to this general pattern of allowing private control of enterprises. A decision of 29 August 1945, for example, commandeered the equipment of the Hanoi Water Hydrant Company and placed it under a state committee; and on 8 September further decisions confiscated for government use the wireless equipment of Air France and the machinery of the 'Metallurgie' company.[89] These were measures essential to the maintenance of social utilities or to the immediate work of government, rather than indications of an economic policy.

The one area in which state enterprise seems to have been decided on from the start was that of the manufacture of armaments. On 7 September 1945 a decree empowered the Director of Minerals and Industry (not named) to set up an expert committee and to proceed with the production of weapons and ammunition. The decision of the following day regarding the equipment of the metallurgy company may have been related to this. In any case, by another decree (of 6 September 1945) it was permitted to government agencies to requisition materials required for public works, on the basis of compensation at current prices.[90] (This was at an early stage, and the arrangements were much more generous than those decreed at the end of November during the financial crisis, already referred to.) Unfortunately we do not have source material that would enable us to explore the detailed development of the arms industry which began in this way, but by 1954 it was clearly a major element in Viet-Minh achievements.

It is not until November that we find a series of decrees and decisions relating to agriculture. Indeed it was not until 14 November that a Minister of Agriculture was appointed.[91] One possible explanation for this is that there were serious policy differences within the leadership, and it may be significant that it was on 11 November 1945 that the Indochinese Communist Party was obliged by Ho Chi Minh to formally dissolve itself and become the Marxist Studies Association, with Truong Chinh as President. Be that as it may, on 13 November 1945 it was finally decided to issue Proclamation no. 55 on behalf of the People's Administrative Committee of the North (Bac-Bo), signed by its chairman Nguyen Xien.[92] This concerned the reduction of land-rent by 25 per cent for tenants and share-croppers, and at the same time the guarantee of revenues to all categories of land-owner. What is remarkable is that these decisions were originally taken by the Committee at its meeting of 1–3 October 1945, but were only now being published after a six-week delay. Truong Chinh, in the essay already referred to, mentions this measure and also (by the time he was writing, in September 1946) the cancellation of certain kinds of rural debt. But he goes on to remark that 'generally speaking, the relations between landlords and peasants have not changed'.[93] Was it he, perhaps, who held up the final decision on what was after all a very mild policy compared with the wholesale confiscations which the completion of the anti-feudal task would eventually require? We can only speculate on this.

A much more central concern of the Provisional Government in relation to agriculture was the threat of famine in the winter of 1945–46. Here again it was immediate practical needs rather than revolutionary principles which shaped the government's attitude towards private property. The need to reach a decision about rent-reduction in mid-November arose in the context of a food crisis which demanded immediate action. It was calculated that the next fifth month harvest (for which sowing began in September–October 1945) would be seriously deficient owing to the floods of the previous August. In the provinces of Nam-Dinh, Ninh-Binh and Thai-Binh, especially important for the fifth-month rice crop, much of the seed had been lost in the floods and this could only be partially compensated for by government action to distribute 110 tons of seed there during November.[94] In the meantime, the tenth month harvest of late 1945 was yielding only half the normal (or average) level of 1,088,000 tons of paddy; and there were serious losses also in northern Annam where 100,000 tons of paddy were destroyed on the ground by further flooding. This meant that for the period from November 1945 to April 1946, Tongking would have only 500,000 tons of paddy. At the very most this would last only until mid-February 1946, even allowing for strict rationing and severe undernourishment. After that there would be famine, as there had been in the early months of 1945.

There was only one practical possibility for action: to organize the cultivation of dry crops on a massive scale. Potatoes, maize and beans would require only three to five months for growth, but hitherto their cultivation had been very peripheral in a region which relied mainly on two crops a year of rice. The one possibility for survival lay in doubling the area and output of such crops by sowing every available piece of land without delay. The organization of this effort was the principal responsibility of the new Minister of Agriculture, acting in concert with the Minister of National Economy. In addition, on 19 November 1945, there was created a Central Committee for Rapid and Intensive Production. Its task was to organize provincial committees, to bring together local officials and technicians from various services, and to mobilize the administrative committees at district and village level to bring the maximum amount of land into cultivation, and to distribute seeds, farm tools, etc. The Committee even produced its own newspaper to propagate information that would be useful in the production drive.[95] The work of the Ministries and the new Committee was supported by Decision no. 41 of the Minister of National Economy (15 November 1945) which compelled landlords to declare all their rice-lands to the village administrative committee.[96] Any land not actually under cultivation must be made available for loan to anyone willing to undertake cultivation of dry crops, provided they were sown by the end of January 1946; the loan would be effective until the following May, when the land would be returned to its original owner. The Ministry of Social Welfare also became involved, encouraging the formation in the provinces of semi-private Anti-Famine Associations, whose aim was to organize the cultivation of spare land by poor peasants and so to mobilize all available manpower where it was most needed.[97] We have no means of assessing the application of these measures in practice in the various provinces of northern Vietnam, but it seems highly probable that they led to the mobilization of resources in a great many localities. In the minds of the ordinary peasants, and even the townspeople whose hunger was at stake, it is likely that mobilization of this kind, directed towards solving a practical problem of vital importance to everyone, did more for the prestige of the Provisional Government than any amount of revolutionary propaganda or political manipulation. The end result was a vast increase in the output of potatoes, maize and beans. During the years 1938–43 the average area devoted to these three crops had been 145,600 hectares, with a total output of 147,600 tonnes. In 1946 it proved possible to harvest 410,000 hectares, from which the total output was 614,000 tonnes, or the equivalent of 500,000 tonnes of paddy.[98]

There was no famine in the Spring of 1946. But it is not easy to be sure that the only reason for that was the increased production of dry crops. The other factor in the food situation in Tongking was the attempt to secure rice from Cochinchina, the traditional source of supply. On 6 October 1945 the Ministry of National Economy set up a committee to represent it in negotiations for the purchase of grain in the South.[99] Part of the background to this decision is indicated by a press report from Hanoi dated 14 October 1945 (one of the very few before Palmer Hoyt's visit in November), to the effect that the American Relief Mission headed by Col. S. L. Nordlinger had been conferring with both the Provisional Government and the French authorities (in the South) and seemed to be on the verge of completing an agreement which would enable rice to be brought to Haiphong from Saigon. It was reported that his plan would involve the shipment of 25,000 tons of rice, which was estimated to be sufficient to last seven months.[100] We do not know whether the plan was actually carried out; a Chinese source notes that some supplies did reach Tongking from Saigon, despite French attempts to delay shipments as much as possible.[101] But in any case, the amount indicated in the press report would not have been enough to meet the needs estimated by the Vietnamese themselves. It seems unlikely that rice shipments were restored to an adequate level until after the Franco–Vietnamese agreement of 6 March 1946. By then, if there had been no dry-crop programme, the famine would have already begun.

## VI

The source materials which are thus far available tell us a good deal about the formal work of the Provisional Government, especially in the fields of administration, constitutional development, finance, economy and education. They give us very much less information about the politics of the Vietnamese Revolution during the second half of 1945; for example, about the role of the Army, or about the process of decision-making and the work of the Indochinese Communist Party and the Viet-Minh. It is therefore possible to present only a very tentative picture of these aspects of the Revolution.

There seems little doubt that the Army was developing strongly during the second half of 1945, but its relationship to the government is unclear. The *Cong-Bao* records hardly any military decrees and certainly nothing substantial enough for us to see how the Army was organized. The Provisional Government included General Chu Van Tan as Minister of Defence, but his decrees and decisions do not seem to have gone through the same channels as those of other Ministers. The position of Vo Nguyen Giap himself in relation to the army at this stage is not clear. Photographs of him during 1945 do not show him in uniform: for example, that published by Sainteny showing Giap in company with the American officer Major Patti has him in a European suit and tie with trilby hat.[102] It is not until late November that we find him referred to in a *Cong-Bao* item as Deputy Minister of Defence, and it is not impossible that he assumed that post only after some kind of government reshuffle in mid-November (in which the Ministry of Agriculture was created, and also a Ministry of Communications under Dao Trong Kim).[103]

The Vietnam People's Army now celebrates the anniversary of its foundation on 22 December, the day in 1944 when an Armed Propaganda Unit for National Liberation was formed in Cao-Bang province on the instructions of Ho Chi Minh, with Vo Nguyen Giap as its leader. This unit gathered strength and marched southwards between then and the spring of 1945.[104] However, a historian using only the limited contemporary sources (in some cases reprinted later by the government in Hanoi, but excluding memoirs after the fact) might be forgiven if he came to the conclusion that the effective origin of the Vietnamese Liberation Army was the Revolutionary Military Conference of Bac-Bo, convened by Truong Chinh, which met somewhere in Hiep-Hoa district (Bac-Giang) province from 15 to 20 April 1945.[105] There are, indeed, some Vietnamese historical materials which also emphasize the importance of this conference, and one account published in Hanoi is explicit that the date of the formal inauguration of the Vietnam Liberation Army was 15 May 1945.[106] It would appear that the group created by Vo Nguyen Giap was one element within the new Army, but that the latter also included a National Salvation force which had originally emerged from the Bac-Son Rising of autumn 1940; leading figures in that force appear to have included Chu Van Tan and Tran Dang Ninh.[107] The Conference of April 1945 created a new Revolutionary Military Committee for Bac-Bo, whose names are given in a source of 1972 as follows: Vo Nguyen Giap, Van Tien Dung, Le Thanh Nhgi, Tran Dang Ninh and Chu Van Tan. Giap, Ninh and Tan were also members of the Insurrection Committee (along with Truong Chinh) established on 13 August 1945 to carry out the Viet-Minh order for general insurrection.[108] All this would suggest that Giap was, at most, merely one military figure among several at that stage, and perhaps not the most experienced. It was only during 1946 that he began to emerge as the eventual top man of Vietnamese military affairs.

The existence of a Liberation Army by September 1945 is thus clearly attested by the sources. Its actual development and role thereafter are not. Martial law existed in Hanoi during the first ten days of September, by virtue of a decree signed by Vo Nguyen Giap in his function of acting President. After it was lifted, a proclamation or general order (also signed by Giap, on 13 September 1945) laid down the powers of the Liberation Forces in the execution of their duties.[109] At about the same time, Military Tribunals were set up, as we have seen, in which one member was a military officer. But then we have very little reference to military affairs until 21 November 1945, when a decree authorized the Minister of Defence to take over the Radio Services: this was on the eve of the complex period of negotiations with the anti-Viet-Minh parties.[110] Beyond these brief references we can only speculate. It is possible that there was some measure of rivalry between Vo Nguyen Giap and Chu Van Tan, and that by the end of 1945 the latter was losing influence over the Army; certainly he was not made Minister of Defence again in March 1946, when the substantive post went to a non-Party figure, Phan Anh, leaving a great deal of actual power with Giap as head of the Resistance Committee.[111]

A similar frustration arises when one asks about the Party and the Viet-Minh in this period. The Indochinese Communist Party had remained active in the northern part of Vietnam throughout the Japanese occupation, under the leadership of a Standing Committee and a Secretary-General, Truong Chinh (alias Dang Xuan Khu). In May 1941 members of the Central Committee had met Nguyen Ai Quoc at Pac-Bo (Cao-Bang province) for the Eighth Plenum, at which the decision was taken to found the Viet-Minh organization.[112] No source gives very full details of that session, or even a complete authoritative list of those who were full members of the Central Committee at that time. But it is absolutely clear from Vietnamese memoirs relating to the period, written by various people, that afterwards a substantial number of the Committee's members returned to lowland Tongking and that it operated from an area to the north of Hanoi from then until mid-1945. During the years 1941–44, indeed, it is reasonable to distinguish between two groups of leaders within the Party. The Standing Committee (lowland Tongking) included Truong Chinh and Hoang Quoc Viet, and perhaps also (after their escape from Son-La prison in 1943) Nguyen Luong Bang and Tran Dang Ninh.[113] The other group set up a regional committee for the three northern-most provinces, known as the Inter-provincial Committee of Cao-Bac-Lang, which seems to have included (among leaders who subsequently became important) Vo Nguyen Giap, Pham Van Dong and Hoang Van Hoan.[114] These were precisely the people whom Nguyen Ai Quoc first contacted on his 'return' to Southern China in 1940, and they appear to have remained close to him for the remainder of his life; Nguyen Ai Quoc himself was with them in 1941–42 and again in 1944–45, having in the interval taken the name of Ho Chi Minh. But it was not until mid-1945 that both groups joined together in lowland Tongking, and the circumstances of their reunion are far from clear.

The Central Committee of the Party (or its Standing Committee) was taking the lead in March and April of 1945. It was that body which issued the celebrated 'Instructions' after the Japanese take-over of 9 March; and which convened the military conference of April 1945 already referred to. But thereafter, we hear very much less of the Party. The decisions of which texts have been published were taken either by the General Committee of the Viet-Minh, by the Military Revolutionary Committee, or by the Liberation Committee (which eventually became the Provisional Government). The Party held a national congress at Tan-Trao (Tuyen-Quang province) on 13–15 August 1945, followed by a People's Congress organized by the Viet-Minh. But there is no reference in any of the published documents or histories to a Plenum of the Central Committee at this time. Nor does it seem that this Party 'congress' counts in the numbering of congresses: the First Congress had been held in 1935, and the Second was the one which founded the Vietnam Workers' Party in 1951. The next formal mention of the Indochinese Communist Party comes with the well-known meeting of 9–11 November 1945, which culminated in an announcement that the Party had decided to dissolve itself and that its place would be taken by an Association of Marxist Studies.[115]

What role did the Party play in the interval between Spring and November 1945? We have no means of knowing. If, as is generally believed, the Communist objective was to create a nationalist movement based on a union of classes and of political parties, it would be natural for the Party to remain in the background and to organize its following in secret: there can be no doubt that the underground organization maintained during the Japanese period was one of the fundamental strengths of the Viet-Minh and the Provisional Government throughout 1945–46. But was the Party also able to fill the role of leadership in decision-making which has been the hall-mark of the Communist movement throughout its history? Silence about its role may reflect not secrecy but lack of coherence, conceivably lack of importance as a centre of decision-making. Certainly Truong Chinh did not play a very prominent part in the work of the Government; he is mentioned only once in the *Cong-Boo*, as a member of the commission set up to draught a Constitution. Nor did he figure in the speech-making of 2 September 1945; nor as a writer of articles (unless under a pseudonym) in the press. Whatever his role, it was very much behind the scenes. Conceivably he did not at this stage enjoy very great power at all. Such an interpretation would fit in well with the failure of the Provisional Government to carry out the kind of land policies of which he would have approved, and might explain the somewhat critical tone of his essay of September 1946.[116] It might even be reasonable to argue that the dissolution of the Party was in effect a defeat for Truong Chinh, and that various issues were settled soon after that according to the ideas of his rivals. One thing is clear: the dissolution made it impossible for the Party to take on the characteristics of a mass party, at the centre of mass movements in all fields of activity, which it was to have in the years after 1951 when Truong Chinh was at the height of his power.

It would seem, therefore, that the focal point of decision-making, from at least June 1945 to the end of 1946, was the General Committee of the Viet-Minh. The membership of this Committee, as given by Devillers, included eight people: Ho Chi Minh, Vo Nguyen Giap, Pham Van Dong, Tran Huy Lieu, Nguyen Luong Bang, Hoang Quoc Viet, Truong Chinh, and Ho Tung Mau.[117] It appears that it did not include either Chu Van Tan or Tran Dang Ninh, who had figured prominently in key committees in the spring and summer; nor Le Thanh Nghi and Van Tien Dung, who had been members of the April Military Revolutionary Committee. The Viet-Minh, indeed, was led to a considerable extent by men who one way or another had some special connection with Ho Chi Minh. Giap and Dong, as we have seen, had been with Ho in Cao-Bang since 1941 (that is, when Ho was there). Nguyen Luong Bang had worked for Ho in Shanghai in the years 1928–30.[118] Ho Tung Mau had been a leading figure in the Revolutionary Youth League at Canton and Hong Kong in the late 1920s, but had subsequently been working in the Chinese Communist Party.[119] Hoang Quoc Viet had met Ho at Poseh (Kwangsi) in spring 1945 and may have formed some kind of attachment to him at that time, although at other times he seems to have been closer to Truong Chinh.[120] The one man whose position is difficult to place was Tran Huy Lieu, whom we have met earlier in his capacity as Minister of Propaganda, and who may possibly have had a special part to play in relation to the Viet-Minh movement in the South. In any case, as we have seen, he was to lose his influence during 1946. Among these various leaders, a special role was played by Nguyen Luong Bang, who was Secretary-General of the Committee and its spokesman on a number of occasions. He was one of the speech-makers at the Independence Day ceremony of 2 September 1945. Devillers (giving no source) says that in December 1945 Bang made a visit to the Soviet Union, which is the only reference in any of the source material to direct communication between the Provisional Government and Moscow.[121]

The scarcity of information about the Party and even about the Viet-Minh in the second half of 1945 need not surprise us. It is very possible that these institutions functioned so secretly that their activities would leave no trace in any records likely to become available to foreigners. But there is at least the basis for an interpretation that in the complex situation which developed after the seizure of power in Hanoi in August 1945, there was a potential conflict between various possible centres of power and decision-making: the Party, the Viet-Minh, the Army and the Government; and that the conflict was resolved by mid-November to the disadvantage of the Party, leaving the Government machine as the principal centre of organization, the Army as a distinct entity not very firmly controlled by Government or Party, and the Viet-Minh as the source of authority but not really a mass movement. There were also the various National Salvation Associations, which in other circumstances might have been the basis for a mass movement centred on the Party, but which for the time being were not especially important. Within this framework, by the end of 1945 the effective decision-making leadership seems truly to have lain with three men: Ho Chi Minh, Pham Van Dong, and Vo Nguyen Giap.

It lies beyond the scope of this article to analyse all the details of the relationship between the Viet-Minh leaders and the rival nationalist organizations in both North and South; we must be content for the time being with the accounts already given by Devillers and by Chen. As far as the South is concerned, the Viet-Minh did not abandon it at any stage: they merely lost control in Saigon and the other towns, and therefore were not in any position to make administrative or other revolutionary changes there. They had to concentrate their efforts on organizing a political struggle, in circumstances where they had no significant advantage (and indeed many disadvantages) in relation to their rivals. But in the area to the north of the sixteenth parallel, the administrative and constitutional changes which have been outlined were applicable in all areas except those which they did not actively control: that is, the four or five provinces where the VNQDD or the DMH had the upper hand. The Viet-Minh *were* the Government, and their rivals were obliged to concentrate their efforts on securing Chinese help to force their way into a central coalition. Ho Chi Minh must have recognized from the outset that he would need to form a coalition with other nationalists. His concern down to the end of November 1945 was to make sure that when it came, his own side would still have the upper hand. The record of the Provisional Government makes it easier to see how far he succeeded. Not until February 1946 was he obliged to put Viet-Minh power to the test, when the National Assembly met and the Coalition was actually formed.

## Notes

1. Ph. Devillers, *Histoire du Viêt-Nam de 1940 à 1952* (3rd edn, Paris, 1952); B. B. Fall, *The Viet-Minh Regime* (Revised edn, Institute of Pacific Relations: New York, mimeo, 1956), and *Le Viet-Minh* (Paris, 1960); J. T. McAlister, Jr, *Vietnam: the Origins of Revolution* (Princeton, 1969); King C. Chen, *Vietnam and China, 1938–1954* (Princeton, 1969).
2. A copy was consulted by the author in the 'National Library' in Saigon in 1972. It is possible that (uncatalogued) copies exist in one or another of the national collections in Paris. The only writer to use the *Cong-Bao* for published work thus far has been B. B. Fall, and that only to a very limited extent.
3. *Trang Su Moi* ('Pages of Recent History'), published by the National Salvation Cultural Association, Hanoi, n.d. The copy in the US National Archives, Washington, was sent home by the US Consul at Kunming on 25 October 1945, and therefore must have appeared before that date.
4. Consulted at the Archives Nationales, Section d'Outre-Mer, Paris.
5. Consulted at the 'National Library', Saigon, 1972. Other Vietnamese-language newspapers and periodicals from the period are available there and also some at the Bibliothèque Nationale, Newspaper section, Versailles.
6. The fullest coverage in the foreign press is probably that of the *South China Morning Post*, Hong Kong. Consulted at the Public Record Office, Hong Kong.
7. Cf. R. B. Smith, 'The Japanese Period in Indochina and the Coup of 9 March 1945': to appear in *Journal of Southeast Asian Studies* (1978).
8. Documentation on the conflicting views of the British and Americans on this issue is now available in the Public Record Office, London: e.g. FO 371/46304, 46307. It is possible that Ho Chi Minh, who visited Kunming in March–April 1945, was well aware of this difference; but he may have expected the whole of Indochina to fall within the American and Chinese sphere, since at that stage the compromise had not been reached.
9. On Ho Chi Minh's activities in this period, the fullest account is now that by Chen, *Vietnam and China, passim*.
10. See Devillers, *Histoire du Viêt-Nam;* and G. Rosie, *The British in Vietnam* (London, 1970).
11. On the economic development of Vietnam in the Japanese period, see the appendix of C. Robequain, *The Economic Development of French Indochina* (English trans., Inst. of Pacific Relations; New York, 1944); and J. Decoux, *A la Barre de l'Indochine* (Paris, 1949).
12. For a vivid account of the famine by a Vietnamese eyewitness, see Ngo Vinh Long, *Before the Revolution* (Cambridge, Mass., 1973), pp. 220–76.
13. *Cong-Bao*, No. 1, 29 September 1945, p. 7.

Provisional Government of Vietnam, 1945    111

14  *Ibid.*, p. 12. For Vu Trong Khanh's earlier appointment, see *Opinion-Impartial*, 18 July 1945; he should be carefully distinguished from Vu Hong Khanh, the leader of one section of the VNQDD at this time. For the text of the Constitution itself, as finally approved on 8 November 1945, cf. Fall, *The Viet-Minh Regime*, Appendix I.
15  *Cong-Bao*, 13 October 1945.
16  The postponement was authorized by a Decree of 18 December, *Cong-Bao*, No. 16, 29 December 1945, p. 196–7. The postponement was due to the objections of the opposition parties which at that time had Chinese support, and with whom the Viet-Minh had to make a political compromise agreement on 23 December 1945. See *Viet-Nam* (Hanoi), 25 December 1945. For the text of the Election Decree of 17 October, see *Cong-Bao*, No. 5, 26 October 1945.
17  *Viet-Nam*, 25 December 1945; cf. Devillers, *Histoire du Viêt-Nam*, p. 200, where the seventy reserved seats are said to be out of a total of 350.
18  Translation of text in *Breaking our Chains, Documents on the Vietnamese Revolution of August 1945* (Hanoi, 1960), pp. 7–17.
19  *Ibid.*, pp. 45–51.
20  *Ibid.*, pp. 52–7.
21  *Histoire de la Révolution d'Août* (Hanoi, 1972), pp. 86–7.
22  *Ibid.*, pp. 124ff.
23  *Ibid.*, p. 135. For the background to these rival parties, see Chen, *Vietnam and China*, pp. 122–4.
24  *Cong-Bao*, No. 11: Special number consisting of only this decree, 30 November 1945. A supplement to this decree was issued on 21 December 1945 (Decree No. 77), relating to the administrative committees of the municipalities of Hanoi, Haiphong, Nam-Dinh, Vinh-Ben-Thuy, Hue, Danang, Dalat and Saigon; *Cong-Bao*, 29 December 1945, pp. 197ff.
25  He is referred to in this capacity at several points in the *Cong-Bao*, e.g. as signatory of a decision of 10 November 1945 relating to the passage of boats on the Dao river, and of a proclamation dated 13 November 1945 relating to reduction of land-rent which had been decided at a meeting of the Committee of Bac-Bo and provincial committee chairmen of the area early in October. *Cong-Bao*, 24 November 1945, pp. 128–9. He later became a leader of the Vietnam Socialist Party, founded in 1946, but may in fact have been a member of the Communist Party as well.
26  *Cong-Bao*, 29 September 1945, pp. 11–12.
27  *Ibid.*, p. 8.
28  *Ibid.*, p. 10.
29  Devillers, *Histoire du Viêt-Nam*, p. 142. He was later a delegate to the conference at Dalat of April 1946 and to the Fontainebleau Conference of July 1946. *Ibid.*, pp. 256, 291. Later he became Deputy Minister of Finance. He may have been secretly a member of the Communist Party, but in any case the Provisional Government depended for its success on the participation of people with his type of expertise.
30  *Cong-Bao*, No. 16, 29 December 1945, p. 196.
31  *Cong-Bao*, No. 4, 20 October 1945, p. 43.
32  *Cong-Bao*, No. 1, 29 September 1945. p. 11 and No. 2, 6 October 1945.
33  Cf. Fall, *The Viet-Minh Regime*, pp. 30ff. Fall is the one Western scholar to have made significant use of the *Cong-Bao* for this period; presumably, therefore, he had access to it.
34  *Viet-Nam* (newspaper of the VNQDD, Hanoi), 7 and 10 March 1946.
35  *Cong-Bao*, No. 12, 1 December 1945, pp. 140–1.
36  *Contribution à l'Histoire des Mouvements Politiques de l'Indochine Française* (Hanoi, 1934), Vol. IV, pp. 73–6; *President Ho Chi Minh* (in English, published in China, n.d.), pp. 63–5; *Breaking Our Chains*, pp. 64–5.
37  Contributors to *Thanh-Nghi* during the early part of 1945 included: Vu Van Hien (Minister of Finance at Hue, April 1945), Hoang Xuan Han (Minister of Education

in that government) and Phan Anh (Minister of Youth at Hue in April 1945, and later Minister of Industry and Commerce in the Viet Minh government of the 1950s); Nghiem Xuan Yem and Dang Thai Mai (of the Socialist Party); and the historian Dao Duy Anh, who had been a member of the Tan-Viet Party in 1929.
38 Devillers, *Histoire du Viêt–Nam*, p. 178. Hoang Minh Giam was a key official in the Ministry of the Interior, under Giap, in September 1945; cf, *Cong-Bao*, No. 1, 29 September 1945, p. 4. He later became Foreign Minister (1946–54) and Minister of Culture (1954–75).
39 *Cong-Bao*, No. 1, 29 September 1945, p. 8; *ibid.*, p. 12.
40 For his appointment, see *ibid.*, p. 8.
41 *Souverains et Notabilités de l'Indochine* (Hanoi, 1943), p. 92.
42 *Trang Su Moi*, pp. 26–7.
43 *Cong-Bao*, No. 1, 29 September 1945, pp. 14–16. Other decisions recorded there include appointments and transfers of individual teachers, and the holding of examinations; the impression one gains is that the existing educational life of Hanoi at least was not seriously interrupted by the revolution; but certain examinations were postponed to allow for the appointment of new examiners.
44 *Ibid.*, p. 7.
45 *Le Peuple*, 16 June 1946.
46 *Cong-Bao*, No. 6, 27 October 1945, pp. 59–65; No. 7, 3 November 1945, pp. 80ff; No. 9, 17 November 1945, pp. 108–9.
47 For press accounts of his career at different stages see *La Tribune Indochinoise* (Saigon), 16 and 18 July 1930; *Dan Quyen* (Hanoi—probably his own paper), first issue, 7 October 1945.
48 Devillers, *Histoire du Viêt-Nam*, 139.
49 *Cong-Bao*, 13 October 1945.
50 Consulted at 'National Library', Saigon. The editorial board included such figures as Dang Thai Mai, Nguyen Huu Dang and Nguyen Cong My; there was thus a measure of overlap with the educational world. Tran Huy Lieu was not himself a member, but the Party was represented by Bui Cong Trung, who is known to have studied in Moscow in the early 1930s (cf. Archives Nationales, Section d'Outre-Mer, Paris: SLOTFOM III/Carton 131).
51 *Le Peuple*, 17 October 1946; *Tien-Phong*, 1 November 1946.
52 *Trang Su Moi*, p. 25.
53 *Cong-Bao*, No. 1, 29 September 1945, pp. 6–7. Decrees of 10 September (*ibid.*, p. 10) maintained in being the existing régime of indirect taxation, including monopolies and customs, with Trinh Van Binh as Director. However, since trade was not functioning normally there was presumably little revenue from customs.
54 PRO: FO 371/46309/F.9312.
55 Vo Nhan Tri, *Croissance Economique de la République Démocratique du Viet Nam* (Hanoi, 1967), p. 110; he adds that the sum of public debt at that time was 564,367,522 piastres; but it is not clear how much of that could be written off following the defeat of Japan.
56 *Cong-Bao*, No. 1, 29 September 1945, p. 4.
57 B. B. Fall (ed.), *Ho Chi Minh: On Revolution* (New York, 1967), pp. 146–7. Nevertheless Vietnamese sources complain of not having obtained enough Japanese arms at this time.
58 *Breaking Our Chains*, pp. 64–5.
59 *Histoire de la Revolution d'Août*, p. 138–9.
60 Cf. R. Harris Smith, *OSS: the Secret History of America's First Central Intelligence Agency* (Berkeley, 1972), pp. 331ff, 348ff.
61 Truong Chinh, *The August Revolution* (Hanoi, 1960), reprinted in *The Resistance Will Win* (New York, 1963), p. 42.
62 *South China Morning Post*, 28 November 1945.

63 Decoux, *A la Barre de l'Indochine*, p. 445–6.
64 *Bulletin Statistique de la Féderation Indochinoise: Quatrième Trimestre, 1946* (Saigon, 1947), p. 24.
65 *Bulletin Statistique de l'Indochine 1947* (Saigon: Union Française, Haut Commisariat pour l'Indochine, 1948).
66 Vo Nhan Tri, *Croissance Economique*, p. 109.
67 J. Sainteny, *Histoire d'une Paix Manquée: Indochine, 1945–1947* (Paris, 1967), p. 163, giving the text of a proclamation to that effect fixed to the walls of Hanoi.
68 *South China Morning Post*, 28 November 1945.
69 *FEER*, Vol. II, No. 11 (12 March 1947).
70 *South China Morning Post*, 28 November 1945.
71 Sainteny, *Histoire d'une Paix Manquée*, p. 163.
72 For the text of this announcement, see F. Martin, *Heures Tragiques au Tonkin* (Paris, 1948), pp. 220–1. The author was in Hanoi at the time. Cf. also Sainteny, *Histoire d'une Paix Manquée*, p. 159, who says that large quantities of the notes had been printed immediately before the surrender.
73 Ch'en, *Vietnam and China*, p. 135, citing a report by the Chinese official Chu Hsieh, who took part in the negotiations on the Chinese side.
74 Ch'en in *ibid.*, p. 136, accepts the Vietnamese version, which may well be correct; the French source is Martin, *Heures Tragiques au Tonkin*, p. 221–2. Sainteny does not commit himself.
75 Martin, *Heures Tragiques au Tonkin*, pp. 225–6, including an undated quotation from the newspaper *La République*.
76 Ch'en, *Vietnam and China*, pp. 137–8.
77 *Cong-Bao*, No. 13, 8 December 1945, p. 160.
78 *Cong-Bao*, No. 16, 29 December 1945, p. 196.
79 *Cong-Bao*, No. 14, 15 December 1945, p. 170.
80 Vo Nhan Tri, *Croissance Economique*, pp. 109–10.
81 *The August Revolution* (Hanoi, 1962), reprinted in *Primer for Revolt* (New York, 1963) pp. 44ff.
82 Mao Tse-tung, *Selected Works*, Vol. II (Peking, 1967), p. 318: quoted from the essay *The Chinese Revolution and the Chinese Communist Party*, written in December 1939.
83 See especially the account in *Thirty Years of Struggle of the Party* (Hanoi, 1960), Book I.
84 See, for example, Tetsuya Kataoka, *Resistance and Revolution in China: the Communists and the Second United Front* (Berkeley, 1974). It is important to remember that Nguyen Ai Quoc (i.e. Ho Chi Minh), after leaving Moscow in the autumn of 1938, spent some time in Yenan and then in Chungking at precisely the period when the Chinese debate on the United Front was getting under way. He was not, however, involved in any way in the Rectification Movement of 1942–44 in which the Chinese Communist Party accepted the ideas of Mao Tse-tung instead of those of Chen Shao-yu, the Comintern delegate to that Party.
85 *Trang Su Moi*, p. 25.
86 *Cong-Bao*, No. 1, 29 September 1945, p. 10.
87 Charles Fenn, *Ho Chi Minh, a Biographical Introduction* (London, 1973), p. 75; Harris Smith, *OSS, the Secret History of America's first Central Intelligence Agency*, p. 325.
88 *Cong-Bao*, No. 4, 20 October 1945.
89 *Cong-Bao*, No. 1, 29 September 1945, pp. 13, 14.
90 *Ibid.*, pp. 6–7.
91 *Cong-Bao*, No. 10, 24 November 1945, p. 125.
92 *Ibid.*, pp. 128–9.
93 Truong Chinh. *The August Revolution*, p. 45.
94 *Le Peuple* (Hanoi), 21 and 25 April 1946: series of articles entitled 'Comment la Révolution a Triomphé de la Famine', by Hoang Van Duc.

95 *Ibid.*, 25 April 1946.
96 *Cong-Bao*, No. 12, 1 December 1945, p. 146.
97 *Le Peuple*, 25 April 1946.
98 *Ibid.*, 5 May 1946.
99 *Cong-Bao*, No. 4, 20 October 1945, p. 47.
100 *South China Morning Post*, 16 October 1945.
101 Chen, *Vietnam and China*, p. 133.
102 Sainteny, *Histoire d'une Paix Manquée*, opposite p. 96. Sainteny met Giap on 27 August 1945, and the photograph may have been taken on that occasion. Patti remained in Hanoi till late September or early October 1945.
103 *Cong-Bao*, No. 12, 1 December 1945, p. 140.
104 Cf. Giap's own account, in *A Heroic People, Memoirs from the Revolution* (Hanoi, 1965), pp. 141–2.
105 For the text of its decision, see *Breaking our Chains*, pp. 23–42.
106 *Histoire de la Révolution d'Août* (Hanoi, 1972), p. 100.
107 *Ibid.*, and also *Thirty Years of Struggle of the Party* (Hanoi, 1960).
108 *Histoire de la Révolution d'Août*, pp. 100, 119.
109 *Cong-Bao*, No. 1, 29 September 1945, pp. 4, 10, 12.
110 *Ibid.*, No. 12, p. 140.
111 Devillers, *Histoire du Viêt-Nam*, pp. 218, 221. Giap did not become Minister of Defence until November 1946; *Le Peuple*, 7 November 1946.
112 *Histoire de la Révolution d'Août*, p. 31. For an account of the journey to Pac-Bo, from lowland Tongking, made by Truong Chinh, Hoang Quoc Viet and others, cf. Hoang Quoc Viet's account in *A Heroic People*, pp. 196ff.
113 For Nguyen Luong Bang's activities after the escape, see his account in *A Heroic People*, pp. 556ff. Tran Dang Ninh had been involved in the Bac-Son rising of 1940, before being imprisoned; he rose to a high position in the Army before his death in 1955.
114 For this group, see the memoirs by Vu Anh and by Giap himself in *Souvenirs sur Ho Chi Minh* (Hanoi, 1962), pp. 154ff and 172ff.
115 I. M. Sacks, 'Marxism in Vietnam' in F. N. Trager (ed.), *Marxism in Southeast Asia* (Stanford, 1960), p. 158; citing *La République*, 18 November 1945. He suggests in a footnote that the decision was opposed by Tran Van Giau, at that time (but not for very long afterwards) leader of the Communist movement in the South.
116 Cf. p. 596 above.
117 Devillers, *Histoire du Viêt-Nam*, p. 232; he presumably draws his information from French intelligence sources; the context suggests that the information belongs to a date around February 1946.
118 *Souvenirs sur Ho Chi Minh*, pp. 56ff.
119 *Contribution à l'Histoire des Mouvements Politiques de l'Indochine* (Hanoi, 1933), Vol. IV, pp. 15–16, 19–20. He died in 1951.
120 *A Heroic People*, pp. 247–9.
121 Devillers, *Histoire du Viêt-Nam*, p. 202. From 1952 to 1956, Nguyen Luong Bang was Vietnamese Ambassador in Moscow.

# 5 China and Southeast Asia
## The revolutionary perspective, 1951

Source: *Journal of Southeast Asian Studies* 19(1) (1988): 97–110.

I

Controversy still surrounds the question whether the communist-led uprisings which developed across Southeast Asia during the months from March to September 1948 were the outcome of a deliberate international communist strategy or merely the product of coincidental decisions by individual communist parties. Equally controversial, although less frequently discussed, is the suggestion that during the early months of 1950 the Chinese Communist Party took on direct responsibility for sustaining those revolutionary armed struggles which were still continuing in Southeast Asia — in Vietnam, Malaya and the Philippines — and even provided material assistance to allow them to expand. The present paper will examine yet a third period at which it is necessary to consider the possibility of coordinated international decision-making on the communist side in Southeast Asia: the second half of 1951.

The question whether the international communist movement actually devised and executed a coherent strategy across all of South and Southeast Asia in 1950–51 — and if so, what forms of international direction or coordination were involved — is impossible to answer without access to the archives of the communist parties and governments concerned: access which we can be sure will be denied to non-communist scholars, probably forever. Nor, for that matter, is it likely that independent researchers will soon be allowed unrestricted access to the most sensitive Western intelligence records relating to this question. It is possible, nevertheless, to make certain deductions from those government files which have been opened in the past few years. Particular interest attaches to indications that Western assessments of communist strategy sometimes differed not only between but even within governments. It is hardly surprising that the French, for their own reasons, emphasised the danger of direct Chinese intervention in Indochina, and the consequences for Malaya and other parts of the region of Indochina falling under Viet-Minh control. During the summer and autumn of 1951, Marshal De Lattre went to great lengths to try to persuade the United States and Britain to respond to that danger by creating a regional reserve comparable with the forces under North Atlantic Treaty Organization (NATO) command in Europe.[1] On the other hand, we find that the British Foreign Office was by 1951 extremely reluctant to believe that the Chinese Communist Party (CCP) had any hand at all in directing or materially supporting the insurgency in Malaya.

On that issue, the British documents of the years 1950–51 stand in marked contrast to those so far available for 1948 — the year in which the Malayan Emergency began. At that earlier period, we find at least a school of thought within the Foreign Office (as well as within the security services in Malaya) inclined to accept the view that the insurgencies across Southeast Asia had been stimulated by Moscow — even though, in the nature of things, there could be no absolute proof. Those who held that view placed special emphasis on the fact that the Madiun Affair in Indonesia (September 1948) came to a head immediately after the arrival in Java of the old Comintern hand, Musso, who had travelled straight from Moscow.[2] There was also a general willingness to take seriously the idea that the Australian Communist Party leader Lawrence Sharkey, who was known to have stopped in Singapore on his way both to and from the Indian Communist Party's second congress (February–March 1948), had acted as intermediary between Indian and Malayan communists; and that his conversations with the latter played a direct role in changing the Malayan Communist Party (MCP) line at a Central Committee Plenum immediately afterwards.[3]

Two years later, however, British official attitudes seem to have undergone a marked change. By 1951 the British authorities were going out of their way to play down any suggestion of external involvement in the activities of the MCP and the Malayan Races Liberation Army (MRLA). When on 25 September 1951 *The Times* published a report that Chinese reinforcements had recently arrived from China and had succeeded in landing secretly from the sea, the Colonial Office immediately asked the High Commissioner, Sir Henry Gurney, for more information. Gurney assured them that there was 'no truth' in the report, and added that he had sent a note to editors of newspapers to 'discourage publication' of the story. Even if it were completely untrue, it would have had a serious effect on morale. A Foreign Office minute also commented on the article, pointing out that whilst there was 'a certain amount of communication and traffic between the MCP and the CCP', it could not be said that the insurgents were 'taking orders' from the Chinese, nor that China was intervening directly in the conflict in Malaya.[4] It is this last point which gives a clue to the Foreign Office attitude, for it is possible to detect a critical change in Whitehall thinking during the early months of 1950 — in the immediate aftermath of London's decision to recognize the People's Republic in Beijing as the only legal government of China.

The issue had come to a head following reports from Malaya of a marked increase in terrorist activity during January and February 1950 — and the suggestion that this was due to a sharp increase in material support from China. On 25 January 1950, Sir Henry Gurney included in a 'personal and secret' letter to the Colonial Secretary a request for any estimate that might have been made in London concerning relations between the CCP and the MCP. It took until 20 March for a Colonial Office official to reply to that point; by which time the issue appears to have generated some disagreement within the British government. The reply, whilst recognizing the complexity of the issue involved, quoted a Joint Intelligence

Committee (Far East) estimate of November 1949, to the effect that the CCP had been expected then to establish closer contacts with the 'bandits' in Malaya and might seek to send small quantities of material aid. It went on to observe that 'even a small volume of material assistance from China could have a most serious effect on the Malayan war'.[5] Meanwhile, in another despatch to London on 10 February, Gurney indicated that he had strong indication of landings by Chinese communists on the coast of southern Thailand; and that they were beginning to infiltrate into Malaya across the land border. In the records so far released nothing more is heard of that evidence — except that it led to a measure of police cooperation between the Malayan and Thai governments along the border in question.[6] But there is at least a hint that the Colonial Office had a different view of things from that held by the Foreign Office.

That impression seems to some extent confirmed by the Cabinet's decision to establish a Malaya Committee, which had its first meeting on 19 April 1950. A brief for a meeting of that group on 1 May, prepared by the Foreign Office's Southeast Asia Department, was extremely critical both of the Colonial Office and of the Malayan government for being too inclined — rather suddenly it would seem, around February 1950 — to blame external factors for the deteriorating situation.[7] The Foreign Office itself preferred to emphasize the strength and skill of the Malayan communist movement, and warned against taking too seriously the government's own propaganda habit of referring to the MCP merely as 'bandits and ruffians'. The real problem lay in 'the Government of Malaya's failure hitherto to estimate the true strength of the threat with which it was faced'. However, the same document also alludes to what was probably the central concern of the Foreign Office in making these points: the fear that too much talk about Chinese aid to the MCP might affect HMG's relations with the Chinese government in Beijing. Both the Chinese community in Malaya and the government of the United States were critical of the British decision to establish diplomatic relations with Beijing and would have liked to see it reversed. One can only conclude that a tacit decision was reached in London that such pressures must be resisted, and that the Emergency in Malaya must be handled within Malaya, without laying the blame on 'international Communism'. This background of interdepartmental controversy suggests that historians should be cautious before accepting all British official pronouncements on such a complex question — even when they appear in previously secret archives.

These views of British officialdom must be tested against more direct evidence. Although we have no access to communist archives, it is possible to make a careful analysis of information contained in communist publications and broadcasts — both at the time and in subsequent historical revelations. Such publications seldom refer to active coordination between the communist parties of Asia, once the COMINTERN had been formally dissolved in 1943.[8] But communist parties in different countries can sometimes be observed adopting very much the same 'correct line' of policy at a particular juncture of history. That in itself suggests a measure of coordination between them, if only on the basis of an effort by each party's leaders to relate their own 'line' to the Soviet (or Chinese) analysis of the world situation at a given time. This need not have been the result of centralized 'monolithic' decision-making for the international movement as a whole — the much-derided 'orders from Moscow'; but the result was often almost the same. Different parties tended to adopt the same strategy and tactics, in harmony with one another; and to change tack at about the same time.

## II

One point to emerge clearly from the Foreign Office and Colonial Office assessments of 1948 and 1950–51 is that at the earlier date the issue was whether to blame Moscow, whereas by 1950 it was whether to blame Beijing. In 1948, too, the Malayan authorities believed that an important role was being played by the Indian Communist Party, and that the 'leftist' line adopted at its Second Congress in Calcutta (28 February–7 March 1948) had direct consequences for the communist parties of Malaya and Burma. In the case of Malaya, the Calcutta decision was supposed to have been communicated to comrades in Singapore through a leader of the Australian Communist Party. It may not be without significance that these were all parties within the British Commonwealth. In the 1920s and 1930s there had been indications of a close relationship between communist movements in the colonies and the corresponding metropolitan party: for example between those of the Dutch East Indies and the Netherlands, and between the Indochinese and the French communist parties. It is possible that, even as late as 1948, the Indian Communist Party was accorded a significant role in determining the 'correct line' for Asian areas of the British Empire — especially following India's own achievement of independence the year before.

At that stage, China was still in turmoil; and it is generally thought that Stalin remained sceptical about the ability of the CCP to defeat the Kuomintang (KMT) in the foreseeable future. There was thus no reason to make the Chinese Communist Party responsible for guiding the revolution in other parts of Asia — except possibly Indochina, where Ho Chi Minh had long-standing links with the CCP. The 'leftist' line which was adopted by the Indian Party's Second Congress in late 1947 was by no means identical with the 'Maoist' line which prevailed in the CCP by that time. In ousting the 'rightist' leader P.C. Joshi, the 'leftist' group under Ranadive had advocated a more extreme 'anti-bourgeois' line — not an 'armed struggle' based on an anti-imperialist united front.[9] It involved the abandonment of an earlier policy of legal activity and constitutional negotiation, deemed appropriate in the aftermath of the anti-Japanese struggle of World War II; but that did not amount to endorsement of the precise forms of struggle practised in China. As far as India was concerned, the advocates of armed struggle were to be found not among Ranadive's supporters but in the Andhra Party committee, whose views did not prevail until about 1950.

The possibility that Southeast Asian communists were influenced by *both* the Indian 'leftist' line *and* the Chinese 'Maoist' line may help to explain some of the confusion that is evident in the thinking of the Malayan and other communist parties of the region during 1948. By the second half of 1949, however, Stalin was obliged to admit that Mao's strategy had worked in China and that it might have direct relevance for other parts of Asia. It is possible, too, that he was anxious to eliminate any 'Titoist' influence in Asia, following his expulsion of Yugoslavia from the COMINFORM in Europe. Soviet endorsement of the Chinese line was signalled by an article in the COMINFORM journal on 27 January 1950, praising the speech of Liu Shaoqi at a conference of Asian and Australasian trade unions held in Beijing the preceding November.[10]

What is less easily gauged is the extent to which Moscow was able to impose the Chinese line on other Asian communist parties at that point; even, perhaps, to entrust the CCP with responsibility for guiding and disciplining those other parties and providing material support for their armed struggles. Unfortunately channels of communication between communist parties, at least after 1943, are extremely difficult for the outsider to identify and assess; and any information about them collected by Western intelligence agencies is likely to be extremely tightly held. Occasional indications seem to suggest the existence of a complex network of communications between the communists of Southeast Asia in the late 1940s and early 1950s. A report in *The Times* (datelined Singapore, 23 May 1951) mentioned the existence of some kind of regional 'executive committee' at 'the village of Mon Len in Eastern Burma', run by a Vietnamese called Nguyen Van Long.[11] But the main purpose of that report was not to emphasize such links so much as to minimize their importance. In any case, communications on that level need not have depended on any initiative from as far away as Moscow or Beijing. Whilst they might constitute a means of enabling senior cadres in each party (and each locality) to adjust their own operations to a single international communist line, they could not in themselves ensure the maintenance of international discipline.

We have rather more information about communication between the Vietnamese communist leadership and both Beijing and Moscow. Hoang Van Hoan, the one member of the Vietnamese Politburo to defect to Beijing after the Sino-Vietnamese conflicts of 1978-79, has revealed that Ho Chi Minh visited China early in 1950 and secured a precise agreement on Chinese military and political assistance to the Viet-Minh.[12] More recently, a Chinese veteran diplomat revealed that Ho visited Moscow at the same time. Possibly he travelled there in the company of Zhou Enlai on 21 January 1950; certainly he travelled back to Beijing with Mao and Zhou in mid-February. At a banquet, shortly before leaving the Soviet capital, Ho was reported to have suggested ('jokingly') that Stalin might sign a treaty of friendship with the Democratic Republic of Vietnam, along the same lines as that signed with the People's Republic of China on 14 February 1950.[13] Stalin, although he had formally recognized the Democratic Republic of Vietnam (DRVN) on 30 January, was not prepared to do that. Nor, so far as we can tell, did the Soviet Union provide direct aid to the Viet-Minh before 1955. It would appear that Moscow had in effect transferred to Beijing full responsibility for guiding and aiding the Vietnamese revolution; and that the Chinese still held that responsibility when they negotiated the partition of Vietnam — supposedly behind Vietnamese backs — at the Geneva Conference of 1954.[14]

There is no longer any reason to doubt that very substantial military assistance and advice were provided to the Viet-Minh by China during the years from 1950 to 1954, even though assertions to that effect by Western commentators were long denied in Hanoi and Beijing. Some of the information available to British and American officials — often from French or Nationalist Chinese sources — can now be documented from the archives. There was firm evidence, for example, of secret Sino-Viet-Minh aid agreements in January and April 1950; and of an important visit by Vo Nguyen Giap to southern China in January 1951.[15] But in any case, we no longer need to depend solely on information of that kind. In 1979, the Chinese themselves, stung by what seemed like Vietnamese ingratitude, made a number of revelations which were substantiated in more detail by Hoang Van Hoan. He tells us that, following Ho Chi Minh's secret visit to China at the beginning of 1950, agreements were signed under which China trained Viet-Minh troops and helped to organize a campaign to clear the Sino-Vietnamese border of French troops. (The Chinese communists were no doubt also interested in preventing any continuing KMT presence along that border.) Hoan mentions in particular three individuals who played a role in Vietnam at that period. General Chen Geng spent some time in Vietnam during 1950, presumably as an extension of his duties as deputy commander of the People's Liberation Army, Second Field Army and commander of the Yunnan Military District. Luo Guibo, one-time political commissar of a unit in the Second Field Army, led a Chinese group responsible for advising the Viet-Minh on financial and administrative matters. Finally, perhaps at a slightly later stage, a military advisory group was sent to northern Vietnam under the command of General Wei Guoqing, a native of Guangxi and subsequently the top party official in that province.[16]

On the other hand, it is still impossible to answer the question whether the Chinese sent either material assistance or political and military advisers to assist the other revolutionary armed struggles still going on in Southeast Asia in early 1950: in Burma, in Malaya, and in the Philippines. Assistance of the kind implied by Gurney's dispatch of 10 February 1950 is by no means improbable in that context. Certainly by April that year we find vigorous support for the Malayan and Philippine struggles in the Chinese media.[17] But even if assistance and advice were tendered, it would be unwise to assume that the CCP had the means to ensure that the new 'line' (and its own advice) were being correctly followed in a disciplined way. In recognizing the importance of the international dimension for an understanding of the overall trend in communist strategy, in this or any other period, it is not necessary to assume monolithic control over actual decisions. The leaders of the communist movements in Southeast Asia were still the same men who had accepted the 'leftist' line of 1948 in one form or another, basing their first efforts at aimed struggle on a narrow 'class line'. They were not necessarily all convinced 'Maoists'. It seems very likely that even after Stalin had endorsed the Chinese line early in 1950, there was still much confusion and diversity at the grass roots level; and that considerable scope remained for local initiative (and mistakes) by individual parties. It is not certain that, before 1951, the Chinese were able to impose ideological orthodoxy even on the Viet-Minh; nor, for that matter,

China and Southeast Asia, 1951 121

that the central leadership of the Vietnamese Communist Party was able to assert total discipline over its own forces in the southern half of Vietnam. In that regard, however, the year 1951 may have seen important new developments.

## III

By June 1951, it must have been evident that, on the scale thus far envisaged, Chinese aid to the Viet-Minh was not adequate to defeat a French Expeditionary Force which was able to draw on military support from the United States. (American aid to the French in Indochina, including the establishment of a Military Assistance Group in Saigon, had also taken formal shape by the end of 1950.) During the first half of 1951, under the command of Marshal De Lattre, French forces defeated two determined attempts by the Viet-Minh to break through the 'cordon sanitaire' around the Tongking Delta: at Vinh-Yen in January, and at Mao-Khe in March–April. They also inflicted heavy casualties on a Viet-Minh force attempting to gain control of the rice harvest of the southern part of the Tongking Delta in late May and early June.

Some idea of Viet-Minh dissatisfaction with their own efforts at that period can be gleaned from an article by Vo Nguyen Giap, published 7 June 1951, which included criticisms both of military training and of fighting ability and called for more effective mobilization and propaganda programmes.[18] (He did not, of course, mention the role of the Chinese.) There are grounds for believing that the frontal assault strategy pursued earlier in the year had involved the senior political commissar, Nguyen Chi Thanh, more closely than Giap himself. It had been Thanh who spoke out optimistically just after the Vinh-Yen battle; and probably it was he who had contributed an article to the magazine *People's China* in February 1951.[19] If that supposition is correct, Thanh might have suffered a corresponding loss of influence over decision-making during the second half of 1951. But the most important question which must logically have arisen at that point was whether the Chinese were willing to increase their assistance to the Viet-Minh even further, to enable them to cope with increased French capabilities.

It will be recalled that June 1951 was also a turning-point in the Korean War. There, too, the frontal assaults of late 1950 and the early months of 1951 had resulted in heavy Chinese casualties; and by June the Chinese commander Peng Dehuai probably recognized the impossibility of doing more than stabilizing the situation around the 38th parallel. In such circumstances it was inherently unlikely that Mao Zedong would wish to send a large army of Chinese 'volunteers' into northern Vietnam, despite French fears that an early truce in Korea would make direct Chinese action in Indochina more likely.[20] On the other hand, the Chinese certainly could not afford to see the Viet-Minh collapse: at the very least they would wish to provide more weapons (perhaps some of those captured from the Americans in Korea) to enable the Viet-Minh to match French firepower at critical moments.

During August and September there were indications that the Viet-Minh were rethinking their whole strategy, and accepting the implications of a more prolonged war than they had originally contemplated. Another important article by Vo Nguyen Giap, put out by the Vietnam News Agency on 18 September 1951, urged greater attention to the conduct of guerrilla warfare — particularly the establishment of armed bases in rural areas behind the French lines. That would appear also to have been the theme of a Viet-Minh conference held in southern Vietnam sometime in August, presided over by the then military commissar for the South, Le Duan.[21] Continuing along the same lines, Giap (in a further article published on 25 September) emphasized the importance of combining political and economic activity with armed struggle and of knowing precisely when to bring each form of struggle into play. One aspect of the political struggle, discussed by Pham Van Dong about the same time, was the need for more effective propaganda to accompany the collection of the next round of agricultural taxes, and to correct 'mistakes' committed on a previous occasion.[22] Similar emphasis on political activity, and on strengthening the 'national united front', is found in a letter addressed by Pham Hung to the people of southern Vietnam on 23 September.[23] Guerrilla warfare, in all areas, was thus seen to depend on effective political mobilization of the masses.

On the other hand, it was clear that guerrilla warfare alone would not be sufficient to drive the French out of Indochina. The classic three stage interpretation of revolutionary war, normally regarded as essential to the 'Maoist' strategy, implied an eventual transition to a more ambitious 'second stage' of military operations. It was equally clear that, in the circumstances of autumn 1951, the Viet-Minh could not make that transition across the whole country simultaneously; at least, not without much greater Chinese participation than either the Chinese or the Viet-Minh themselves were contemplating. The logical solution was to concentrate effort at one particular point in the hope that Chinese aid on the existing scale would be sufficient to allow a Viet-Minh breakthrough.

French assessments of the situation in late 1951 focused attention on an area to the west and south-west of Hanoi which the Viet-Minh needed to control if they were to link up their base area in the highlands of northern Tongking with the rice-producing lowlands of southern Tongking and Thanh-Hoa. (The province of Thanh-Hoa, part of the Viet-Minh 'Interzone IV' or fourth military region, had not been reoccupied at all by the French since 1945.) In November 1951, in order to forestall a Viet-Minh campaign to gain control of the territory between those two key areas, De Lattre ordered French units to occupy the town of Hoa-Binh and part of the Black River valley. The Viet-Minh responded with a determined effort to capture Hoa-Binh, and by early February 1952 they had succeeded in forcing a French withdrawal. That victory — coinciding as it did with the death of De Lattre in mid-January — can probably be regarded as the most significant turning-point of the whole anti-French war.[24] It opened the way for the Viet-Minh to consolidate their control of the area to the west of the southern Tongking Delta, and to prepare further campaigns against a French force whose morale was now in sharp decline.[25]

The Hoa-Binh operation was, indeed, the most ambitious Viet-Minh campaign thus far. Although the Chinese role in it has not been described in detail, there can be little doubt that Chinese assistance was of vital (if not decisive) consequence. A combination of guerrilla warfare, behind French lines in the Tongking Delta, with a growing capability for large-scale operations in the uplands might eventually be sufficient to defeat the French in the northern half of Vietnam without direct Chinese military intervention. However, it was clear that a similar level of Chinese military assistance could not be provided to Viet-Minh forces in Central and South Vietnam, to allow them also to go beyond the stage of guerrilla warfare and link up base areas in those regions.

A specific communist decision to differentiate between the northern and southern halves of Vietnam might not have yet been taken at the time of Le Duan's southern conference in August 1951. By the end of the year, however, we find several indications that a separate strategy had been devised for the South — albeit one which might not have been entirely to the liking of southern Viet-Minh cadres. The most important document suggesting this interpretation is a long statement made by Le Duc Tho to the 'second conference' of the Vietnam Workers' Party in South Vietnam (probably Nam-Bo), parts of which were published in the southern edition of *Nhan-Dan* and then put out by the Vietnam News Agency (in Vietnamese) on 18–20 December 1951. A second piece by Tho — or possibly a continuation of the same statement — was broadcast by the 'Voice of Nam-Bo' radio early in the new year.[26]

Le Duc Tho's critique of guerrilla warfare in the South echoed some of the themes of Vo Nguyen Giap's September article. He recognized that one reason for lack of progress was the 'difficult situation' in the South: in particular, communications were not easy and existing forces were split up into a number of different sectors. But he also took to task 'many responsible cadres' who were too preoccupied with grand ideas about 'regular troops' — as well as with a 'spirit of formalism' — instead of concentrating on guerrilla warfare and the conduct of propaganda. Cadres trained in 'military schools' were inclined to give 'purely military instruction'. The remedy for these past shortcomings lay in ensuring that the 'people's forces' were more closely allied to 'the people'. Whilst recognizing that the armed forces must train themselves for eventual open warfare, Tho insisted that the guerrilla struggle must remain the principal form of activity in the South for the time being; and that 'rash' military operations should be avoided. Regarding supplies, it was necessary to capture them from the French rather than depend on resources provided by 'superior echelons'. In later portions of the statement, he went on to urge that the united front become more active in French-held areas (particularly in Nam-Bo) where it was important to improve propaganda techniques in order to 'stimulate patriotism and hatred of the enemy'. The level of political education among cadres in those areas was too low, and 'some comrades' had failed to carry out the party's orders. On the other hand, Tho was willing to praise the achievements of the 'liberated zones' of Central and South Vietnam in bringing about a temporary redistribution of riceland and in increasing agricultural production.

These points fit in with other broadcast statements monitored in the latter part of 1951. The strengthening of the 'united front' in the South was one of the main points in Pham Hung's letter of 23 September. An important element in the Southern 'united front' was the overseas Chinese community and on 1 October (the second anniversary of the creation of the People's Republic of China) an appeal to the Chinese community of the Saigon area was broadcast by Pham Ngoc Thach, chairman of the Viet-Minh committee for Saigon-Cholon. He urged them to pay taxes to the 'people's regime', to facilitate the execution of 'traitors', and to help in sabotage operations.[27] We have no means of knowing whether the Chinese population of Vietnam were also being mobilized by the Chinese Communist Party; but it seems more than probable that some among them were actual members of the Chinese rather than of the Vietnamese Party. Pham Hung again played a prominent role at a southern (Nam-Bo) conference on economic and financial questions, held from 23 October to 2 November 1951.[28]

It is impossible to tell who, precisely, was being criticized by Le Duc Tho. But the man who had commanded Viet-Minh forces in the South since 1946 was Nguyen Phuong Thao, better known as Nguyen Binh. A native of Tongking he had originally joined the Vietnam Quoc Dan Dang (the Vietnamese equivalent of the Chinese Kuomintang) and had gone South in 1929 to establish cells for that party in Saigon. The following year he was arrested by the French and then spent several years in prison — during which time he was probably recruited into the communist party. Very probably he was now being blamed for the situation which Le Duc Tho found unsatisfactory. But on 12 January 1952 the Vietnam News Agency reported that he had recently been 'killed in action' and that Ho Chi Minh had awarded him a posthumous decoration at a special commemorative ceremony.[29] Many non-communist Vietnamese later believed he had been eliminated for political reasons, and the background of political differences within the party in the South lends some credence to that suspicion. What seems certain is that his death coincided with a significant reorientation of the southern struggle.

The possibility of sharp conflict over the new party line also emerges when we come to look at events during this period in Central Vietnam: the area of Quang-Nam, Quang-Ngai and Binh-Dinh provinces, which the Viet-Minh designated 'Interzone V'. A conference to establish a regional organization for the VNWP was held there in late September; but already by 20 October the official report of the meeting was being openly criticized by the VNA for not indicating sufficiently clearly the 'lessons' learned from it. A fuller report, published in *Nhan-Dan* and broadcast in the 'Voice of South Vietnam' on 23 December 1951, indicates that the cadres and people of 'Interzone V' were being urged to follow much the same line as that laid down by Le Duc Tho. In criticizing earlier military actions, and in emphasizing the need for more political training in the army, specific mention was made of the need to understand Mao Zedong's ideas about revolutionary warfare. A week later a new school was opened to train party cadres.[30] No senior party figures were mentioned by name, either as authors or as targets of criticism. We know that in fact Nguyen Duy Trinh had been appointed party leader in 'Interzone V' in mid-1950, and that he remained in charge there until 1954: presumably, therefore, no significant 'purge' took place as a result of the change of line in Central Vietnam.

To sum up, the evidence so far available suggests that by the end of 1951 (and in principle perhaps as early as the end of September that year) the Vietnam Workers' Party took a deliberate decision to downgrade the military struggle in the southern half of the country — at the same time as they were developing a more ambitious military strategy for the North, which depended on substantial Chinese assistance and advice. We have no means of knowing whether this decision was inspired by the Chinese themselves. But its consequences were far-reaching. In the event, after another three and a half years of bitter fighting, the Viet-Minh found themselves still unable to intensify or expand the scale of their armed struggle in the southern provinces. By the spring of 1954 the international situation, as interpreted by the Russians as well as by the Chinese, dictated an end to hostilities in Indochina. Soon afterwards the Geneva Conference agreed to the virtual partition of Vietnam.

## IV

Turning to the wider context of this redefinition of Viet-Minh strategy in the second half of 1951, it is immediately apparent that the line enunciated by Le Duc Tho had several points in common with the criticisms and directives formulated by the Malayan Communist Party at a plenary session of its own Central Committee in October 1951.[31] It is not possible to attempt a point-by-point comparison, if only because the situations of the two areas were so different: but the same essential principles seem to have applied in both cases. Directing its attack against 'leftist' deviations, the MCP was particularly concerned about the failure to relate guerrilla action, terrorism and sabotage, to the actual feelings of the masses: or, conversely, to use propaganda and other political methods to mobilize the masses and to secure effective support for the armed struggle. Criticism of too much coercion of the population in the past was matched by determination to ensure a greater measure of voluntary support for the struggle in future. Another important issue was the party's attitude towards the 'middle bourgeoisie' and the need to broaden the 'united front'.

All of these points can be paralleled, either in Le Duc Tho's statement or in the articles by Pham Van Dong and Vo Nguyen Giap published earlier the same year. The main difference between Malaya and Vietnam was that the latter already had extensive 'liberated zones' in which the Viet-Minh controlled the administration and were producing their own food and even simple weapons. The main focus of Vietnamese criticism was on past failure to develop both guerrilla bases and political mobilization in areas still under French 'occupation'. In that sense one could argue that almost all of Malaya was still under British 'occupation': even the central area of Pahang, where the MCP Central Committee had its headquarters during 1950–51, was not a 'liberated zone' as the Viet-Minh understood the term. One further comparison is worth noting: Le Duc Tho's criticism of military cadres who paid too little attention to guerrilla warfare, and of 'some cadres' who ignored party instructions, finds significant parallel in a growing number of MCP references to Mao Zedong's resolutions at the Gutian Conference of 1929: the first occasion on which Mao had enunciated the principle that the party must 'command the gun'.[32]

It might be argued, indeed, that in this and other respects the new line that was being imposed both in Malaya and in southern Vietnam at this time was a purer form of the 'Maoist' concept of armed struggle than either area had previously pursued. The 'leftist' line adopted by the MCP in 1948, which had led directly to the decision to embark on violent struggle against British 'imperialism', had implied a rather narrower class basis for struggle than that favoured by Mao. It had assumed that the whole of the 'bourgeoisie' would cooperate with the British and that only workers and squatters were sufficiently reliable to be recruited to the struggle: everyone else must be coerced. Mao's approach — at least during the periods when Liu Shaoqi was working closely with him — emphasized the need to mobilize as wide a class following as possible, and to hold together a broad 'united front' by means of political education and effective propaganda. Within that framework, it was necessary also to ensure party leadership over the 'people's liberation army'. The 'leftist' line, whilst it paid more attention to class purity and to coercion than to political education, carried with it the danger that the 'people's armed forces' would become *too* concerned with violence and hence too divorced from the masses. That was precisely what was said to have happened in Malaya (and in southern Vietnam) in the period before 1951.

It is possible also to make comparisons with communist developments elsewhere in Asia. In the Philippines, a meeting of the 'Huk' leadership in December 1951 appears to have accepted the conclusion that the 'revolutionary current has abated' and that more attention should now be paid to political work amongst trade unions and students. The party would now have to adjust to the likelihood of a long, protracted struggle.[33] Even in India, where the attempt to mobilize the peasantry for armed struggle against Nehru's Congress government had clearly failed by the end of 1950, it is possible to recognize in the line adopted by the Indian Communist Party in May 1951 the same essential elements as those already discussed. Whilst the renewal of violent struggle was indefinitely postponed, under the leadership of Ajoy Ghosh (elected secretary-general at that time) the concept of a 'united front' of many different classes was fundamentally similar to that of Mao and Liu. The 'leftist' line which had been pursued by Ranadive, between late 1947 and early 1950, had now been left behind completely.

In considering the evolution of the Malayan Communist Party 'line' after 1945, it is possible to identify three phases: a 'rightist' line under the leadership of Loi Tak, and for a short time under his successor Chin Peng; followed by the adoption of a 'leftist' line in March 1948, without any obvious change of leader; followed later still by the gradual acceptance of the 'Maoist' line. It is not impossible that one reason for the criticisms of October 1951 was that, even at that late stage, some MCP cadres were still pursuing a 'leftist' line in the sense that they continued to rely on too narrow a class base for the struggle.

Perhaps the true significance of what was happening during the latter part of 1951 was that, for the first time, the CCP was at last able to impose both its own line *and* a measure of real discipline on communist parties throughout

Southeast Asia — presumably with the continuing approval of Stalin. The Vietnam Worker's Party had fully accepted the 'Maoist' line on the united front and the class basis of armed struggle, when it was 'reestablished' in February 1951. The 'second congress' had been followed by a decision to merge the Viet-Minh front of 1941 (comprising only workers, peasants and intellectuals) with the Lien-Viet front, founded in 1946, which included the patriotic bourgeoisie and some landed elements. Relations between the DRVN and the People's Republic were further strengthened in the summer and autumn of 1951 by the visit to China and North Korea of a Vietnamese delegation led by Hoang Quoc Viet, a close associate of Truong Chinh.[34] But it took until later that year to impose effective discipline on the southern areas of Vietnam; a step which was finally achieved by Le Duc Tho's mission to the South, and which was possibly confirmed by the elimination of Nguyen Binh. The next logical move would be for the CCP also to impose firmer discipline on the Malayan Communist Party. Conceivably the Chinese even sent some kind of delegation to the MCP Central Committee Plenum held early in October 1951 — which might be the explanation for the supposed 'landings' reported on 25 September, shortly before the meeting took place.

At this point in the argument, it may be permissible to bring in evidence drawn from Chinese Nationalist intelligence sources, as indicated by Radio Taibei. Such testimony would not on its own prove anything; but when it fits in with a pattern already emerging from other sources, it may in fact help us to fill in certain details. On 5 January 1951, Radio Taibei cited the (KMT) Military Information Service for reports of a recent 'order' from the CCP to the communist parties of Malaya, Indochina, India, Burma and the Philippines, instructing them to send delegations to Beijing to sign a secret agreement on allocations of military assistance. But it was observed that in all countries *except* Vietnam, the agreement would insist that the cost of military action within each country must be borne by each individual Party. The Chinese (and, it was said, the Russians) would bear only the cost of training personnel. The following day, the Central News Agency (also Taibei) reported that in December 1951 a meeting of Soviet, Chinese and Vietnamese representatives, somewhere in northern Indochina, had been presided over by Gao Gang: at that time the head of CCP administration in the Northeast (Manchuria) and also a senior member of the Chinese Politburo.[35] The implication of these two reports, taken together, is that the Chinese were now ready to increase their military commitment to the Viet-Minh; but that beyond the northern areas of Indochina they were anxious to apply a principle of 'self-reliance' which would make it impossible for the armed struggle in those areas to grow beyond the level of continuing guerrilla warfare. In India and Indonesia it was assumed that the armed struggle would be abandoned altogether for the foreseeable future.

Such a decision, taken at the highest level of international communist deliberation, would certainly have made sense in relation to the larger situation then emerging in the world as a whole. The strategy which had been pursued in Korea since mid-1950 had obviously failed — in that it had provoked concerted action by the West under United States leadership — and had also helped to revive the international capitalist economy. There was little to be gained by continuing that war in its original form. On 26 November 1951 an agreement was reached at Panmunjon on a ceasefire line, which would become definitive if an armistice could be signed within the next month.[36] But despite the apprehensions of the French, Mao Zedong had no intention of immediately creating a 'Korean' situation in Indochina, which would almost certainly have galvanized the United States, Britain and France into establishing a virtual equivalent of NATO in Southeast Asia. The struggle in Indochina had to be continued in a form which would lead ultimately to French defeat; but on a scale which would not bring the whole Western alliance into the war.

It would be going too far to suggest that the struggles in Malaya and the Philippines were thereby written off. But both Moscow and Beijing probably recognized that in the longer term their goal must be to wean Indonesia, Burma and India away from their post-imperial associations with the West. In those countries, a peaceful communist strategy would now be oriented towards that end. Thus was born what, by 1955, would be recognizable as China's 'Bandung Strategy'. As far as Vietnam itself was concerned, the decisions of late 1951 were tantamount to a recognition that the Viet-Minh might have to be content to 'liberate' only half the country, as a result of the current struggle. In 1954 the Chinese did indeed accept in Vietnam the same 'temporary' solution they had been obliged to accept in Korea: partition.

## Notes

1. The possible consequences of a Chinese 'invasion' of Indochina were discussed at the Phoenix Park conference of 15–18 May 1951: see FO 371/93085 (FZ1197/102). For a British official's minute on the question, including the possibility of a 'theatre reserve' in Southeast Asia, see FO 371/92416 (FF 10317). None of the papers on that subject, however, deals with the question of possible links between the communist struggles in Indochina and Malaya.
2. See particularly a Foreign Office paper by P.F. Grey, 29 Sept. 1948: FO 371/69695 (F. 13733/727/61); and one by J.H. Watson, 8 Nov. 1948: FO 371/69695 (F. 17015/727/61).
3. Noted in a chronology of recent events, sent by the Commissioner-General's Office in Singapore to the US Consulate-General in Singapore on 24 November 1948, of which a copy found its way into Foreign Office files: FO 371/69695 (F. 17253/727/61). It will be noted that the most important meeting in Calcutta was that of the Indian Communist Party — not the 'Calcutta Youth Conference' held shortly before, which is something of a red herring in this discussion.
4. FO 371/93010 (FZ 1016/82), and *The Times* (London), 25 Sept. 1951.
5. A copy of this reply (J.D. Higham to Sir Henry Gurney, 20 March 1950) appears in FO 371/84479 (FZ 1018/5). I found no complete copy of Gurney's letter of 25 January 1950; but an extract, including the relevant passage appears in FO 371/84477 (FZ 21016/7). It should be noted in passing that FZ 1018 (in FO 371/84479) originally included four other items on this question, all of which have been 'retained by the Department'.
6. This despatch is mentioned by Anthony Short, *The Communist Insurrection in Malaya, 1948–60* (London, 1975), p. 227, although he is not inclined to take it seriously. I have

not succeeded in locating the despatch in the Colonial Office files (nor in FO 373); but a brief résumé, together with a note of arrangements made with the Thai authorities in consequence, is included in 'Weekly Report on Malaya', No. 55, 10–16 February 1950: FO 371/84475 (FZ 1015/9). The subject is not referred to again in subsequent issues of that report.

7 FO 371/84478 (FZ 1017/8); the brief in question was prepared for the Minister of State at the Foreign Office by R.H. Scott, head of the Southeast Asia Department. Unfortunately this file does not contain the views of the Colonial Office.

8 An interesting exception, relating to a somewhat later period, is the almost casual revelation in Hanoi's 'White Book' (October 1979) that in September 1963 Zhou Enlai presided over a meeting in Guangzhou of representatives from the communist parties of Vietnam, Laos, and Indonesia (*SWB/FE*/6238/A3/5). It can be confirmed from monitored broadcasts at the time that Zhou Enlai and D.N. Aidit were in fact in Guangzhou at the date in question; we do not know who represented Vietnam or Laos.

9 For a detailed analysis of the changes of line of the Indian Communist Party between 1947 and 1951, see J.H. Kautsky, *Moscow and the Communist Party of India* (New York and London, 1956). He analyses at length the contrast between the 'leftist' line adopted in late 1947 and the different versions of the 'Maoist' (or 'Chinese') line which evolved during 1950–51.

10 Kautsky, op. cit., pp. 102–104. A possible Yugoslav role in promoting revolution in Asia, suggested by the attendance of three Yugoslavs at the Calcutta Youth Conference in February 1948, was discussed in British Foreign Office telegrams at that time: FO 371/69694: F. 3475/727/61 and F. 3467. See also C.B. McLane, *Soviet Strategies in Southeast Asia* (Princeton, 1966), p. 375, note 31, for evidence of a Yugoslav role in Burma in 1948.

11 *The Times* (London), 24 May 1951; the report is attributed merely to 'our own correspondent'.

12 Hoang Van Hoan, 'Distortion of Facts about Militant Friendship between Viet Nam and China is Impermissible', *Renmin Ribao*, 27 Nov. 1979; translated in *Beijing Review*, 7 Dec. 1979, p. 12; Hoan was in exile in Beijing from mid-1979. For the text of the Vietnamese 'White Book' of 4 October 1979, to which he was replying, see BBC: *Summary of World Broadcasts, Far East*: nos. 6238 and 6242. It contained a long series of accusations about Chinese attitudes to Vietnam, going back to 1954, and alleged that China had used the Vietnamese for their own purposes throughout the 1950s and 1960s.

13 Wu Xiuquan, *Eight Years in the Ministry of Foreign Affairs: Memoirs of a Diplomat* (Beijing, 1985, English-language edition), pp. 19 and 23.

14 For details of that issue, see the Vietnamese 'White Book' of 1979, cited in note 12 above.

15 See, for example, cables from US consulates in Saigon and Hanoi to State Department during 1950, cited in *Declassified Documents Reference System: Retrospective Collection*, pp. 549: A, B, D; 553: G; 554: A. Also British Foreign Office reports, e.g. FO 371/92194: FC 1015/43, for Giap's visit to Guangzhou in January 1951. I am grateful to Miss Laura Calkins for drawing my attention to these references. Her doctoral thesis, currently in progress at the School of Oriental and African Studies, will explore more fully this and other aspects of Sino-Vietnamese relations in the 1950s. For an indication of the information on this subject to be gleaned from secret Chinese Nationalist sources, see also K.C. Chen, *Vietnam and China 1938–1954* (Princeton, 1969), pp. 254ff.

16 For Hoang Van Hoan's article, see note 12 above. For biographical details of the three Chinese figures mentioned here, see D.W. Klein and A.B. Clark, *Biographic Dictionary of Chinese Communism, 1921–1965* (Cambridge, Mass., 1971). Luo Guibo was appointed China's first ambassador to the Democratic Republic of Vietnam in 1954.

17 See, for example, broadcasts from Beijing around 11–13 April 1950, monitored in *SWB/FE*/52.

18 *Nhan-Dan*, 7 June 1951. For text, as broadcast, see *SWB/FE*/115: p. 75; a copy can also be found in FO 371/92410 (FF 1017/3) at the Public Record Office. For accounts of the Vinh-Yen, Mao-Khe and Day River engagements of 1951, see B.B. Fall, *Street Without Joy* (Harrisburg, 1962), pp. 26–47.
19 Truong Son, 'The Growth of the Viet Nam People's Army', *People's China*, 16 Feb. 1951. 'Truong Son' (the Vietnamese name of the Annamite Chain) is believed to have been the pseudonym either of Nguyen Chi Thanh himself or of someone very close to him; it reappears on articles of the mid-1960s, when Thanh was (from 1964–67) senior Party commissar in South Vietnam. For Thanh's press conference of 20 Jan. 1951, at which he was still optimistic about victory at Vinh-Yen, see *SWB/FE*/93: p.68.
20 See comment on his views in a British Foreign Office minute of 1 Aug. 1951: FO 371/92416 (FF 10317/64). For a CIA assessment of 7 Aug. 1951 (including the estimate that at that time there were 10,000 Chinese personnel serving with Viet-Minh units), see *Foreign Relations of the United States: 1951: Asia and the Pacific*, Pt. I, pp. 469–76, The Americans believed large-scale Chinese intervention was unlikely, at least during the rest of 1951.
21 Le Duan's conference was reported briefly by the 'Vietnam Information Service, Saigon' on 9 September 1951; fuller information about it seems to have been available to the British representative in Saigon (H.A. Graves) by early September; FO 371/92401 (FF 1013/16). For Giap's article of 18 Sept. 1951, see *SWB/FE*/128: pp. 73–74.
22 For these two articles, *SWB/FE*/129: pp. 67, 69.
23 The letter was not reported by VNA until 14 Oct. 1951: *SWB/FE*/131: p. 62.
24 For a detailed account of the Hoa-Binh campaign, see B.B. Fall, *Street without Joy*, pp. 49–60. Further insight into French thinking can be gained from British reports from Saigon at the time, including one based on a press conference given by General Salan in Tongking on 16 Jan. 1952: see FO 371/101609 (FF 1092/2 and 3).
25 Declining morale in Paris was noted by the British naval attaché there as early as 24 January 1952: FO 371/10169 (FF 1092/5); in marked contrast with reports from Saigon in the latter part of 1951.
26 *SWB/FE*/140: p. 74; no. 141: p. 67; no. 143: pp. 81–83. The Vietnam Workers' Party had been reestablished, under that name, at a meeting in Tongking in February 1951; the occasion was always referred to as the 'Second Congress' of the party, the first having been held in Macau in 1935. The precise status of the second conference' in Nam-Bo, sometime in the second half of 1951, is not clear.
27 *SWB/FE*/129: pp. 60–62.
28 *SWB/FE*/140: p. 76. The fact that both Le Duc Tho and Pham Hung were prominent in the South in the latter part of 1951 may indicate a close association between them within the VNWP leadership. It will be recalled that they also cooperated closely during the final phase of the 'Vietnam War', which ended with the fall of Saigon on 30 April 1975.
29 *SWB/FE*/144: p. 85. For the earlier career of Nguyen Binh, see P. Devillers, *Histoire du Viet-Nam de 1940 à 1952* (Paris, 1952), p. 247; and *La Tribune Indochinoise*, 16 July 1930.
30 *SWB/FE*/132. p. 77; no. 141: p. 66; and no. 143: p. 81.
31 Summarized in A. Short, op. cit., pp. 318ff. The British records so far released do not contain a full version of the deliberations of that plenum; but a political intelligence report for October–November 1951 does indicate awareness of a change in MCP tactics at that time: notably greater efforts to penetrate legal trade unions, to form illegal ones, and to 'woo' Indian workers and Malay peasants. See 'Malaya: Monthly Political Intelligence Report, no. 22' in CO 537/7343 (1951-55404/5).
32 Short, op. cit., pp. 320–21.
33 C.B. McLane, *Soviet Strategies in Southeast Asia* (Princeton, 1966), p. 429. The source for this information appears to be the testimony of a 'Huk' cadre who surrendered soon

after the meeting; and also the text of a 'political transmission' issued by the meeting itself.
34 See Chen, op. cit., p. 251. Hoang Quoc Viet arrived in Beijing on 23 July 1951 and held talks during August. He was again in the Chinese capital, on the way back from North Korea, during October. Meanwhile another Vietnamese delegation, headed by Ton Duc Thang, attended the Chinese national day celebrations in Beijing on 1 October 1951: *SWB/FE/*131: p. 62.
35 *SWB/FE/*143: p. 36.
36 No armistice was concluded within the stated interval, however, and the war in Korea eventually resumed. Nevertheless in the immediate aftermath of the definition of a ceasefire line, most ground fighting appears to have come to a halt: see *The Times* (London), 27 and 29 Nov. 1951.

# 6 The TET crisis of 1967–1968 in perspective

Source: Extracted from an unpublished Research Paper delivered in Washington 1998.

The Communist offensive of Tet Mau-Than (January–February 1968) was one of the most important turning points of the Vietnam War, and also a focus of subsequent controversy on both sides. Most Americans agreed, however, that the element of 'surprise' in both the timing and the nature of the offensive required some explanation – and possibly the condemnation of those who had been 'to blame'. For many civilian commentators, the very fact that the nation-wide offensive occurred at all was taken as vindication of their view – already established by mid-1967 – that the war was 'un-winnable' and that the only sensible path was for the United States to withdraw as soon as possible on whatever terms could be negotiated. To the American generals, on the other hand, the outcome of the offensive appeared as a major setback for the Communist side – which US forces should have been able to follow up with an offensive of their own which could then have inflicted decisive defeat on the Communists. But in the event, the Communist offensive produced a 'moment of truth' in Washington's continuing debate about further escalation of the war, and it set the scene for the critical decisions announced in President Johnson's televised address of 31 March 1968.

In approaching the new information that has emerged in publications from both Hanoi and Ho Chi Minh City since 1980, three lines of questioning are likely to be uppermost in the historian's mind.

First, what exactly happened, on the Communist side, during the critical phase of the offensive itself? Were Hanoi's forces (and those of the southern PLAF) conscious of having suffered a major setback?

Second, what can be learned about the purpose of the offensive from information about the sequence of events that culminated in Hanoi's decision to launch it? And what were the attitudes of Moscow and Beijing to the decision on launching this kind of offensive at this stage of the war?

Third, in the larger context of the anti-imperialist struggle, how were the objectives of the offensive related to perceptions of United States global difficulties?

## (1) The events of the actual offensive in January–February 1968

American impressions that the Communists did not achieve their initial objectives, at least in the Saigon area, were supported at the time by a number of captured documents – of which the most striking was a communication to senior cadres issued by the chief of the Central Committee Office in South Vietnam (Pham Hung) as early as the morning of 1 February 1968. That document acknowledged serious shortcomings during the initial stage and pointed to the danger that the American and South Vietnamese government forces might soon recover their strength and counterattack.[1] It also became evident during the first few days that – except for the city of Hue – the 'general offensive' against major cities and towns had failed to spark off a 'general uprising'. The government and armed forces of the Republic of Vietnam, which appeared to have been the primary target of the offensive, had survived largely intact.

In reappraising the course of events on the basis of new Vietnamese evidence, it has been possible to gain a better understanding both of the detailed planning and actual execution of offensive operations, and of the nature of the uprising they were intended to bring about. Insight into these questions has been gleaned from a series of articles and memoirs published in Hanoi in the period 1986–89, used in the analyses attempted by Ngo Vinh Long (1993) and R. E. Ford (1995).

What emerges very clearly from these memoirs of twenty years later is that the principal objective of the offensive was Saigon. One important article – by Tran Van Quang, who in 1968 had been commander of the 'Tri-Thien-Hue front' – tells us that the main targets of the 'TCK/TKN'[2] offensive were the cities of Saigon, Hue and Danang. He indicates that Hanoi's plan envisaged two principal theatres of operation, of which the primary one was Eastern Nam-Bo (the B-2 theatre, including Saigon) and the secondary one was Tri-Thien-Hue. The 'Highway 9 front', which by late 1967 was under separate command from that of Tri-Thien-Hue, was also important. Tran Van Quang's account suggests that although the initial purpose of operations there was to attract US forces away from other areas, there was also an intention 'when conditions permitted, to break a section of the enemy defensive line . . . paving the way for an advance to the South'.[3] Such a breakthrough might have permitted a full liberation of Hue and Danang.

All of this would seem to imply that the Central Highlands (Tay-Nguyen) front and the Mekong Delta were much less significant operational theatres. While the overall pattern of the offensive seems to show that one of its objects was to achieve nearly simultaneous attacks throughout the country, it may well be that there was no intention to hold towns in those areas for any length of time. Nevertheless the fighting for Pleiku and Kontum was very fierce; it may have been part of the plan to force a major American effort to defend those cities.

Another 1988 article – by Van Tien Dung, chief of staff of the PAVN from 1953 to 1980 – states categorically that 'not until 21 January was the actual decision taken to launch the offensive at midnight on the eve of the 1968 lunar new year of Mau-Than'.[4] One possible interpretation of this statement is that the final order depended on the PAVN commanders knowing for certain that their strategy of drawing US troops to northern I Corps (especially Khe Sanh) had actually worked, and that they themselves were capable of sustaining offensive operations there (which opened on 20 January). However, there is also a possibility that it was only on 21 January 1968 that the actual timing of the urban offensives – the early hours of 31 January – was finally decided. Such an interpretation is suggested by two other 1988 articles, which say that the original plan had been to launch the offensive shortly after the end of the Tet truce on 3 February.

A book published in Ho Chi Minh City in 1988, under the title *Mau Than Saigon*, includes articles by two southern Communist leaders: Tran Bach Dang, who commanded part of the forces which attacked Saigon from the South on 31 January 1968; and Pham Chanh Truc, at that time secretary of the (Viet Cong) Saigon Youth League. Both writers indicate that the date originally planned for the offensive in Saigon was 5 February, and that on the evening of 4–5 February there was to have been a large demonstration in the park near the Independence Palace to commemorate the 'Emperor Quang Trung Tet festival'. Pham Chanh Truc was in charge of planning this. It would appear that the plan was for a series of sapper attacks – on the US embassy, the Independence Palace and other targets – to be followed by an expansion of the mass demonstrations as well as the advance of PLAF 'vanguard units' into the city to take over places captured by the sappers. The latter would in turn be reinforced by larger main-force units waiting in the surrounding area. Tran Bach Dang says that the Politburo decided at the last minute to advance the date of the offensive, 'for some unexplained reason'; and Pham Chanh Truc's plans had to be abandoned.[5]

Ford speculates about one possible reason for the change, on the basis of the memoirs of a Hanoi spy on the staff of President Thieu (also published in 1988). He suggests that on 16 January 1968 a decision was taken by Thieu and Westmoreland to cut short the Tet truce, which would consequently end at 6.00 a.m. on 31 January. The decision was not announced until the 29th or 30th; but Ford argues that it was reported to Hanoi immediately, by the spy; and that the Politburo changed its own timetable accordingly on 21 January.[6] Such speculation cannot yet be confirmed, but it would fit in with the statement of Westmoreland that on 10 January – following new evidence of Communist troop movements around Saigon produced by the commander of the US Army's II Field Force – he issued an order to abandon earlier plans for the deployment of more US troops toward the Cambodian border and instead ordered a partial pull back to the Saigon area.[7] A decision to cut short the truce may well have been made soon afterwards. Moreover, even if the Americans had had some precise intelligence of what was planned for 5 February, they would still have been surprised when the offensive was actually launched on 31 January. Knowledge of the change of plan certainly helps to explain the confusion and sense of urgency on the Communist side that is evident from several of the captured documents.

The memoirs of the southerners imply, therefore, that the offensive in the Saigon area did not go according to plan. In a slightly later article, published in July 1988, Tran Bach Dang went further than before in criticising the strategy (presumably that of the Party Centre) of making Hanoi in 1945 or Leningrad in 1917 the models for a 'general uprising'. The model should have been that of the continuous uprisings in Ben Tre province in 1960.[8] An article by Tran Do (another senior military commander in the South) also includes wider reflections on the question of the kind of uprising that was practicable in the circumstances of 1968. He too suggests that what ought to have been attempted was a continuous mass uprising rather than one which sought to take over (or 'liberate') some urban areas completely. The Communist forces were not strong enough to resist the counter-attacks, which the second strategy would provoke. Tran Van Quang again emphasises that the meaning of 'uprising' was a continuing process, not a once-and-for-all event. Only complete military superiority, and complete disintegration of the 'puppet' forces could have permitted an effective liberation of Hue.[9]

The memoirs by Tran Bach Dang and by Tran Do indicate that some of the southern leaders, including Dang himself, were summoned to COSVN headquarters on 5 February 1968. They also tell us that Le Duc Tho went south at that time to hear their reports. One reason why things went wrong subsequently was that the southern commanders reported only their successes and did not allow Tho to know how much had gone wrong on the ground. That may have been the basis on which Hanoi eventually confirmed the decision to press ahead with further stages of the offensive later in the spring and early summer.[10]

Three other sectors of the 1968 offensive are much less adequately covered by the twentieth anniversary revelations: those of Khe Sanh and Highway 9; of the city and environs of Danang; and the fighting in the Mekong Delta.

There seems no longer any reason to doubt that the essential purpose behind the siege of Khe Sanh, and the various other attacks along Highway 9, was to oblige Westmoreland to concentrate ever larger numbers of troops in that area, leaving the lowlands and urban areas less adequately protected. Even so, it seems reasonable to ask whether Hanoi's plans did not also include the objective of inflicting very much heavier casualties on those forces than proved possible in the event. At Khe Sanh itself the experimental use of new tactics in B-52 bombing, and of anti-personnel sensors designed originally for use on the Ho Chi Minh trail, enabled the Americans to destroy far more of the besieging forces than the PAVN commanders could have expected; with the result that the US 1st Cavalry division was able to relieve the Marine base remarkably smoothly in early April. Had things gone differently, there would have been enough PAVN troops in the Highway 9 area to inflict massive casualties on that division. In the circumstances of early 1968, even casualties on the same scale as those in the Ia Drang Valley in 1965 would have been seen as a major disaster. But speculation along these lines will not be resolved unless Hanoi provides a detailed account of its own intentions and troop movements during the Highway 9 campaign.

The fighting round Danang is also difficult to assess, but it too may have been more significant than is suggested in most accounts of the period. Danang was one of the places (all in Central Vietnam) where the offensive began on the night of 29–30 January, 24 hours earlier than at Hue, Saigon and elsewhere. News agency reports during the following day indicated serious damage to American aircraft in mortar attacks on American bases in the area, but also the rapid defeat of an attack by local guerrilla forces on Danang city.[11] Simultaneously an attempt to take over Hoi An town, south of Danang, was also defeated in a matter of hours.

However, starting on 7 February a much more substantial advance toward Danang from the South was attempted by the 2nd division of the PAVN. That threat was taken very seriously by Westmoreland, who was obliged to send reinforcements to meet it. It took three days of heavy fighting before the PAVN abandoned the attempt on 10 February and withdrew.[12]

That engagement illustrates clearly what seems to have been one of the most serious problems of the whole Tet Mau Than offensive: the difficulty, in a fast changing situation, of ensuring proper coordination between local Communist forces – recruited in various parts of South Vietnam – and North Vietnamese main force units operating under a different command structure. The problem was acknowledge by Tran Van Quang in his article of 1988: writing of his own experience at Hue he noted that in planning the Tet Mau Than offensive, Communist leaders had 'made light of the all round preparations necessary for combining the people's war with the combat operations of main force units'. He went on to observe that this shortcoming had been overcome by the time of the Spring Offensive of 1972, in which he was himself again involved.[13]

The offensive in the Mekong Delta, where most of the provincial towns came under attack, may also have been 'diversionary' in the sense that its main purpose was probably to tie down ARVN forces which might otherwise have been moved to counter the assault on Saigon. The attacks on the Delta towns all failed, but there is evidence to suggest that the outcome might have been more serious for the Saigon side. In several places there seems to have been a deliberate intention to coerce ARVN commanders into changing sides by kidnapping them and their families during the Tet holiday. A prisoner who was interrogated following an unsuccessful guerrilla attack on the home of the commander of the 9th ARVN division at Sa Dec, revealed a plan to capture the general and his family, to blackmail him into summoning his immediate subordinates, and then to force him to turn over his division to the PLAF or face immediate execution. The commander of the 7th ARVN division also narrowly escaped a similar plan.[14]

Unfortunately we do not have any detailed accounts of the Delta battles from the Communist side. But we should note the proximity of the Mekong Delta to the Cambodian border, across which supplies could have moved more freely if some of the towns had fallen. Particularly important in this respect was the battle for Chau Doc, very close to the border, which was saved largely by the presence in the area of US Navy SEAL teams. The fighting there was important enough for Rostow to bring it to the direct attention of President Johnson on 2 February.[15]

The above points will be sufficient to indicate that the information so far available from the Communist side on the operational level is still only fragmentary. Even so, it is important to take such evidence into account when trying to assess new materials relating to the higher levels of decision-making. In attempting to build up a multi-faceted Communist perspective, we should be careful not to repeat the mistake – evident in many of the American writings – of allowing the study of decision-making to become largely divorced from studies on the operational level. The articles published in 1988 suggest that the view from Hanoi is not enough for an understanding of the events of 1968.

## (2) The sequence of decision-making in Hanoi

A logical starting-point for the exploration of decision-making in Hanoi, throughout the period 1954–75, is the official history published by the PAVN itself in 1980. Regarding the origins of the offensive of Tet Mau Than, that account emphasises two stages of decision-making by the Vietnam Workers' Party leadership. In June 1967 'the Party Central Committee met to evaluate our people's great victory in inflicting a very basic defeat on the US imperialists' limited war ...' and to consider the next stage. In December, 'the Politburo met and issued the historic resolution on "transforming our revolutionary war in the South to a new phase – the phase of winning a decisive victory" ', which was then 'approved by the [14th] Plenum of the Party Central Committee in January 1968'.[16] However, it is clear from the memoirs appearing in Communist publications of the period 1986–89 that the actual sequence was more complicated. The 1980 account was probably intended to mask the more controversial aspects of the Hanoi debate. In addition to the articles used by Ford and by Ngo Vinh Long, there is also a fairly detailed account of the decision-making sequence in the second volume of the official history of the PAVN published in 1988.[17]

The first stage of the sequence unfolded between April and June (or perhaps the first week of July). Already by April it was becoming apparent – to officials and military leaders in Hanoi and Washington alike – that the situation on the battlefield in South Vietnam was approaching a stalemate; and that, despite the optimism of Communist propaganda, this could not be left to continue for year after year. The starting-point of Hanoi's reassessment seems to have been a meeting of the Party Politburo and Central Military Commission in April 1967 to consider 'how to secure a decisive victory'.[18] By June, according to the 1988 official history, the Politburo approved a 'strategic resolution' which included two objectives: to 'win a decisive victory in a short period of time' and to 'force the Americans to admit defeat, militarily'.[19] But it is by no means clear that this resolution amounted to a precise plan for implementing such a decision. Another important source, however, suggests that the leadership was already contemplating action of some kind in the urban areas. On 1 July, Party first secretary Le Duan, after reading reports from the South by Tran Bach Dang, sent a letter to the Zone Committee (*khu-uy*) of Saigon-Gia Dinh which attempted a thorough analysis of the urban struggle, its techniques and opportunities, starting from a critique of the failure of the 1966 Buddhist uprising in Danang-Hue.[20]

The end of this first stage coincided with the death of one of the two leading generals on the Communist side, Nguyen Chi Thanh, officially reported as taking place in Hanoi on 6 July 1967.[21] Since at least 1964 he had been in command of Communist main forces in the South as well as secretary of the Central Committee's Office in South Vietnam (COSVN), but he had travelled North in April in order to take part in the Politburo's review of the situation. A major issue in several American analyses of the Hanoi debate and decisions of mid-1967 has been the question of Nguyen Chi Thanh's relationship to the most senior Vietnamese Communist leader Vo Nguyen Giap. It was given especially strong emphasis by Patrick McGarvey (of the CIA) in an analysis of 1969, and later by Philip Davidson (chief of MACV's intelligence operations in 1967–68) in a history of the war published in the United States in 1988.[22]

There is every reason to believe that as early as the 1950s the rivalry between Vo Nguyen Giap and Nguyen Chi Thanh was well known among their subordinates. From 1950 to 1961 Thanh was head of the general political directorate of the PAVN, which put him in charge of political education and political authorisation of decisions – in a system where the Party must 'command the gun'. Giap, as commander in chief was more concerned with the professional modernisation of Vietnamese military capabilities, which involved training and other assistance from the Soviet Union as well as China. It seems probable that the promotion of Thanh to be full general in 1959, giving him the same rank which Giap alone had enjoyed until then, was an attempt by someone (perhaps Le Duan) to put a break on Giap's prestige and influence within the leadership. It is also known that Nguyen Chi Thanh – perhaps as early as 1961, certainly by the end of 1964 – was given secret responsibility for over-seeing the southern struggle; which may well have reduced Giap's direct involvement in the South before mid-1967. As early as 1963, Thanh's articles show him as a strong advocate of defying the power of the United States rather than giving in to it – which was the line actually adopted by Hanoi in 1963–4 and sustained over the following three years.

What is much more questionable is the suggestion, by both McGarvey and by Davidson, that Vo Nguyen Giap was (in Davidson's word's) 'adamantly and consistently opposed' to the plan for the Tet Offensive as it was taking shape in the latter part of 1967. In the debates of April–June, before the death of Thanh, they place Vo Nguyen Giap and Truong Chinh on one side of the argument (opposing the offensive) with Le Duan and Nguyen Chi Thanh on the other (in favour of it). More generally, Davidson suggests that throughout the period 1960–67 Giap and Truong Chinh were 'North firsters', in that they believed in giving priority to building and protecting the North and leaving the revolution in the South to be resolved by the southerners, whereas Le Duan and Thanh were 'South firsters' who believed in massive military involvement by PAVN regular forces to ensure the final victory of the revolution in the South.

It is certainly possible to speculate that Giap *may* have had doubts about the extent to which the North would be left vulnerable if too many PAVN regulars were sent south; his own task was, above all, to defend the North. It is also possible to *speculate* that Giap was unhappy about the need for North Vietnam to rely on Chinese military support for its own defence, and about the presence inside North Vietnam of between 30,000 (1965) and 170,000 (early 1968) Chinese PLA troops. But we have no firm knowledge of this; nor is it part of Davidson's argument.

We need, nevertheless, to deconstruct the McGarvey–Davidson hypothesis as it stands – not least because it raises important issues about the kind of interpretation of published Communist statements that is permissible as we approach the task of relating them to previously secret archival materials and to the revelations contained in memoirs. We need, above all, to be clear about the general nature of the relationship, in the 1960s and 1970s, between high-level decision-making and the output of the Communist news media. Party decision-making almost certainly involved serious disagreements at the highest level, behind closed doors. But once, a decision was reached, the consensus had to be maintained: everyone must support and implement the 'correct line'. Divergences of implementation might arise as a result of complicated command structures or of failures in lower-level cooperation. But it was not permitted for one leader to publicly challenge a course of action once it had been agreed. It is therefore extremely risky to 'read between the lines' in the hope of using published articles to discern the actual thoughts and opinions of individual leaders. Both Giap and Thanh were members of a Politburo whose decisions must be accepted.

An important element in McGarvey's 1969 analysis was his interpretation of an article by Nguyen Chi Thanh, which had appeared one year before the mid-1967 meetings, in the July 1966 issue of the Party journal *Hoc-Tap*. He focuses particularly on a passage in which Thanh openly criticised people who 'mechanically copy ... past experiences or experiences of foreign countries' and who worry too much about numerical superiority over the enemy.[23] McGarvey sees this as a veiled attack on Vo Nguyen Giap. But neither McGarvey nor Davidson takes adequate account of the wider background of the article. The passage in question had originally occurred in a speech by Le Duan at a 'Determined to Win' conference of young recruits to the PAVN on 18–19 May, but not reported until 26 July 1966. On 4–5 August, Giap's own speech to the same conference was also reported.[24] It is true that Giap's speech did not include the reference to 'foreign experiences, etc', and that he placed special emphasis (as always) on the virtues of protracted war. But it was nonetheless an aggressive speech, essentially in keeping with the ideas expressed by Le Duan and by Thanh.

I have argued elsewhere that the speeches at the 18–19 May 1966 conference, and the timing of their publication in late July and early August, should be seen in the light of events in China and their implications for Vietnam.[25] There had been a sharp contrast during 1965 between the military ideas expressed by the PLA chief of staff Luo Ruiqing (pro-Stalinist, believing in vigorous military attack) and by the Chinese minister of defence Lin Biao (advocating protracted, low-level guerrilla warfare). The apparent Chinese 'strategic debate', however, was overtaken in 1966 by the Cultural Revolution, in which Luo was purged and Lin Biao's ('Maoist') line triumphed. The removal of Luo (and also that of Peng Zhen) was made known to Chinese Party members on 16 May 1966; and Mao's own triumph was publicly evident by 26 July, following his swim in the Yangtzi. The real target of the speeches by Le Duan and by Giap (and of Thanh's article) seems to have been the Lin Biao line in China – and those in the Vietnamese Party who wanted to follow the Chinese model by reverting to 'protracted war' in the South rather than continuing to use heavy weapons to attack the Americans. It is quite possible that Giap was less impressed than Thanh by 'frontal assault' tactics against the Americans; but there is no reason to imagine he was advocating the Lin Biao line. If anything he was an admirer of the 'Soviet model' rather than of any

'Chinese model'. My argument is that all the top PAVN leaders were in favour of continuing the PAVN role in the South at this point; but they could not afford to offend the Chinese by openly attacking Lin Biao.

Returning to 1967, there certainly seems to have been a major strategy debate in Hanoi (starting in April–May) about how to overcome the 'stalemate' situation, and how to resolve the conflict in a relatively short period of time. But we have no knowledge concerning the views expressed by either Nguyen Chi Thanh or Vo Nguyen Giap behind closed doors. We must accept that we simply do not know if the rivalry between them extended to a direct confrontation over what ought to be done about the situation in the early summer of 1967. Nor, even if a conflict occurred, do we have any evidence to indicate the precise issues being debated or the different 'solutions' being proposed. We know only that some kind of offensive was envisaged by the time of Thanh's death in early July, but that a great deal more analysis had to take place before a complete 'plan' emerged. We do not know for certain that a final decision to attack the cities had actually been made *before* the death of Thanh; we certainly have no basis for suggesting that Giap opposed it.

The month of July itself was probably crucial. It may well be that in the aftermath of Thanh's death – and also in the light of an improvement in Soviet–American relations in late June – a serious effort was made by some leading figures in Hanoi to explore the possibility of a negotiated solution. There may have been Soviet pressure urging Hanoi in that direction. We should also take note of what was happening in China, where the Cultural Revolution had led to growing political chaos in many provincial cities. Almost a year after Mao's celebrated swim in the Yangtzi, he was again at Wuhan in July 1967 – but this time in order to deal with a major factional conflict which at one point looked as though it might lead to a breakdown of central control in that city.[26] The importance of Wuhan as a focal point of Chinese internal communications had been greatly enhanced in 1957 with the building of the rail and road bridge there, making it the lowest point at which the Yangtzi could be crossed without depending on ferries. Loss of the bridge would have seriously weakened Mao's control over southern China – a fear reflected soon afterwards in his urgent command to build another bridge, at Nanjing, as rapidly as possible.

We have no knowledge of any Vietnamese analysis of events in China at this critical moment; but even if Hanoi's concern about the situation was short-lived, there was certainly reason during the second half of July to avoid exclusive dependence on Chinese military support in the continuing war against the United States. Slightly more is known about Soviet attitudes at this juncture. Moscow's concern about the level of Chinese influence in Hanoi has been documented by Ilya Gaiduk, who found records of three relevant exchanges: on 13 June 1967 the Soviet ambassador in Hanoi (Shcherbakov) had a conversation on the subject of Chinese aid to Vietnam with a PAVN general, Nguyen Van Vinh. A month later, on 14 July, a memorandum from the Soviet defence ministry to the CPSU Central Committee, estimated that the number of Chinese troops in Vietnam at this time numbered 60,000 to 100,000. In the meantime a Soviet Memorandum of

30 June – entitled 'Some new Moments (*sic*) in the attitude of the VNWP to the Vietnamese Problem' – included the estimate that by then the PAVN had deployed around 120,000 regular troops – out of a total main force of 300,000 – in South Vietnam.[27]

Soviet policy at this time was probably governed principally by a desire to undercut Chinese influence in Vietnam. But that could be done in either of two ways: by encouraging a negotiated solution, if the Americans could be persuaded to compromise; or by giving more Soviet military assistance to allow Hanoi to step up the war. A logical combination of the two alternatives might be possible, however: the Russians could assist – if not actively encourage – the Vietnamese to mount one more major offensive in the South, on a sufficient scale to inflict a short-term defeat on the Americans, which would convince them of the futility of continuing the conflict. We should not, therefore, assume that the Russians were necessarily seeking to restrain Hanoi from a military plan that was designed to hasten the end of the war rather than to prolong it indefinitely.

The first alternative may have been tried in July, in the aftermath of the Glassboro meeting between President Johnson and the Soviet premier Kosygin (23–25 June 1967). Moscow may at that point have made one last attempt to persuade both Washington and Hanoi to seek a negotiated solution. On 23 July the Chinese newspaper *Renmin Ribao* carried a sharp attack on the 'insidious collaboration policy' of the Soviet Union towards the United States in relation to Vietnam.[28] This happened to coincide with the first move in what the Americans later dubbed the 'Pennsylvania' peace initiative. On 24 July premier Pham Van Dong, together with President Ho himself, received an unofficial French delegation in Hanoi, consisting of the leftwing scholars Raymond Aubrac and Herbert Marcovitch, who had been in touch with the Harvard political scientist Henry Kissinger at a recent Pugwash Conference.[29] Nothing came of that initiative in the end, despite the seriousness with which it was taken by the White House between mid-August and October; but Pham Van Dong's remarks on 24 July may possibly have been a sincere attempt to bring about a negotiated solution.

Alternatively, the whole episode may have been an exercise in deception, designed to keep alive Western liberal hopes for negotiations while concealing Hanoi's real plans for the coming months. In any case, the Aubrac–Marcovitch visit was secret; North Vietnam's public 'line' was moving in the opposite direction. On 22 July the PAVN newspaper *Quan Doi Nhan Dan* carried an article by the deputy head of the general political directorate, Le Quang Dao. Under the title: 'The Anti-US National Salvation Struggle is very violent but will certainly achieve complete victory', it insisted that 'there is no alternative' to waging 'an extremely violent revolutionary struggle', and that 'if one deviates from the path of revolution through violence, he will enter the path of reforms and compromise'.[30] The one firm piece of evidence that suggests there may actually have been a 'peace party' in Hanoi at this time, reflecting a serious division within the Party, was the arrest on 27 July of the ideologist Hoang Minh Chinh, who had been identified as a supporter of 'peaceful coexistence' as early as 1963–4.[31] After the end of July, there seems to have been no possibility of negotiations until the planned offensive in the South had run its course.

The next stage in the decision-making sequence can be identified as that of detailed operational planning and directives, lasting from July to the end of October 1967. The first clear formulation of 'plans to carry the revolutionary war to the highest stage, that of General Offensive, General Uprising (*TCK/TKN*)' was probably that contained in a report to the Party Politburo and CMC by the PAVN General Staff, sometime in July. It defined a series of objectives which included: 'surprise attacks on the cities of Saigon, Hue and Danang'; 'striking at main forces of the "puppets" and at mobile forces of the US on the battlefronts of mountain and forest areas' and to 'disintegrate an important part of the US-puppet forces'; to 'overthrow the puppet administration'; and to 'break the aggressive willpower of the Americans'.[32] Also in July a decision was taken to establish a 'Fourth Front' within Military Region V (*Quan khu* V), to focus on attacking Danang; included three battalions of infantry and one regiment of artillery, with rockets.[33]

By the beginning of September, judging from the date of a document later captured in Tay Ninh province entitled 'Instructional material to help understand the new situation and our new task', southern cadres were being indoctrinated on the tasks of the three-pronged offensive, whose objectives were those of defeating the forces of ARVN, destroying military and political institutions of the GVN, and achieving a general uprising. The document also made reference to the establishment of a coalition government.[34]

A significant stage in military planning seems to have been completed by mid-September. A memoir of 1980 gives 10 September as the date of instructions given to Hoang Minh Thao, the PAVN general who was being sent to take command of the B-3 Front and to open the 'Dak To campaign', whose aim was to force the Americans to deploy more troops to Central Highlands.[35] A few days later, on 14–16 September, *Quan Doi Nhan Dan* published the celebrated article of Vo Nguyen Giap, 'The Big Victory, the Great Task', on which American intelligence analysts based their supposition that Giap favoured 'protracted war' and was opposed to the new offensive strategy.[36] The article seems to have been an indoctrination text, intended to be read by PAVN officers, to make them aware of the weaknesses of the Americans and the possibilities of military and political success in general terms. The reason why it does not give any account of the strategy to be followed in the coming offensive is probably that the details had not yet been fully worked out at that stage.

The main body of the offensive plan for TCK/TKN, as it affected the southern cities, seems to have been completed by late October. It was embodied in the Central Committee's 'Resolution 14' for which the precise date of 25 October is given in a book published in HCM City in 1988, with reference specifically to the attacks planned against Saigon and the towns of the upper Mekong Delta.[37] Tran Van Tra, commander of forces of the B-2 Front, also gives late October or early November as the date at which COSVN was informed of the 'Politburo Resolution' ordering the TCK/TKN offensive.[38] This chronology would fit, too, with the date (30 October 1967) on which the DRVN National Assembly Standing Committee approved the 'Decree on Punishment of Counter-revolutionary Crimes', which was promulgated by President Ho on 10 November 1967.[39]

Soon after 25 October, the Party first secretary Le Duan – accompanied by Vo Nguyen Giap and Nguyen Duy Trinh – left for Moscow to attend the fiftieth anniversary of the Russian October Revolution. Ho Chi Minh did not go, but on 4 November TASS reported that he had been awarded the Order of Lenin. Also on that day *Nhan Dan* published Le Duan's article for the anniversary: 'Forward under the glorious banner of the October Revolution', which with hindsight can be seen as giving a much clearer picture than Giap's article of the actual thinking of the VNWP Politburo on the next stage of the war. It analysed the relationship between armed and political struggle, and placed special emphasis on the need to coordinate the struggle in the countryside with that in the cities: 'The seething struggle of the urban masses has created highly favourable conditions for uprisings in the countryside and the extension of people's war'.[40] What is yet to be revealed, but is no doubt contained in the Soviet archives, is the answer to the question whether Le Duan and Vo Nguyen Giap discussed their plans for the coming offensive with their Soviet comrades.

## (3) The wider perspective and the global vulnerability of the Americans

Two tentative conclusions emerge from the above analysis:

First, the essential objective of the Tet Mau Than offensive – the sense in which it aimed at 'a decisive victory' – was probably to break the confidence of the Americans in their own ability to achieve military victory; and with it, their will to continue the war. This objective was to be achieved by means of: (a) disintegrating the Saigon government structure, by attacking its nerve centres in the cities and by forcing its military commanders to capitulate; and (b) creating circumstances favourable for a Communist-led political uprising in Saigon and elsewhere, which would lead in turn to a political crisis and the formation of a coalition government. The success of such a strategy would undercut the opposition of the United States in South Vietnam, by depriving them of a non-Communist regime to which they could commit their support. The offensive was thus in line with the analysis made by Le Duc Tho and by Nguyen Van Vinh in their early 1966 interpretations of the 12th resolution of the VNWP Central Committee. They acknowledged that Vietnamese main forces could never inflict absolute military defeat on those of the United States. But neither was that necessary: their aim must be to destroy the Saigon regime, militarily and politically.[41]

In the circumstances of mid-1967, however, it was unlikely that the US will to continue would be broken completely by this strategy alone. It was also necessary to inflict unacceptable casualties on American combat divisions. This could be achieved by means of a series of attacks in the upland areas, to which the Americans would have no choice but to respond: notably on the Highway 9 and B-3 (Central Highlands) fronts. The combination of a political-military offensive against the cities and military campaigns in the uplands would leave the Americans with no choice but to negotiate on Communist terms. In some respects the Tet offensive as a whole – not just the battle for Khe Sanh – was comparable with the battle of Dien Bien Phu in 1954. Both were campaigns designed to break the will of the enemy, in the context of anticipated negotiations which it was hoped would bring the conflict to an end on terms acceptable to the Communist side.

Secondly, it would appear that this offensive strategy – designed to force the Americans to accept a negotiated withdrawal – had the full support of Moscow, whose strategy of detente with Washington would provide the diplomatic framework necessary to allow the Americans to 'save face'. This impression is reinforced by a Chinese document recording a conversation in Beijing on 29 June 1968, between Zhou Enlai and the Vietnamese Politburo-member Pham Hung (who had taken over Nguyen Chi Thanh's role as chief Party secretary of COSVN). That conversation, which took place in the aftermath of a second series of attacks in Saigon in May–June, implies that Zhou Enlai regarded the attacks on the cities as a Soviet idea; and one which did not have full Chinese approval. He contrasts the 'tactics of using the countryside to encircle the urban areas' (which the Chinese preferred) with the Soviet opinion that 'lightning attacks on big cities are decisive'.[42]

The Soviet analysis of the situation depended on more than their perception of the stalemate in Vietnam. In the wider perspective of global anti-imperialism, the Tet offensive had an additional significance: as a means to weaken further the global power of the United States. The question of Soviet, North Vietnamese and also Chinese perceptions of American global weakness is one which we might usefully approach, at least in the first instance, by way of public statements rather than still secret archives. This can be done on the American as well as on the Communist side.

One of the most important public statements about United States strategy in Vietnam, relating it with remarkable candour to America's global difficulties, was Lyndon Johnson's celebrated address of 31 March 1968. In addition to announcing a cutback of the bombing of North Vietnam and offering to enter into negotiations, Johnson indicated the close relationship between the ability to deploy more American troops to Vietnam and the seriousness of the United States economic and financial dilemma. The cost of the war was now weighing heavily on the US budget, leading to a deficit, which could only be remedied by a tax surcharge – a measure strongly opposed by the Congress. In the absence of a reduction of the deficit, and in a situation where the American balance of payments was also in trouble, any decision to put another two hundred thousand troops into Vietnam would have had disastrous consequences for the whole United States position in the world.

International pressure on the value of the dollar, in terms of the dollar price of gold in the world market, had been growing since the devaluation of sterling in November 1967. It reached a peak in mid-March 1968, when world central bankers met in Washington to decouple the private gold market from the Bretton Woods arrangements between central banks, which depended on the price of gold remaining fixed at $35 per ounce. By the end of March, Johnson knew that the immediate gold crisis had been resolved, and that the International Monetary Fund had finally agreed to the creation of 'special drawing rights', which would ease longer term pressure on the dollar as the world's principal reserve currency. But the condition of a return to stability was – in effect – an end to the escalation of the war in Vietnam. Johnson had no choice but to limit further troop commitments to a level of 13,500, instead of the 206,000 requested by Westmoreland. It meant, too, an end to the search-and-destroy strategy in Vietnam and – in effect – any possibility of an eventual military victory.

In this sense, one might argue that in spite of the failure of the offensive itself to work out according to Hanoi's plans, and despite the survival intact of the Saigon regime and its armed forces, their strategy had achieved its one most important objective of convincing the Americans they could not win; and – it seemed – of the need for negotiations. The question which then arises is: how far were these wider aspects of United States vulnerability an element in the strategy itself? How far was the real target of Tet Mau Than the global weakness of the United States, whose Achilles heel was now displayed for all to see in South Vietnam?

Chinese awareness of the link between Vietnam and the global monetary and financial crisis facing the United States was already being expressed early in the year: notably in an article in the 26 January issue of *Peking Review*, which commented that 'from the financial and economic point of view the war of aggression against Vietnam is like a bottomless pit'. It went on:

> What warrants particular attention is the fact that the position of the dollar has become increasingly precarious since the devaluation of the pound. The continuation of the war of aggression against Vietnam will only speed up the deterioration of U.S. finance and its international payments. This is another contradiction, which U.S. imperialism, obstinately bent on expanding the war of aggression, can never solve.[43]

In Hanoi, Vo Nguyen Giap was also aware of this dimension of the war. One of the most important passages in his article of mid-September 1967 reads as follows:

> As for the enemy, although his economic and military potential is great, it is obvious that the more he intensifies the war of aggression in Vietnam, the more weakened he becomes and the more difficulties he encounters. Although great, the U.S. military forces have been scattered in many parts of the world. The U.S. imperialists must cope with the national liberation movement, with the socialist bloc, with the American people and with other imperialist countries. [They]...cannot mobilise all their forces for the war of aggression in Vietnam. The present mobilisation level has far exceeded initial U.S. forecasts and is at variance with U.S. global strategy. At present the U.S. does not have enough troops to meet Westmoreland's requirements.

146  *Communist Indochina*

In another passage, he refers to the opening of a 'new front' in the Middle East for the Americans to worry about; and a little further on to the 'growing budget deficit, troubles with the Congress, with the allies, and with the dollar'.[44]

The Tet offensive, whose first objective was to bring about the political collapse of South Vietnam, also had the larger purpose of forcing the United States to admit that its problems in the global arena, both military and financial, were too great to allow continuation of the war in Vietnam. It is difficult to tell, even with hindsight, what the United States might have done if the offensive had indeed succeeded in achieving its objectives, and if the Saigon regime had actually collapsed.

## Notes

1. Translated in P. J. McGarvey, *Visions of Victory: Selected Vietnamese Communist Military Writings 1964–1968* (Stanford: Hoover Institution, 1969), pp 252–6.
2. These are the Vietnamese initials used in many of the documents as an abbreviation for 'General Offensive/General Uprising'.
3. R.E. Ford, Tet 1968: *Understanding the Surprise* (Portland, Oregon, 1995), pp. 118–19.
4. The same article confirms that 'Saigon-Gia Dinh was the main target'; and that the purpose of 'powerful attacks all along Route 9' was 'to draw US main force troops away from the cities'; Ford (1995), p. 209; also pp. 106 and 107.
5. Ngo Vinh Long, 'The Tet Offensive and its Aftermath', in eds Jayne Werner and David Hunt, *The American War in Vietnam* (Cornell Univ. SEA Program, 1993), p. 35; and Ford (1995), pp. 124–5, 127–8.
6. Ford (1995) pp. 126 and 143 n.32.
7. Wm. C. Westmoreland, *A Soldier Reports* (New York, 1976; 2nd edn 1989), p. 318.
8. Ngo Vinh Long (1993), p. 34.
9. Ford (1995) pp. 122 and 135–6.
10. Ford (1995) pp. 130, and 142 n.5.
11. These reports received little attention after being overtaken by the more dramatic news from Saigon early on the 31st; I am grateful to friends at the Reuters Archive in London for allowing me to see copies of the original news agency reports about Danang.
12. See MACV Command History 1968: vol ii, Annex A, pp. 884–5; consulted at Military History Institute, Carlisle Barracks, Pennsylvania.
13. Ford (1993), p. 123.
14. Information obtained by the MACV deputy commander Creighton Abrams, during a visit to the Delta, and reported by Westmoreland in a message to Washington on 4 February 1968: Lyndon Johnson Library: Papers of Wm. C. Westmoreland: Box 16, item 55.
15. Lyndon Johnson Library, National Security Files: Rostow Memos to the President: Box 28, vol. 59, item 85. The memo relates mainly to intelligence concerning preparations for the attack on Chau Doc, but is unfortunately heavily sanitized. For a brief account of the SEAL operation, see T.L. Bosiljevac, *SEALS: UDT/SEAL Operations in Vietnam* (New York, 1990), pp. 86–8.
16. *The Anti-US Resistance War for National Salvation 1954–1975: Military-Events*. Vietnamese original completed 30 May 1980 by War Experiences Recapitulation Committee of the High Level Military Institute, and published by the People's Army Publishing House in Hanoi; English translation in JPRS 80968 (Washington DC, 1982), pp. 100–1.
17. Ministry of Defence, Institute of Vietnamese Military History: *Lich-Su Quan-Doi Nhan-Dan Viet-Nam, tap. ii, quyen mot* ('History of the People's Army of Vietnam', vol. 2, part 1), Hanoi, 1988; referred to below as *LSQDND* (1988).

18 *LSQDND* (1988), pp. 369–70. This meeting, placed in April or May, is also referred to in 1988 articles by Tran Van Quang and by Van Tien Dung who refer to it as approving Politburo Resolution no. 13; Ford (1993), pp. 123–4 and 206.
19 *LSQDND* (1988), p. 370.
20 Le Duan, *Thu vao Nam* (Hanoi, 1985), pp. 158ff.
21 Hanoi radio reports to this effect at the time are now confirmed by Bui Tin's memoir, *Following Ho Chi Minh, the Memoirs of a North Vietnamese Colonel* (London, 1995), pp. 61–2.
22 McGarvey (1969), P.B. Davidson, *Vietnam at War: the History 1945–1975*, (Novato, California, 1988)
23 The text of the article is translated by McGarvey (1969) pp. 61–71; his commentary appears on pp. 11–12.
24 Translated in BBC, *Summary of World Broadcasts*: FE/2234, 2235 and 2237. For the broadcast of Thanh's article, on 24 July 1966, see *ibid*. FE/2234.
25 *An International History of the Vietnam War* vol. iii (Macmillan, London, 1991) pp. 337 and 354–5. The importance of Le Duan's speech at the May conference, as indicating a Vietnamese military line independent of that favoured by China in 1966, was first noted by D.S. Zagoria, *Vietnam Triangle: Moscow, Peking, Hanoi* N.Y. (1967).
26 For a detailed account of the Wuhan Incident, which came to a head on 20 July 1967, see Yen Chia-chi and Kao Kao, *Ten Year History of the Chinese Cultural Revolution* (1988); based partly on the memoirs of Chen Zadao, the PLA commander at Wuhan.
27 I.V. Gaiduk, *The Soviet Union and the Vietnam War* (Chicago, 1996), pp. 60 and 64–5.
28 Translated in *Peking Review*, 28 July 1967.
29 United States–Vietnam Relations 1945–1967, VI.C.4: reproduced in G.C. Herring (ed.), *The Secret Diplomacy of the Vietnam War* (Austin: University of Texas, 1983), pp. 717–25.
30 Quoted in P. McGarvey (1969), p.22.
31 Hoang Minh Chinh's statement of 27 August 1993. See paper by Judy Stowe (later published as 'Revisionisme au Vietnam' in *Approaches Asie*, no. 18, 2003).
32 *LSQDND* (1988), pp. 370–1. We do not know whether this report was made before or after the death of Nguyen Chi Thanh on 6 July; in any case, the *LSQDND* account does not indicate any final decision to adopt the above proposal at this stage.
33 *LSQDND* (1988), p. 378.
34 Translated in *Vietnam Documents and Research Notes* (US Embassy, Saigon), no 20. Also on 1 Sept. 1967, a Special Congress of the NLFSVN approved a new political programme aiming at coalition.
35 Hoang Minh Thao, in article of 1980 cited by Ford, (1995) pp. 97, 98.
36 Broadcast by Hanoi Radio, 17–20 Sept. 1967. An English translation was published by Praeger, New York in spring 1968, with introduction by David Schoenbrun; also translated in P. McGarvey (1969).
37 A collection of memoirs entitled *Mau Than Saigon*: see Ford (1995), p. 79. The same resolution is referred to as 'the October Resolution of the Party Central Committee' in the article of Tran Van Quang, commander of the Tri-Thien-Hue military command: Ford (1995), p. 81.
38 Tran Van Tra' article of 1988, translated in J.S. Werner and Luu Doan Huynh, *The Vietnam War: Vietnamese and American Perspectives* (Armonk, NY M. E. Sharpe, 1993) pp. 39ff. He gives details of the resolution, but not its precise date.
39 Not published till late March 1968; text translated in *Vietnam Documents and Research Notes* (DS Embassy Saigon), no 26, April, 1968. See Stowe (2003) for its significance.
40 Translated in BBC, *Summary of World Broadcasts*, FE/2616/c/1–17; also in *Vietnam Documents and Research Notes*, no 9, Dec. 1967.
41 See discussion in R.B. Smith, *An International History of the Vietnam War*, vol. iii (1991), pp. 237–40.

42 I am grateful to Odd Arne Westad and Chen Jian for allowing me to see a copy of this document, which is to be included in a forthcoming selection of Chinese Party and diplomatic documents.
43 *Peking Review*, 26 Jan. 1968, pp. 18–19. A later article, in the issue for 5 April 1968, offered a penetrating short analysis of the dollar crisis as a whole.
44 General Vo Nguyen Giap, '*Big Victory, Great Task*' (New York and London, 1968), pp. 90, 97.

# 7 The international setting of the Cambodia crisis, 1969–1970

Source: *The International History Review* 18(2) (1996): 253–504.

> This is why we have renounced U.S. aid and accepted extreme poverty. But although we are miserable, the Khmer Reds still say that we have sold out the country to the Americans. This is not true. And if the Khmer Reds still continue to accuse us in this way, they will drive the Sangkum into a corner ... We are still continuing to struggle, and if they stop their activities so much the better. But if they go on creating insecurity and waging war in all the provinces, that will be the end of it. In that event – I must tell the priests – it will be necessary to dissolve the Sangkum and to hand over power to the military authorities, which would be led by Lon Nol, who will be like Suharto in Indonesia ... It will be up to him to decide whether we should accept U.S. aid again.
>
> Prince Norodom Sihanouk[1]

The emotions generated by the United States war in Indo-China have bedevilled the writing of its history. This is especially true of President Richard M. Nixon's decision to send US combat units beyond the border of South Vietnam, at the end of April 1970, to destroy a series of Vietnamese Communist military bases which had previously enjoyed the status of sanctuaries in supposedly neutral Cambodia. As has happened so often in the historiography of 'Vietnam', little attempt has been made to analyse the course of events as an episode in the continuous history of a war: as a sequence properly understood only when its military, political, and diplomatic dimensions are examined– so far as the sources allow – from all sides. The military story is told only in a handful of works dealing with specific aspects of the campaign, or with the role of individual American units;[2] no official history has yet given a comprehensive account of the combined United States– South Vietnamese operations. The decision itself has been set mainly into the highly charged context of US politics and the exercise of presidential power; and so far, apart from the memoirs of those in office at the time, it has been examined without the benefit of access to the national security files of the Nixon White House.[3] On the Communist side, North Vietnam's role has been treated largely as a response to US actions, rather than as the result of its own long-standing ambitions.

Sufficient evidence is now available to show that Nixon reached his decision to invade the sanctuaries between 17 and 26 April 1970. In time, access to the archival record will permit detailed analysis, day by day and even hour by hour, of the high-level debates and planning sessions that took place in Washington, Honolulu, and Saigon. This article will not attempt to forestall that endeavour, but will place the decision – and the campaign that followed it – in the wider context of the events of the preceding eight months.

By the autumn of 1969, the Nixon administration had reached two conclusions. First, the United States had given up the hope – if it had ever been realistic – of winning a decisive military victory in Vietnam: a solution would depend on a negotiated agreement. Second, the United States could not sustain indefinitely the level of over 500,000 troops currently committed to the ground war in South Vietnam: with or without an agreement, these forces would gradually be withdrawn. On the other hand, it *was* still assumed to be possible – indeed necessary, from the point of view of US global credibility – to prevent the enemy from winning a military victory: North Vietnam must be compelled to negotiate an end to the fighting on terms acceptable to the United States. It remained a moot point in Washington whether the United States should try to ensure the survival of an independent, non-Communist South Vietnam – at least for long enough to allow its population an opportunity for genuine self-determination through free elections. This aim certainly featured in Nixon's first major public pronouncement on the Vietnam War, when on 14 May 1969 he outlined his thoughts on a negotiated settlement.[4]

The remarkably coherent US strategy in Vietnam, as it had evolved by October 1969, contained four key elements. First, pending a negotiated settlement, US forces would be withdrawn unilaterally, at a pace determined by Washington. The first step in the 'redeployment' had been announced by Nixon and the president of the Republic of Vietnam, Nguyen Van Thieu, at a meeting on Midway Island on 8 June; a second step, lowering the number of US troops to 484,000 by mid-December, was announced by the White House on 16 September. At this stage, however, detailed plans had not been made for the period beyond July 1971, when the United States would still have 260,000 men in Vietnam.[5] A new debate would begin within the Pentagon when the secretary of defence, Melvin Laird, asked the joint chiefs of staff on 10 November to suggest how the South Vietnamese forces might be further enlarged, so as to require only a small US advisory force by mid-1973. Whereas the military doubted whether this timetable was feasible, the civilians in the Pentagon were eager to speed up the withdrawal.

Second, as the US forces withdrew, the armed forces of the Republic of Vietnam (ARVN) would have to be both expanded and trained and equipped to take over the combat role hitherto performed by Americans. The US administration believed that, given sufficient time, the ARVN could be made strong enough to deal with armed opposition originating inside South Vietnam, but not with regular North Vietnamese (PAVN) combat forces, if the latter were allowed to remain in the South.[6] Hence Nixon's insistence in May on *mutual* withdrawal of United States and North Vietnamese forces from South Vietnam, a demand sustained until the spring of 1971.

Third, the United States would deny the Communists the opportunity to continue recruiting their own forces within South Vietnam by strengthening the combined United States–South Vietnamese rural pacification and development programme; in particular, the campaign to root out the Viet Cong infrastructure (known in Vietnamese as *Phung Hoang* and in English as *Phoenix*). The groundwork for this campaign had been laid by Robert Komer, in charge of pacification programmes in Saigon, in the summer and autumn of 1967, but the opportunity to develop it had followed in the wake of the Communist offensives of 1968, which, despite the contrary impression given by the media, had left the South Vietnamese countryside more open to penetration by the Saigon government than at any time since 1963. The success of the campaign would be monitored by the Vietnam Special Studies Group, set up under the national security council (NSC) in September 1969.[7]

The optimism in Washington about the pacification programme was buttressed, later in the year, by a report which Nixon commissioned from the British counter-insurgency specialist, Sir Robert Thompson; and by the views of Colonel John Paul Vann, in charge of US pacification support in the Mekong Delta, who was summoned to the White House on 22 December.[8] Nixon himself took an interest in land reform in South Vietnam, responding favourably to a letter advocating that policy from Senator Robert Packwood (Rep.–Oregon) on 20 October. The president's enthusiasm (and that of the NSC staff) may have helped to resolve a debate at lower levels of the administration, in which some analysts argued that land reform would not affect the outcome.[9] Although *Phoenix* was even more controversial, its effectiveness in weakening Communist capabilities at the grassroots was reflected in the propaganda campaign against it mounted by the Communists themselves, who sought to undermine it in every way possible.[10]

Fourth, the United States would negotiate. The conference at Paris on ending the war in Vietnam, which opened on 26 January 1969, remained nominally in session until the signature of the Paris Agreements of 27 January 1973. Although it no longer seemed likely that the conference would reach a settlement quickly – secret negotiations between Washington and Hanoi, should they ever take place, were more likely to succeed – the form of the conference had itself pointed to the likely form of an eventual agreement. The conference might best be described as a four-party negotiation conducted on two levels. On one level – which dealt with the political future of South Vietnam – not only the United States and North Vietnam but also the 'two parties' from the South were involved. Despite the fact that neither recognized the legitimacy of the other, representatives of the government in Saigon (formally the Republic of Vietnam) sat down with those of the Provisional Revolutionary Government of the Republic of South Vietnam (PRGSVN), which had been formally inaugurated on 10 June 1969.

This structure differed markedly from the situation after the Geneva conference of 1954, when there had been an effective (albeit temporary) equivalence between the Viet Minh (in Hanoi) and the Republic of Vietnam (in Saigon), which was accepted in practice as the successor to the French regime. By 1969, simply owing to the general acceptance of the structure of the conference, Hanoi had already achieved one of its principal goals: equivalence between its own and the US delegations, and hence *de facto* equivalence between Saigon and the PRGSVN. It was already too late for the Nixon administration, even had it wished, to insist on reverting to the notion that Hanoi and Saigon were the only equal Vietnamese parties. Nor, it would seem, did the United States try to negotiate in secret directly with the PRGSVN once the Paris talks had begun.

There were two other important differences between the Paris and Geneva conferences. First, the Paris conference was not truly international. At Geneva in 1954, the principal negotiations – between Great Britain, France, China, and the Soviet Union, and to a limited extent the United States – had taken place within the framework of a single conference. In 1969 (and until 1973), diplomatic relations between the United States and North Vietnam's two major Communist allies – the Soviet Union and China – had to take place outside the Paris framework, subject to pressures and 'linkages' having little to do with Indo-China.

Second, the agenda of the Geneva conference had dealt with the whole of Indo-China, whereas the Paris conference dealt only with Vietnam. The French had been determined at Geneva to obtain separate cease-fire agreements for Cambodia and Laos, and the Chinese premier, Zhou Enlai, to the dismay of the Viet Minh, had agreed. The outcome was an Indo-China-wide settlement guaranteeing in principle the existence of Laos and Cambodia as independent and neutral states free of any Vietnamese military presence. In 1969, however, it was assumed that cease-fire agreements governing Laos and Cambodia must follow agreement over Vietnam; that they would be negotiated at separate meetings involving the 'two parties' in each country. Despite the Communists' dependence on the Ho Chi Minh trail, running through southern Laos, and on base areas inside both Laos and Cambodia, the North Vietnamese had never acknowledged their military presence there, at least since 1962. Thus, the Paris conference was unable to devise an agreement containing an explicit promise of withdrawal. Although Nixon had called on 14 May for a North Vietnamese withdrawal from both countries, there was a serious discrepancy between his declared objectives and the diplomatic machinery available for achieving them as part of a negotiated settlement. Nor could a reaffirmation of neutrality and territorial integrity by the Laotian or Cambodian parties themselves be made within the Paris framework.

As far as Vietnam itself was concerned, the chances of early agreement seemed, in any case, remote. On 4 August, following a US initiative some weeks earlier, the national security adviser, Henry Kissinger, held a secret meeting with the head of the North Vietnamese delegation at Paris, Xuan Thuy, who presented a clear statement of Hanoi's demands: a coalition government in Saigon (excluding Thieu and other anti-Communist figures); a simultaneous settlement of both political and military issues, which tied not only the cease-fire, but also the release of prisoners of war, to the acceptance of the coalition government; and the withdrawal of all US and other foreign troops from Vietnam within a specified period. Thus, an independent South Vietnamese regime was to be denied the opportunity to continue the war. Lastly, the elections following the settlement would be supervised by the coalition government: in effect, by the Communists and the non-Communist politicians acceptable to them. For his part, Kissinger conveyed a message from Nixon warning that, if no progress towards an agreement was made by 1 November, the United States would have to consider 'steps of grave consequence'.[11]

By mid-September, as he announced a further withdrawal of troops and set up the Vietnam Special Studies Group, Nixon was becoming impatient. He appears at this point to have contemplated a strategy of trying to speed up the negotiations by threatening a major use of force against North Vietnam of the kind frequently recommended to his predecessor, Lyndon Johnson, by the joint chiefs of staff during 1966–8, and which Nixon himself finally authorized in response to the North Vietnamese offensive of April–May 1972. In his memoirs, he makes several vague references to 1 November as a deadline for progress in Paris, implying some kind of 'ultimatum' to Hanoi. Kissinger is a little more explicit: during the weeks following a national security council meeting on 12 September, he and his staff explored the requirements and ramifications of re-escalating the war; and the joint chiefs of staff worked on a new military plan for action against North Vietnam. These contingency plans bore the name *Duck Hook*.[12] More precise evidence for them is to be found in back-channel messages (now declassified) in the papers of General Creighton Abrams, the commander of US forces in South Vietnam. They were reports to the chairman of the joint chiefs of staff, General Earle Wheeler, from the operations chief of the joint chiefs of staff, Rear-Admiral Bardshar, who by 19 September was on his way to Saigon with the task of devising a way to bring systematic military pressure to bear on Hanoi. Known to the joint chiefs as *Pruning Knife*, the plan which emerged included not only the resumption of heavy bombing of targets throughout North Vietnam, but also the naval bombardment of coastal areas and the mining of Haiphong and other harbours.[13]

Whether or not Nixon seriously contemplated giving North Vietnam an ultimatum is impossible to tell but, if he did, clearly he gave up the idea around 17 October. On that day, Kissinger tells us, he sent a memorandum to Nixon recommending that he 'defer consideration' of *Duck Hook*. One possible reason may have been the international situation, in particular the reaffirmation of Soviet support for Hanoi. The Vietnam News Agency reported on 17 October the substance of the Soviet foreign minister, Alexei Kosygin's, remarks to the premier of North Vietnam, Pham Van Dong, who was visiting Moscow. While the Russians believed that an 'equitable' settlement would prove possible in the end, they were willing in the meantime to provide all the help Hanoi might need. On the same day in Hanoi, the newspaper *Nhan Dan* expressed gratitude for Soviet aid, more detail of which was given in a communiqué on the 20th.[14] The North Vietnamese had also recently signed another aid agreement with China, which, if less generous than they had hoped, nevertheless gave them a measure of continued support.

Although it is unlikely that this round of aid negotiations had left Hanoi able to embark on a massive offensive in the South during the coming winter–spring season, or that China and the Soviet Union wanted to see that happen, together they had promised enough aid to enable North Vietnam and the Communist forces in the South to continue the war. They would not have to give way to the United States at the negotiating table. Given these Soviet and Chinese commitments to Hanoi, therefore, Nixon could not have re-escalated the war in Vietnam without risking world-wide confrontation.

Nixon was undoubtedly impatient with the failure of the Soviet Union to give the United States more help to reach an acceptable diplomatic solution in Vietnam: he had been disappointed by the Soviet foreign minister, Andrei Gromyko's, negative reaction to his speech at the United Nations on 18 September. He reiterated these feelings, in the strongest terms, when the Soviet ambassador, Anatoly Dobrynin, called at the White House on 20 October. At the same meeting, however, Dobrynin told him of the Soviets' willingness to set a date for strategic arms limitation talks (the first step towards SALT-I).[15] Kissinger, who was ready to 'link' the various issues entering into an eventual Soviet–American *détente*, knew that extreme actions by the United States could prejudice it altogether.

On the same day (20 October), the Soviet and Chinese deputy foreign ministers, Vasily V. Kuznetsov and Qiao Guanhua, began a new round of Sino-Soviet talks in Beijing.[16] It was essential for the success of Nixon's long-term China strategy that the talks should fail. In view of what came later, it might be suggested that the chairman of the Chinese Communist Party, Mao Zedong, and Zhou Enlai were playing a Soviet 'card' to tempt Washington. If they were, the ploy does not seem to have been recognized as such by Nixon or Kissinger, who appear to have been deeply concerned about the possibility of a Sino-Soviet *rapprochement*. Its likelihood would certainly have been increased by a resumption of the bombing of North Vietnam after Nixon's supposed 'deadline' of 1 November.

In their memoirs, Nixon and Kissinger make no connections of this kind. Nixon himself offers three explanations for his decision not to re-escalate the war: first, the war was relatively quiet, making it difficult to justify an escalation; second, Hanoi might possibly have changed its policy on negotiations, following the death of Ho Chi Minh in early September; and third, he was influenced by a meeting with Thompson, also on 17 October, who emphasized that without pacifying the South, action against the North would be futile.[17] Some will also argue that Nixon's options were seriously restricted by the large-scale anti-war protests which occurred across the United States during the Vietnam Moratorium of 15 October. Certainly the mood in the country would have made it difficult to build a consensus behind a programme of re-escalation.

Nixon had announced on 13 October that he would make another televised address on Vietnam on 3 November. Although he again took a tough line, he did not threaten military action against North Vietnam. He concentrated instead on winning the support of the 'silent majority' among the American people, although aware that, by doing this, he would jeopardize the chances of progress at the Paris conference. When Henry Cabot Lodge, the leader of the US delegation in Paris, announced his resignation 20 November, Nixon decided for the time being not to replace him by anyone of comparable stature.

Of the four elements in the American strategy outlined above, therefore the main emphasis would be placed on Vietnamization and pacification The question awaiting an answer was whether those programmes would be allowed sufficient time to succeed. Laos and Cambodia began to play a more important role in the strategies of both sides.

The pattern of conflict in Laos and Cambodia by the late 1960s had two dimensions: geographical and political. The Vietnamese Communists depended on border sanctuaries and supply lines in both countries to sustain the war in Vietnam: both men and supplies were sent along the Ho Chi Minh trail to support Communist forces in the South, and important base areas (or sanctuaries) were set up on the Laotian side of the border with South Vietnam's I Corps Tactical Zone. In Cambodia, even larger base areas were set up along the borders with II and III Corps Tactical Zones; the latter included the provinces of Phuoc Long and Tay Ninh, which had to be defended if the United States and South Vietnam were to head off the threat of a Communist attack on Saigon. These sanctuaries depended increasingly on supply lines running through the heart of Cambodia for illegally procured Cambodian rice, and weapons and ammunition smuggled through the port of Sihanoukville.[18]

The ability of US forces to counter the North Vietnamese beyond the borders of South Vietnam was restricted by the Geneva Agreements of 1954 (on Cambodia) and 1962 (on Laos), which required all of the great powers to respect the independence and neutrality of both countries. A double standard, however, made it internationally acceptable for North Vietnam to violate the territory of its neighbours so long as it did not formally acknowledge it; but prohibited the United States from doing so – at least on the ground – without risking counter-moves by the Soviet Union and China. In Cambodia, the head of state, Prince Norodom Sihanouk, who had rejected US aid and broken off diplomatic relations in 1965, was determined to remain neutral. The price he paid was acquiescence in the growing Vietnamese Communist military presence in Cambodia and the existence of covert supply lines. In Laos, on the other hand, the government headed by Prince Souvanna Phouma interpreted neutrality in terms that allowed the United States both to bomb Vietnamese forces inside Laos and to seed electronic sensors to monitor truck traffic on the Ho Chi Minh trail.

The political dimension of the conflict in Laos and Cambodia related to the long-term future of the two countries. For twenty years, the Vietnamese Communists had treated first Laos, and later Cambodia, as part of a single Indo-Chinese battlefield, a policy endorsed at meetings of the Indo-Chinese Communist Party as early as 1948 and 1950. At a plenum of the Party's Central Executive in August 1948, the commander of the People's Army of Vietnam, Vo Nguyen Giap, was reported as saying: 'If the Rhine was the first line of defence for Britain, the Mekong River was Vietnam's first line of defence.' By 1950, the Viet Minh had also decided that both Laos and Cambodia needed mass revolutionary movements of their own, but as their own societies and revolutions were less advanced than Vietnam's, they would need Vietnamese leadership.[19]

In 1954, the Viet Minh were obliged to accept a settlement which not only partitioned Vietnam but also – with the approval of China – set up independent, neutral regimes in Vientiane and Phnom Penh. When the Vietnamese Communists resumed the armed struggle in 1959–60, therefore, they were obliged to confine their guerrilla war ostensibly to South Vietnam, making only clandestine use of the territory of Laos and Cambodia. Although their ultimate objective had to be temporarily shelved, it had not been abandoned: they were still determined to bring about a Communist revolution in the whole of what had once been French Indo-China. As would become apparent later on, the two Vietnamese leaders in the Vietnamese party politburo most deeply committed to the objective of a Communist Indo-China under Hanoi's control were Le Duan and Le Duc Tho, whose political stars were rising in 1969–70.

In Cambodia, between 1965 and 1969, both Hanoi and Beijing used their influence to restrain the Kampuchean Communist movement (by now under the leadership of Saloth Sar, alias Pol Pot) from embarking on full-scale armed struggle against the Sihanouk regime in Phnom Penh. None the less, Pol Pot did carry on his own small-scale armed struggle from early 1968, even though it could not hope to succeed without substantial Vietnamese aid.

The situation in Laos was in some ways simpler, in others more complicated. By 1969, Laos formed two distinct battlefields. In the north, the future of the government in Vientiane and, more immediately, control of the contested plain of Jarres was at stake, with the North Vietnamese providing regular army support to the Communist-led Lao People's Liberation Army (or Pathet Lao forces), owing to the close relationship between the Laotian Communist movement (effectively led by the half-Vietnamese Kaysone Phomvihane) and the Vietnamese Workers' Party in Hanoi. In southern Laos, the United States was employing all means short of invasion on the ground to obstruct the flow of men and supplies along the Ho Chi Minh trail. The government of Souvanna Phouma was willing to allow the United States not only to bomb targets in northern as well as southern Laos, but also to conduct clandestine operations, including the recruitment and support of guerrilla forces among the Meo (or Hmong) minority population, led by Vang Pao, and the maintenance of a secret 'Air America' base at Long Cheng.

Neither the North Vietnamese nor the US role could be openly acknowledged; but no one was in any doubt that what was taking place was ultimately a struggle between Hanoi and Washington, in which the Americans found themselves on the defensive. After an offensive by the North Vietnamese and Pathet Lao in May and June 1969 drove the Laotian government forces out of the plain of Jarres, a counter-attack by Vang Pao's Hmong forces designed to diminish the pressure on Vientiane recaptured Muong Soui and Xieng Khouang in late August and September. The United States would be in grave difficulties should Souvanna Phouma prove unable to maintain his own position and his policy of co-operation with Washington.

It was in Washington's interest, therefore, to preserve neutral governments in both Vientiane and Phnom Penh, rather than risk further destabilization leading to a possible Communist take-over. To that end, the Nixon administration had taken steps towards re-establishing diplomatic relations with Cambodia. As Sihanouk was willing, despite knowing about the secret US bombing of the sanctuaries which began in March,[20] relations were re-established on 11 June, although the

US embassy at Phnom Penh did not reopen until August. Sihanouk, to balance the decision, formally recognized the PRGSVN, inaugurated on 10 June, but in August allowed the political situation in Cambodia to shift in a direction likely to favour US interests, by convening a congress to choose the members of a new 'government of salvation'. Formed on 12 August, it was headed by Lon Nol (already a deputy premier and minister of defence) and included as first deputy premier the right-wing Prince Sirik Matak, Sihanouk's cousin and rival within the royal family. Its first task was to solve an economic crisis, of which the only logical solution lay in restoring economic ties with the West in the hope of increasing government revenues.[21]

The new government did not wish to abandon Cambodia's longstanding policy of neutrality nor to weaken its relations with Hanoi and Beijing. It may, however, have wished to contain the Vietnamese Communist military presence in order to prevent the war from spreading further. On 9 September, Sihanouk, in Hanoi to attend the funeral of Ho Chi Minh, had talks with Pham Van Dong that may have included an appeal for Vietnamese restraint in the use of Cambodian territory. He may also have proposed a new trade agreement governing the supply of rice and other Cambodian materials to the North Vietnamese troops that would earn his government more money. An agreement was signed on 25 September 1969[22] at precisely the same time as a new aid agreement between Hanoi and Beijing, which suggests that Chinese financial assistance played a part in the new arrangements. Cambodia's own friendly relations with China were reaffirmed when Lon Nol travelled to Beijing to attend the parade in Tiananmen Square commemorating the twentieth anniversary of the People's Republic on 1 October 1969,[23] and possibly also to seek China's help in persuading the Vietnamese Communists not to drag Cambodia into the war.

The situation in Laos and Cambodia mattered more to the United States during the last quarter of 1969 for two reasons. First, both Vietnamization and pacification would be seriously disrupted, if not altogether prevent by a Communist military offensive in late 1969 or 1970, especially if it threatened the security of Saigon – Hanoi's ability to mount such an offensive would depend on its use of the base areas and their supply lines through Laos and Cambodia. An attempt by the North Vietnamese to expand their military presence in either country would have to be countered effectively by the Americans, if Vietnamization was to succeed.

Second, the Americans remained worried about the influence of the Vietnam War throughout South-East Asia. The 'domino theory' was still being applied, even though in July 1969 Nixon had reformulated US policy terms of the 'Guam Doctrine', which placed on Asian countries themselves the main burden of defence against Communist aggression. The possibility of a negotiated compromise over Vietnam, and the need to withdraw some of the US forces, with or without a settlement, were bound to have repercussions. Although the easing of tensions elsewhere had permitted the creation in August 1967 of the Association of South-East Asian Nations, its foundations were fragile and several of its members faced internal threats to their long-term stability. In Thailand, a 'Maoist' armed struggle, some years old, was stepped up towards the end of 1969; in Malaysia, the political fabric was shaken by the Malay–Chinese clashes of 13 May. The Malayan Communist Party, eager to take advantage, inaugurated its own radio station – the 'Voice of the Malayan Revolution' – on 28 November, In the Philippines, the 'New People's Army', founded in March, began its own 'Maoist' armed struggle with some support from Beijing.[24] Thus, Laos and Cambodia represented a bridge across which the anti-imperialist revolution might quickly spread to Thailand and Malaysia – perhaps beyond – in the event that a settlement in Vietnam looked like a defeat for the United States.

Lastly, there was growing apprehension among US critics of the war – especially in Congress – that without a diplomatic settlement in Vietnam, ties to Laos and Cambodia might entangle the United States more deeply, instead of furthering the disengagement from Indo-China to which the administration was supposedly committed. The concern was expressed frankly, although not yet publicly, at congressional hearings on Laos conducted by a subcommittee of the senate committee on foreign relations between 20 and 28 October,[25] during which – in 'executive session' – the assistant secretary of state, William Sullivan, explained the US objectives, and military and intelligence officials provided highly sensitive information about the extent of US covert operations. The committee was upset by the recent fighting in Laos and by the likelihood that the Communists would make another attempt to control the plain of Jarres – compelling the United States to provide more support for Laos. In December, therefore, Senators John Sherman Cooper (Rep.–Kentucky) and Frank Church (Dem.–Idaho) introduced a legislative amendment designed to prevent the administration from sending ground combat forces – as opposed to covertly controlled special forces – into Thailand or Laos. The amendment became law on 29 December, when Nixon signed the bill to which it was attached.[26]

These concerns were difficult to reconcile. Stability in Laos and Cambodia, valued for its effect throughout South-East Asia, could best be obtained by combining diplomacy with limited programmes of economic and military assistance. On the other hand, containing – perhaps even temporarily destroying – the Vietnamese sanctuaries and their supply lines would require large-scale military operations likely to be politically destabilizing, if the Communists responded by challenging the governments of Cambodia and Laos. At that point, congressional reluctance might block the US aid programmes needed to ensure the survival of neutral regimes.

In Vietnam itself, there was a lull in Communist-initiated military activity between 18 August and the end of October. Senator Mike Mansfield (Dem.–Montana) was reported as saying on the 21st that a virtual cease-fire was in effect. A week later, however, the *New York Times* drew attention to a captured Communist document which pointed to an offensive around the middle of November: a significant date for the administration, as a massive anti-war demonstration was planned in Washington for the 15th. US intelligence hesitated to predict Hanoi's likeliest next moves and, in particular, whether the Communists would prove strong enough – or would even try – to launch an offensive in the South to disrupt the US withdrawal and the Vietnamization programme. One likely reason for the hesitation was the difficulty in measuring the content and consequences of the autumn agreements with China and the Soviet Union. Another was the possibility that the death of Ho Chi Minh would lead to a struggle over the succession in Hanoi.

The first half of November did see an upsurge in fighting in some areas of South Vietnam, as well as rocket and mortar attacks against targets across the country on the 4th and 7th. The most significant occurred in the northern part of III Corps Tactical Zone near the Cambodian border, which covered Saigon itself: the US 1st Cavalry Division and the 11th Armoured Cavalry Regiment repulsed attacks near the special forces camps at Bu Prang and Duc Lap, and in northern Tay Ninh province. By the 7th, they were able to counter-attack, to force PAVN units back across the Cambodian border. After further successes on the 9th and 10th, and on 3 December, for the next few months they were able to block the movement of men and supplies into Tay Ninh and Phuoc Long provinces.[27] Their task was made easier by the continued bombing operations, code-named *Menu*, of the Cambodian sanctuaries. These remained secret for the most part, although one series of especially heavy attacks in Mondolkiri province on 16–17 November was reported in the press. It led to a sharp public response from Sihanouk a week later.[28]

By mid-November, the Communists had probably decided that a major offensive was impracticable. On the 12th, a new directive from the secret headquarters of the Vietnamese Workers' Party for South Vietnam, usually known as COSVN, on the importance of guerrilla warfare and the need to prevent pacification, was passed down from higher- to lower-level party officials in South Vietnam. By December, other captured documents showed that an earlier pronouncement on the same theme was being recommended for urgent study.[29] The leadership was not abandoning its offensive strategy, however, nor scaling down the armed struggle: it was recognizing the need to play a waiting game in order to encourage the United States to continue withdrawing its forces, while gathering strength for operations designed to forestall the Vietnamization programme. The sanctuaries still had a key role to play.

At the same time, the Communists decided to infiltrate PAVN units into the Mekong Delta (the IV Corps Tactical Zone), in order to forestall the pacification programme there. Equally important for the Communists was an effective guerrilla presence in the province of Hau Nghia, situated between the Delta and northern III Corps Tactical Zone, which held the key to long-term co-ordination of the struggle in the two areas. It bordered on the Cambodian province of Svay Rieng, whose southernmost tip was known to the Americans as the 'Parrot's Beak'.[30]

By the end of 1969, therefore, it was clear that the war in Indo-China could not be ended by negotiation short of a US surrender. That being so, it was logical for the United States to carry out its new strategy with as much vigour as possible. The withdrawal of another 50,000 troops was announced on 15 December, and the White House publicized Thompson's optimistic report on the prospects for pacification and Vietnamization. Meanwhile, Nixon's attempt to revive the dialogue with China had had a small success: new contacts were made between the US ambassador and the Chinese chargé d'affaires at Warsaw,[31] Walter Stoessel and Lei Yang, whereas the Sino-Soviet border talks, begun in October, appeared to have broken down. Even if this turn of events was unlikely to produce immediate dividends, it might eventually provide the opportunity for what Kissinger called 'triangular diplomacy' between Washington, Moscow, and Beijing. Nevertheless, the danger of a North Vietnamese offensive remained; and that possibility left the situation in Laos and Cambodia as complicated and unpredictable as ever.

The crisis that began in Cambodia on 11 March 1970 must be set against the background of events throughout Indo-China during the preceding four weeks. When Laird visited Saigon from 10 to 13 February, he found the usual debate in progress about the Communists' current strategy and their likeliest next move.[32] There appeared to have been a massive increase in the quantity of military supplies – as opposed to troops – moved southwards along the Ho Chi Minh trail during the previous two months. Among the possible explanations were the difficulty of moving supplies through Cambodia, and the fear that Cambodia would soon create more difficulties. What was not clear was why extra supplies were needed, or how they might be used. Possibly the Communists were still planning a major offensive in South Vietnam; alternatively, they were simply preparing for all contingencies.

There were two principal areas of fighting in South Vietnam in mid-February: the provinces of Quang Tin and Quang Nai, where it was feared that the Communists might be preparing an offensive against Danang, and, once again, the part of III Corps Tactical Zone that bordered on Cambodia. There was less activity in the Central Highlands: the record of *Menu* operations inside Cambodia shows that one of the principal targets between mid-January and April 1970 was Base Area 609, the sanctuary laying astride the borders of Laos, Cambodia, and Vietnam and the key to the movement of troops into the provinces of Pleiku or Kontum.[33] Nor was there much sign of an imminent attack in the Mekong Delta. A press report of 22 February, probably derived from US intelligence, noted that one of the PAVN regiments that had penetrated the delta and been very active in January had been withdrawn to Cambodia. It is impossible to tell from this whether the Communists had already decided on some form of offensive action in the Cambodian provinces to the south and east of Phnom Penh.[34]

The offensive that actually materialized began in Laos, where a PAVN buildup had already been observed by late January. Starting on 12 February, the combined forces of the Pathet Lao and the North Vietnamese moved rapidly to recover control of the plain of Jarres, which they had lost to government forces the previous September. Since then, another 13,000 North Vietnamese troops had been deployed in Laos to reinforce the 50,000 already there, and were in a position to threaten, if not to capture, the secret base of Vang Pao's Hmong forces at Long Cheng. Souvanna Phouma appealed to the United States for additional support, with the result that, for the first time, on the 17th, B-52s bombed northern Laos. Although they averted a Communist advance on Long Cheng, both Xieng Khouang and Muong Soui were abandoned by the 24th.[35] Meanwhile, press reports of the raids provoked an outcry in Congress. On the 25th, a number of senators criticized

*International setting of the Cambodia crisis, 1969–1970* 161

the administration's deepening involvement in Laos and called for the publication (at least in part) of the hearings held the previous October. Two days later, the national security council decided to prepare a White House statement on the US role in Laos, which was issued on 6 March.[36]

The offensive in Laos coincided with a new, but highly secret, phase in Kissinger's attempt to negotiate an end to the war in Vietnam. Le Duc Tho, a member of the North Vietnamese politburo, who had arrived in Paris at the end of January to attend a congress of the French Communist Party, let it be known on 16 February, through the US defence attaché at the embassy in Paris, General Vernon Walters, that he was willing to meet secretly with Kissinger on the 20th or 21st. When Kissinger agreed, the two men held the first of their series of meetings on the 21st at Choisy-le-Roi – the day Xieng Khouang airfield fell to the Pathet Lao, and one day after the 136th Sino-American ambassadorial meeting in Warsaw.[37] It is difficult to tell what Kissinger expected of the meeting. All that happened was that Le Duc Tho repeated – more authoritatively but just as negatively – the irreducible demands made the previous August by Xuan Thuy. For his part, Kissinger could not even mutter vaguely about an 'ultimatum'. On the defensive from the beginning, his only encouragement lay in the fact that the meeting took place at all; and that Tho agreed to meet again on 16 March.

Nor was it likely that anything would come of a new round of public exchanges on Laos. On 28 February, Souvanna Phouma protested to Britain and the Soviet Union as co-chairmen of the Geneva conference against the presence of North Vietnamese troops in his country. On 6 March, the United States made a similar protest to the Soviet Union, at the same time as Nixon issued his statement on Laos. The Lao Patriotic Front responded the same day with a statement that denounced US escalation of the war and put forward an uncompromising five-point proposal for a 'solution'. On the 9th, Souvanna Phouma agreed to receive an emissary bringing a message from the leader of the Communist Pathet Lao forces, Prince Souphanouvong. But a formal note from Britain to the Soviet Union of 9 March, proposing that they begin 'consultations', evoked a reply from Kosygin a week later that such an approach was 'unrealistic' so long as the United States continued to expand its armed intervention in Laos.[38]

At that point, although fighting continued in Laos for the rest of the month, attention began to shift to events in Cambodia, where a political crisis had been building for several months during which effective control of the government had passed into the hands of Sirik Matak. Lon Nol was away in France between 30 October 1969 and 18 February 1970; Sihanouk too, left for France on 6 January. His own influence in the government had been virtually purged at the end of 1969. Between 27 and 29 December, he presided over a national congress of his own political movement, the Sangkum Ryastr Niyum (People's Socialist Community), at which he condemned legislation designed to permit foreign and private banks to operate in Cambodia, and allowed the three Sangkum ministers still in the government to demonstrate their disapproval by offering their resignations. However, Sihanouk lost this confrontation with the government-dominated national assembly: the resignations were accepted and the legislation passed. At the same time, on 31 December, Cambodia was admitted to membership of the International Monetary Fund, a necessary preliminary to seeking economic aid.[39]

During January and the first half of February 1970, Sirik Matak took other steps designed to weaken Sihanouk's influence in Phnom Penh. In particular, he challenged the group attached to Sihanouk's wife, Princess Monique, which included her half-brother Colonel Oum Manorine, the secretary of state for ground defence and therefore commander of the national police; Colonel Sosthene Fernandez, the secretary of state for national security, who had the power to turn a blind eye to shipments of arms to the Vietnamese Communist bases; and Khek Vandy, who ran the state casino and controlled the state marketing of luxury imports. In January, Sirik Matak closed down the casino and also the National Office of Mutual Aid, in which Princess Monique herself was believed to have a direct interest.[40] He also arranged live broadcasts of meetings of the national assembly on 4 February, and of the cabinet council on the following day, at which critical statements were made about the 40,000–60,000 Vietnamese Communist troops on Cambodian soil and about the trade agreement with the PRGSVN.[41]

Sirik Matak's next move had to wait until the return of Lon Nol to Phnom Penh on 18 February. The following day, it was announced that all 500-riel notes would be replaced by the national bank before 7 March, making the old ones no longer legal tender, and that diplomatic bags would be searched during the period to prevent the smuggling of counterfeit notes. As the Vietnamese Communists were believed to have accumulated a large stock of counterfeit notes in Hong Kong to pay for their purchases in Cambodia, the measure was likely to deprive them of significant resources.[42]

As soon as the currency change had been completed, Sirik Matak was ready to take a more direct step against the Vietnamese Communists by staging demonstrations against their presence in Svay Rieng province on 8 March, followed by larger anti-Vietnamese demonstrations in Phnom Penh that culminated in the sack of the North Vietnamese and PRG diplomatic missions on the 11th. Meanwhile Lon Nol, on 6–7 March, made his own visit to the north-eastern province of Ratanakiri, the remote area bordering on South Vietnam. The timing of these moves was determined by Sihanouk's announcement on 22 February that he planned to return home soon, by way of Moscow and Beijing, and that he would arrive in Phnom Penh shortly after 10 March.[43] A crisis at that point was all but inevitable.

Studies of the Cambodian crisis have focused on the question whether the United States – specifically the central intelligence agency (CIA) – was directly responsible for the Phnom Penh 'coup' of 18 March 1970. This idea, first propagated in the Communist press as early as the 20th, gained greater currency when Sihanouk, in collaboration with the pro-Moscow journalist Wilfred Burchett, published his own memoir in 1973, alleging that Lon Nol had conspired with the CIA during his stay in France.[44] But unless fresh evidence emerges, there is no reason for historians to take the anti-American propaganda of the early 1970s as the foundation for a scholarly hypothesis that a US conspiracy removed Sihanouk from power.

There can be no doubt, however, that the United States had actively encouraged Lon Nol and Sirik Matak to change the direction of Cambodia's domestic policies by becoming less accommodating towards the Vietnamese Communists. It is equally clear that the United States was not yet (in early March) planning to target the Communist sanctuaries inside Cambodia, nor was it willing to provide direct military assistance to the Cambodian armed forces. The time for that had probably passed. It was more logical to seek a diplomatic solution that would buttress the neutrality of Cambodia and Laos and oblige the Vietnamese to withdraw from both countries.

Too little attention has been paid hitherto to Cambodia's relations with other South-East Asian countries whose leaders had a direct interest in its political future, and who were seeking a neutralist regime in Phnom Penh that would afford them some protection against Vietnamese dreams of exporting the Marxist–Leninist revolution beyond their own borders. Thailand and Malaysia, especially anxious, were already arming themselves against a new threat of armed struggle by the Malayan Communist Party. On 7 March 1970, the prime minister of Malaysia, Tun Abdul Razak, visited Bangkok to sign a new Thai–Malaysian Border Cooperation Agreement. Meanwhile, Indonesia, too, was promoting regional co-operation: between 16 and 22 March, President Suharto visited Kuala Lumpur and Bangkok, precisely as events were coming to a head in Cambodia.[45] There is no reason to suggest that any of these countries played a direct role in the overthrow of Sihanouk, but their leaders must have been watching events in Phnom Penh very carefully.

It might not be inappropriate to compare the Phnom Penh 'coup' with the events in Indonesia in 1965–6. The comparison is not, of course, a neat one. Indonesia is a far larger country than Cambodia, and its politics have always been more complex. By contrast with Sukarno's Indonesia, Cambodia under Sihanouk lacked both a strong army and a powerful Communist Party operating openly as a mass organization. And Cambodia lacked the oil and other natural resources that might make its politics a matter of vital importance to the world economy. Both countries, however, had developed friendly relations with China in the early and mid-1960s and, in both cases, the CIA was accused of playing a key role in securing an outcome favourable to US interests. Perhaps, however, such developments are better seen primarily in terms of the autonomous politics of Asian states, whose own leaders often play the decisive role.

Sihanouk himself had formerly been conscious of the similarity between his own anti-imperialism and Sukarno's, whom he had regarded as a friend in the days of the 'Beijing–Phnom Penh–Jakarta Axis'. He had entertained Sukarno in Phnom Penh and at Angkor in January 1964 and, in August, had been present in Jakarta to hear Sukarno's famous 'Year of Living Dangerously' speech, and had then visited Bali. Four years later, after Sukarno had been overthrown, Sihanouk made at least one half-prophetic speech in which he contemplated his own resignation and compared Lon Nol's likely policies with Suharto's.[46]

The outline of events in Phnom Penh between 11 and 18 March 1970 is well known. Following the sack of the two Vietnamese embassies on the morning of 11 March, the national assembly met later in the day to express sympathy with the demonstrators and to call on the government to 'use all means to defend the territorial integrity of Cambodia as an independent and sovereign country ... and to increase and strengthen the national forces'.[47] On the 12th, Sirik Matak announced that the government had sent a formal note to the Vietnamese apologizing for the damage to their property but also demanding the withdrawal of their troops from Cambodian territory within three days. It had also decided to suspend deliveries of rice under the trade agreement with the PRGSVN. On the same day, Lon Nol wrote to Sihanouk reporting these decisions, and proposing to increase the armed forces to 100,000 troops.[48] These events prompted a CIA intelligence report, also dated the 12th, predicting the possibility of a coup in Phnom Penh if Sihanouk tried to 'exert pressure on the government'.[49]

Sihanouk was still in Paris, where he met the Soviet ambassador on the 9th and the president, Georges Pompidou, the following day. On the 11th, he wrote to his mother, Queen Kossomak, telling her that he would return to Phnom Penh immediately, to compel 'the nation and the army' to choose between his policy of neutrality and the group who wanted to 'place our country into the hands of an imperialist and capitalist power'.[50] In fact, however, he did not change his plans to visit Moscow and Beijing on the way home: leaving Paris on the 13th and spending two or three days in each, he planned to be home around the 18th. Meanwhile, in Phnom Penh, the queen on the 13th intervened to put an end to continuing attacks on Vietnamese houses, shops, and places of worship, earning the approval of a group calling itself the 'counter-cabinet' which issued a communiqué on the 14th.[51] Had Sihanouk returned at that moment, events might have taken a different course; as it was, on arriving at Moscow, he declined the Soviet president, Nikolai Podgorny's, offer of an airplane to take him home immediately. In fact, he prolonged his visit by two days.

Events remained in the balance during the 14th and 15th. The North Vietnamese were optimistic that, despite the incidents of the 11th, outstanding issues might still be settled by negotiation. Their representative in Phnom Penh, together with his PRGSVN colleague, met the Cambodian foreign minister, Norodom Phurissara, on the 14th, and agreed that negotiations should begin two days later. One meeting was held before the negotiations were interrupted – as it turned out, permanently.[52]

In Paris on the 16th, Kissinger had a second secret meeting with Le Duc Tho. So far as one can tell, they did not talk much about Cambodia, although Tho was already blaming the United States for instigating the anti-Vietnamese demonstrations in Phnom Penh. They did talk about Laos, but their main business seems to have been to reaffirm their incompatible positions regarding a settlement in Vietnam. Nevertheless, despite the lack of progress, they agreed to meet again on 4 April.[53] Presumably the Soviet leaders knew that the talks were taking place, and although we have no means of knowing whether they expected a breakthrough to a settlement, it seems unlikely that either they or the North Vietnamese told Sihanouk about them.

Meanwhile, on the 15th, Sihanouk had changed his travel plans yet again, deciding – apparently at the request of the Soviets – to stay two days longer in Moscow for more talks with Kosygin and to meet the secretary-general, Leonid Brezhnev. In his memoir, Sihanouk claims that the Soviets were ready to give military aid to Cambodia. It may, however, have been conditional on his going straight home to Phnom Penh and to side with Moscow rather than with Beijing thereafter. Instead, after a further exchange of letters with Zhou Enlai on the 15th or 16th, Sihanouk decided to continue with his planned visit to Beijing from the 19th to the 24th. No more was heard of the Soviet military aid.[54]

By the time these events took place in Paris and Moscow, events in Phnom Penh had begun (given the difference in time zones) to enter a new and more decisive phase. On the morning of the 16th, the national assembly met again. While it continued to discuss the Vietnamese bases, a clash developed between 'rightist' deputies (Sim Var, Doue Rasy, In Tam, and others) and the 'leftist' ministers Oum Manorine and Sosthene Fernandez (Khek Vandy was visiting Japan), The two ministers were accused of illegally importing cloth from Hong Kong, and they, in turn, blamed junior officials and a Chinese merchant. After an investigation was agreed upon, the assembly decided to reconvene on the 18th to vote on a resolution expressing confidence in Oum Manorine and Sosthene Fernandez.[55]

The lines were now drawn between two factions, but in such a way that neither Sirik Matak nor Lon Nol was directly involved in the issue immediately at stake. Oum Manorine's only means of defending himself lay in using his control over the police to stage a coup of his own before the next meeting of the assembly. On the night of 16–17 March, he appears to have tried to do so, and to arrest Lon Nol and Sirik Matak. As they had the army on their side, they were able to outwit him: Oum Manorine himself was arrested and forced to resign on the 17th, which gave control of the police to his enemies. Sosthene Fernandez, now alone, could do little to prevent his own dismissal when the assembly next met.[56] Thus, a relatively bloodless coup was possible. A show of military strength ensured that, when the national assembly met on the 18th, the deputies endorsed a resolution removing Sihanouk as head of state and appointing Cheng Heng as his acting successor.[57] Sihanouk learned of the decision from Kosygin as he was being driven to the airport in Moscow.

A full understanding of these few days would require more detailed information than is likely ever to be available, as Sirik Matak and Lon Nol are both dead. What is known is compatible with the assumption that they (and the 'rightists') acted on their own initiative; and that their decisions were governed at least in part by the fear that only decisive action would prevent a reversal of their recent policies – and possibly their own dismissal – once Sihanouk returned. Their biggest mistake may have been to assume that the United States would be eager to provide them with generous economic and military assistance. The evidence from the US side suggests that Nixon himself was keen to welcome the 'coup', but faced resistance from the state department and the civilians in the Pentagon.

Kissinger may be telling the truth when he says that he paid no attention to events in Phnom Penh until 17 March and, even then, was not clear what was happening.[58] The decision to remove Sihanouk as head of state does not seem to have been part of anyone's deliberate planning in Washington. Nor was it immediately clear what the consequences would be.

In looking at events during the next phase of the crisis, between 19 and 25 March, we need to shift the focus away from Phnom Penh to Beijing, Hanoi, and Washington. The uncertain course of events during the first few days after the coup suggests that senior officials in all three countries had been taken by surprise. Each government was watching the others – as, no doubt, were the Russians – before deciding what to do next.

Sihanouk arrived in Beijing, after a stopover at Irkutsk, on the morning of 19 March, to be met at the airport by Zhou Enlai; a member of the politburo, Li Xiannian; the commander of the PLA air force, General Wu Faxian; and – according to the broadcast report – the minister of public security, Xie Fuzhi, whose responsibilities for border defence had given him a long-standing role in relations with the countries of Indo-China and southern Asia. However, we are immediately faced with a mystery, for this is the last mention made of Xie until 1972, when he was reported to have died 'after a long illness'. Shortly after his death, it was alleged in a Hong Kong newspaper that an attempt had been made on Zhou's life as the motorcade returned from the airport; but that his car was not travelling in its usual position, with the result that Xie's car was hit by mistake.[59] The truth of the story cannot be confirmed; but the mere fact of Xie's disappearance illustrates the turmoil within the Chinese leadership. Cambodia was only one of many issues about which Zhou and his colleagues may have disagreed.

The Chinese may have been disturbed by the events in Phnom Penh. The New China News Agency did not mention the sacking of the Vietnamese missions until early in the afternoon of the 16th, and did so then only owing to the need to deny rumours circulating in Phnom Penh that a Vietnamese crowd had damaged the Cambodian embassy in Beijing.[60] The Chinese were obviously reluctant to comment on a possible dispute between two countries in Indo-China seen as firm allies, even though Cambodia was not Communist. Had Sihanouk arrived in Beijing on the 16th, as originally scheduled, Zhou might have echoed Podgorny, telling him return home as quickly as possible. By the 19th, it was too late. Sihanouk had to decide whether he would accept his removal from power and retire to France permanently, or lead the opposition to the Lon Nol–Sirik Matak regime. If he chose the latter course, he would have to ally himself not only with the Kampuchean Communists but also with Hanoi.

The North Vietnamese seem to have been uncertain how to react to the coup: the Hanoi media did not mention it until the 22nd.[61] It was claimed later that the COSVN decided immediately, on the 19th, to begin moving its headquarters staff away from Base Area 353 deeper into Cambodia. The accuracy of the claim cannot be confirmed; the decision may have been taken a few days later. Contact was immediately made between Hanoi and Beijing, however, and on the 21st, the Vietnamese premier, Pham Van Dong, flew to Beijing to meet Sihanouk. By then Sihanouk had issued two statements to the press (on the 20th and the 21st) denouncing his overthrow as illegal and defending himself against the charges of corruption made in the national assembly. After more talks with the Chinese leaders and with Pham Van Dong, Sihanouk issued on the 23rd his first 'Message to the Nation', in which he dissolved the Lon Nol government and the national assembly, declared his intention to establish a new government, and proclaimed the 'National United Front of Kampuchea'.[62]

If we can believe Kissinger's account, the same interval was marked by continuing uncertainty in Washington. A meeting of the Washington Special Actions Group (WSAG) on the 19th devoted some time to events in Cambodia, in particular to a report that a US ship carrying weapons to Sattahip in Thailand had been hijacked at sea by two self-proclaimed antiwar activists and forced to put in to Sihanoukville on the 13th. This incident has frequently been cited as 'evidence' of 'possible' US involvement in the overthrow of Sihanouk, on the unverifiable supposition that the two 'activists' were really CIA agents. It is unlikely that Lon Nol needed such help at that stage; even less likely that bombs suitable only for B-52s would be of much use in a *coup d'état*. On the other hand, the loss of the shipment was a matter of legitimate concern to WSAG. It was finally handed back to the Americans by Lon Nol on the 30th, after his forces had secured control of the port.[63]

The WSAG meeting paid more attention to the situation in Laos, which remained critical. On the 16th, the Soviet Union had made a formal reply to the British proposal of the 9th for 'consultations', as well as to Nixon's statement of the 6th. Kosygin placed the blame for the escalation of fighting on the United States, and therefore rejected consultations as 'unrealistic', a view echoed in *Nhan Dan* on the same day.[64] The next day, the PAVN resumed its offensive with an assault on the outlying base of Sam Thong, not far from Vang Pao's (and Air America's) headquarters at Long Cheng. The US personnel there were rapidly evacuated and, by the 20th, Sam Thong was in PAVN hands. In the following days, North Vietnamese forces advanced within three miles of Long Cheng, which was narrowly held owing to heavy B-52 bombing and the Thai troops who reinforced Vang Pao's men on the ground. Although the most critical fighting came on 23–24 March, the area was not fully secure again until the end of the month.[65]

Meanwhile, Nixon, on the 19th, urged Kissinger to instruct the director of the CIA, Richard Helms, to develop a plan for 'maximum assistance to pro-US elements in Cambodia'. Kissinger, however, moved slowly: he did not pass on the message until the 23rd. For several days, he seems to have been uncertain whether Sihanouk might not manage to return to Phnom Penh as part of a last-minute compromise.[66] On the 20th, moreover, Cambodia's acting foreign minister, Yem Sambaur, told the US chargé d'affaires, Lloyd Rives, and other heads of mission that his government's policy of neutrality would continue unchanged.[67] The following day, a CIA report noted that Lon Nol's forces were still 'avoiding friction' with the Vietnamese Communists.[68] Not until the publication of Sihanouk's message of the 23rd, therefore, was the position clear and the die cast.

A new phase in the Cambodia Crisis began around 25–26 March, when North Vietnam issued a formal statement supporting Sihanouk and the 'patriotic struggle of the Cambodian people' and stressing the 'unity of the Indochinese peoples'. In the same spirit, statements supporting Sihanouk were released by the PRGSVN on the 26th and the Lao Patriotic Front the next day, and on the 27th, both North Vietnam and the PRGSVN withdrew their diplomats from Phnom Penh.[69] The Chinese, however, merely broadcast a summary of Sihanouk's message. Nor did they immediately publicize the statement made on the 26th by the Khmer Rouge leaders in Cambodia, Khieu Samphan, Hou Yuon, and Hu Nim.[70] They continued well into April to negotiate with an envoy from Lon Nol, in the hope of preserving Cambodia's neutrality.

In Cambodia itself, the five days from 26 to 30 March were marked by demonstrations in support of Sihanouk in three provinces – Kompong Cham, Takeo, and Prey Veng – in which peasants attacked government buildings and burned records, and tried to march towards Phnom Penh. The government reacted with considerable force, firing into crowds and reportedly killing several hundred demonstrators.[71] At the beginning of April, this form of opposition was abandoned as suddenly as it began, when Sihanouk issued a statement advising unarmed peasants not to take such risks on his behalf.

During this phase, Lon Nol's army began to co-operate with the ARVN, and fighting between Cambodian government forces and the Vietnamese Communists became more widespread. A number of incidents involving cross-border action by South Vietnamese forces occurred during the week of 20–27 March; ARVN planes certainly attacked targets inside Cambodia and the first major ground assault by the ARVN against a Vietnamese Communist sanctuary area occurred on the 27th.[72] The same day, according to the minister of justice in the PRGSVN, Truong Nhu Tang, B-52 raids on the base area containing his own and other PRGSVN ministries forced them to withdraw across the border into Cambodia, where they were attacked on the 30th by ARVN ground forces.[73] Other, more secret, ground penetrations of PAVN sanctuaries may explain the decision of the joint chiefs of staff on the 25th to suspend the round of *Menu* bombings inside Cambodia approved for that week. No B-52 raids on Base Areas 351, 352, or 353 took place between 22 March and 5 April, although raids on Base Area 609 (far to the north) were resumed on 29 March.[74]

US ground forces remained firmly restricted to South Vietnamese territory. Although the US 1st Cavalry Division and the 11th Armoured Cavalry Regiment had succeeded in containing attacks from the sanctuaries bordering on northern III Corps Tactical Zone, the pressure remained, and around 26–29 March the two units suffered heavy casualties in two attacks on their fire-support bases in the 'Dogs Head' area of north-western Tay Ninh province. Despite the fact that the base areas posed a significant threat to the strategy of Vietnamization, even limited ground operations across the border, especially if they were openly acknowledged, would raise the issue of Cambodia's continued neutral status.

This was probably a more sensitive issue for the state department than for the Pentagon – or the White House – and it appears to have created some tension within the administration towards the end of March. The state department was still looking for a diplomatic solution to the problems created by the coup in Phnom Penh. On 28 March, the assistant secretary of state for East Asian affairs, Marshall Green, sent a memorandum to the secretary of state, William P. Rogers (and ultimately to Nixon), urging them to take up French proposals for an international conference: it was 'too risky to try to solve the North Vietnamese problem in Cambodia by force'.[75] Precisely what happened next is not entirely clear, but it would seem that, on the 30th, the US ambassador at Saigon, Ellsworth Bunker, persuaded Thieu to 'hold cross border operations in abeyance' for the time being. Possibly Rives had a similar conversation with Lon Nol on the same day because, on the 31st, Lon Nol issued a statement reaffirming the 'strict neutrality' of Cambodia and adding that neither South Vietnamese nor US forces were authorized to operate on Cambodian territory.[76]

US aid to the Lon Nol regime was also being discussed in Washington by this time, even though no formal request had been received. It might have been possible, in principle, to form with Cambodia the kind of relationship the United States had had since 1964–5 with the theoretically neutral government of Laos; but that option appears not to have been regarded as feasible. As direct military assistance would infringe Cambodia's neutrality, the state department was cautious. Laird, although probably more cautious than the generals, nevertheless raised with Rogers by the 31st the need to take some action to help the Lon Nol government to establish itself more firmly in power, lest the situation should develop 'in a way which we would wish to avoid'. He mentioned as one possibility an attempt to persuade the Thai government to ease the pressure on Cambodia's western and northern borders, allowing Lon Nol to redeploy some of his forces to the eastern and southern areas of the country. Another possibility was to ask the Australians to provide military advisers for the Cambodian armed forces. One thing Laird wanted done immediately: a CIA station should be set up in Phnom Penh to secure communications. Even that move, however, seems to have been resisted by the state department.[77]

What Laird was not yet permitted to discuss with anyone in the state department was the secret planning for military operations being undertaken in the Pentagon and in Saigon. On 26 March, Wheeler sent a back-channel message to the commander-in-chief of US forces in the Pacific, Admiral John McCain in Honolulu, and to Abrams at Military Assistance Command Vietnam (MACV) in Saigon, directing them to develop contingency plans for combined ground operations against the sanctuaries. Wheeler was looking for plans able to be implemented on seventy-two-hours notice, and asked for a reply by the 30th. Two possible operations were envisaged, at that stage seen as alternatives. The first would attack Base Area 353 – just beyond the northern borders of Tay Ninh province in the area sometimes referred to as the 'Fish Hook' – which was correctly believed, until the evacuation of the 19th, to include the headquarters of COSVN itself. The second option would simultaneously attack Base Areas 367 and 706, in the 'Parrot's Beak' area of Svay Rieng province, and Base Area 704 closer to the Mekong.[78]

Abrams's reply on the 30th to Wheeler set out the advantages and disadvantages of each option, and its chances of success. The second option could be mounted largely by ARVN forces, with US logistic and air support; but involved a higher risk of civilian casualties. The first option – which he believed should also include Base Area 352 – would require a substantial commitment of US ground forces, but would risk few civilian casualties and might destroy COSVN's headquarters. This option was the one recommended. The proposals were immediately forwarded by Wheeler to Laird, and on 3 April embodied in a formal memorandum from the joint chiefs of staff.[79]

Thus, by the end of March, the first steps had been taken towards operations inside Cambodia, in which use of American ground-combat units – notably the 1st Cavalry Division and the 11th Armoured Cavalry Regiment – was envisaged from the outset. The date of these messages seems to confirm that such plans were not being made by MACV *before* the events of 11–18 March in Cambodia; they were a response to the changing situation, rather than preliminary to the change. On the other hand, it seems unlikely that Kissinger would have been unaware of Wheeler's message of 26 March to MACV, even though he was away from Washington when the reply was due. Although one cannot tell what happened to the joint chiefs' recommendation during the next two weeks, it is not true that no one at the highest levels in Washington was contemplating military operations of the kind eventually authorized.

However, the preparation of contingency plans does not necessarily lead to their implementation. As of 3 April, the plans could have gone the same way as many earlier recommendations for cross-border operations during the Johnson years, and likewise the *Pruning Knife/Duck Hook* plans of September–October 1969. The decision to invade the sanctuaries must still be attributed, therefore, principally to the course of events during the first half of April; and to Nixon's response to a situation which could not have been foreseen at the beginning of March.

One element in US calculations was the fragility of the military situation in South Vietnam at the beginning of April. Abrams's message to Wheeler on 30 March recognized the possibility that, in the event of an invasion of Cambodia, the Communists might retaliate by an offensive of their own in northern I Corps Tactical Zone, which the United States would be unable to contain if they withdrew any more troops. The point was well taken. By 20 April, when Nixon announced further troop withdrawals, he had decided on a one-year programme for the withdrawal of 150,000 troops, most of whom would not leave until after the end of 1970. Therefore, when the decision was finally made to implement both options in an attack on the sanctuaries at the end of April, it was also decided to bomb targets north of the 17th parallel; even the temporary destruction of stores and dislocation of supply lines in that area would hamper PAVN plans for an offensive south of the demilitarized zone.[80] The danger that US forces might become overstretched was illustrated on the night of 31 March, when the Communists attacked across

*International setting of the Cambodia crisis, 1969–1970* 171

all four Corps areas, followed in the first week of April by serious fighting south of the demilitarized zone.[81] This was perceived to be the most serious offensive since mid-November 1969, and almost certainly had an impact on US thinking in the following weeks.

The offensive coincided, moreover, with Kissinger's third meeting with Le Duc Tho at Choisy-le-Roi on 4 April, when Tho was more uncompromising than ever. No further meetings were arranged. Tho was particularly critical of the US role in Cambodia, blaming the United States for everything and rejecting the possibility of a new international guarantee of Cambodian neutrality. As the Cambodian people, who had responded to Sihanouk's appeal for support, would fight to overthrow the Lon Nol regime, the unity of 'the three Indo-Chinese peoples' made Vietnam, Laos, and Cambodia into a single battlefield. Kissinger had to admit to the failure of his diplomacy.[82]

Tho's private views were echoed in a public declaration the same day by Sihanouk, still in Beijing. In his second 'Message', he proclaimed his faith in the 'progressive' younger generation, called for full-scale armed struggle against Lon Nol, and insisted on the need for solidarity with China and North Vietnam, without 'falling on our knees before them'.[83] At this moment, the Chinese finally decided to back Sihanouk: the following day (5 April), Zhou left for a two-day visit to Pyongyang, where both he and the North Korean head of state, Kim Il Sung, henceforth a close ally of Sihanouk, promised him their support.

These developments probably implied some kind of formal agreement between the armed forces of the Khmer Rouge and those of North Vietnam and the PRGSVN. Many years later, in September 1978, Pol Pot revealed that he himself was also in Beijing at this time, after visiting Hanoi in late 1969 or early 1970 – he had gone to North Vietnam to try to persuade Le Duan and his colleagues to support the struggle against the government in Phnom Penh. According to Pol Pot, the Vietnamese turned him down; after the events of late March 1970, however, they sang a different tune. They were now not only willing to support an armed struggle in Cambodia but wanted to lead it: Pol Pot claims that he had to resist pressure for a joint military command, amounting to Vietnamese control.[84] Evidence of increasing Vietnamese Communist military activity inside Cambodia was noticeable by 3 April, especially in the eastern provinces of Prey Veng and Svay Rieng. On the 10th, a battle between Cambodian and Viet Cong units at Prasaut (near Svay Rieng) ended with a massacre of Vietnamese civilians. From the 13th, the fighting – in effect, by now, a Vietnamese Communist offensive – spread to the provinces of Kampot and Takeo, south of Phnom Penh. It was unlikely that Lon Nol's forces would be able to cope with this challenge on their own.[85]

Against this background, Lon Nol finally appealed for direct military support from both South Vietnam and the United States. He placed the ball firmly in Nixon's court. Ten days later, Nixon decided that the only way to meet the challenge effectively was by means of a full-scale combined operation against the sanctuaries.

## Notes

1. Phnom Penh Radio, 28 Feb. 1968 [British Broadcasting Corporation], S[ummary of] W[orld] B[roadcasts]: F[ar] E[ast] 2710/A3/9–10.
2. For a detailed study of the role of the US 1st Cavalry Division before and during this campaign, see J. D. Coleman, *Incursion* (New York, 1991); also important is K. W. Nolan, *Into Cambodia* (Novato, 1990). Other works with useful military details on the US side are three monographs in the US Department of the Army 'Vietnam Studies' series: J. J. Tolson, *Airmobility, 1961–1971* (Washington, 1973); D. E. Ott, *Field Artillery, 1954–1973* (Washington, 1975); D. A. Starry, *Mounted Combat in Vietnam* (Washington, 1978). For a South Vietnamese account, see Tran Dinh Tho, *The Cambodians Incursion* (Washington, 1979).
3. We are still dependent on more or less polemical exchanges between Nixon and Kissinger, on the one hand, and their various critics on the other: *The Memoirs of Richard Nixon* (New York, 1978); Henry Kissinger, *The White House Years* (Boston, 1979), ch. xii; W. Shawcross, *Sideshow: Kissinger, Nixon, and the Destruction of Cambodia* (London, 1979); S. M. Hersh, *The Price of Power: Kissinger in the Nixon White House* (New York, 1983).
4. Nixon's televised address of 14 May 1969, repr. in *Department of State Bulletin*, 2 June 1969, pp. 457–61.
5. See J. J. Clarke, *United States Army in Vietnam: Advice and Support: The Final Years, 1965–1973* (Washington, 1988), p. 355.
6. This point is also discussed in ibid., pp. 353–6.
7. Mentioned by Kissinger, *White House Years*, p. 434. The Vietnam Special Studies Group was set up on 16 Sept. 1969 by National Security Decision memorandum no. 23, and held its first meeting on 20 Oct. 1969. See Joint State–Defense–CIA telegram to Saigon, 7 Nov. 1969 (declassified 10 July 1987). I am grateful to William Gibbons for this reference.
8. Thompson met Nixon on 17 Oct. 1969; he completed his report by 3 Dec., and its conclusions were publicized in a presidential statement on 15 Dec. 1969. See Sir Robert Thompson, *Peace Is Not at Hand* (London, 1974), pp. 71–2. On Vann's meeting with the President, see Neil Sheehan, *A Bright Shining Lie* (New York, 1988), pp. 734–6. Sheehan does not, however, share the optimistic views which Vann developed during 1968–9 and which governed his career until his death in 1972 preferring to dwell on the pessimism his hero had enunciated before 1967. In a biography of over 800 pages, only thirty are devoted to the period of Vann's real achievement in South Vietnam, 1969–71.
9. See R. L. Sansom, *The Economics of Insurgency in the Mekong Delta of Vietnam* (Cambridge, Mass., 1970), esp. ch. 12. By Oct. 1970, Sansom was a member of the NSC staff and played a part in the work of the Vietnam Special Studies Group. For the Packwood letter and other not very sensitive papers on land reform, see US National Archives, Nixon Presidential Materials Project, White House Central Files (Special Files), Subject Files, CF Box 10 (CO 165, Vietnam, July–Nov. 1969). A useful summary of the background to the South Vietnamese 'Land to the Tiller' Law, finally promulgated by Thieu on 26 March 1970, appears in *Keesing's Contemporary Archives: 1969–70*, xvii. 23, 505–6 and 24, 356.
10. The most useful history of the subject is Dale Andrade, *Ashes to Ashes: The Phoenix Program and the Vietnam War* (Lexington, Mass., 1990).
11. The meeting is described, in its essentials, by Kissinger, *White House Years*, pp. 280–1. Xuan Thuy was not a member of the politburo and not empowered to negotiate matters of substance.
12. Kissinger, *White House Years*, pp. 284–5; Nixon, *Memoirs*, pp. 393–4, 398–400.
13. [Creighton] Abrams Papers: 1969–1970 Messages. Consulted at US Army Military History Institute, Carlisle Barracks, Sept. 1991.

14 See *Yearbook on International Communist Affairs, 1970* (Stanford, 1971), pp. 707–8. For Kosygin's talks in Hanoi at the time of Ho Chi Minh's funeral in Sept. 1969, see *SWB* FE/3174/C/11.
15 Kissinger, *White House Years*, pp. 145, 187; Nixon, *Memoirs*, pp. 405–7.
16 *Peking Review*, 24 Oct. 1969.
17 Nixon, *Memoirs*, p. 404.
18 Kissinger, *White House Years*, pp. 241–2, notes disagreement between the CIA analysts and military intelligence specialists (presumably at the M[ilitary] A[ssistance] C[ommand] V[ietnam in Saigon]) over the relative importance of the Ho Chi Minh trail and the Cambodian supply route. CIA emphasized the route through Laos and questioned MACV's emphasis on Cambodia, but Kissinger says that evidence found in the border sanctuaries themselves, when the Americans invaded in April–May 1970, 'indicated that shipments through Cambodia far exceeded even the military's highest estimates'. For a detailed MACV analysis of the importance of Sihanoukville, the routes through Cambodia, and the role of Chinese businessmen in the system, see 'VC/NVA Use of Cambodia for Logistics Support', 22 Nov. 1968 (originally top secret, declassified 18 May 1983), US Army Military History Institute, MACV Files I-E 13.
19 See Motoo Furuta, 'The Indochinese Communist Party's Division into Three Parties: Vietnamese Communist Policy toward Cambodia and Laos, 1948–1951', originally published in Japanese *in Ajiya Kenkyu*, xxix (1983); trans. in *Indochina in the 1940s and 1950s*, ed. T. Shiraishi and M. Furuta (Ithaca, 1992), esp. pp. 147–52. Furuta visited Hanoi in 1982 and was allowed to consult Vietnamese documents relating to these two meetings, as well as to others of the period.
20 The bombing operations, code-named *Menu*, were highly controversial when it became known, in 1973, that they had been conducted in such a way as to keep them entirely secret from the US Congress and public. There is no longer any reason, however, to doubt the administration's version of relations with Sihanouk in this period, as given in Kissinger, *White House Years*, pp. 241–54. For JCS memoranda relating to the bombing programme, see *Declassified Documents Quarterly Catalog, 1979* [Washington, 1979], pp. 390–401.
21 See *Keesing's Contemporary Archives, 1969–70*, xvii. 24,015ff. For an informative account of Cambodian politics in this period, see D. Kirk, *Wider War: The Struggle for Cambodia, Thailand, and Laos* (New York, 1971), part II; on the developments of summer 1969, D. P. Chandler, *The Tragedy of Cambodian History: Politics, War, and Revolution since 1945* (New Haven, 1991), pp. 187ff.
22 Kirk, *Struggle for Cambodia*, p. 84. For the radio report of Sihanouk's visit to Hanoi and his talks on 9 Sept. 1969, see *SWB* FE/3174/C/13. It is possible that the prince also met Li Xiannian, who led the Chinese delegation to Hanoi for the funeral.
23 *Peking Review*, 3 Oct. 1969, p. 9. The same account indicates that Pham Van Dong was also present, having arrived on 27 Sept. For the Sino-Vietnamese aid agreement signed by Li Xiannian and Le Thanh Nghi on 26 Sept., see *SWB* FE/3189/A3/1–2.
24 The Chinese media gave prominence to these various struggles: see *Peking Review*, 12 Dec. 1969, pp. 24–5; 16 Jan. 1970, pp. 28–9, and 13 Feb. 1970, pp. 19–24. A useful survey of China's relations with revolutionary struggles across the region is to be found in Jay Taylor, *China and Southeast Asia* (New York, 1976).
25 *United States Security Agreements and Commitments Abroad: The Kingdom of Laos* (US Senate, Committee on Foreign Relations, Washington, 1970). The hearings, held on 20, 21, 22, 28 Oct. 1969, were part of a series undertaken by the Subcommittee on US Security Agreements and Commitments throughout the World, chaired by Senator Stuart Symington (Dem.–Missouri). They were held in executive session, with the senators and all others present sworn to strict secrecy. But, by early 1970, there was pressure on the administration to allow a 'sanitized' version of the hearings to be published, which was finally authorized on 3 April 1970. The published version did *not* include any of the testimony given on 28 Oct. by Richard Helms for the CIA.

174  Communist Indochina

26 This first Cooper–Church amendment was attached to the Defense Appropriations Bill for FY 1970 (HR 15090), which became Public Law 91–171. It should be distinguished from the subsequent amendment, relating to Cambodia, introduced by them in May 1970 and finally enacted in Jan. 1971.
27 In addition to press reports of the more important engagements, the US fighting in this area is covered in some detail by Coleman, *Incursion*, pp. 160ff.
28 *International Herald Tribune*, 30 Nov. 1969 for Sihanouk's protest on 22 Nov., *Peking Review*, 5 Dec. 1969, p. 16. In another statement, however, on 15 Dec. 1969, Sihanouk admitted that the Vietnamese Communists had started the incident by firing on the Americans from Cambodian territory: *SWB* FE/3257 and 3259.
29 The earlier of the two directives on this theme, COSVN Resolution No. 9, July 1969, had already been captured by US forces in the field; a translation was released by the US embassy at Saigon on 15 Dec. The directive passed down to lower levels on 12 Nov. was COSVN Resolution No. 14, 30 Oct. 1969: for text, see *Vietnam Documents and Research Notes*, no. 81 (US mission, Saigon, July 1970).
30 For the Communists, much of Hau Nghia was still part of the province of Long An, as it had been in the French period. Writing many years later, the southern Communist commander Tran Van Tra noted the fierceness of the struggle in Long An during 1969–70, and the bravery of the 320th PAVN regiment sent to operate there: see Tran Van Tra, *Concluding the Thirty Years War* (Vietnamese original, Ho Chi Minh City, 1982; US translation in *Southeast Asia Report*, no. 1,247 [Washington, Feb. 1983]: JPRS 82783), pp. 39ff. For a recent study of the war in Hau Nghia province, see Eric M. Bergerud, *The Dynamics of Defeat* (Boulder, 1991).
31 This led to the holding of the 135th formal ambassadorial meeting in Warsaw on 20 Jan. 1970. See Kissinger, *White House Years*, pp. 188–191, 684ff.
32 Melvin Laird, draft memorandum for the president, 17 Feb. 1970, declassified 18 Aug. 1977, (incomplete) copy, National Security Archive [Washington, D.C.].
33 See memos from the chairman of the JCS to the secretary of defence seeking authorization for *Menu* operations against specific base areas: *Declassified Documents Quarterly Catalog, 1979*, pp. 396–400. For operations in northern III Corps area, see Coleman, *Incursion*, pp. 193ff.; Starry, *Mounted Combat*, p. 159. Individual engagements in Quang Ngai province and the area immediately south of Danang were reported in the press on 13, 15, 20 Feb. 1970.
34 *International Herald Tribune*, 23 Feb. 1970.
35 For a short account of the Laos offensive and the US response, see Kissinger, *White House Years*, pp. 448–57. An extract from a declassified USAF commander's account of the loss of the plain of Jarres and of Muong Soui is reprinted in J. C. Pratt, *Vietnam Voices: Perspectives on the War Years* (New York, 1984), pp. 422–3.
36 Kissinger, *White House Years*, pp. 454–5.
37 Ibid., pp. 438ff., 688–9.
38 These exchanges are mostly covered in *Keesing's Contemporary Archives, 1969–70*, xvii. 24,093; see also Kirk, *Struggle for Cambodia*, pp. 250–1.
39 See *Keesing's Contemporary Archives, 1969–70*, xvii. 23,796 and 24,015; see also Kirk, *Struggle for Cambodia*, pp. 87–8. Interestingly, the US mission seems to have underestimated the significance of what amounted to a serious – if not decisive – defeat for Sihanouk: see Chandler, *Cambodian History*, p. 352 n. 92, citing telegram no. 287, US embassy, Phnom Penh, to state dept., 31 Dec. 1969.
40 For Princess Monique's 'coterie', see Kirk, *Struggle for Cambodia*, pp. 85ff.; also Chandler, *Cambodian History*, p. 193, citing *Réalités Cambodgiennes*, 18 Jan. 1970 and Airgram A-45, US embassy, Phnom Penh, to state dept., 12 Feb. 1970.
41 *SWB* FE/3319/A3/4–5; FE/3320/A3/3. It later became known that Cambodian troops clashed with the 'Viet Cong' in Svay Rieng province between 2 and 6 Feb. 1969; FE/3330/A3/3 and FE/3331/A3/8.

42 *International Herald Tribune*, 23 Feb. 1970; see also Kirk, *Struggle for Cambodia*, pp. 89, 91.
43 *SWB* FE/3313/1; also noted by Kissinger, *White House Years*, p. 461. For the first report of the Svay Rieng demonstrations by Phnom Penh Radio, on 10 March 1970, see FE/3327/A3/3.
44 Norodom Sihanouk (as related to Wilfred Burchett), *My War with the CIA: Cambodia's Fight for Survival* (London, 1973). The idea was later accepted by Hersh, *Kissinger in the Nixon White House*. It was also entertained by Shawcross, *Kissinger, Nixon, and the Destruction of Cambodia*, although he was unable to find any hard evidence of US involvement; for his part, Kissinger, *White House Years*, responded to the allegation by insisting that the events of 18 March came as a complete surprise both to himself and to Nixon.
45 See reports in *SWB* FE/3332/A3/9; FE/3334/A3/1; FE/3337/A3/1. On 19 March, the Indonesian government issued a statement emphasizing that the latest developments in Phnom Penh were 'entirely Cambodia's internal affair': FE/3335/A3/6. For the Thai–Malaysian agreement of 7 March, see FE/3325/A3/8.
46 The relevant passage from this speech, delivered in Jan. 1968, is quoted at the head of the present paper. On Sukarno's visit to Cambodia, 11–15 Jan. 1964, see *SWB* FE/1450/A3/1; FE/1458/A3/1–3; for Sihanouk's visit to Jakarta and Bali, 14–21 Aug. 1964; FE/1633/A3/2–3; FE/1637/A3/9.
47 A live broadcast of part of the proceedings was monitored: see *SWB* FE/3327/A3/3 and FE/3328/A3/1.
48 This, too, was broadcast live by Phnom Penh Radio: see *SWB* FE/3329/A3/9 and FE/3331/A3/5–6.
49 Noted by Shawcross, *Kissinger, Nixon, and the Destruction of Cambodia*, pp. 118–9; this report was presumably compiled in Washington; there was no CIA station in Phnom Penh at this stage.
50 The text was broadcast by Phnom Penh Radio: *SWB* FE/3328/A3/2.
51 This communiqué was not broadcast by Phnom Penh, although it was picked up by the Agence France Presse correspondent there; it was reported by NCNA from Beijing on 16 March, in its first reference to events in Phnom Penh since 11 March. For Sihanouk's travel plans, see *SWB* FE/3328/A3/2; FE/3329/A3/8, 12; FE/3330/A3/1; Sihanouk/Burchett, *My War with the CIA*, pp. 21ff.
52 Optimistic articles on Vietnamese–Cambodian solidarity, and the need to defeat US efforts to undermine it, appeared in the Hanoi daily *Nhan Dan* on 14, 15, 16 March 1970: *SWB* FE/3330/A3/2, FE/3331/A3/7.
53 Kissinger, *White House Years*, pp. 445, 468.
54 Sihanouk/Burchett, *My War with the CIA*, pp. 24–6. For the exchange of messages with Zhou Enlai, as broadcast by Phnom Penh Radio on the evening of 16 March (Phnom Penh time), sec *SWB* FE/3332/A3/1.
55 The proceedings were broadcast live: see *SWB* FE/3331/A3/4 and FE/3333/A3/10; cf. also Kirk, *Struggle for Cambodia*, p. 97.
56 These events are described by Kirk, *Struggle for Cambodia*, pp. 97–8, but his statement that the assembly met again on the 17th is wrong. Oum's arrest was reported briefly by Phnom Penh Radio on the evening of the 17th: *SWB* FE/3333/A3/9. Sosthene Fernandez subsequently made his peace with Lon Nol and was again given a post in the government.
57 This time the proceedings were not broadcast live, although a recorded version was put out that evening. The vote of no confidence in the head of state was passed at 1.00 p.m. (Phnom Penh time); first news of it came in the form of a government communiqué and a statement by Cheng Heng, put out four hours later: *SWB* FE/3333/A3/7, 10; and FE/3334/A3/3–5.
58 Kissinger himself was in Paris on the 16th, He quotes a memo which he sent to the president on 17 March 1970, presumably on his return, which included a reference to

Lon Nol's proposal to expand the Cambodian armed forces. This drew forth a comment from Nixon, urging efforts to assist that expansion. See Kissinger, *White House Years*, pp. 463, 465.

59 The story was reported in the Hong Kong newspaper *Xingtao Ribao*, 3 April 1972: see *Translations on People's Republic of China* (Joint Publications Research Service), no. 188, 19 May 1972, pp. 3–5. Lin Biao was believed to have been responsible for the assassination attempt. We know from Sihanouk/Burchett, *My War with the CIA*, p. 29, that Sihanouk was driven from the airport with Zhou. For the published reports of his arrival at the airport (including reference to Xie) and his initial talks with Chinese leaders the same morning (*not* including Xie), see *SWB* FE/3334/A3/2 and FE/3335/A3/5.

60 *SWB* FE/3331/A3/1.

61 This silence is noted by Kissinger, *White House Years*, p. 47.

62 These documents were reprinted in *Peking Review*, 27 March 1970, pp. 13–19. The Chinese allowed Sihanouk to broadcast his message immediately from Beijing, in Cambodian: *SWB* FE/3338/A3/11. They did not, however, themselves formally endorse Sihanouk's position until early April.

63 The meeting is covered by Kissinger, *White House Years*, p. 465. The most balanced assessment of the *Columbia Eagle* affair is probably that given in Malcolm Caldwell and Lek Tan, *Cambodia in the Southeast Asian War* (New York, 1973), pp. 259–60; although convinced of US involvement in the coup, those authors were ready to accept the anti-war credentials of the two hijackers.

64 *SWB* FE/3331/A3/8–9; for Kosygin's letter of 16 March 1970, see *Keesing's Contemporary Archives, 1969–70*, xvii. 24,093.

65 See ibid.; Kirk, *Struggle for Cambodia*, p. 244.

66 Kissinger, *White House Years*, pp. 464–5.

67 This was reported by Phnom Penh Radio, which on the same day broadcast a message to the nation from Lon Nol, also reaffirming Cambodian neutrality: *SWB* FE/3336/A3/7. Yem Sambaur, already a deputy premier, was confirmed as foreign minister on the 22nd: FE/3337/A3/8.

68 Cited by Shawcross, *Kissinger, Nixon, and the Destruction of Cambodia*, pp. 124–5.

69 All three statements were eventually reproduced in *Peking Review*, 3 April 1970, pp. 18–22. The Chinese, however, were at this point still focusing attention on Laos: the same issue gave more prominence to a Chinese foreign ministry statement of 26 March, denouncing the Americans and Thais for expanding the conflict there.

70 B. Kiernan, 'The 1970 Peasant Uprisings against Lon Nol', in *Peasants and Politics in Kampuchea, 1942–1981*, ed. Ben Kiernan and Chanthou Boua (Armonk, 1982), p. 75. The statement was eventually published in China on 10 April 1970.

71 For a detailed account, see ibid., pp. 206ff. See also Kirk, *Struggle for Cambodia*, pp. 112ff.

72 See *Peasants and Politics*, ed. Kiernan, pp. 304–5, citing *Cambodia and the Vietnam War*, ed. H. Kosut (New York, *Facts on File*, 1971). For Phnom Penh government communiqué on clashes with 'Viet Cong' forces on 27, 28 March 1970, see *SWB* FE/3340/i.

73 Truong Nhu Tang, *Journal of a Viet Cong* (London, 1986), pp. 177ff. (US ed., 1985, *A Viet Cong Memoir*). The PRGSVN headquarters were eventually established in Kratie province, deep inside Cambodia; as was the COSVN, whose staff – again according to Tang – had begun to move out of Base Area 353 as early as 19 March, the day after the coup.

74 Wheeler to Laird (CM-4983-70), 25 March 1970, *Declassified Documents Quarterly Catalog, 1979*, p. 399C; for reports of actual raids, see p. 400A and E.

75 Shawcross, *Kissinger, Nixon, and the Destruction of Cambodia*, p. 129, based on his interviews with Green as early as spring 1970.

## International setting of the Cambodia crisis, 1969–1970    177

76 These moves are noted by Kissinger, *White House Years*, p. 488; he also tells us (p. 489) that immediately afterwards Laird intervened with Nixon to get a resumption of approval for South Vietnamese cross-border raids; but with what result is not clear. Kissinger himself was 'on holiday' for a week after 27 March.
77 Laird to Rogers, 31 March 1970, declassified 18 Aug. 1977, National Security Archive, consulted Autumn 1991. This document was also used by Shawcross, *Kissinger, Nixon, and the Destruction of Cambodia*, p. 130, but perhaps without his appreciating its full significance. On the establishment of a CIA station in Phnom Penh, see Kissinger, *White House Years*, p. 466: Nixon gave a formal order for it on 1 April 1970, but found that no action had been taken as late as 16 April.
78 CJCS to CINCPAC and COMUSMACV: message no. 04213, 19.41 GMT, 26 March 1970; supplemented by a further message requesting additional details (no. 04266), 17.36 GMT, 28 March 1970, Abrams Papers, 1969–1970 Messages, Military History Institute, Carlisle Barracks, Sept. 1991. The same box contains Abrams's reply (MACV 4159) sent from Saigon at 10.14 GMT, 30 March 1970.
79 CM-2005-70, 30 March 1970 and JCSM-149-70, 3 April 1970; both summarized in 'JCS Recommendations and SecDef Actions with respect to Cambodia, 1 January 1969 to 15 February 1975', prepared by Historical Division, Joint Secretariat, JCS, 26 Feb. 1975, declassified 23 Nov. 1990, National Security Archive, consulted Autumn 1991.
80 It may have been intended to keep this action secret; but it was immediately reported by William Beecher in the *New York Times*, 3 May 1970. For a discussion of the steps leading to the 20 April troop decision, see Kissinger, *White House Years*, pp. 477–81.
81 Apart from press reports at the time, there appears to be no account of this offensive from the US side. For a Communist assessment of its opening phase – a captured directive, 3 April 1970 – see *Vietnam Documents and Research Notes*, no. 88 (US mission, Saigon, Dec. 1970), doc. no. 4.
82 The meeting is again covered by Kissinger, *White House Years*, pp. 446, 468–9.
83 Repr. in *Peking Review*, 10 April 1970, p. 21, together with reports of Zhou's visit to North Korea and the joint communiqué of 7 April endorsing Sihanouk's position.
84 Democratic Kampuchea: Ministry of Foreign Affairs, *Black Paper: Facts and Evidences of the Acts of Aggression and Annexation of Vietnam against Kampuchea* (Phnom Penh, Sept. 1978: English trans. repr. by 'Group of Kampuchean Residents in America', n.d.), pp. 32ff. This is generally believed to be a memoir written by Pol Pot himself.
85 Kirk, *Struggle for Cambodia*, pp. 113–18, based partly on his own encounters with Vietnamese Communist troops inside Cambodia, as early as 3–5 April; also Kissinger, *White House Years*, pp. 467, 472.

# 8 Cambodia in the context of Sino-Vietnamese relations

Source: *Journal of the Royal Society for Asian Affairs* 72 (1985): 273–287.

THE SIX YEARS following the Vietnamese conquest of Cambodia and the Sino-Vietnamese war, early in 1979, have been a period of equilibrium during which the pattern of conflict in that area has remained relatively unchanged.[1] The conquest of Cambodia has remained incomplete, in that the government of Democratic Kampuchea has retained a substantial measure of international recognition whilst Cambodian guerrilla forces have continued to resist Vietnamese control. At the same time, the pro-Vietnamese government of Heng Samrin has strengthened its administrative authority throughout much of Cambodia – as well as participating in the close relations which now exist between the "three Indochinese states" under the leadership of Hanoi. Meanwhile the border area between Vietnam and China has remained tense, with renewed fighting from time to time – and with an apparent correlation between the intensity of military action on the Sino-Vietnamese and Thai–Cambodian borders in each campaigning season. The pattern is reinforced by the willingness of ASEAN (with varying degrees of commitment among its individual governments) to continue recognising Democratic Kampuchea; to campaign on its behalf at the United Nations; and to supply a measure of material assistance to anti-Vietnamese guerrillas. In the midst of all this, the Socialist Republic of Vietnam has found its military and political resources overstretched and its economy stagnating – despite a close alliance with the Soviet Union and the countries of COMECON. But there has been no sign of any willingness on the part of Hanoi to abandon its essential objectives in Cambodia; and any pressure there may have been from Moscow towards encouraging a compromise has certainly not been visible to the outside world. The Chinese government, for its part, continues to regard the Vietnamese presence in Cambodia as an obstacle to the restoration of fully harmonious relations between itself and the Soviet Union.

On the face of things it would appear that this state of affairs was the product of the three to four years after the fall of Phnom Penh and Saigon to Communist rule in April 1975; and more particularly, of the two years immediately following the death of Mao Zedong in September 1976. However, revelations made by Hanoi and Peking since the autumn of 1979 suggest that the conflicts run much deeper and that they were already present throughout the period when the world at large was conscious only of the "principal contradiction" between the Communist powers and the United States.[2] Indeed, it is now clear that we must look for the origins of the situation at least as far back as the early 1950s.

Among the issues raised in the "White Book" published by Hanoi in October 1979 – and elaborated upon in a similar document put out by Phnom Penh in July 1984 – was Zhou Enlai's conduct of the negotiations leading to the Geneva Agreements of 1954. Two allegations were made against him. First, he had been willing to compromise with the French at a time when, according to Hanoi's later version of events, the Viet-Minh had been heading for complete victory throughout the country. In that respect, the resentment of Le Duan, Le Duc Tho and other Communist leaders (who had been in charge of the struggle south of the seventeenth parallel) is easy to understand. Secondly, Zhou had given in to French demands that the Geneva Conference should separate the problems of Laos and Cambodia from that of Vietnam, and had in effect recognised the existence of neutral governments in those two countries at the expense of their Viet-Minh-sponsored front organisations. The result was to allow the separate political development not only of South Vietnam but also – with complete legal justification – that of Laos and Cambodia. In the case of Laos, genuine neutrality proved difficult to establish; by 1961 that country was also virtually partitioned between rightist and leftist elements – with the Vietnamese Communists playing an important role alongside the Pathet Lao. But in Cambodia Prince Sihanouk was able to create a truly neutralist regime, with which the Chinese developed friendly relations independently of their "fraternal" support for North Vietnam. The People's Revolutionary Party of Cambodia faded into the background, although an important element within it was given political and military training in Hanoi during the Sihanouk years.

The arguments put forward by the ruling group in Hanoi in 1979 suggest that, fifteen years earlier, Le Duan and his closest associates had been profoundly unhappy with the decision of Ho Chi Minh and Truong Chinh (Party Secretary-General before 1956) to accept the terms of the Geneva settlement. But they were overruled by the majority in the Vietnamese Politburo and Central Committee; and despite the suggestion that Zhou Enlai was principally responsible for the settlement, it also had at least the acquiescence of Molotov and the Soviet leadership. Nevertheless, it seems highly probable that Le Duan's own ambitions for the future pattern of relations in Indochina had already taken shape by 1954; and that they required the eventual reversal of the main features of the Geneva Agreements.

It can be argued, indeed, that there were always two strands of opinion within the Vietnamese Communist movement on the question of relations with the other two countries of Indochina, and that a potential conflict between them had existed from the Party's earliest days. When Ho Chi Minh held his famous meeting in Hong Kong in February 1930 to "unify" the various Communist groups already in existence, he insisted on the name "Vietnamese Communist Party". But one of the groups had already, the previous summer, founded an "Indochinese Communist Party", and in October 1930 the latter name was restored and accepted by the whole organisation.[3] The distinction was more than merely academic; it probably reflected a difference of principle. The label "Indochinese" implied a revolution throughout the territories of French Indochina: a movement that was first and foremost anti-colonial, – in which the principal ally of the Indochinese Communist Party would be the Communist Party of metropolitan France. It is impossible to know the inner workings of the Vietnamese Communist movement at that or any other period. But there seems every likelihood that Le Duan belonged to that "Indochinese" element within the Party; and certainly he seems to have had little or nothing to do with China before the late 1950s. Ho Chi Minh, on the other hand, was not only a Moscow-trained Comintern agent but also had close links with – if he was not actually a member of – the Chinese Communist Party. He may well have shared with the Chinese a perception of revolution in South-East Asia which was independent of the pattern of Western colonial rule and did not require sponsorship of colonial Communist Parties by those of the metropolitan countries. In that perspective, Vietnam, Laos and Cambodia would appear as national entities alongside Siam, Malaya and Burma. Ho himself operated in Thailand for a time in the late 1920s (as did Hoang Van Hoan in the 1930s) and is said to have played a role in the foundation of the Malayan Communist Party.[4] Neither Laos nor Cambodia had its own Communist Party as early as 1930; but the eventual creation of such Parties was allowed for.

The Indochinese Communist Party was formally dissolved in 1945. At the time it reemerged in 1951, it adopted the name "Vietnam Workers Party". We now know that in June of that year the Cambodian People's Revolutionary Party was also founded, although a similar Laotian Party did not emerge until 1955. Ho Chi Minh and Truong Chinh thus imposed a pattern of three separate Parties. At the same time they established three front organisations, together with a joint committee whose role was presumably to coordinate their strategy.[5] It was these Cambodian and Laotian fronts which were excluded from the Geneva Conference three years later; and which were thereby prevented from participating in state power and from acquiring the same international status as the Democratic Republic of Vietnam. The decisions taken in 1951 amounted to a compromise between the various points of view within the Indochinese Communist Party. We shall never know whether in other circumstances they would have led to a very loose form of unity between the three countries – of a kind the Chinese would have found acceptable; or whether, in due course, the "Indochinese" school of thought would have imposed a tighter form of unity which would have obliged the Chinese to deal with all three countries through Hanoi.

These issues were left unresolved in the years following the Geneva settlement. The period from the mid-1950s to the late 1970s was dominated by the consequences of the American decision to support a regime friendly to the West in Saigon, and to maintain a presence in Laos as the means of protecting a pro-Western government in Thailand. The United States commitment to South Vietnam, leading eventually to the escalation of American involvement after 1964, led all Communist Parties with an interest in Indochina to form a united front whose first aim was to defeat "US imperialism". The underlying tensions between different schools of thought regarding the eventual future of the region did not evaporate completely; but they did not have to be resolved yet.

The leaders of the Vietnam Workers' Party had no wish to become embroiled in the "Sino-Soviet Dispute" which was bedevilling international Communist relations by 1963–64. Ho Chi Minh succeeded in maintaining a Vietnamese "line" which opposed any compromise with "imperialism" without going so far as to identify anyone in the Soviet leadership as "revisionist". The Vietnamese refused to follow Peking into open revolt against Moscow, thereby making it difficult, if not impossible, for the Chinese to establish an independent Communist movement in Asia. Those Western commentators who at the time analysed Hanoi's position in terms of continuing rivalry between two "factions" – failed to come to grips with the true nature of proletarian internationalism and of Marxist–Leninist decisionmaking. It is very likely that by 1960 Le Duan was "pro-Soviet" and that Hoang Van Hoan was "pro-Chinese"; but the majority in Hanoi followed Ho's line of seeking friendly relations with all Communist Parties throughout the world. The acid test was the VNWP Central Committee's 9th Plenum (December 1963) at which Le Duan took an "anti-revisionist" position which was anything but "pro-Chinese"; after which he undertook an important mission to Moscow in February 1964. Some of the confusion in the minds of Western observers may have arisen from an assumption that being "anti-revisionist" was the same as being "anti-Soviet" at that time. In reality, Le Duan found his allies amongst Khrushchev's opponents in the CPSU itself; and in October 1964, Khrushchev was overthrown.[6]

As far as Cambodia was concerned, throughout this period from the Geneva settlement to the late 1960s Hanoi and Peking followed essentially the same policy of friendship towards Sihanouk's neutral regime – so long as he turned a blind eye to the use of territories along his borders as "Viet Cong sanctuaries". Sihanouk's method of maintaining himself in power was ingenious. As a born diplomat, he was able to travel the world seeking friendship with every major power involved in that part of the world – and to convince everyone from Kennedy to Zhou Enlai that a stable and neutral Cambodia was in their interests. Even Brezhnev accepted an invitation to Phnom Penh on one occasion, although the visit did not take place. At home, Sihanouk was able to add to the natural charisma of an ex-King the argument that he alone was capable of maintaining Cambodia's independence and neutrality in the wider world; and that his organisation (the *Sangkum*) should therefore rule unchallenged. For fifteen years, it worked. Even in 1965, as the war in Vietnam escalated, he persuaded the Chinese and the North Vietnamese to agree that Cambodian neutrality was of more use to them than a Cambodian revolution. Yet beneath the apparent calm of his own country, which for a few years presented a striking contrast with war-torn Vietnam, Sihanouk knew that Vietnamese ambitions for an Indochina-wide revolution were only dormant.

Meanwhile a serious split developed within the Cambodian Communist movement. Saloth Sar, who later took the name Pol Pot, emerged as secretary-general of the Party inside Cambodia sometime in 1963. He would later claim that his own Communist Party (which supplanted the People's Revolutionary Party of 1951) had been founded at a secret conference in Phnom Penh in September 1960.

We now know that in the latter part of 1965 he visited both Hanoi and Peking to seek support for a resumption of the armed struggle in Cambodia. At that point he was overruled by both the Chinese and the North Vietnamese leaders.[7] (But neither did General Lon Nol, Sihanouk's army commander, secure any major increase in Chinese military assistance to Phnom Penh, when he visited China in late 1965.) Cambodia was left on one side for the time being. It was not until 1967–68 that Sihanouk began to face a significant revolutionary challenge to his rule inside Cambodia. By that time Hanoi would appear to have lost all control over the leadership of the Kampuchean Communist Party Central Committee.

A number of significant changes occurred in the international situation as it affected South-East Asia in the late 1960s. Some were changes in the Communist world. In China the "cultural revolution" passed through a series of critical phases between early 1967 and the middle of 1970. In the Soviet Union the "Brezhnev Doctrine" combined a policy of detente towards the United States with one of tighter international discipline among the "socialist" countries of the world. The result was a more acute phase of the "Sino-Soviet Dispute", reflected in growing revolutionary rivalry between Moscow and Peking throughout the third world. One aspect of the conflict between them was the emergence of two very different perceptions of the revolution in South-East Asia.

It would appear that the Soviet line, accepted by Le Duan, involved concentrating all military efforts on Vietnam itself until the Americans were forced to withdraw. By contrast the Chinese favoured a less intensive military struggle, extending across a much wider area: if possible to every country in South-East Asia. That would oblige the Americans to spread their forces widely, making it impossible for them to win victory in Vietnam or anywhere else. That was the significance of Lin Biao's famous essay of September 1965: *Long live the Victory of People's War*. It implied relatively self-sufficient guerrilla struggles in Thailand, Burma, the Philippines and Malaya; and, of course, in Cambodia. As Lin Biao's influence grew, during the years 1967–69, that was the revolutionary line which China sought to encourage in South-East Asia; and which was therefore accepted by those Communist groups that looked to Peking for guidance, including the Kampuchean Communist Party.

The escalation of the Vietnam War during 1965 forced Hanoi to depend increasingly on the technologically more advanced military assistance (SAM missiles and MIG fighters) which the Soviet Union could provide more effectively than China. Chinese aid was still important, especially in maintaining and guarding railway communications; but China alone could not have protected North Vietnam against the "graduated pressure" inflicted on it by the United States Air Force and Navy. One result was that during the years 1965 to 1970 the influence of Le Duan increased and that of Hoang Van Hoan probably declined – at a time when Ho himself was growing too old to maintain a balance between rival second generation leaders. Ho's death in September 1969 strengthened Le Duan's hand even further and made it likely that in the long run the Vietnamese would accept the "Brezhnev line", and with it an even closer relationship to Moscow. This did not, however, mean that Hanoi immediately became eager to renew armed struggle in Cambodia.

These developments coincided with a growing crisis in the United States, where President Johnson faced increasingly difficult decisions. The commitment to Vietnam, although it had achieved greater military success than critics would allow, was proving too costly and too unpopular for the President to contemplate a further extension of the "big-unit war" beyond the borders of South Vietnam. From the spring of 1967 to early 1968 he carefully avoided authorising the large increase in troop deployments which his generals were asking for: a "ceiling" of 700,000 rather than 500,000 American troops. In the aftermath of the Tet offensive, and under the impact of a serious gold crisis in March 1968, he finally decided against such action. It was immediately evident that the United States would not now be able to deploy ground combat troops to Cambodia and Laos, which was the logical "next step" of the Westmoreland strategy.[8] The question for Hanoi, and for Pol Pot's Communists inside Cambodia, was whether to respond to this new situation by reactivating the revolutionary struggle in Cambodia straight away – or to allow Sihanouk to remain in power unchallenged until Vietnamese Communist forces were themselves ready to intervene to "liberate" Cambodia. The Cambodian *Black Paper* of 1978 indicates that Pol Pot was again at loggerheads with the Hanoi leadership on this issue. But this time he was powerful enough inside the country – and, although he does not say so, had sufficient encouragement from Peking – to ignore Hanoi's advice and to embark on an independent armed struggle.

The first revolt against Sihanouk's government had occurred in the spring of 1967. Starting in the district of Samlaut in Battambang province, it had spread to a number of neighbouring provinces but had been finally quelled in August that year. Sihanouk attributed it to a particular group of Cambodian Communists, led by Khieu Samphan and Hou Yuon who had disappeared from Phnom Penh in late April. The rural revolt was coordinated with student demonstrations in Phnom Penh, which by late June reflected the themes of the Chinese cultural revolution, and it is possible that these at least had been inspired by extreme radical elements in China – the "May 16 Group" – whose bid for power was finally defeated in September 1967. The Pol Pot group in the leadership of the Kampuchean Communist Party later denied all responsibility for the Samlaut affair; and it is probable that their own links in China were with elements that came to the fore in Peking in 1968. On 18 January 1968 the Pol Pot group itself embarked on armed struggle against the Sihanouk regime; and by the end of February several provinces were affected.[9]

Sihanouk made a number of speeches in different parts of the country appealing to the "Red Khmers" not to destroy the fragile independence which he had built up. On one occasion he went so far as to threaten that if they went on creating "insecurity" in various places he would have no choice but to dissolve the *Sangkum* (his own political movement) and hand over power to Lon Nol, whose policy would be similar to that of Suharto in Indonesia.[10] He assumed, of course, that the Americans would be only too willing to give aid to a pro-Western regime. It was impossible at that stage to know how limited the United States commitment to Cambodia would turn out to be.

Events moved rapidly in the direction Sihanouk predicted. By the time he left for France at the beginning of January 1970 he had already lost most of the power he once enjoyed: government decisions were largely in the hands of his princely rival Sirik Matak and of pro-American military and civilian officials. His failure to return home to resume power on 18 March 1970, often described as a "coup", was in reality the failure of a counter-coup. Even then the Americans may have been in some doubt how far to commit themselves to Lon Nol. Only when they sent their own combat units into the border areas of Cambodia on 30 April did it become clear to everyone that the Nixon administration was willing to provide active support to the new regime in Cambodia. And only after that, on 5 May 1970, did Peking break off relations with Lon Nol. The Vietnamese "White Book" of 1979 actually accused the Chinese of having tried to do a deal with him. Nor should we forget Lon Nol's earlier ties to China: he had been in Peking as recently as October 1969.[11]

If we put together the information contained in Pol Pot's *Black Paper* and that from Phnom Penh's "White Book" of 1984, we begin to get a clearer picture of the uncertainties affecting decision-making in Peking during the six weeks following Sihanouk's arrival from Moscow on 19 March 1970. Unbeknown to him, Pol Pot was also in Peking at that time; so too was Pham Van Dong, who did meet Sihanouk. It would appear that it took Sihanouk himself several days to make up his mind to collaborate with the leftist forces inside Cambodia (led ostensibly by Khieu Samphan) and to issue his statement of 23 March establishing the Front Unifié National de Kampuchea (FUNK). It then took the Chinese some weeks to commit themselves to backing that organisation openly. According to Pol Pot, the eventual outcome was a new alliance of forces in Cambodia, which Hanoi at last felt it could support. He tells us that when he visited North Vietnam at the end of 1969 he quarrelled furiously with Le Duan, who at that stage disapproved of the armed struggle in Cambodia. But on his return there in late April 1970, on the way back from China, he found a completely different atmosphere. He implies that the Vietnamese were obliged by events in Phnom Penh, and by the new relationship between Lon Nol and the Americans, to change their line on Cambodia. But he also indicates that in doing so, Hanoi expected to be able to restore the same relationship it had had with the Khmer united front before 1954. In practice Pol Pot's group was strong enough to resist the creation of a new joint command and began to devise its own strategy. The effect was a continuing separation between the pro-Vietnamese Communist network in Cambodia and the "indigenous" groups existing in various provinces. The lack of full centralised control over the latter may explain a good deal about the ultimate fate of the Kampuchean Revolution.

The decisions of March–April 1970 were followed by another period during which Hanoi drew upon both Soviet and Chinese aid in order to step up the war in Vietnam: first, to defeat (or at least to stall) the South Vietnamese invasion of Laos in early 1971; later, to mount the spring offensive of 1972. But by the latter date China had resolved its internal conflicts sufficiently to make up its mind on rapprochement with the United States. The Vietnamese "White Book" accused the Chinese of increasing their aid to Vietnam, and offering to build a better road network, simply in order to establish firmer control over the Vietnamese war effort as a basis on which to negotiate with the United States to bring about an end to the war. (No mention was made, in that 1979 context, of the fact that the Soviet Union also wished to improve its relations with the United States and was equally anxious to resolve the conflict in Indochina as a prelude to détente. In fact, Kissinger's strategy depended on simultaneous diplomacy with Moscow and Peking: only a double détente could permit the negotiating sequence which led to the Paris Agreement of January 1973.)

For Cambodia, the tragedy of the situation which had developed by then was that no one had sufficient control over the situation to produce a parallel Agreement on ending hositilities there too. The armed forces of the Front (FUNK) were strong enough to carry on fighting on their own, but not yet to win; whilst Sihanouk lacked sufficient control within FUNK for any diplomatic initiatives in his direction to produce results. Neither the Chinese nor the Vietnamese (that is, Hanoi) had any interest in promoting an agreement that might ultimately work to the advantage of the other. All this made it impossible to include Cambodia within the scope of the Paris Agreement. Pol Pot later accused the Vietnamese of hoping that the intense American bombing of Cambodia between February and August 1973 would be sufficient to destroy the "indigenous" Cambodian resistance movement; but it was not. As a result the war in Cambodia remained a complicating factor throughout 1973–75. According to the Phnom Penh "White Book" (1984), the Pol Pot group sought additional military assistance from China in late 1974. The Chinese refused direct aid, but asked Hanoi to give additional assistance; which was no doubt of considerable importance in the ability of the "Khmer Rouge" to launch their successful attack on Phnom Penh shortly afterwards.

Pol Pot himself – making no mention of that aid – says that the Vietnamese did not believe his forces had enough ammunition to defeat Lon Nol. He insists that the fall of Phnom Penh on 17 April 1975 took the Vietnamese Communist leadership by surprise; the implication being that the Khmer Rouge saw themselves in a race against time to capture Phnom Penh before Van Tien Dung's divisions reached Saigon. Success would make it unnecessary for the Vietnamese then to go on to "liberate" Cambodia. Moreover, the "White Book" of 1984 tells us that, even after the fall of Phnom Penh, Pol Pot controlled only the central organs of the Party – not the grass roots power bases, and especially not those in the cities (where the "pro-Vietnamese" network probably remained strong). This would give credence to later claims by Pol Pot and Ieng Sary that the decision to empty the Cambodian cities was motivated primarily by desire to forestall a Vietnamese takeover of the new regime. If so, they had every reason to proceed with maximum speed; which, as is well known, they did.

The resulting chaotic situation was one in which the Vietnamese had no chance to restore their own control over the Cambodian Communist movement. Control remained in the hands of "indigenous" leaders, who probably had effective power only in their own localities. Internecine warfare between the different leaders seems to have continued throughout the next three and a half years, with Pol Pot finally asserting his own control in September 1977 after an extremely bloody purge. It is not part of the purpose of the present paper to analyse the consequences of that period of conflict inside Cambodia; nor to enter into the controversy over how many people were killed, and in what circumstances. But there can be little doubt that the background to those events was far more complicated than most commentators have assumed; and that the tragedy was deeply rooted in the history of the Indochinese Communist movement. It is clear, too, that the initial destabilisation of Cambodia antedated not only the incursion of United States ground troops in the spring of 1970, but even the "secret bombing" of the country from March 1969. To lay blame for everything that happened in Cambodia after 1973 on American actions before that date is to ignore these equally important aspects of the situation. It will be evident from what has already been said that the situation following the almost simultaneous "liberation" of Phnom Penh and Saigon was extremely tense. On the one hand the Vietnamese Communists retained their earlier ambition to lead, if not to control, the revolution throughout Indochina. Le Duan was by now firmly established as Party leader, even though still only *primus inter pares*; and Le Duc Tho's power had been enhanced by the success of the southern campaign for which he and Van Tien Dung had been responsible. There was thus every chance that the Vietnamese Party would move towards an exclusive alliance with the CPSU; and that the Russians would eventually support Vietnamese ambitions. In the short term, however, since "pro-Vietnamese" elements in the Kampuchean Communist Party were in no position to seize power, Hanoi had to come to terms with the revolutionary regime actually in control inside Cambodia. Le Duan's visit to Phnom Penh in August 1975 probably did no more than establish a *modus vivendi*. For their part the new rulers of Cambodia turned to China, and Khieu Samphan secured various aid agreements when he visited Peking later the same month.[12]

From the point of view of Vietnamese–Cambodian relations, the period from August 1975 to late 1978 can be divided into three phases. During the first phase, until March or April 1977, the *modus vivendi* seems to have remained in force. The principal hope of the Vietnamese was that the internal conflicts within the Kampuchean Party would eventually bring to the fore a group more willing to cooperate with Vietnam. Pol Pot later alleged that the Vietnamese made several attempts to assassinate him. But in due course it was he who began the great purge, including the arrest of Hu Nim in April 1977 and his execution the following July. Hu Nim was the effective Party boss in Kompong Cham province; his removal made it possible for Pol Pot and his allies to control (and purge) that and other regions. Another important development was the purge and reorganisation of the Siem Reap area.[13]

The second phase of Cambodian–Vietnamese relations, beginning in April 1977, was characterised by the growth of conflict along the Cambodian–Vietnamese border – for which, as is hardly surprising, each side blamed the other as the aggressor. The Vietnamese appear to have been responsible for a larger incursion into Cambodia in September 1977; and another at the end of the year, which led to the formal breaking-off of relations between the two governments.[14] By May 1978 there was a chance that the Vietnamese might succeed in establishing an alliance with the rulers of Eastern Cambodia, who were ready to rebel against Pol Pot. But the revolt, led by So Phim, was brutally suppressed and another bloody purge followed. That led to the third phase, from May to December 1978, in which the Vietnamese appear to have used the border conflict as a means to put more and more pressure on the armed forces of the Pol Pot regime – until they were eventually too weak and disorganised to resist a further uprising, supported by massive Vietnamese intervention.

Placing these events into the wider international context, it is possible to see a relationship between Vietnam's conflict with Cambodia and its policy towards the Soviet Union and China. Not for nothing did President Carter's top adviser Brzezinski refer to the Vietnamese–Cambodian conflict at the end of 1977 as a "proxy war" between the two principal Communist powers. Here too, it is possible to see the spring and summer of 1977 as an important stage in Vietnamese decision-making. Until that point it still seemed possible that Vietnam would pursue a moderate, if not conciliatory policy towards all countries and would seek a wide range of economic relations. Hanoi received the Woodcock Mission – which also included the Senator Mansfield – in March 1977; it also published an investment code designed to impress capitalist investors. In April it sought aid from the Asian Development Bank, just as Pham Van Dong was signing an aid agreement in Paris. But by then it must have been apparent that the Vietnamese would have great difficulty in reconciling all the international demands being made upon them: by the capitalist countries (particularly Japan), by China, and above all by the Soviet Union.

The leading Soviet Politburo-member M. A. Suslov, who had attended the Vietnamese Party's fourth national congress in December 1976, had already made it clear that Vietnam – having accepted so much Soviet aid during the war – was now expected to participate in the "international division of labour": in other words, to meet the needs of Eastern Europe in specific fields and to develop its own economy accordingly.[15] Suslov, of all Soviet leaders, was probably the principal architect of the Brezhnev Doctrine of tight unity among socialist countries; Le Duan was the Vietnamese leader most likely to respond, and his power was greater than ever. But the closer Vietnam aligned itself with Moscow the more difficult it would become to develop independent economic relations with capitalist countries; the more difficult, too, to meet the demands of the Chinese. In February 1977 the Chinese informed Hanoi that they were unwilling to start any new aid projects. The following June, on his way through Peking Pham Van Dong received a memorandum from Li Xiannian setting out the issues that would have to be resolved if Sino-Vietnamese relations were to be improved.[16] By the time Dong returned home in July (having also visited Moscow) the Vietnamese faced some difficult choices which could no longer be postponed.

Also in June and July 1977, Vo Nguyen Giap made a tour of China during which he met Chen Xilian and other Chinese generals. On his return he made a speech to military cadres calling for the rapid modernisation of Vietnam's defence industry.

He remarked at one point that: "If an aggressive war occurs in the future, our enemy will very possibly have larger numbers of troops and more modern weapons than before;" and that "some comrades believe that because we defeated the Americans no other enemy will dare to touch us."[17] In view of what happened a mere eighteen months later, this now seems like prophecy. But it is by no means certain that Giap expected a conflict with China to come soon; nor that he was in favour of Vietnam adopting a completely defiant attitude towards Peking. What *is* clear is that by this time the Russians had no intention of financing the development of heavy industry in Vietnam. They were more interested in arrangements with Vietnam that would provide Soviet military facilities in return for specific military assistance, within the framework of the kind of friendship treaty actually signed on 3 November 1978. Economic development would take place within the framework of the CMEA (COMECON), which Vietnam finally joined as a full member in June 1978. By that time it was clear that Hanoi no longer had any chance of the kind of independent military and economic line envisaged by Giap. But the danger of conflict with China was very much greater.

In the meantime relations between Cambodia and China became closer than ever and were further strengthened by visits of two leading Chinese figures to Phnom Penh: Chen Yongkui in December 1977 and Deng Yingchao (widow of Zhou Enlai) in January 1978. These coincided with an escalation of the border war between Cambodia and Vietnam, as we have seen. When it became apparent that there was no hope of an early diplomatic solution to that conflict, the Chinese stepped up their military assistance to Pol Pot during the first half of 1978. That was probably the main reason why he was able to defeat the revolt of the eastern provinces in May that year. It was in May 1978, too, that relations between China and Vietnam began to deteriorate even more sharply with the result that the breach between them became public knowledge. In that same month, the visit to Peking by Zbigniew Brzezinski opened the way towards final 'normalisation' of relations between China and the United States.[18] By mid-year the Vietnamese had decided to abandon their long-standing policy of trying to maintain friendship with both Moscow and Peking. As large numbers of Chinese residents left Vietnam, Peking announced first the restriction (and later the termination) of its economic aid to Vietnam. It lies beyond the scope of the present paper to decide whether, at that point, the Vietnamese still had any real choice in the matter or were merely victims of global circumstance.

The question of Cambodia must now have become an issue in China's own debate about global and economic strategies. If Vietnam became more closely allied with the Soviet Union, and if Moscow proved willing to support Hanoi's ambitions in Indochina as a whole, how far were the Chinese prepared to go in providing military support for Cambodia? How far should they risk a larger and more direct confrontation with the Russians? These were questions of more than local significance; and they may have served as the catalyst which brought to a head the conflict within the leadership, between Deng Xiaoping and the PLA, about strategic and economic priorities. Peking's decisions on Cambodia were taken against a background of acute internal crisis.

On 29 July 1978 the Cambodian defence minister Son Sen arrived in Peking and was given a warm welcome by Generals Chen Xilian and Wang Shangrong. Next day, in addition to formal talks with Chen, he met Deng Xiaoping. At a formal banquet there were impressive speeches emphasising Sino-Cambodian solidarity; and on 31 July the Cambodian delegation was received by Hua Guofeng. They then went off to visit a number of places outside Peking and did not return to the capital until 4 August. In the meantime it was reported on 1 August that Li Xiannian had received another Cambodian leader, Ieng Sary. The next few days may have been critical in all respects. All that is known for certain is that the reports of Son Sen's farewell banquet on 4 August, and of his departure the following day, were in very much lower key; he was seen off by much less senior figures than Chen Xilian. On his return to Phnom Penh he disappeared from public view and it was later rumoured that he had lost face by failing to obtain a significant expansion of Chinese military support.[19]

One other development of this period may also have had some significance for the Cambodian issue: it was announced on 8 August, after an unexplained delay, that five days earlier the leading general Luo Ruiqing had died. It was Luo who, as chief of staff of the PLA, had advocated a more vigorous Chinese defence strategy than Mao was willing to sanction in 1965; and who had been dismissed towards the end of the year (at about the time when Lon Nol seems to have asked for Chinese military assistance). Luo's final disappearance from the scene on 3 August 1978 must surely have weakened the position of other PLA generals willing to take the strategic risks involved in a commitment to defend Cambodia at all costs.[20] There can be no doubt at all that China's actual decision was against such a course. This may even have been the turning-point in Deng Xiaoping's whole campaign for more moderate policies, based on a new relationship with Japan and the United States: a line which was eventually confirmed at the CCP Central Committee's Third Plenum in December.

It is impossible to tell how quickly the Vietnamese, for their part, recognised the direction Chinese policy was now taking; but they must surely have begun to make plans for the eventual Cambodian operation long before it actually began on 25 December 1978. It would be logical for them to be encouraged in that decision by indications that Peking did not intend to provide further massive assistance to the Pol Pot regime. On the other hand, they may have been worried by signs of Chinese diplomatic activity pointing in the direction of a Peking-sponsored rapprochement between Bangkok and Phnom Penh. By November, when Deng Xiao Ping visited Thailand at the same time as security minister Wang Dongxing visited Phnom Penh, it had probably been decided that the Khmer Rouge would have to defend their country on the basis of a "people's war" strategy – perhaps losing control of Phnom Penh and other major cities but retaining control of the countryside. Such a strategy would be the more effective if Thailand was willing to provide cross-border support. That being so, the Vietnamese had every reason to act quickly. In early December they encouraged the formation of a pro-Vietnamese "National Salvation Front"; and three weeks later they were ready to act swiftly and decisively in support of a "Cambodian uprising" against Pol Pot. The publication of the communiqué of the Chinese Communist Party's Third Plenum on 22 December, which indicated Deng's political victory over his opponents, may well have served as the "signal" for Vietnamese action. It is difficult to believe that Pol Pot was in a position to mount a frontal invasion of Tay-Ninh province on that day, as was later alleged by Hanoi propaganda.[21]

The Chinese probably expected Vietnamese action of some kind at that point. On the other hand, they may well have been surprised by the speed with which Van Tien Dung's forces captured all the main centres in Cambodia – within about a fortnight – and anxious that Pol Pot's forces might prove unable to establish an effective resistance. That may have been the reason why the Chinese decided, after all, to undertake their own "punitive" action against the northern-most provinces of Vietnam. But there were good reasons why it could not begin before the middle of February. One was the timing of Deng Xiaoping's visit to the United States, in late January and early February. Another was that 15 February 1979 was the date on which the Chinese were obliged formally to notify Moscow that they did not intend to renew the thirty-year Sino-Soviet Friendship Treaty signed in 1950. Consensus on that decision may have been achieved only at the last minute, on the basis of Deng's reports from Washington and Tokyo. The invasion of Vietnam began two days later.

China's overall strategy did not include a large war with Vietnam, and for that reason the Russians saw no reason to intervene. Had the Chinese intended to prevent a Vietnamese conquest of Cambodia at all costs, they would have done so the previous autumn. In fact, what they intended to achieve was precisely the kind of stalemate which came into being as a result of what actually happened between December 1978 and March 1979. The Russians and the Americans were prepared to live with that outcome. For a time at least, the "focal point of world contradictions" – as Sukarno had described it in 1964 – moved away from South-East Asia towards the Middle East, the Gulf and Afghanistan.

## Notes

1 The final version of this paper was completed at the end of 1984. It originated in a lecture at a meeting of the Royal Society for Asian Affairs on 25 April 1979. Since then, much new information has become available, making possible a complete revision of that initial presentation.
2 Particular mention should be made of three sources: (i) *Facts about Vietnam–China Relations over the past Thirty Years* ("White Book" put out by the Vietnamese Ministry of Foreign Affairs, Hanoi, October 1979), of which the text appears in BBC, *Summary of World Broadcasts/Far East/*6238 and 6242 (Caversham, 6 and 11 October 1979); (ii) *The Chinese Rulers' Crimes against Kampuchea* ("White Book" of the People's Republic of Kampuchea Foreign Ministry, July 1984), translated in *SWB/FE/*7703/C: special appendix (Caversham, 24 July 1984); (iii) Hoang Van Hoan, "Distortion of Facts about Militant Friendship between Vietnam and China is Impermissible," originally published in *Renmin Ribao* ("People's Daily") on 27 November 1979, and subsequently translated in *Beijing Review* (7 December 1979), pp. 11–23. Also important was a document issued by the government of

Kampuchea (the Pol Pot regime): *Black Paper: Facts and Evidences of the Acts of Aggression and Annexation of Vietnam against Kampuchea* (Democratic Kampuchea, September 1978).

3 The most detailed study so far written about the early stages of the Indochinese Communist Party is that of Huynh Kim Khanh, *Vietnamese Communism 1925–1945* (Cornell University Press, Ithaca, 1982); on the question of the Party's name, see pp. 123–9.

4 For the suggestion that Ho Chi Minh (then known as Nguyen Ai Quoc) was present at the foundation of the Malayan Communist Party in April 1930, see C. B. McLane, *Soviet Strategies in Southeast Asia* (Princeton, 1966), p. 136. A good idea of the international Communist milieu in which Nguyen Ai Quoc operated at that period is given by D. J. Duncanson, "Ho Chi Minh in Hong Kong, 1931–32," *China Quarterly,* no. 57 (January–March 1974).

5 For an early broadcast reference to the existence of this "Joint People's Committee of Vietnam, Laos and Cambodia", on the occasion of its first anniversary on 3 March 1952, see BBC, *Summary of World Broadcasts/FE*/151. pp. 68–9. The foundation of the Cambodian PRP on 28 June 1951 was revealed in 1984: see *SWB/FE*/7703/C/5.

6 For a more detailed account of the VNWP 9th Plenum and its significance, see R. B. Smith, *An International History of the Vietnam War:* Volume II, *The Struggle for South-East Asia 1961–65* (Macmillan, London, 1985), chapter xiii.

7 The disagreement between Pol Pot and the Vietnamese Communist leadership in 1965 is described in the *Black Paper* cited in note 2 above (pp. 25–6); his visit to China is mentioned in the Phnom Penh "White Book" of 1984 (*SWB/FE*/7703/C/11); that of Lon Nol to China, in November–December 1965, was known publicly at the time: see *Peking Review*, 3 Dec. and 17 Dec. 1965. For a Vietnamese account of the Cambodian Party split of 1960–63, see *Nhan-Dan* (Hanoi), 26 May 1981. Pol Pot's own account of the founding of the Kampuchean Communist Party and its subsequent history is given in his speech to commemorate its 17th anniversary in September 1977: *SWB/FE*/5629/C/1–9.

8 No full account exists of what was planned by the US Army if the additional 200,000 men had been sent to Vietnam; but some impressions can be gleaned from William Westmoreland, *A Soldier Reports* (New York 1976).

9 For a detailed study of the events of 1967 and early 1968, see B. Kiernan and Chantou Boua, *Peasants and Politics in Kampuchea 1941–1981* (London and New York, 1982), chapter 7, Pol Pot's version, concentrating especially on the events of 1968–70, is to be found in the *Black Book* of 1978.

10 Speech of Sihanouk at Chhouk, Kampot Province, 28 February 1968: *SWB/FE*/2710/A3/9–10. Other speeches of that period were monitored in *FE*/2709, 2715 and 2719. He again named Khieu Samphan as the instigator, but made no mention of any members of the Pol Pot group; it is impossible to tell how much he knew about the inner decision-making of the "Khmer Rouge" at that stage. The reference to Suharto in Indonesia may reflect Sihanouk's belief that once Sukarno had been toppled, he himself was bound to be next.

11 *Peking Review*, 3 Oct. 1969. For the relevant passage in the "White Book" of 1979, see *SWB/FE*/6242/A3/5. The account which follows, dealing with events from March 1970 to April 1975, is based largely on the sources cited in note 2 above.

12 For Le Duan's visit to Phnom Penh, see Communiqué of 3 Aug. 1975: *SWB/FE*/4973/A3/1–2; on the same day, *Nhan-Dan* wrote of the "great friendship between Vietnam and Cambodia." Khieu Samphan and Ieng Sary visited China from 15 to 19 Aug. 1975; the former then went on to Pyongyang: *FE*/4983/A3/l; *FE*/4989/A3/l.

13 These purges are discussed, on the basis of information gleaned from interviews with Cambodian refugees in Thailand in 1980, in M. Vickery; *Cambodia 1975–1982* (Sydney and Hemel Hempstead, 1984). For evidence relating to the arrest, torture and execution of Hu Nim, see *New Statesman* (London), 2 May 1980.

14 For statements by both sides, indicating the evolution of the border conflict down to the end of 1977, see *SWB/FE/5703/A3/1–10*.
15 For Suslov's speech at the VNWP Fourth National Congress, December 1976, see *SWB/FE/5392/C/11–14*.
16 The Li Xiannian Memorandum, dated 10 January 1977, was published in *Renmin Ribao* on 23 March 1979 and in *Beijing Review* 30 March 1979; see also *SWB/FE/6075/A3/1*.
17 *Tap-Chi Cong-San* (Hanoi), October 1977: translated, as broadcast, in *SWB/FE/5647/C/1–8*.
18 For an "inside" report on the Sino-American talks of May 1978, see Z. Brzezinski, *Power and Principle: Memoirs of the National Security Adviser 1977–81* (London 1983), Chapter 6.
19 For details of Son Sen's visit, as broadcast at the time, see *SWB/FE/5857, 5879, 5880, 5882, 5884*. The impression that he was told that Cambodia must ultimately pursue a "self-reliant" strategy is noted by Nayan Chanda, in a long account of the Vietnamese invasion of Cambodia, which appeared in *Far Eastern Economic Review*, 19 Jan. 1979, p. 12.
20 For Luo Ruiqing's views in 1965, see M. Yahuda, "Kreminology and the Chinese Strategic Debate," *China Quarterly*, xlix (1972), pp. 32–75. In May 1965 he praised Stalin's strategy in the second world war, which was in marked contrast to the line put forward by Lin Biao the following September. It is impossible to confirm the hypothesis that Luo actively favoured Chinese intervention to save Cambodia in 1978; but the eventual outcome of the Chinese "debate" in the latter year seems fairly clear in the light of what actually happened.
21 See, for example, the "White Book" of October 1979: *SWB/FE/6242/A3/13*.

# 9 Vietnam from the 1890s to the 1990s

Continuity and change in the longer perspective[1]

Source: *South East Asia Research* 4(2) (1996): 197–224.

The [chapter] seeks to define and explore some of the problems in the evolution of Vietnam as a country during the past one hundred years, focusing on institutional and economic continuity and change rather than on political conflict and war; and emphasizing the internal perspective rather than that of international relations. Its four sections deal, first with some general aspects of change and continuity in the period 1890–1990; with the importance of the village, of the Confucian élite, and of clan networks in 'traditional' Vietnam; with economic development and monetary issues before, during, and after the colonial period — including the contrast between North and South in the two decades of partition after 1954; and finally with economic and social opportunities and failures in the period since the early 1970s — particularly the consequences of choosing a Soviet economic alignment in preference to links with Japan and capitalist Asia, and the effects of the loss of a succession of élites, owing to revolution and war, which has left many of the most qualified Vietnamese living as ideological or economic exiles in Australia, Europe, and North America.

## I

During the past two or three decades, Western writing on the modern history of Vietnam has been dominated very largely by three themes: the impact of French colonial rule leading to the growth of anti-colonialism; the rise of the Vietnamese Communist Party and the progress of the Revolution; and the course of international conflict after 1945, culminating in the 'Vietnam War' and its aftermath. The purpose of the present paper is to go beyond those well-worn themes and to consider the problems of Vietnam as a country — rather than merely as a 'nation' in the political sense — during the whole of the twentieth century. I am conscious of the need ultimately to focus on an even longer time-span: certain of the fundamental characteristics of Vietnam have been shaped by experiences going back to the eleventh or twelfth centuries and beyond; and its geographical complexity, shaped partly by physical features, also stems from the diversity of a pre-nineteenth century cultural heritage involving more than the history of the Vietnamese people themselves. Here, however, I propose to concentrate on the past hundred years or so — with occasional reference to the two centuries before that — in order to establish a better perspective for understanding Vietnam's problems in the 1990s.

For most of that period — indeed, since 1802 — the country which is now Vietnam has been a recognizable unity in all major respects: geographically, administratively, culturally, and politically. Only in the context of that essential unity can we talk about Vietnam's transformation into a French colony between 1859 and 1885; its occupation by Japanese forces from 1941 to 1945; and its 'partition' into two independent states — both distinctively Vietnamese — from 1954 to 1975. While emphasising the theme of continuity during the 'long' twentieth century, we cannot altogether ignore the interaction between the national and international perspectives. However, it will best serve our present purpose to focus on those discontinuities which were of greatest consequence for the evolution of the country itself, rather than on those whose importance derives from the course of international events.

By starting in the 1890s, of course, we are taking the French presence largely for granted. It is worth suggesting, none the less, that conquest by France might conceivably have been avoided if the court of Hué had been more accommodating to the Europeans in the mid-1850s. At that time France and Britain were cooperating in a diplomatic effort to 'open up' the ports of China, Vietnam, and Siam. It would have been possible at that stage for 'Dai Nam' to agree to treaties with both those powers, then to follow the same path with other Western governments. It was by accepting such treaties with several countries almost simultaneously — Britain, France, the United States, Denmark, the Hanseatic League, etc. — that Siam was able to escape colonial conquest by any single power during the later years of the nineteenth century. Even China had treaties with enough countries to retain its sovereignty, although not all of its power, until the formal establishment of an 'open door' policy after 1898. Vietnam, however, rejected the advances of both the French ambassador Charles de Montigny and the British official Thomas Wade in 1856–57. By refusing to trade with foreigners at all at that critical juncture, Vietnam found itself, by 1859, having to deal with the colonial ambitions of a single European power. Thereafter, Britain and other Western powers were content to leave France to pursue its own ambitions in Vietnam and Cambodia; and up to a point, even in Laos. By the start of our period, therefore, in the 1890s, Vietnam was gradually coming to terms with an unprecedented form of foreign domination which, having established itself in the South a generation earlier, was now beginning to make itself felt in the Centre and North.

During the period since the 1890s it is possible, from Vietnam's own point of view, to identify three — perhaps four — key moments of social and political discontinuity. The first such moment occurred around 1916: the year which saw the final abolition of the Confucian examination system as a means of recruiting

Vietnamese 'mandarins'. Until that point there was still some sense of continuity with a tradition dominated by classical Chinese texts and an imperial bureaucracy. A notable Hué scholar of the early French period was Cao Xuan Duc (1842–1923): governor of a key area of 'Tonkin' in the early 1890s, then head of the Office of History (*Quoc Su Quan*) from 1903 to 1908 and subsequently minister of education (1908–13).[2] In 1909 he produced the third and last edition of the standard geography of the kingdom of 'Dai-Nam', which had first been commissioned by Tu Duc in 1865; he also compiled a biographical dictionary of successful examination laureates of the Nguyen period. Such works reflected a kind of continuity which declined rapidly after 1916. That year also witnessed the last involvement of the throne at Hué in an anti-French revolt, leading to the forced abdication and exile of the emperor Duy-Tan. His successor, Khai Dinh, had no such connections with revolutionary radicalism; and by 1945 the abdication of Bao-Dai merely confirmed that the throne could have no significant role in a genuinely national revolution.

The revolution of 1945, coming as the climax of a transition starting in 1940, marks the second moment of discontinuity. Its most essential aspect at the time was not so much the emergence of a Communist-led provisional government in Hanoi, which would eventually control the whole country, as the sudden eclipse of French power following the Japanese coup of 9 March: an eclipse which totally disrupted France's system of colonial exploitation of the country and lasted long enough to permit an eventual seizure of power by the Vietnamese. That dislocation could not, in the end, be reversed by the war which France chose to fight between 1946 and 1954 in the hope of recovering control. The revolution itself opened the way to competition among rival Vietnamese movements for leadership of an independent Vietnam: a struggle which eventually became the focus of international conflict as well as calling for national mobilisation on a scale never previously attempted; and which eventually led to control of the whole country by the Vietnamese Communist Party.

The third moment of discontinuity occurred in two stages: in the North in 1954–55, with the victory of a Marxist–Leninist movement dedicated to socialist transformation of the economy and elimination of the class system; in the South not until 1975, when the same revolutionary principles could at last be applied nationwide. In the interval an alternative pattern of change began to take shape in the South, although it was prevented by war from becoming firmly established. None the less, the delay in achieving a Marxist transformation south of the seventeenth parallel left that part of the country less securely socialist when further changes came along in the late 1980s. It remains to be seen whether, in the longer perspective of Vietnamese history, future historians will feel justified in regarding 1989–91 as a fourth moment of discontinuity. Certainly those years saw a transformation of the global economic and political context in which the Vietnam of the 1990s has been obliged to chart a new course, without entirely abandoning its socialist principles.

As well as these temporal discontinuities, we must also take account of the physiographic complexity of Vietnam, and the serious problems of transport and communication to which it has given rise. Before the twentieth century, the principal lines of communication depended on inland waterways and on small-scale shipping between coastal ports (both of which remain important even today). That made communicating between distant localities, in an expanding kingdom, a slow and uncertain business. An important theme of twentieth century change has been gradual improvement in this sphere: first in the period from 1900 to 1945; then in the 1950s and 1960s; and even more markedly during the present decade. The first railway lines had already been built before Paul Doumer became Governor-General of Indochina in 1898; but it was his programme which led to the construction of rail links with China and from Hanoi to Saigon. Even then, the latter project — the 'Transindochinois' — was not completed until 1936. Meanwhile a network of roads was also created in the 1930s. The last major contribution of the French was the introduction of radio-broadcasting, again in the 1930s. Following partition, the post-war reconstruction of communications in the 1950s was undertaken separately in North and South Vietnam. Most notably, the Chinese provided assistance to restore and expand the railways of the Democratic Republic; while the Americans promoted the building of roads in the territory controlled by the Saigon regime.

During the war of 1961–75, both sides experienced acute logistical problems arising from the sheer length of the country. The US Army found itself needing large numbers of support troops to sustain a logistics system based on five depots stretched out along the coast of South Vietnam; while the People's Army of Vietnam steadily built up the Ho Chi Minh trail through Laos. Both sides also created networks of electronic communication, of which many details remain secret even now: the longer-term effects of the war in that respect are still difficult to assess. More recently, however, the electronic revolution of the 1980s and 1990s has been a world-wide phenomenon. In that context Vietnam, although to some extent lagging behind its neighbours, has entered yet another phase in the evolution of its communications system. (The problem now, for all Asian countries with a strong sense of national culture, is how to respond to an expansion of genuinely global communications which may threaten rather than reinforce national unity.)

All of these developments have helped to transform Vietnam into a more unified country and society. Nevertheless, the regional diversity of the country has remained important in the twentieth century. The pattern of French conquest led to a broad distinction between three regions (known in the French period as the three *ky*, but in present-day usage as the three *bo*): the North corresponding to the French protectorate of 'Tonkin'; the Centre to the French 'Annam', also a protectorate; and the South to 'French Cochinchina', which the French claimed as a fully-ceded colony. The contrasts between them, however, have much deeper historical roots.

The North (and part of the Centre as far south as Nghe-Tinh) corresponds broadly to the region once controlled by Tang China, as well as to the territory of the Trinh *chua* in the seventeenth and eighteenth centuries. The remaining provinces of the Centre, conquered gradually by Vietnam between the twelfth and the seventeenth centuries, were previously controlled by a series of Cham principalities — and as such were strongly influenced by Indian Mahayana Buddhism. In the seventeenth and eighteenth centuries they were the territory of the Nguyen *chua*, and became the point of departure for further southward expansion by the Vietnamese. (The question of continuity between the Cham and the Vietnamese cultures is one which has still to be fully explored.) Culturally, the North was the most strongly 'Confucianized' area of Vietnam, as well as probably the most literate; the Centre was culturally more fragmented, and more deeply influenced by Buddhism than other regions. The Centre was also the region most resistant to the impact of French culture, and it produced some of the most staunchly anti-colonial leaders of the twentieth century. But linguistically it was northern Vietnamese which eventually became the standard for the country as a whole, gradually overcoming the pronounced differences between regional dialects.

The South, being the area most recently conquered and settled by the Vietnamese as well as the first to be dominated by the French, was doubly different from the other two regions. Originally part of Cambodia, it had only gradually been brought under Vietnamese control between *c.*1660 and *c.*1840 and remained something of a frontier region even in the second half of the nineteenth century. The French were thus able, to a remarkable extent, to shape the pattern both of its economic exploitation and of its continued settlement by the Vietnamese. Already in the 1890s the digging of canals was allowing large new areas of rice production to be opened up, on the basis of government concessions to large landowners: a process which continued until the 1920s, producing in some areas a pattern of landownership and tenure quite uncharacteristic of traditional Vietnam. In the early twentieth century comparable French encouragement was given to large-scale rubber planting in the northern part of 'Cochinchina'. These developments contributed in turn to the growth of Saigon-Cholon as a major commercial centre, with Saigon itself becoming a predominantly French-style city at its core.[3]

Another significant feature of the society and economy of the South was the much higher percentage of Chinese residents there than elsewhere. Over the centuries Chinese settlement had contributed a great deal to the life and culture of Vietnam as a whole; but the South was unusual in that Chinese communities already existed at Bien Hoa, My Tho, and Ha Tien even before the Vietnamese first established administrative control. Further migration occurred in the colonial period. By the mid-1930s, out of a total of 217,000 inhabitants counted as Chinese by French statisticians, as many as 171,000 lived in 'Cochinchina'.[4]

In addition to these differences between the principal lowland regions of Vietnam, a further distinction must be made throughout the country between lowland and highlands. The latter areas were traditionally inhabited by non-Vietnamese 'hill-peoples', of various ethnic origins, and were markedly separate from 'Vietnam proper'. However, the trend in the twentieth century has been towards integrating the highlands more fully into the economic and social life of Vietnam as a whole. Large numbers of Vietnamese have been encouraged to settle there in the past thirty or forty years, and their presence has tended to blur the distinction between the two types of region. The highlands were also the scene of some of the most violent battles of the various wars fought on Vietnamese soil between 1945 and 1980, and their strategic importance cannot be ignored by any Vietnamese regime.

Finally, we should note the steady increase that has occurred in the population of Vietnam over the past hundred years. Accurate population figures for the late nineteenth and early twentieth century are not available for Vietnam as a whole. Relatively precise census estimates were possible in French Cochinchina, but were not attempted elsewhere at that early stage. After 1950, efforts to count numbers of inhabitants were made difficult by the disruption of revolution and war. Nevertheless it is possible to indicate the general trend of population growth in the country as a whole; and also to observe how the rate of growth has increased dramatically during the past quarter century (see Table 1).

Population growth at the rate that has prevailed during the 1980s and 1990s — the estimated population is by now over 70 million — cannot be sustained without parallel economic growth. Already in the 1930s and 1940s there was concern about overpopulation in certain areas, notably lowland 'Tonkin' and the region of Nghe-Tinh; it was a contributory factor to the famine of 1944–45. But in present circumstances economic expansion on a scale hitherto unprecedented is an urgent necessity for Vietnam, transcending all differences in the political and ideological spheres.

## II

It is impossible to do justice in a single paper to all aspects of the history of Vietnam during the past century. In pursuing the question of continuity and long-term change, I propose to concentrate on two main themes: first, the continuing importance of 'traditional' social and political relations, shaped over several

*Table 9.1* The population of Vietnam, 1914–89

|  | *1914 (est.)* | *1936–37 (census)* | *1960–61 (census)* | *1989* |
|---|---|---|---|---|
| North ('Tonkin') | 6,119,724 | 8,700,000 | – | 3,643,000 |
| Centre ('Annam') | 5,200,000 | 5,656,000 | – | 7,714,000 |
| South ('Cochinchina') | 3,050,785 | 4,616,000 | – | 2,201,000 |
| Vietnam | 14,370,509 | 18,370,509 | 30,800,000 | 63,367,000 |

*Notes*: The figures for 1914, based on official French estimates, are taken from *French Indochina*. London: HMSO for Foreign Office, 1920; those for 1936–37, based mainly on census returns in January 1937, are from *Annuaire Statistique de l'Indochine 1936–37*.

The figure for 1960–61 combines data from a census in North Vietnam in 1960 with an estimate for the South made in 1961.

Figures for the census of April 1989 are calculated from a summary given in *Far East and Australasia 1991*. London: Europa, 1990; note that the total population of 64,411,668 frequently quoted for the 1989 census included 1,045,000 Vietnamese living overseas.

centuries before the 1890s and still only partially transformed by colonial conquest and socialist revolution; second, the theme of economic 'development', past and present, and the question of foreign economic relations.

Accounts of Vietnam's 'traditional' society usually focus on three essential elements: the Confucian bureaucracy, the autonomy of the village, and the importance of the clan. Sometimes attention is also given to Buddhism and to the proliferation of Chinese-style religious sects outside the Confucian framework. Invariably these things are discussed against a background of strong awareness of 'Chinese influence' on the evolution of Vietnamese culture and institutions. Even in the twentieth century the Vietnamese have tended to define their national independence in terms of their former subjection to China and their subsequent ability to defeat invading Chinese armies. The use of classical Chinese in so many 'Sino-Vietnamese' documents and literary works, down to the late nineteenth century, makes it impossible to study Vietnamese history before that date without a firm knowledge of Chinese literary and institutional traditions. The Confucian bureaucracy of eighteenth century Hanoi or nineteenth century Hué represented the highest point of similarity between Vietnamese and Chinese practices, and the importance of the 'Chinese model' in the latter period has been thoroughly explored in Alexander Woodside's classic study.[5] Chinese influence was also much in evidence among the first generation of Vietnamese scholars to confront the 'loss of the country' after 1885. Later on, however, China's own lack of an effective response to Western imperialism down to the 1920s — and the growing influence of Japanese modernization and of French political theory — contributed to the decline of the Confucian model as a continuing source of inspiration; and hence to the lack of continuity between the 'mandarinal' system and the eventual emergence of two independent Vietnamese governments in 1954–55.

What matters particularly, from our present point of view, is the continuing influence of the Confucian attitude to law — which depended more on respect for powerful and supposedly virtuous individuals than on the impersonal application of general principles. China did not impose on Vietnam the kind of legal system which was stamped by the Roman Empire on what subsequently became the independent states of Europe; nor did the monarchy of Dai-Viet develop the kind of relationship which the rulers of feudal Europe had with their vassals, which generated a tradition of parliamentary legislation. The French colonial presence upset Vietnam's Confucian traditional practices, but it did not lead to the universal adoption of a French (derived from Roman) legal system. What France imposed was an extension of the principle of extra-territoriality, for its own citizens and institutions, combined with an arbitrary system of penalties for ordinary crimes and a relatively traditional approach to peasant litigation. For most Vietnamese, *droit* remained an alien concept. The residual influence of 'traditional' attitudes to law and institutions, despite the revolution of 1945, remains a factor in Vietnam's problems even in the late twentieth century.

This emphasis on Confucianism is not, in any case, the only way of perceiving pre-colonial Vietnam: it is equally possible to regard it as one of the countries of South East Asia. Certain features of Vietnamese society and culture find just as close parallels in Java, and even Bali, as in southern China, All of South East Asia has experienced the influence of one or another external source of religious and literary tradition. In the case of Vietnam, that source happens to be China; and whereas in other parts of the region such external influences have come by sea, Vietnam has an actual land border with China. One might argue that the extent to which direct Chinese rule shaped the future kingdom of Dai-Viet between the first and ninth centuries A.D. is comparable with the kind of influence exerted by Spain during the 'Hispanization' of the Philippines between the mid-sixteenth and the nineteenth centuries. The Vietnamese, in the end, are no more Chinese than the Filipinos are Spaniards.

Confucian influence in shaping the Vietnamese 'traditional' élite must be balanced against the fundamental importance of the village at the grassroots of Vietnamese society. Despite the adaptation of Chinese terminology, the traditional Vietnamese village had far more in common with villages in certain parts of South East Asia (notably Java and Bali) than with those of China. Its focal points were the *dinh*, serving both as meeting hall and as shrine to the village 'deity'; and the *cong-dien* ('communal land'), which was regularly parcelled out among the inhabitants and which at the same time served to guarantee the village's collective obligations to the state. The village had its own hierarchy of 'officials' and its own 'ruling class' of richer families who by the nineteenth century owned private rice land as well as participating in the *cong-dien*. The pattern of village administration and society in the North, in the years immediately following the French conquest, was described in some detail by one of the early French district officials.[6] In this, as in other aspects of Vietnamese society, there were inevitable differences between North, Centre, and South; but accounts of villages in the two latter regions leave no doubt that the same essential features were taken south and reproduced in a new environment, not abandoned in the course of the *Nam-tien*.[7]

The principle that 'the laws of the emperor give way to the customs of the village' — *phep vua thua le tang* — is well known. P. Ory found that principle clearly reflected in the *xa* (village) archives which he had been able to inspect. At least four types of register were usually kept: two for the benefit of higher-level officials, the other two for use solely within the village. In the former category were the *dien-bo* ('register of fields') on which the assessment of land tax was based; and the *dinh-bo* ('register of obligations'), which — although listing only some of the inhabitants — formed the basis of the village's assessment for *corvée* and personal taxes. The other two records, kept secret from outsiders, were the *so-thu-thue* ('tax collection list') used to allocate the tax burden among the inhabitants; and the *so-hang-xa* ('categories of people list') used for the actual allocation of communal lands. These records indicate a system of control over land and labour very different from that which existed in 'feudal' Europe, where 'lords' derived wealth and power from hereditary 'manors'.

It is possible, using sources of this kind, in conjunction with the record of imperial decrees over several centuries, to give an impressionistic account of the 'typical' village and its customs. What is not yet possible is to get a comprehensive picture of the grassroots pattern of society across the country as a whole. Beneath the broad picture of institutional conformity there was probably considerable diversity in actual village arrangements: particularly regarding differences of origin and size, and patterns of power and wealth involving the dominant village families. Some villages, for example, had a substantial area of communal land; in others its extent had been eroded, leaving a large proportion of land in private ownership. Villages might also differ in the nature of their economic livelihood: for example in lowland 'Tonkin' there were villages whose inhabitants, as well as growing rice, specialized in different manufacturing activities. A number of records surveying the actual obligations of all Vietnamese villages province by province — rather than single villages, typical or otherwise — have survived for certain dates in the period from 1806 to the 1840s; but they have not yet been systematically examined by historians. By the time the French came to attempt their own more thorough statistical survey of landownership and distribution — not until around 1930 — they were no longer interested in village structures but only in the application of 'modern' categories of individual (or household) ownership, tenure, etc.[8]

Nor do we have a very full picture of the relationship between villages and mandarins in pre-colonial Vietnam. Most existing studies tend to focus on 'the village' and 'the bureaucracy' as ideal types — in the Weberian sense — while leaving something of a gap with regard to the nature of actual relations between the two. Records of the Confucian examination system indicate the procedures by which a small number of individuals, drawn probably from the wealthier element in their respective villages, could rise to become powerful mandarins at the provincial level or above. And we have a fairly clear picture of what is likely to have occurred when higher officials visited individual villages to settle disputes or to assess obligations. But that does not give us an adequate picture of the real structure of power in nineteenth century Vietnam. At any one time, probably fewer than two thousand individuals performed 'mandarinal' functions as full laureates of the examination system: a rather small number of administrators for a society of perhaps nine or ten million people. A great many people who cannot be categorized as either village leaders or scholar-mandarins must have held influential positions. What of district level officers, for example, performing tasks not requiring scholarly status? Or the officers who led units of the armed forces? What relationships existed among these 'invisible' categories of people?

Some of the answers to these questions may lie in a better understanding of the traditional role of the family or clan, whose importance is often recognized in principle but whose actual history proves extremely difficult to study in depth. Important families had impressive ancestral shrines and kept their own records, sometimes in the form of *gia-pha* (family genealogies). But such records were too informative for outsiders to be allowed access to them, and even now it is probable that many have been kept hidden. Such sources could have value to historians not merely for their biographies of successful individual family members, but even more for the information they might provide about networks of clan relationships linking officials in different parts of the administrative system and also leading figures in different villages. Almost certainly those families which produced scholars and high officials would assign other clan members to look after the family shrine and estate, and perhaps to control affairs in the clan's native village. At present, unfortunately, the study of traditional Vietnamese society in these terms is too difficult to undertake. But without such studies our understanding must remain very limited.

Neither is it possible, in the present state of our knowledge, to test the now-famous hypothesis of James C. Scott that life in the pre-colonial villages of South East Asia was governed by a 'moral economy', which broke down under the impact of colonial administration and economic materialism. It seems fairly clear that in general the formal tax burden on Vietnamese peasant families, measured both in money terms and in relation to rice yields, increased significantly between the 1890s and the 1930s; and there is a strong likelihood that the local power of wealthier families would ensure that the increased burden was less than equitably distributed between rich and poor in each village community. Attempts to impose any kind of 'progressive' direct taxation in rural areas were doomed to failure, given the limitations of rural administration. On the other hand *corvée* obligations were, in principle at least, commuted to cash payments; and the colonial authorities also did their best to eliminate formal exemptions from personal tax on the ground of official status. Even so, there was a growing shortfall of colonial revenue, which was made up by the imposition of indirect taxes, including those raised from the notorious alcohol, opium, and salt monopolies. There again, an opportunity was created for the dominant 'rich' element in each village to use its power to the disadvantage of poorer families.[9] Unfortunately this evidence concerning the rising taxes payable under successive colonial decrees cannot be balanced against detailed information about actual rural incomes in this period.

The one other element in the situation which seems fairly well attested is a growing materialism amongst better-off Vietnamese, in the countryside as well as in the towns, and their increasing demand for types of consumer goods unimagined in earlier periods — including automobiles. That in turn increased the incentive to add to family income wherever possible, leading to unprecedented levels of exploitation of poorer neighbours and tenants. In 'Tonkin' around 1930 Pierre Gourou notes specific cases where already rich landowners were able to expand their estates by taking advantage of the need of small proprietors to borrow more than they could repay, when faced with the sudden effects of flooding.[10] In the Mekong delta the opportunities opened up by an expanding export market for rice, especially in the newly settled areas of the Transbassac, led to the emergence of even more commercially-oriented attitudes towards landownership and tenancy — in some places completely transcending the traditional village structure. The changing economic dimensions of southern society were explored by Robert Sansom, in the course of a study designed to establish the background to the land reform of Ngo Dinh Diem in the 1950s.[11]

The various strands of institutional and agrarian history which have been mentioned, all too briefly, in the foregoing paragraphs suggest the need for a new and more comprehensive attempt to analyse the structure of power in Vietnamese society, during both the pre-colonial and colonial periods, before attempting to define its fundamental character in terms which are too simple to do justice to the reality.

In studying a country whose eventual rulers adopted thoroughgoing Marxism–Leninism, for a generation and more after 1954, it is perhaps also relevant to consider the ways in which Vietnam's traditional society, and its development under colonialism, have been analysed in Marxist terms; as well as the Party's actual policies for achieving a socialist transformation. The whole question of Marxist–Leninist analysis of traditional power structures in Asia has been bedevilled by the 'Stalinist' debate on the distinction between 'feudal' and 'Asiatic' modes of production. Karl Wittfogel, who was roundly condemned in Moscow in the 1930s, argued that Marx should have unequivocally recognized the officials of traditional 'oriental' bureaucracies as a ruling class in the fullest sense of the term — deriving their ability to exploit the agricultural surplus of such societies from a distinctive system of class relations. The ambiguity of both Marx and Lenin on that issue allowed Stalin to insist, on the contrary, that all pre-capitalist societies must be regarded as 'feudal': that is, their political structures invariably depended on the power of a landlord class.[12]

In Vietnam, Marxist historians writing in the 1950s and 1960s conformed with that orthodoxy in equating the 'Confucianization' of Dai-Viet in the fourteenth and fifteenth centuries with the rise of a landlord class — in place of the 'princely' (slave-owning) class who had supposedly been dominant since the eleventh century or before. This new 'landlord' class was deemed to have produced both the scholar-officials of the Le dynasty and the pattern of court politics of the Trinh and the Nguyen *chua*. After surviving a challenge to its power from the 'revolutionary forces' of the Tay-Son period, it was seen to reach the height of its political domination under the 'reactionary' Nguyen dynasty of the nineteenth century. This interpretation of Vietnamese history has a bearing on the way the Party handled revolutionary strategy in practice after 1954. In terms of propaganda, it found it relatively easy to denounce French imperialism and the 'comprador bourgeoisie' which had directly served its interests, as well as the owners of large plantations and rice lands in the South. However, the Communists came to power first in the North and were not immediately given the opportunity of eliminating the relatively easily identifiable 'landlord class' of French Cochinchina. Faced with the problem of seizing power in practice, they found it much more difficult to devise an effective strategy of revolutionary transformation in the villages of North Vietnam. They turned to the Chinese model of land reform, which was based not merely on the expropriation and redistribution of land but also on the denunciation and disgrace of the 'ruling class' in every locality.

The controversial consequences of Truong Chinh's land reform of 1953–56 are well known and need not detain us here; nor need it any longer be doubted that a good deal of killing and imprisonment of 'landlords' took place in the course of the rural seizure of power.[13] Underlying those events lay a fundamental contradiction between the revolutionary practice of mobilizing poor peasants to establish Party control in each village and the ideological principle that rural power lay in the hands of a landlord class. Serious problems arose from the fact that, in many villages in the North and northern Central provinces, village power was in the hands of people whose actual property did not justify their classification as landlords in any meaningful sense. Worse still, for Party unity, was the fact that many of the 'richer' families had sent sons to fight for the Viet Minh.

It is logical to ask, nevertheless, how far 'socialist transformation' really did transform village life — as opposed to merely placing new people in control of institutions too deeply rooted to be changed overnight. For the first few years, down to 1959, the redistribution of land appears to have led to a significant improvement in the livelihood of many villages: Andrew Vickerman has shown that in North Vietnam, rice yields per hectare actually increased during that period, before declining in the 1960s. But the purpose of transformation was not merely to bring about grassroots political change; it was to establish a basis for economic growth. In Marxist–Leninist terms that meant ensuring that the 'surplus' accumulated through higher agricultural production would be diverted away from unnecessary consumption and devoted to economic development — including industrialization. To that end, from 1959 the Party set about implementing the next stage of its revolution: the creation of agricultural collectives, in conjunction with the use of Soviet and Chinese aid to build an essential infrastructure. Ultimately, socialist Vietnam would have to sustain its own capital accumulation and its own economic growth.[14]

Adam Fforde has examined in depth the situation which actually emerged by the 1970s. North Vietnam did not follow China down the path of creating 'communes' but it succeeded in establishing a limited number of model 'higher level co-operatives', in which a measure of managerial control was accompanied by technological innovation — giving at least the promise of improved agricultural performance. Unfortunately that was achieved by concentrating all available resources on those places at the expense of the large majority of villages, where co-operative management remained at the level of 'brigade' production teams and where there was neither sufficient high-level co-ordination nor sufficient incentive to increase productivity. The renewal of the war in South Vietnam after 1960 may also have been a factor in this situation, to the extent that it drew potentially skilled labour away from the fields into unproductive military and logistical operations. As the war moved towards its climax, the policy of socialist construction in the North was reaffirmed in 1974; regulations were tightened up, and by 1977 it was possible to embark on serious social transformation in the South.[15]

In the South, the situation of the mid-1970s was already quite different from that which had existed in 1954, having passed through three phases of change. First, in 1956 the regime of Ngo Dinh Diem had introduced a measure of land reform designed to limit the size of estates to between 100 and 150 hectares. Although widely circumvented by landlords, it led to the elimination of the enormous estates of the French period; and by 1960 the French agreed to underwrite the compensation of all French owners of rice land in the South. (Plantations were a separate issue.) Some of the lands acquired in this way were used to resettle refugees from North Vietnam, but only a relatively small proportion of the expropriated land had actually been distributed to new owners when the 'armed struggle' was resumed in 1960–61. The second phase, from then till around 1968, was dominated by the political and military activities of the NLFSVN, which succeeded in carrying out rent reductions and even redistribution in some areas; and in making many other areas too insecure for landowners to collect any rents. By 1969, as the Thieu regime began to recover control of significant areas of the countryside, there was no longer so much resistance to a properly planned 'land-to-the-tiller' programme. A third phase began, with American financial support, allowing the implementation of Thieu's programme in much of the Mekong delta during 1970–72. That redistribution, where it occurred, was the basis of the land system existing at the time of reunification in 1975. It was supplanted by the co-operativization which began in 1977 — but which this time was carried out by bureaucratic methods rather than by the hysteria of mass mobilization.[16]

Yet by the early 1980s — after a major food crisis in 1979 — it was clear that socialism in the countryside was not working as it should. The adoption of a 'three contract' system within co-operatives proved to be the first step towards their virtual dismantling — which was completed following the sixth Party Congress of December 1986 and a final series of decisions in April 1988. Although Vietnam remains a socialist republic and has not formally abandoned the principle of collective agriculture, the decisions of 1988 amounted to a reversal of the co-operativization process. Economically it led to a marked increase in agricultural output, assisted by effective use of fertilisers and new strains of rice, with the result that by the early 1990s Vietnam was once more a major exporter of rice in the world market. But the longer term effects of this change on village society remain to be seen. Should we expect to see the 'traditional' pattern of village relations re-emerge — but on a higher plane of material wealth and technical achievement than was possible in earlier periods? Much will depend on the nature of the relationship between countryside and cities, in the larger context of rational economic growth and political change.

## III

The theme of economic development also deserves to be studied in terms of the longer historical perspective. A comprehensive study of economic development in Vietnam before the colonial period has still to be written; but sufficient work has been done to permit a few observations which may have relevance for our present enquiry. It is a sphere in which Vietnam's external relations have always had special importance. Unlike states of comparable size in Western Europe, the Vietnam of the seventeenth and eighteenth centuries did not develop a capability for accumulating capital through long-distance trade conducted on its own terms. There does appear to have been a significant expansion of trade in the South China Sea during the seventeenth century, but Vietnamese participation depended for the most part on Chinese, Japanese (till 1636), and European mercantile enterprise.

The Dutch and the English both had factories in 'Tonkin' in the later years of the seventeenth century; Dutch interest, in particular, was related to demand for Vietnamese products in Japan — where they alone among the Europeans could still trade after 1636.[17] But European interest declined in the eighteenth century, leaving the field open to the Chinese whose trade in Vietnam probably continued to expand. The lively activity of the ports of Pho Hien and Hoi An (Faifo) in this period has been the subject of recent research involving collaboration between Vietnamese and foreign scholars.[18] Hoi An played an especially important role in the seventeenth and early eighteenth centuries in helping the Nguyen court to resist successive invasions of its territory by the Trinh; and that, in turn, gave the Nguyen a base from which to expand into lower Cambodia.

It is impossible to make any precise measurement of the impact of external trade on Vietnam's own economy in the pre-colonial period. A significant element in the benefit derived by Vietnamese from foreign trade probably took the form of taxes and bribes paid to officials. In certain areas, however, trade also stimulated Vietnamese economic enterprise and presumably therefore contributed something to rural incomes. Local production of raw silk and lac, for example, led some villages in the North to start manufacturing silk cloth and lacquerware for export. Other places produced relatively coarse pottery, for which there was a demand elsewhere in South East Asia. It has also now been demonstrated that the exploitation of the Mekong delta to produce rice for export began in the second half of the eighteenth century, long before the French conquest of Gia-Dinh.[19] The relationship between trade and the production of export items became much more important, of course, under colonial rule; but the degree of continuity with earlier periods should not be underestimated.

Despite the expansion of trade, however, the rulers of pre-colonial Vietnam exerted only limited control over the money which circulated in their country. Late seventeenth century accounts by English traders refer to the circulation of copper 'cash' in considerable quantities — much of it brought in from China. That appears to have been the main currency of Vietnam itself. By then substantial amounts of silver were already coming in, in the form of bars, to pay for Vietnamese produce; but Samuel Barron tells us that most of it was allowed to leave the country again in return for Chinese copper currency.[20] A continuing shortage of copper in the eighteenth century led to frequent debasement of coins, mixing copper with zinc; and eventually, in the 1740s, to the payment of soldiers and officials in silver. That raised the question, never adequately resolved, of defining a stable rate of exchange between copper and silver. By the early Nguyen period the government was minting its own silver coinage for internal use, but there remained a shortage of silver. By then, too, silver mines were being operated in 'Tonkin', mainly by Chinese entrepreneurs — a large part of the output being illegally exported to China. Vietnam's shortage of both copper and silver was part of a regional problem, and there was little the Vietnamese government could do to assert effective control over the various forms of money circulating within its own territory.[21] By the late nineteenth century, the French faced analogous problems in attempting to deal with the circulation of Mexican trade piastres: their decision to allow the Banque de l'Indochine to issue its own silver piastre coins was only the first step towards a partial solution.

This brief excursion into Vietnamese economic activity before the 1890s indicates three principal dimensions which would continue to shape the country's development — and problems — during the twentieth century: expansion and control of trade; investment in production for export; and regulation of the supply and value of money. During the period from 1885 to 1945 the Vietnamese had no way of preventing the French from dominating all three of these spheres, with the Chinese also playing an importent role in trade, both internally and externally. By the late 1930s it can be argued that Vietnam was still in part a 'traditional' society and economy, but in part a component of the economy of the French empire. It did not really have a 'national' economy of its own. Nor were the French concerned to promote Vietnam's balanced economic development as a country.

As is well known, substantial French investments transformed both the infrastructure of Indochina and also its capacity to produce primary commodities for export. The building of canals, allowing more effective water control in the Mekong delta, opened up large new areas for rice production. Although the French probably owned no more than about 15 per cent of the rice lands there, they benefited hugely from the expansion of exports. They also developed rubber planting on a large scale, as well as coffee plantations; while French investment in mining led to the exploitation of coal, tin, zinc, wolfram, and phosphates. On the other hand, businessmen in France actively discouraged significant investment in manufacturing industry in Vietnam, with the result that only a few factories were allowed to produce textiles, matches, and cement. The pre-colonial pattern of industrial handicrafts in 'Tonkin' was still represented in 1934 by around 250,000 peasants (7 per cent of the labour force) engaged in small scale industries.[22] But for the most part Vietnamese consumer demand was met by imports from France and elsewhere. These developments have been studied in some depth and the details need not concern us here.[23] What is remarkable is that while French Indochina as a whole had a substantial annual trade surplus, its balance of payments was usually in deficit owing to the transfer of profits from piastres into francs (and also the transfer abroad of Chinese commercial profits). It has been calculated that from 1934 to 1938 the trading surplus was on average 67.3 million piastres, whereas the balance of payments as a whole ran an average annual deficit of 11.2 million piastres.[24]

French commercial interests also governed decisions regarding the monetary system. Until the late nineteenth century, most currencies and exchange rates in Asia were geared to a silver standard — even though the gold standard prevailed in Europe. In Indochina, the main object of French policy from 1885 to 1900 was to establish the silver trade piastre of the Banque de l'Indochine as the main currency of Indochina, in place of the Mexican dollar; and to regulate the exchange rate between it and the copper coinage still used by the mass of the population. Its value against the franc, based on gold, was allowed to fluctuate. But by 1900 the depreciation of silver against gold was leading many parts of Asia to abandon the silver standard altogether: British India in 1893, Japan in 1897,

Thailand in 1902. Should Indochina do the same? Different interests had different views — there was conflict between importers of French goods into Vietnam and exporters of Indochina's own produce — but in 1904 it was decided to remain on a silver standard, with the modification that Indochinese trade piastres could not be exported. A further debate led to changes in 1919, but the *vase clos* system was restored two years later. Not until 1930 was the piastre firmly tied to the French franc, and therefore to gold.

For a brief while, in 1940–42, there was a possibility that French Indochina might become a focal area within Japan's 'Great East Asia Co-Prosperity Sphere'. Between the fall of France in mid-1940 and the Japanese conquest of most of South East Asia in early 1942, there was a moment when it seemed as if Japan would devote special attention to exploiting the resources of French Indochina (and also Thailand) and would seek to develop its economy to meet Japan's own needs. The French were obliged to sign a trade agreement with Tokyo in May 1941, which was followed by a major survey of Indochinese resources and seemed to presage a new era of investment. But that possibility was forestalled by Japan's move into the rest of South East Asia — leading to an intensification of the war and the consequent unavailability of investment funds for Vietnam. New monetary arrangements were also agreed, to allow the piastre to be linked to the yen as well as to the franc; and there was a reorientation of Indochina's trade towards Japan and its dependencies — although the total volume of trade fell sharply in the later part of the war. By 1945, however, Japan was defeated. In the meantime the French colonial system had been seriously disrupted and the economy of Vietnam was little better off than before.

One of the major questions following the Revolution of 1945 was whether Vietnamese independence — under whatever form it was finally achieved — would permit the emergence of genuinely national economic development. In the event the following three decades were consumed by revolution and war, which damaged even further the prospects for significant economic growth. Labour and other resources which might have been mobilized for more balanced and independent economic growth were instead mobilized for political and military purposes. French preoccupation with the war against the Viet Minh meant that there was no renewal of the flow of investment of the earlier twentieth century. The eventual French defeat left the field open to others. The partition of 1954–55 did not, however, give either half of the country genuine economic independence. Such investment and post-war reconstruction as was possible in the North depended on Chinese and Soviet aid; while the South relied heavily on American support. By 1959 the North had restored its transport system and its agricultural productivity had risen; while the South was able to export around 350,000 tons of rice in 1960 (compared with a pre-war 'peak' of 1,673,000 tons in 1928). Had the Vietnamese leaders in Hanoi opted for Khrushchev's policy of 'peaceful competition', the two 'zones' of Vietnam might have experienced a steady continuation of economic growth through the 1960s. Beyond that, it is impossible to speculate. But the reality was an ever-escalating war between 1962 and 1972, followed by an abortive peace agreement (1973), then a further round of war (1974–75): in short, an environment of economic destruction rather than development.

## IV

When we come to examine the situation and choices of Vietnam in the 1990s it is remarkable how much similarity, if not continuity, we find with different periods of the past. The country itself has essentially the same boundaries as in the mid-nineteenth century, and — with a vastly larger population — remains predominantly agrarian. It also continues to embrace considerable regional diversity. The unity of the whole, despite regional differences of economic experience, was increased by the improvement of communications during the French period; and the highland areas have for various reasons become more closely integrated into the rest of the country during the twentieth century. In the 1990s there is again a prospect of a complete overhaul of the transport and communications system, on the basis of a new wave of foreign investment in infrastructure projects; as well as of improved communications with neighbouring countries. The development of a national electricity grid will contribute further to the practical interdependence between regions. Nevertheless, following the two decades of partition from 1954 to 1975, certain differences between North and South persist — both of temperament and of opportunity. There is also the possibility of tension between Hanoi, as the centre of government, and Saigon as the city best placed for international commercial development: a situation unusual in South East Asia, where in most countries the political capital is equally the centre of business activity. (An analogy could, however, be drawn with the relationship between Beijing and Shanghai.) Part of the problem lies in the fact that the pre-1975 experience of Saigon may prove to be more relevant than that of the North to the needs of Vietnam in the world of the 1990s.

There is something to be said for the view that the fundamental turning-point in Vietnam's economic opportunities in the second half of the twentieth century actually occurred in the early 1970s. For Vietnam, as for the world as a whole, the roots of the situation of the 1990s must be sought not merely in the 'end of the Cold War' since 1989 but even more in the global economic transformation which began nearly twenty years before. Unlike other countries of the South East Asian region, however, Vietnam lost fifteen to twenty years before starting to exploit the changing situation.

The key to the transformation was oil, and the possibility that more advanced techniques of offshore drilling might lead to significant new discoveries off the coasts of Thailand, Vietnam, and southern China. Oil companies themselves were aware of that possibility as early as 1969–70 — and also of the likelihood of a world oil shortage in the 1970s. It was in those circumstances that the South Vietnamese national assembly approved legislation in December 1970, authorizing the granting of licences to international oil companies for offshore exploration. Negotiations followed during 1971–72, leading to acceptance of a number of oil company 'bids' and the start of actual drilling in 1973. By early 1975, when Mobil discovered oil off Vung Tau, the Thieu government had already received US$47 million in return for drilling rights.[25]

It was logical for South Vietnam to take the initiative at that stage, since the likeliest offshore locations were well to the south of the seventeenth parallel. But in the aftermath of the Paris Agreement of January 1973 there was a possibility that North Vietnam would also encourage oil exploration, by Japanese companies, in the Bac-Bo Gulf. In September 1973, as Japanese and DRVN representatives in Paris held talks on establishing formal diplomatic relations, the firm of Nissho Iwai negotiated an initial agreement on oil exploration in Hanoi. That was followed in November by a visit to Tokyo on the part of Hoang Quoc Viet, still an important figure in North Vietnam although no longer a Politburo-member.[26] However, other leaders in Hanoi were unwilling to make political sacrifices for economic gain; these contacts were eventually undermined by an insistence that Japan recognize the PRGSVN and break off relations with Saigon. Nevertheless, there is ample evidence that if the Paris Agreement had been allowed to take lasting hold, the exploitation of oil resources would have figured prominently in post-war reconstruction — with Japanese as well as American participation. The price, of coarse, would have been a further period of partition.

Oil became an even more significant factor in the situation by the start of 1974, when OPEC succeeded in quadrupling the price per barrel in the aftermath of the Middle East crisis. The opportunity thus created was immediately exploited by Indonesia, Malaysia, and Brunei, and in due course by Thailand. Had a more peaceful situation prevailed, South Vietnam would have been able to benefit too. The Chinese recognized the implications very quickly, and in January 1974 acted to secure control of the Paracel Islands by driving out South Vietnamese forces. Perhaps, too, the prospect of an eventually enriched South Vietnam, able to survive and to arm itself without any further need of United States assistance, was a factor in Hanoi's decision during 1974 to bring about a rapid military solution in the South, in order to secure reunification as soon as possible. In the process, however, the opportunity for effective exploitation of oil resources — by either half of Vietnam — was destroyed for a decade and more. Conflicting interpretations will no doubt place blame for the delay, respectively, on the United States' imposition of an embargo on economic relations with Vietnam (from 1975 to 1993) or on Hanoi's own decision (in 1977–78) to align the economy of a unified Vietnam exclusively with the planning structures of the Soviet Union and the Council for Mutual Economic Assistance.

As far as future economic development is concerned, Vietnam as a country remains as dependent on the investment of foreign capital — in some form or other — as it was throughout the French period and again in the 1950s. Despite the optimism of the Communist five year plans of 1961–65 and the period 1971–85, socialist Vietnam failed to accumulate significant capital of its own by means of Soviet-style planning. Such economic construction as was possible depended on Soviet and (until 1978) Chinese aid. By 1980, moreover, Vietnam had been obliged to accept its place in a socialist 'international division of labour', under which any hope of industrialization would depend on planning decisions within the whole CMEA. As late as June 1985, at the time of Le Duan's last visit to Moscow, a major expansion of Soviet aid was announced — including support for oil exploration, a steel plant, and other industrial projects.[27] But during the next eighteen months, Gorbachev's *perestroika* led to tougher evaluation of such aid. In the run-up to the VCP sixth Congress in late 1986, Truong Chinh, speaking as Le Duan's temporary successor as Party leader, admitted that Vietnam had 'wasted' a great deal of the aid it had received from the Russians and other allies. In the event, however, attempts to place aid projects on a sounder footing were overtaken by the formal end of Soviet assistance in 1990–91. That left Vietnam, like Russia itself (and other elements of the former Soviet Union) to rebuild its economy on the basis of new patterns of trade with 'hard currency' areas, and of efforts to attract the investment of foreign capital.

Vietnam began to make some progress towards such a transition by increasing its agricultural exports — over one million tons of rice in 1989 — and by exporting limited quantities of unrefined oil, mainly to Japan. But its markets for light industrial products and for rubber had been in other socialist countries; only a higher level of capital investment in those sectors would enable them to compete effectively in other parts of the world. By 1993–94 investors from Taiwan, Hong Kong, South Korea, and Malaysia were taking the first steps towards establishing special 'export processing zones' in the vicinities of Saigon, Hanoi, and Danang, as well as investing in individual enterprises. In the more immediate future, however, the best hope of attracting capital lay in granting new contracts for offshore oil and gas exploration to Western and Japanese companies. A few grants were made as early as 1988; by the early 1990s they involved such major companies as Mitsubishi, which found oil in the 'White Tiger' field in mid-1994; and British Petroleum, which made a major discovery of natural gas a little later in the year. American companies, with Mobil in the lead, re-entered the field after the lifting of the 'embargo' in 1994.

By comparison with other countries in the Asia-Pacific region the degree of Vietnamese dependence on outside capital was likely to be extreme. Its per capita GNP in the early 1990s was estimated at roughly US$200, compared with Thailand's $1,570, Malaysia's more than $2,500, and Taiwan's $8,788. There may be something of a paradox in reports, side by side with such depressing economic indicators, that many individuals in Vietnam are believed still to have secret hoards of gold and dollars stashed away; yet even if those resources could be attracted into an investment market, it would be a one-time occurrence which would not completely transform the overall situation. One economic estimate, made in 1993, suggested that foreign credits and investment to the tune of perhaps US$20 billion would be required to enable Vietnam merely to double its per capita income by the year 2000.[28]

Another aspect of continuity with the past is to be found in the sphere of Vietnam's monetary relations. From the mid-1970s to the mid-1980s socialist Vietnam maintained a semblance of stability by linking the dong to the Russian rouble. But the rouble, unlike the French franc in the 1930s, was not itself a 'hard' currency. The price of membership of the Soviet payments system, moreover, appears to have been the transfer of a considerable quantity of Vietnamese gold to Moscow to repay previous debts. The only possibility of securing control over the monetary system of a unified Vietnam lay in a series of currency 'reforms', which destroyed past savings by declaring old notes no longer valid and controlling the issue of new ones. (Ironically, the Banque de l'Indochine had sought to use a similar technique against the Viet Minh in 1945, by declaring its own 500-piastre notes no longer valid.) But it was impossible during the 1980s to prevent the continued use of American dollars inside Vietnam for many transactions — and as a form of savings — the eventual result being runaway inflation of the black market exchange rate between the dollar and the dong. The country was no closer than the Vietnam of Gia Long or Minh Mang to establishing a purely Vietnamese currency which could command confidence among the population as a whole, including the prosperous as well as the poor.

Of course, the concept of any individual government having full authoritarian control over its 'own' money, without reference to world markets, is long since past. Vietnam, like all other countries, must come to terms with the globalization of banking and finance; it must command international confidence. By 1990, with a certain amount of French technical assistance, Hanoi was able to make its peace with the International Monetary Fund and the World Bank — to which it had failed to keep up payments since 1979 — and so to take the first steps towards rejoining what used to be called the 'free world' economy. Only by meeting IMF and other international capitalist criteria could Vietnam hope to attract 'hard currency' investments. This would require, among other things, a stable banking system in which the national bank would confine itself to the roles of issuing and regulating the currency and of controlling interest rases, leaving other banks — both Vietnamese and foreign — to take deposits and make loans in a secure monetary environment. Some progress towards that restructuring occurred in 1992–93. In 1994 moves were also under way to ensure that regular foreign exchange transactions would take place through the banks, rather than on the black market.

The problem of monetary regulation is in a sense merely one dimension of the much larger problem — again reflecting continuity with the past — of reforming Vietnam's whole legal system. The contrast between the Confucian tradition and the Western approach to law was, as we have seen, a major issue in the latter part of the nineteenth century. The conflict between them was never wholly resolved, in that French administration tended to erode tradition without replacing it by genuine respect for its own *droit*: from the Vietnamese point of view the French system was too arbitrarily colonialist. Then came American influence in the South, which by the early 1970s had had possibly more success than its critics — especially radical Americans — allowed. But both French and American ideas of law were swept away by the conscious imposition of a 'dictatorship of the proletariat'. Having ruled since 1954 (or since 1975, in the South) on the basis of Marxist–Leninist ideology, the Communist Party found itself being obliged after 1990 to devise legislation — at least in certain spheres — which would be acceptable to the international capitalist community. Quite apart from questions of 'democracy' and of 'human rights', the readiness of foreign investors to part with their money depends increasingly on the 'transparency' of laws governing commercial and financial operations.

This is certainly one of the most important — and fascinating — aspects of both the modern history and the current dilemmas of Vietnam. It raises, in a new form, the time-honoured question of interaction between the 'custom of the village' and the 'laws of the emperor'. It may prove to be the case that, in the longer term, the 'revolution' had only a superficial impact on the deeper ways of thinking of the vast majority of rural Vietnamese. If so, 'law' in a great many situations will continue to depend on the recognition of an authority derived from personal virtue and attainment, rather than from either political ideology or elaborate but impersonal legislation. But in the cities, and in situations where international business is involved, the new 'emperors' must be able to establish — and to enforce — their own version of something like extraterritoriality. The administration of such law might depend, in turn, on the evolution of a new kind of Vietnamese élite — capable, like the emerging élites of other Asia-Pacific countries, of understanding both the subtleties of their own tradition and the even greater subtleties of an ever-changing international environment.

It is perhaps this need for a new kind of élite which offers the greatest challenge of all to Vietnam in the 1990s. It is also the level on which there has been more discontinuity than continuity in Vietnam's recent history. Unlike other countries in the region, apart from China, it has a history of successive eliminations of old élites in the interests of modernization, of revolution, or of class conflict. After about 1916 the Confucian scholars had to give way to a new generation with either a French education or an admiration for Japan (or both). After 1954, in the Communist North, both Confucian survivors and French-influenced elements were dismissed as either 'reactionary' or 'bourgeois'; whilst in the South, the French-educated élite was overtaken by a new generation more receptive to American ideas. The latter, in turn, had to flee or to accept 're-education' in 1975. To make matters worse, many educated and skilled Chinese residents had to flee after 1978–79. The result was that by the early 1990s a great many of the best-educated and most experienced Vietnamese were living outside Vietnam; whilst the 'ruling class' inside the country had been trained for a different kind of world from that in which they would now have to live. There are no simple solutions to that almost unprecedented situation.

## Notes

1 The original draft of this paper was prepared for the sixth conference of the Northwest Regional Consortium for Southeast Asian Studies, Seattle, November 1994. I am grateful to Professor C.F. Keyes for his encouragement and comments on that occasion.
2 See his long obituary by C. Patris in *Bulletin des Amis du Vieux Hue*, 10, 4, 1924; *cf.* also R.B. Smith 'Sino-Vietnamese sources for the Nguyen period', *Bulletin of the School of Oriental and African Studies*, 30, 3, 1967, pp. 600–21.

3 For a recent analysis of the French transformation of the central and western provinces of 'Cochinchina', see Pierre Brocheux, *The Mekong delta: ecology, economy and revolution, 1860–1960*. Madison: University of Wisconsin-Madison, 1995.
4 Figures from *Annuaire Statistique de l'Indochine 1936–37*. The figures were never static, since Chinese migrants continued to come and go in significant numbers. There were also families that could be identified as Sino-Vietnamese (*minh-huong*); of the 73,000 inhabitants placed in that category in 1936, as many as 62,000 were in the South (Cochinchina).
5 Alexander B. Woodside, *Vietnam and the Chinese model: a comparative study of Nguyen and Ch'ing civil government in the first half of the nineteenth century*. Cambridge, Mass.: Harvard University Press, 1971.
6 P. Ory, *La commune annamite au Tonkin*. Paris: A. Challamel, 1894.
7 See, for example, Gerald C. Hickey, *Village in Vietnam*. New Haven: Yale University Press, 1964, describing the history and institutions of a village in Long An province, south of Saigon. Brocheux, however, is more inclined to emphasize the contrast between the villages of the Mekong delta and those of other regions of Vietnam (*cf.* note 3, above).
8 For example Yves Henry. *Economie agricole de l'Indochine*. Hanoi: Impermerie d'Extrême-Orient, 1932, published for the International Colonial Exhibition in Paris in 1931. On the *dia-bo* of Gia Long and Minh Mang, see Nguyen Dinh Dau, 'Remarques préliminaires sur les registres cadastraux des six provinces de la Cochinchine', *Bulletin de l'Ecole Française d'Extrême-Orient*, 78, 1991, pp. 275–85; also the article by Smith cited in note 2, above.
9 For discussion of the impact of colonial taxes in general on the Vietnamese peasantry, see Ngo Vinh Long, *Before the revolution: the Vietnamese peasants under the French*. Cambridge, Mass.: MIT Press, 1973; Martin J. Murray, *The development of capitalism in colonial Indochina (1870–1940)*. Berkeley: University of California Press, 1980, chapter 2. A series of more detailed studies of the subject can be found in the *Revue indochinoise Juridique et Economique* for 1939–40: by R. Pinto (nos. 10–11, 1939); by J. Boyer (no. 11, 1939); and by Vu Van Hien (no. 13, 1940).
10 Pierre Gourou, *Les paysans du delta Tonkinois*, Paris: Les Éditions d'Art et d'Histoire, 1936, pp. 362–63.
11 Robert L. Sansom, *The economics of insurgency in the Mekong delta of Vietnam*. Cambridge, Mass.: MTT Press, 1970, chapter 2.
12 See Karl A. Wittfogel, *Oriental despotism: a comparative study of total power*. New Haven: Yale University Press, 1957, chapter 9.
13 The standard account of the Vietnamese land reform of the 1950s remains Edwin E. Moise, *Land reform in China and North Vietnam: consolidating the revolution at the village level*. Chapel Hill: University of North Carolina Press, 1983; but see also Vo Nhan Tri, *Vietnam's economic policy since 1975*. Singapore: Institute of Southeast Asian Studies, 1990, chapter 1. Tri, who worked in North Vietnam from the 1950s to the 1970s, found documentary evidence pointing to an estimate of 15,000 people killed during land reform.
14 Andrew Vickerman, *The fate of the peasantry; premature 'transition to socialism' in the Democratic Republic of Vietnam*. New Haven: Yale Center for International and Area Studies, 1986. Yale University, Southeast Asia Studies Monograph Series 28.
15 Adam Fforde, *The agrarian question in North Vietnam, 1974–1979*. Armonk, N.Y.: M.E. Sharpe, 1989.
16 On the agrarian history of the South between 1955 and 1968, see Sansom, op. cit., chapter 3; also Stanford Research Institute, *Land reform in Vietnam*. Menlo Park, California, 1968. For a brief assessment of the Thieu land reform, see Douglas C. Dacy, *Foreign aid, war and economic development: South Vietnam 1955–1975*. Cambridge: Cambridge University Press, 1986, pp. 112–13; he estimates that by 1975 only 300,000 hectares (out of over 2 million hectares under cultivation) were occupied

by tenant farmers. The Thieu reform itself is described in *Asian Survey*, 10, 8, 1970: special issue devoted to Vietnamese land reform.
17 On Dutch and British trade in seventeenth-century Vietnam, see W.J.M. Buch, 'La Compagnie des Indes Néerlandaises et l'Indochine,' *Bulletin de l'Ecole Française d'Extrême-Orient*, 36, 1, 1936, pp. 97–196; 37, 1937, pp. 121–237; and Ma Yi Yi, 'English trade in the South China Sea 1670–1715', Ph.D. thesis, University of London, 1958.
18 See, for example, Association of Vietnamese Historians, *Pho-Hien, centre of international commerce in the XVIIth–XVIIIth centuries*. Hanoi: The Gioi Publishers, 1994.
19 For an important new analysis of the economy of southern Vietnam in that period, see Li Tana, '"The Inner Region": a social end economic history of Nguyen Vietnam in the seventeenth and eighteenth centuries', Ph.D. thesis, Australian National University, 1992.
20 Samuel Barron, *A description of the kingdom of Tonqueen*. London, 1732; original edition, 1686; cf, also William Dampier, *Voyages and discoveries*. London, 1729; new edition, London: Argonaut Press, 1931.
21 On Vietnamese monetary history, see the pioneering contribution by John K. Whitmore, 'Vietnam and the monetary flow of eastern Asia, thirteenth to eighteenth centuries', in J.F. Richards (ed.), *Precious metals in the later medieval and early modern worlds*. Durham, North Carolina: Carolina Academic Press, 1983; on the silver problem under the Nguyen dynasty, see also Woodside, op. cit, pp. 276ff.
22 P. Gourou, *L'utilisation du sol en Indochine française*. Paris: Hartmann, 1940, pp. 312–14.
23 See, for example, Charles Robequain, *L'évolution economique de l'Indochine française*. Paris: Hartmann, 1939; also the work of Martin J. Murray, cited in note 9, above.
24 Figures calculated by Vo Nhan Tri, *Croissance économique de la republique démocratique du Vietnam, 1945–1965*. Hanoi: Éditions en Langues Étrangères, 1967, p. 71.
25 Figure given by Dacy, op. cit., p. 18, citing no other references (cf. note 16, above). The growing importance of oil for Indochina and Thailand was reported by Jacques Decornoy in *Le Monde*, 8 January 1971, and quickly attracted the attention of the anti-war radicals: see, for example, *Vietnam International* (London), 5, 3, 1971.
26 These contacts were fully reported in the Japanese press; see Yvonne Tan, 'The limits to stability: the economic implications of the Paris Agreement on Vietnam, January 1973–August 1974'. Ph.D. thesis, University of London, 1991.
27 Joint declaration of 28 Jane 1985: BBC, *Summary of World Broadcasts: Soviet Union*, 7991.
28 See *Far Eastern Economic Review, Asia 1994 Yearbook*. Hong Kong, 1994. pp. 14–15 and 223. For a recent examination of international investment trends in Vietnam, by Michael Vatikiotis, see *Far Eastern Economic Review*, 22 September 1994.

# Index

Abrams, C. 146n14, 153, 169–70
agreement(s) 34, 37, 41–5, 64, 88, 99–100, 105, 111n16, 128, 150, 159, 163, 171, 75n45; aid 120, 153, 173n23, 186–7; cease-fire 152; defense 43; economic 35; Franco-Vietnamese 105; Geneva 155, 179; secret 127, 185; trade 157, 162–4, 208–10
agriculture 7, 9, 54–5, 86, 101–6, 122–3, 202–5, 208–9, 211, 215n16
aid 57, 61, 117, 119–22, 140, 149, 153–8, 162–5, 169, 173, 182–8, 204, 208–11
Allies 39, 41, 43, 49, 60–1, 64, 78–80, 102, 146, 152, 166, 181, 186, 211
Annam 5, 11–12, 16–27, 36, 39, 44, 47–51, 54–58, 63, 77, 88, 90, 104, 130n19, 196–8
armaments 35, 46, 61–4, 77, 96–103, 112n57, 121–6, 138–9, 142, 155–7, 162, 167, 188
Armed Forces of the Republic of Vietnam 133, 136, 142, 150, 168, 170
Asia: capitalist 193; colonies in 74; communism in 8, 10, 15, 21, 25, 28, 74, 117–19, 126, 129n10, 182; countries of 157, 163, 196; enterprise in 6; finance and 207; intelligence and 4; standards in 80
Aung San 37, 78
Australia 116, 118, 169, 193

Bank(s) 144, 161, 212; agricultural 55; Asian Development 187; of Indochina 35, 62, 69n137, 82, 98–100; national 162; Paris 96; the World 212; the Yokohama Specie 97
Bao-Dai 39–40, 45, 50–3, 57, 59, 62, 73, 80, 85, 87, 93, 95, 195
Borodin 15

Brezhnev, L. 165, 181–2, 187
Britain 8, 26, 40–6, 62–3, 70–4, 82, 85–6, 96, 102, 115–20, 125–8, 151–5, 161, 167, 194
Brzezinski, Z. 187–8
Buddhism 137, 197, 199
bureaucracy 56, 71, 92, 101, 195, 199, 201, 203–5
Burma 21, 36–7, 42, 47, 73–4, 77–8, 85, 118–20, 127–8, 180, 182
business *see* commerce

Caodaist(s) 36, 38–40, 58, 64
Cambodia 44, 47, 49, 57, 73, 134–6, 152, 155, 158, 163–4, 178, 194; border sanctuaries in 155, 159; China and 166, 184, 188–90, 192n20; and Communism 180–5, 191n7; crisis in 160–2, 168; 19th century 72; neutrality of 149, 168, 176n67, 179; and self-reliance 192n19; and the US 156–7, 167, 169–71, 173n18, 174n26 n39, 175n44; and Vietnam 186–7, 191n12, 197, 206
capitalism 6, 7, 13, 17, 28, 128, 164, 187, 193, 203, 212; Western 8
Central Committee's Office in South Vietnam (COSVN) 135, 137, 142, 144, 159, 166, 169–70, 176n73
Ceylon *see* Sri Lanka
the Cham 73, 197
Chau Van Liem 24, 27
Chen, K.C. 84, 109
Chen Xilian 187, 189
Cheng Heng 165, 175n57
Chennault, C. 42–3, 86
Chiang Kai-shek 42
Chin Peng 126
China 72–3, 101–2, 138, 152–4, 163, 176n59, 178, 180, 189, 194–6, 199, 213;

Cambodia and 157, 166, 171, 182–6; Comintern and; 6, 9–10; Communist movement in 71, 113n 84, 118, 124; and the DRVN 127–9, 129n12 n16, 139, 147n25, 153–55, 187–90, 191n7, 204; and the Korean War 121; and the US 159; labour movement in 8; Malaya and 116–17; south 11–12, 19, 22–3, 34, 61, 98, 107, 140, 209; the Viet-Minh and 119–20; and Vietnam 199–200, 206; WWII and 42, 46, 85–6
Chu Van Tan 59–61, 106–8
clan(s) 192, 199, 201–2
clandestine activities 12–14, 18, 23–4, 29n14, 33n84, 40–4, 49–51, 58, 61–3, 75, 79–81, 88–91, 108–9, 111n29, 116, 120, 127, 138, 156, 159–61, 164, 168–9, 173n20 n25, 181, 186, 196, 200, 211; *see also* intelligence; secret societies
Cochinchina 13–27, 36–9, 47–50, 54–9, 63, 75–8, 85, 88–90, 105, 196–8, 203, 214n3 n4
coinage 206–7
colonialism 58, 70, 76, 194 200–7; Dutch 73; French 46, 51, 72, 77–8, 85, 88, 193–9, 208, 212; the Japanese and 51; and Malaya 116–18, 128–9n6; revolutionary movement and 6–10, 20–5, 59, 71, 79, 101, 180
COMINFORM 119
COMINTERN (Communist International) 5–28, 29n14, 30n37, 32n74, 33n79, 75, 100–2, 113n84, 116–17, 180; *see also* Viet-Minh
commerce 34–5, 40, 53, 73, 97, 102–3, 112n37, 197, 164, 173n18, 196, 202, 207–9, 213
communications 9, 18, 80, 106, 119, 123, 140, 169, 182, 196, 209; radio 38, 45, 58, 80, 107, 117, 123–4, 127, 158, 162, 166, 168, 176n67, 196
Communist Party of the Philippine Islands 8, 78; *see also* The Philippines
Communist Party of the Soviet Union 140, 181, 186; *see also* Soviet Union
Communist strategy 16, 25, 28, 115–17, 136, 143, 180, 183, 204, 159
Conference(s) 8, 24, 27, 32n74, 57, 111n29, 119, 122–4, 128n1, 129n10, 130n26, 139, 169, 181; the Geneva 119, 125, 151, 161, 179–80; the Paris 152–4; the Pugwash 141; the Revolutionary Military 60, 106–7; the Second Quebec 42; the Supreme War Leaders' 44–8
Confucianism 51–2, 56, 71–2, 76–7, 193–4, 197–203, 212–3
Constitutionalists 38, 59, 76; *see also* Party
co-operatives 204–5
corruption 54–5, 167, 206, 94
Cu Huy Can 87, 95
culture 52, 71, 84–7, 93; Vietnamese 51, 71, 94–5, 196–9
Cuong-De, prince 37–9, 50, 52, 65n 15, 76–7
currency 86, 97–100, 145, 162, 206–7, 211–12

Dai-Viet movement 39, 52, 62, 72, 79, 199–200, 203
Dang Thai Mai 87, 93, 95, 112n37 n50
Dang Xuan Khu 87, 94
Dao Duy Anh 12, 112n37
Davidson, P. 138–9
De Gaulle 41–2
De Lattre, Marshal 115, 121–2
Decoux, J. 34–6, 38, 41–5, 48, 51–3, 86, 102
Democratic Kampuchea 156, 166–7, 178, 182–6, 190, 191n7; *see also* Cambodia
The Democratic People's Republic of Korea (North Korea) 127, 131n134, 171, 177n83
The Democratic Republic of Vietnam (North Vietnam) 14, 87, 119, 180, 136, 138, 141, 144,149–71, 179–84, 198, 203–5, 210
demonstrations 14, 21, 30n32, 36, 50, 58, 68n112, 99, 134, 154, 158, 162–4, 168, 183
Deng Xiaoping 188–90
development 187, 203; economic 193, 199, 204–10; industrial 188; political 179
Devillers, P. 36–40, 58, 84, 108–9
Do Ngoc Du (aka Phiem Chu) 20–3
Ducoroy 36, 55, 58
Duong Bach Mai 11, 75
Duong Hac Dinh 16–17, 21, 23
the Dutch 7, 47, 70, 73–4, 76, 102, 112, 206
Dutch East Indies *see* The Netherlands East Indies; Indonesia

East Asia 6, 34–6, 46–7, 56, 63, 71, 86, 157, 169, 199–200, 208; *see also* South-East Asia

economy 34–6, 54, 57, 74, 80, 86–9, 97–105, 122–4, 128, 144–5, 157–65; 178, 187–8, 193–212
education 11, 16–18, 23, 27, 29n19, 39, 51–8, 73, 81, 86–7, 91–4, 105, 112n43 n50, 116, 123–4, 180, 195; Confucian 77; French 12, 50, 74, 213; political 123, 126, 138; Western 6
election(s) 59, 74–5, 87–90, 95, 126, 150, 152
elite 7, 12, 53, 56, 71–6
England 5, 206
Europe 6, 34–6, 51, 63, 73, 77, 97, 101, 106, 115, 119, 187, 193–4, 199–200, 205–7

Fall, B. 84, 96
family 37, 136, 157, 201–2; *see also* clan
famine 54–5, 86, 89, 104–5, 198; *see also* food, grain, rice
feudalism 6–9, 101–2, 104, 199–200, 203
finance 20, 25, 29n14, 34, 44–5, 53, 80, 86, 91, 95–100, 103–5, 120, 124, 144–6, 157, 188, 205, 212–13
Ford, R.E. 133–4, 137
Fforde, A. 204
food 54–5, 81, 86, 104–5, 125, 202, 205; *see also* famine; grain
France 6, 11–12, 21, 34–41, 47–58, 74–7, 86, 103, 128, 152, 161–2, 166, 180–4, 194–5, 199, 207–8
(the) French 10, 13, 16–17, 20, 27, 34–64, 70–105, 115, 118, 120–8, 141, 151–2, 156, 169, 197–213; business 13, 28; Communists 7, 11–12, 21–2, 161; Sûréte 5, 9, 14, 18, 25, 62; and Vietnam 212

Gaiduk, I. 140
geography 30n32, 42, 72–3, 80, 155, 193–5
Germany 34, 41
globalism 6–7, 28, 132, 143–6, 150, 188, 195–6, 209, 212
gold 25, 96, 98, 144–5, 183, 207–8, 211–12
grain 104–5
Green, M. 169, 176n75
Guangzhou (Canton) 10–20, 23, 25, 27, 74, 109, 129n8 n15
Gurney, H. 116–17, 120

Ha Huy Tap 13–14, 75
harvests 54–5, 86, 104–5, 121
Hatta 70, 74, 77, 79–80
Hayashi H. 40, 47, 52, 65n26

history 6, 61, 70–1, 81, 95–6, 106, 108, 112n37, 117, 132, 162, 198, 201–2, 213, 214n7; of the CCP 8; of the DRVN 137; ICP 5, 28; Kampuchean Communist Party 191n7; of the PKI 75; of Vietnam 50, 52–3, 64, 71, 84, 193–5, 199, 203; of the Vietnam War 138, 149; VCP 6, 15, 186
Hmong forces 156, 160
Ho Chi Minh (Nguyen Ai Quoc) 6, 10–17, 20, 23–8, 31n38, 32n74, 33n79, 41, 59–61, 68n123, 70, 73–5, 79–87, 91–2, 96–8, 101–9, 110n8, 113n84, 114n121, 118–20, 124, 134–5, 143, 152, 154–57, 159–60, 173n18, 179–81, 191n4, 196
Ho Huu Tuong 11, 81
Ho Tung Mau 12–13, 16–27, 108–9
Ho Van Nga 58–9
Hoang Minh Giam 93–4, 112n38
Hoang Quoc Viet 13, 17, 21, 107–9, 127, 131n34, 210
Hoang Van Hoan 5, 15, 23, 28n3, 107, 119–20, 129n12, 180–2
Hoang Xuan Han 51, 53, 11–12n37
Hong Son 12, 16–19, 23–4, 27
Hou Yuon 168, 183
Hu Nim 168, 186
Hukbalahap 78, 126, 130–1n33
Huynh Phu So 39, 75

imperialism 6–10, 126, 137, 164, 181, 199, 203; anti- 25–8, 100–2, 118, 132, 144, 158, 163; US 137, 145, 185
independence 38, 46, 50, 56, 74, 77, 82; Annamite 11, 36, 44, 46; Burmese 36; Cambodian 49, 73, 181, 183; DRVN 79, 84; Indonesian 70, 80; Korean 26; Vietnamese 6, 47, 51, 54, 58, 63, 72, 85, 91–3, 109, 134, 155, 199, 208
India 8, 26, 38, 41–4, 71–4, 116, 118, 126–7, 128n3, 129n9, 130n31, 197, 207
Indonesia 7–10, 40, 56, 70–80, 116, 127–8, 129n8, 149, 163, 175n45, 183, 191n10, 210; *see also* Netherlands East Indies
industry 6, 8, 13, 17, 35, 53, 86, 89, 93, 102–3, 163, 188, 197, 204–11, 215n25
intellectuals 12, 22, 51, 53, 71, 79, 81, 92–3, 95, 127
intelligence 61, 115–19, 130n31, 134; British 41, 46, 62, 78; Chinese Nationalist 127; French 114n117; Japanese 40; US 45, 61, 79–82, 103, 138–42, 158–69, 173 n25
investment 97, 187, 207–13

Ishizawa 48, 66n46
Islam 71–3, 76–7

Japan 8, 34, 41, 47–61, 70–1, 76–85, 92, 96, 99, 107–8, 118, 165, 187–9, 193–5, 199, 205–8; and business 40, 210, 211, 213; and Caodaists 36, 39; cultural influence of 56; and diplomacy 35; and the military 34, 37–46, 62–4, 86, 89, 97
Java 21, 25, 40, 72–3, 80, 116, 200
Johnson, L.B. 132, 136, 141, 144–5, 153, 170, 183

Kha Van Can 58–9
Khek Vandy 162, 165
Khieu Samphan 168, 183–6, 191n10 n12
Khmer Rouge 168, 183–6, 191n10 n12
Khrushchev, N. 181, 208
Kim Il Sung 171
Kissinger, H. 141, 152–4, 160–1, 164, 166–7, 170–1, 173n18, 175n58, 177n76, 185
Kosygin, A. 141, 153, 161, 165, 167
Korea 10, 25–6, 46, 71, 121, 127–8, 131n36, 171, 177n83
Krestintern 8, 10, 15

labour 5–10, 13–17, 20–2, 70, 75, 87, 100, 108, 123–7, 130n26 n31, 137, 156, 159, 180–1; 200, 204, 207–10; *see also* Profintern
Laird, M. 150, 160, 169–70, 177n76
Lam Duc Thu 12, 16
land 25, 81, 102, 104, 107, 117, 122–3, 133–5, 142–3, 197–200; communal 72, 201; policies 108; reform 101, 151, 202; rent 103, 111n25, 172n9; urban 98
landlords 55, 102, 104, 197, 201–9; feudal 9, 101
de Langlade, Major 42, 44
Lao People's Liberation Army (Pathet Lao) 156, 160–1, 179
Laos 39, 44, 49, 57, 73, 129n8, 152, 155, 156–71, 173n18, 176n69, 179–84, 194–6
Lau, A. 27, 33n83
Le Duan 122–3, 137–9, 143, 147n25, 156, 171, 179–81
Le Duc Tho 123–7, 130n28, 135, 143, 156, 161, 164, 179, 186
Le Duy Diem (aka Le Huy Diem and Le Loi) 16–18
Le Hong Phong 11–12, 19, 29n20, 75
Le Hong Son 16, 18, 23–4, 27

Le Quang Dat 12, 16–18, 23, 27
Le Thanh Nhgi 33n87, 106, 108, 173n23
Le Van Hien 87, 100
legal system 7, 11, 50, 53, 56–7, 75, 87, 91–4, 99, 106, 116, 118, 130n31, 155, 158, 162, 165–7, 172n9, 174n26, 179, 199–200, 206, 212–13
Lenin 96, 143
Leninism 6, 16–17, 163, 181, 195, 203–4, 212
Li Lisan 9, 28
Li Xiannian 166, 173n22 n23, 187, 189
Lin Biao 139–40, 176n59, 182, 192n20
Liu Shaoqi 119, 126
Lon Nol 149, 157, 161–71, 175n56 176n58, 182–5, 189
Luo Guibo 120, 128n16
Luo Ruqing 139, 189, 192n20

Macau 17, 23, 27, 130n26
Machijiri, General 38, 43, 47
Malaya 7–8, 13, 21, 25–6, 47, 78, 115–20, 125–8, 158, 163, 180, 191
Malayan Races Liberation Army (MRLA)
Malaysia 72, 157–8, 163, 210–11; *see also* Malaya
Mao Zedong 9, 28, 101–2, 119–25, 128, 139–40, 157–8, 178, 189
Maoists 8, 118–22, 126–7, 129n9, 139–40, 154
Marxism-Leninism 13, 17, 71
Marxist(s) 6, 8, 11–12, 15, 87, 94, 103, 108, 163, 181, 195, 203–4, 212
Matsumoto S. 35, 43–9
Maurras, C. 51, 55
Middle East 146, 190, 210
military 34, 40–9, 54–6, 60, 73, 76, 80, 86, 89–91, 106–8, 122, 124–5, 134–7, 142, 145–6, 149–58, 169–71, 173n18, 178, 183–4, 187, 204–5, 208, 210; assistance to Cambodia 163, 165, 179, 182, 185, 189; assistance from US 121; Chinese 119–20, 123, 127, 138–40; operations 37; rule 35, 78; schools 12, 23; the Soviet 141, 188; training 38, 77; *see also* armaments; war
mining 6, 8, 17, 33n87, 89, 103, 153, 206–7
Minoda Fujio 49, 57–8, 78
monarchy 37, 47–50, 77, 149, 155–7, 161–4, 179, 181, 199
monopolies 35, 112n53, 202
Mordant, General 41–5

Mountbatten 85
Musso 75, 116

the nationalist movement 14, 36–41, 50–3, 58, 63, 69n141, 70–79, 82–4, 96, 100, 108–10, 120, 127, 181
The Netherlands 74–5, 118
The Netherlands East Indies 35, 47, 73–4, 80
news sources 10, 12, 21–2, 36, 38, 45–6, 53–9, 63, 80–1, 84, 91, 94, 97, 104, 107, 116–17, 120–4, 127, 129n8, 135, 139, 141, 145, 151–3, 158, 162, 166–8, 175n57, 196
Ngo Dinh Diem 39–40, 52–3, 77, 202, 204
Ngo Gia Tu 13, 17, 23–4, 27, 31n55
Ngo Thiem 14–15, 17
Ngo Vinh Long 54, 133, 137
Nguyen Ai Quoc *see* Ho Chi Minh
Nguyen An Ninh 12, 14
Nguyen Binh (Nguyen Phuong Thao) 124, 127, 137, 139–40
Nguyen Chi Thanh 121, 130n19, 137, 144
Nguyen Cong My 93, 112n50
Nguyen Duc Canh 13, 18, 23–6
Nguyen Duy Trinh 14, 124, 143
Nguyen dynasty 37, 72, 194, 203, 206
Nguyen Huu Dang 95, 112n50
Nguyen Luong Bang 13, 20, 24, 59, 68n122, 87, 95, 101, 107–9
Nguyen Nghia (Thieu) 16, 20, 27, 31n42
Nguyen Tuan 16, 18
Nguyen Van Sam 37, 59, 81
Nguyen Van Tao 7, 11, 75
Nguyen Van Thieu 134, 150, 152, 169, 205, 210
Nguyen Van Vinh 140, 143
Nguyen Xien 81, 90, 103
Nixon, R.M. 149–61, 165–7, 169–71, 172n2 n3, 175n44, 176n58, 184
North Korea *see* The Democratic People's Republic of Korea
North Vietnam *see* The Democratic Republic of Vietnam

oil *see* petroleum
Oum Manorine 162, 165, 175n56

Party: the Annam Communist 20, 23; the Chinese Communist 9, 19, 109, 113n84, 115, 120, 124, 154, 190; the French Communist 11–12, 21–2, 161; the Indian Communist 118, 128n3, 129n9; the Indochinese Communist 5–6, 10, 16–18, 24, 27, 31n44, 32n74, 41, 59–61, 73–5, 78–9, 87–9, 95, 101–7, 112n50, 119, 180; the Indonesian Communist 7, 74; the Kampuchean Communist 182–3, 165–6; the Malayan Communist 8, 78, 126, 158, 163; the Tran-Trao 92; the Vietnam Workers' Party 70, 108, 123–7, 130n26, 137, 156, 159, 181; the Vietnamese Communist 25–6, 28, 37, 121, 134, 138–44, 147, 179, 187, 193–5, 203–5, 211, 212; the Vietnamese Nationalist 84
Patti, A.L. 79, 82, 106
The People's Army of Vietnam 133, 136–42, 150, 159–60, 167–70
The People's Republic of China *see* China
petroleum 13, 102–3, 163, 209–11, 215n25
Phan Anh 53, 55–6, 62, 107, 112n37
Phan Boi Chau 11–12, 15, 21, 37
Phan Ke Toai 50, 62
Pham Cong Tac 38–9
Pham Hung 122, 124, 144
Pham Ngoc Thach 41, 58, 79–81, 124
Pham Quynh 51–2
Pham Van Dong 14–17, 24, 59, 61, 75, 96, 101–2, 107–9, 122, 125, 130n28, 133, 141, 153, 157, 167, 173n23, 184, 187
Phiem Chu 13, 18, 20, 23
The Philippines 7–10, 13, 21, 36, 42, 47, 72–4, 77–8, 85, 115, 120, 126–8, 158, 182, 200
plantations 6–8, 203, 206–8
Podgorny, N. 164, 166
Pol Pot (Saloth Sar) 156, 171, 181, 183–90, 191n7, 191n10
police 14, 19, 29n21, 36, 40, 49, 70, 91, 117, 162, 165
politics 8–9, 11, 14, 22–7, 36, 40, 46, 51, 55–6, 58, 63, 71–80, 84–9, 92–4, 101, 105, 108–9, 111n16, 119–26, 130n31, 138, 140–3, 146, 149–63, 178–9, 183, 190, 193–5, 198–9, 203–5, 208–10, 213
population 35, 77, 85–8, 96, 101, 124–5, 150, 156, 198, 207–9, 212
Profintern 6, 8, 13
proletarian movement 7–10, 13, 15–16, 19–20, 27–8, 74–5, 102, 181

# Index  221

propaganda 8, 20, 26, 39, 59–60, 86–95, 105–6, 109–17, 121–6, 137, 151, 162, 190, 203
Provisional Government of Vietnam 41, 84–6, 92–5, 97–110, 111n29, 195

Quinn-Judge, S. 30n37, 32n74

railway(s) 25, 54, 140, 182, 196
Ranadive 118, 126
regional cooperation 163, 178
The Republic of China *see* Taiwan
The Republic of Korea 211
The Republic of Vietnam 53, 133–7, 143–6, 149–62, 168–71, 178–84, 196, 204, 209–10
revolt 6–10, 12, 23–5, 28, 37, 43, 59–60, 62, 70, 74–81, 90, 106, 114n113, 115–16, 133–7, 151, 181–3, 187–8, 195
revolutionary activity 7, 10–12, 20, 25, 28, 60–2, 71, 74–6, 81, 85–92, 96, 101, 104–9, 115, 120–26, 137, 141–3, 151, 155, 173, 179–86, 195, 203; *see also* revolt; Than Nien association
rice 13, 53–7, 60, 86, 89, 104–5, 121–3, 155–7, 164, 197, 200–11
Rissine 9–10
Rives, L. 167, 169

Sabattier, General 43–6, 66n35
Sainteny, J. 51, 98–9, 106, 113n74, 114n102
scholarship 41, 50, 56, 62, 71–2, 76, 84, 88, 93, 98, 108, 115, 134, 141, 163, 195, 199, 201–3, 206, 213
secret societies 12, 27
sect(s) 63–4, 75, 78, 80, 90, 199
security 43, 62, 91–2, 116, 149, 151–3, 157, 161–2, 166, 189
Siam 7, 15–17, 19, 21, 23–7, 30n38, 180, 194; *see also* Thailand
Norodom Sihanouk 49, 149, 155–68, 171–3, 174n28 n39, 176n59 n62, 179–85, 191n10
Singapore 8, 25–6, 29n11, 37, 52, 58, 116, 118–19
Sirik Matak 157, 161–6, 184
Amir Sjariffuddin 75, 78
Socialist Republic of Vietnam 178, 184–215
Sosthene Fernandez 162, 165, 175n56
sources 6, 11, 24, 40, 45, 59, 71, 90, 95, 99, 103, 103–7, 109, 112n57, 127, 129n15, 137, 149, 162–3, 199, 201;

archival 31n39, 35–7, 43, 46, 61–2 64n5, 66n36, 89, 115–17, 120, 138, 143–4, 150, 200
South-East Asia 6–7, 10, 20, 24–5, 30n38, 42–4, 48, 70–4, 78, 85, 115–20, 127–9, 158, 163, 180–2, 190, 193, 202, 206, 209
South Korea *see* the Republic of Korea
South Vietnam *see* the Republic of Vietnam
Souvanna Phouma 155–6, 160–1
Soviet Union 5–11, 28, 45, 48, 62, 71, 94, 101–2, 109, 117–19, 127, 138–44, 152–5, 159–61, 164–5, 167, 178, 181–90, 193, 204, 208–12
Spain 72–3, 200
Sri Lanka 42, 63
Stalin, J. 11, 28, 118–20, 127, 192n20
strike(s) 6–8, 12–13, 17, 25, 28, 57, 99
Suharto 149, 163, 183, 191n10
Sukarno 70, 74, 77–80, 163, 190, 191n10

Taiwan 26, 38, 40, 47; Republic of China 211
taxation 28, 53–7, 91, 95–6, 103, 112n53, 122–4, 144, 200–2, 206, 214n9
technology 20, 104, 182, 204–5, 209, 212
Terauchi, H. 34–5, 42–3, 47, 63, 69n141, 79–82
the Tet Offensive 138, 144–6, 183
Thailand 23, 28n3, 35, 47, 72–3, 117, 129n6, 157–8, 163, 167, 169, 176n69, 178–82, 189, 208–11, 215n25; *see also* Siam
Than Nien association 12–27
Thompson, R. 151, 154, 159
Ton Duc Thang 13, 15–17, 131n34
Tongkin 20, 35–63, 85, 88–91, 94–9, 104–7, 114n112, 121–4, 130n26
trade 7–9, 17, 34, 53, 73, 98–9, 119, 126, 130n31, 157, 162–4, 194, 202, 206–8, 211
Tran Bach Dang 134–5, 137
Tran Dang Ninh 60–1, 106–8, 114n113
Tran Do 134–5
Tran Huy Lieu 30n34, 75, 87, 94–5, 108–9, 112n50
Tran Phu 17, 26–8, 29n20, 33n82
Tran Quang Vinh 36, 38
Tran Trong Kim 37, 52–3, 57–8, 62, 77, 80, 85, 87, 92
Tran Van An 37–8, 40, 58–9, 80
Tran Van Cung 16–17
Tran Van Giau 69n139, 79, 81, 114n115

Tran Van Quang 133, 135–6, 147n18 n37
transportation 35, 44–5, 54–7, 86, 135, 140, 152, 155–6, 160, 173n18, 185, 195–6, 208–9; *see also* railways
Trin Dinh Cuu 18, 23–7
Trinh Van Binh 91, 112n53
Troskyists 11, 30n22, 80–1
Truong Chinh (Dang Xuan Khu) 59–61, 69n137, 75, 79, 81, 87, 89, 96–7, 101–3, 106–9, 114n12, 127, 138, 179, 180, 211
Truong Van Lenh 12, 23, 27
Tsuchihashi, General 43, 47–9, 52, 57, 67n75, 82

USSR *see* the Soviet Union
United Kingdom *see* Britain
United States of America 6, 34, 43–8, 61, 70, 73, 78–9, 82, 85, 96–9, 102–6, 110n8, 120–1, 130n20, 132–7, 139–67, 170, 173n 18 n25, 180–90, 193, 196, 205, 208, 210–13

Van Tien Dung 106–8, 133, 147n18, 185–6, 190
Vang Pao 156, 160, 167
Viet-Minh 38, 53, 56, 59–64, 80, 84–110, 115, 119–28, 130n20, 179

Vo Nguyen Giap 59–61, 68n123, 75, 81–7, 92–5, 101–2, 106–9, 120–5, 137–45, 155, 187
Vu Dinh Hoe 56, 87, 92
Vu Trong Khanh 87, 92
Vu Van Hien 55–6, 111n37

war(s) 13, 21, 25, 34–9, 42, 45–9, 56, 59–3, 70–8, 82, 85–6, 89–96, 116–19, 121–8, 31n36, 132, 136–46, 149–61, 171, 178, 181–90, 192n20, 193–6, 198, 204, 208–10
Westmoreland, W. 134–6, 145, 183
women 14, 16, 53, 87, 162
workers *see* labour

Xie Fuzhi 166, 176n59
Xuan Thuy 152, 161, 172n11

Yem Sambaur 167, 176n67
Yokoyama M. 40, 45, 49–50
Yoshizawa K. 35, 43
youth movements 10, 12, 25, 36, 41, 53–62, 74, 77–80, 87, 92, 109, 112n37, 128n3

Zhou Enlai 102, 119, 129n8, 144–52, 154, 165–6, 171, 176n59, 177n83, 179–81, 188

# eBooks – at www.eBookstore.tandf.co.uk

## A library at your fingertips!

eBooks are electronic versions of printed books. You can store them on your PC/laptop or browse them online.

They have advantages for anyone needing rapid access to a wide variety of published, copyright information.

eBooks can help your research by enabling you to bookmark chapters, annotate text and use instant searches to find specific words or phrases. Several eBook files would fit on even a small laptop or PDA.

**NEW:** Save money by eSubscribing: cheap, online access to any eBook for as long as you need it.

### Annual subscription packages

We now offer special low-cost bulk subscriptions to packages of eBooks in certain subject areas. These are available to libraries or to individuals.

For more information please contact webmaster.ebooks@tandf.co.uk

We're continually developing the eBook concept, so keep up to date by visiting the website.

## www.eBookstore.tandf.co.uk